Designing Large-Scale LANs

Kevin Dooley

O'REILLY®

Beijing · Cambridge · Farnham · Köln · Paris · Sebastopol · Taipei · Tokyo

Designing Large-Scale LANs
by Kevin Dooley

Copyright © 2002 O'Reilly & Associates, Inc. All rights reserved.
Printed in the United States of America.

Published by O'Reilly & Associates, Inc., 1005 Gravenstein Highway North, Sebastopol, CA 95472.

O'Reilly & Associates books may be purchased for educational, business, or sales promotional use. Online editions are also available for most titles (*safari.oreilly.com*). For more information contact our corporate/institutional sales department: 800-998-9938 or *corporate@oreilly.com*.

Editor:	Jim Sumser
Production Editor:	Jeffrey Holcomb
Cover Designer:	Ellie Volckhausen
Interior Designer:	Melanie Wang

Printing History:

January 2002:	First Edition.

Library of Congress Cataloging-in-Publication Data

Dooley, Kevin.
   Designing large-scale LANs / Kevin Dooley.
      p. cm.
   ISBN 0-596-00150-9
      1. Local area networks (Computer networks) I. Title.

TK5105.7 .D66 2001
004.6'8--dc21   2001045924

[CS]

Table of Contents

Preface vii

1. Networking Objectives **1**
Business Requirements 1
OSI Protocol Stack Model 5
Routing Versus Bridging 10
Top-Down Design Philosophy 12

2. Elements of Reliability **14**
Defining Reliability 14
Redundancy 17
Failure Modes 44

3. Design Types **50**
Basic Topologies 50
Reliability Mechanisms 61
VLANs 66
Toward Larger Topologies 70
Hierarchical Design 81
Implementing Reliability 113
Large-Scale LAN Topologies 115

4. Local Area Network Technologies **126**
Selecting Appropriate LAN Technology 126
Ethernet and Fast Ethernet 130
Token Ring 141
Gigabit and 10 Gigabit Ethernet 146
ATM 149

FDDI   154
Wireless   155
Firewalls and Gateways   160
Structured Cabling   162

5. **IP** **169**
IP-Addressing Basics   170
IP-Address Classes   173
ARP and ICMP   175
Network Address Translation   177
Multiple Subnet Broadcast   179
General IP Design Strategies   182
DNS and DHCP   191

6. **IP Dynamic Routing** **193**
Static Routing   194
Types of Dynamic Routing Protocols   196
RIP   197
IGRP and EIGRP   206
OSPF   213
BGP   228

7. **IPX** **234**
Dynamic Routing   236
General IPX Design Strategies   242

8. **Elements of Efficiency** **247**
Using Equipment Features Effectively   248
Hop Counts   249
MTU Throughout the Network   250
Bottlenecks and Congestion   252
Filtering   253
Quality of Service and Traffic Shaping   254

9. **Network Management** **273**
Network-Management Components   273
Designing a Manageable Network   275
SNMP   280
Management Problems   288

10. **Special Topics** **306**
     IP Multicast Networks   306
     IPv6   319
     Security   333

Appendix: Combining Probabilities **341**

Glossary **344**

Bibliography **364**

Index **369**

Preface

Computer networks are like any complex engineering project. A small network can be slapped together quite successfully with minimal experience. But a larger network requires careful thought and planning. As with many types of engineering projects, this planning and design phase is best served by an organized and disciplined design philosophy. The trouble with design is that it is difficult to differentiate between personal or near-religious biases and sound ecumenical strategies that can result in better usability, stability, security, and manageability.

Everyone has religious biases when it comes to network design. This is because most networks are so complex that a feeling of black magic falls over anybody trying to understand them. They tend to be too large and too intricate to hold in your mind all at once. So when some particular incantation appears to work miracles, it is adopted as an article of faith. And when a vendor's equipment (or support engineer) saves the day in some important way, it can turn into a blanket belief in that vendor as savior.

So, in the interests of making plain my assumptions and biases, let me explain right from the start that I am a network agnostic. I have used equipment from most of the major vendors, and I believe that every individual piece of gear has its pluses and minuses. I prefer to use the gear that is right for the job, rather than expressing a blind devotion to one or another. So this book is vendor neutral.

I will discuss some proprietary protocols and standards because these are often the best for a particular situation. But in general I will try to lead the reader towards open industry standards: I believe that it is unwise to lock your technology budget to one particular vendor.

In the mainframe-computing era, many firms spent large amounts of money on one company's equipment. Then they found that this required them to continue spending their hardware budget with that company unless they wanted to abandon their initial investment. All incremental upgrades merely reinforced their dependency on this one vendor. This was fine unless another manufacturer came along with gear that would be better (cheaper, faster, more scalable, etc.) for important business requirements of the company. It is wise to avoid the "fork-lift" upgrade where the entire infrastructure has to be replaced simultaneously to improve performance.

In practice, most LANs are multivendor hybrids. This may be by design or by chance. In many cases a best-of-breed philosophy has been adopted so that a particular type of Ethernet switch is used in the wiring closets, another type at the backbone, with routers from another vendor, while ATM switches and long-haul equipment are provided by still other vendors. In other cases, the multivendor nature of the network is more of an historical accident than intention. And there are also cases where all or nearly all of the network hardware comes from the same manufacturer. If this is the case, then the choice should be made consciously, based on solid technical and business reasons. Having stated my biases here, I leave the reader to make these decisions freely.

Because computer networks are large and complex engineering projects, they should be designed carefully and deliberately. There are many important questions to ask about how a network should function and what purposes it needs to serve. And there are even more questions to ask about how best to meet these objectives. This book will serve as a guide to this process.

Audience

This book is intended for anybody who needs to build or maintain a large-scale network. It is not a theoretical book for classroom use, and it isn't intended to help programmers with designing applications. Instead it is a hands-on set of rules, guiding principles, and useful tips for people who build networks.

So it should be useful for network-operations people who need to understand the overall logic of their network. It should also be helpful to engineers who need to think about upgrading parts of an existing network in a logical way. And it is particularly relevant for network designers and architects.

In short, this is the book that I always wanted to read when I was starting to work on large networks.

Organization

The book begins in Chapter 1, *Networking Objectives*, by discussing the most important question of all: why build a network in the first place? The answers to this question shape everything that follows. This first chapter also reviews several of the basic networking concepts used throughout the book.

Chapter 2, *Elements of Reliability*, discusses reliability in networks, the factors that lead to a solid network. This includes discussion of how to find the single points of failure in your network. It also includes an important section on how to evaluate the stability of your network and its components statistically.

Chapter 3, *Design Types*, describes many of the most successful design types and their strengths and weaknesses. This chapter should help you to decide on the large-scale shape of the network you build. It includes many ideas for ensuring both reliability and scalability in a large-scale network.

Chapter 4, *Local Area Network Technologies*, delves into the technologies commonly used on LANs. This is intended as a guide to the network designer and implementer, rather than the engineer building the hardware. There are many other books that provide that higher level of detail, which is beyond the scope of this book. The intent here is to provide the information that a network designer needs to make appropriate decisions.

The same is true of Chapter 5, *IP*, which begins a three-chapter discussion of the various Layer 3 and 4 protocols that are commonly used on LANs, focusing in particular on TCP/IP (see Chapter 6, *IP Dynamic Routing*) and IPX (see Chapter 7, *IPX*). At the same time, these chapters look at good ways of implementing networks based on these protocols, as well as appropriate dynamic routing protocols.

Then in Chapter 8, *Elements of Efficiency*, I turn to efficiency. What is meant by efficiency in a network? How it is it achieved? In particular, I discuss how to implement Quality of Service (QoS) through a network to ensure that low-priority traffic doesn't interfere with the delivery of important data.

Chapter 9, *Network Management*, is devoted to network management. But, rather than looking at how to manage a network, this section focuses on how a network's design can make it either easier or more difficult to manage. There are several key design decisions that have implications on how the network will later be managed. Since manageability is one of the keys to reliability, it is important to design networks so that they can be managed effectively.

Chapter 10, *Special Topics*, discusses other important considerations that may not be relevant to every network. These include issues of LAN security, designing for multicast capabilities, and inclusion of the new IPv6 protocol.

The Appendix describes in some mathematical detail how to combine statistical probabilities. This is important for estimating failure rates in a complex network. This information is particularly used in Chapter 2 in the section on calculating "Mean time between failures."

The Glossary is a listing of networking terms. Networking has unfortunately become bogged down with highly technical jargon that often makes it difficult to understand things that are actually relatively simple. So this glossary is included to help prevent that from being a problem.

Conventions Used in This Book

I have used the following formatting conventions in this book:

Italic

> Used for emphasis and the first use of technical terms, as well as email and URL addresses.

`Constant Width`

> Used for MAC and IP addresses.

Comments and Questions

Please address comments and questions concerning this book to the publisher:

> O'Reilly & Associates, Inc.
> 1005 Gravenstein Highway North
> Sebastopol, CA 95472
> (800) 998-9938 (in the United States or Canada)
> (707) 829-0515 (international/local)
> (707) 829-0104 (fax)

There is a web page for this book, which lists errata, examples, or any additional information. You can access this page at:

> *http://www.oreilly.com/catalog/lgscalelans/*

To comment or ask technical questions about this book, send email to:

> *bookquestions@oreilly.com*

For more information about books, conferences, Resource Centers, and the O'Reilly Network, see the O'Reilly web site at:

> *http://www.oreilly.com*

Acknowledgments

There are several people who were instrumental in helping me get this book completed. Most important was my editor, Jim Sumser. Jim was extremely encouraging, which was important because of the aggressive schedule that I wanted to follow. He also really helped me organize and present these (often scattered) ideas in a rational way.

I'd like to thank my technical reviewers, who each pointed out more than one serious blunder. Andre Paree-Huff made a number of encouraging comments about the book. Ian J. Brown, CCIE# 3372, showed his vast depth of technical knowledge in his comments, which allowed me to make significant improvements to the quality of the information presented. And Scott M. Ballew offered many important structural, as well as technical, suggestions for which I am grateful.

In addition, I'd like to thank the following people at O'Reilly: Sheryl Avruch, Mary Brady, Claire Cloutier, Emma Colby, Tatiana Apandi Diaz, Jeffrey Holcomb, Mihaela Maier, Jessamyn Read, Ann Schirmer, Ellie Volckhausen, Melanie Wang, Rachel Wheeler, and Sue Willing.

And, I am particularly grateful to Sherry Biscope for her unconditional support and encouragement throughout this project.

CHAPTER 1

Networking Objectives

The American architect Louis Henry Sullivan described his design philosophy with the simple statement "form follows function." By this credo he meant that a structure's physical layout and design should reflect as precisely as possible how this structure will be used. Every door and window is where it is for a reason.

He was talking about building skyscrapers, but this philosophy is perhaps even more useful for network design. Where building designs often include purely esthetic features to make them more beautiful to look at, every element of a good network design should serve some well-defined purpose. There are no gargoyles or frescos in a well-designed network.

The location and configuration of every piece of equipment and every protocol must be carefully optimized to create a network that fulfills the ultimate purposes for which it was designed. Any sense of esthetics in network design comes from its simplicity and reliability. The network is most beautiful when it is invisible to the end user.

So the task of designing a network begins with a thorough study of the required functions. And the form will follow from these business requirements.

Business Requirements

This is the single most important question to answer when starting a network design: why do you want to build a network? It sounds a little silly, but frequently people seem confused about this point. Often they start building a network for some completely valid and useful reason and then get bogged down in technical details that have little or nothing to do with the real objectives. It is important to always keep these real objectives in mind throughout the process of designing, implementing, and operating a network.

Too often people build networks based on technological, rather than business, considerations. Even if the resulting network fulfills business requirements, it will usually be much more expensive to implement than is necessary.

If you are building a network for somebody else, then they must have some reason why they want this done. Make sure you understand what the real reasons are. Too often user specifications are made in terms of technology. Technology has very little to do with business requirements. They may say that they need a Frame Relay WAN, or that they need switched 100Mbps Ethernet to every desk. You wanted them to tell you why they needed these things. They told you they needed a solution, but they didn't tell you what problem you were solving.

It's true that they may have the best solution, but even that is hard to know without understanding the problem. I will call these underlying reasons for building the network "business requirements." But I want to use a very loose definition for the word "business." There are many reasons for building a network, and only some of them have anything to do with business in the narrow sense of the word. Networks can be built for academic reasons, or research, or for government. There are networks in arts organizations and charities. Some networks have been built to allow a group of friends to play computer games. And there are networks that were built just because the builders wanted to try out some cool new technology, but this can probably be included in the education category.

What's important is that there is always a good reason to justify spending the money. And once the money is spent, it's important to make sure that the result actually satisfies those requirements. Networks cost money to build, and large networks cost large amounts of money.

Money

So the first step in any network design is always to sit down and list the requirements. If one of the requirements is to save money by allowing people to do some task faster and more efficiently, then it is critical to understand how much money is saved.

Money is one of the most important design constraints on any network. Money forms the upper limit to what can be accomplished, balancing against the "as fast as possible" requirement pushing up from below. How much money do they expect the network to save them? How much money do they expect it will make for them? If you spend more money building this network than it's going to save (or make) for the organization, then it has failed to meet this critical business objective. Perhaps neither of these questions is directly relevant. But in that case, somebody is still paying the bill, so how much money are they willing to spend?

Geography

Geography is the second major requirement to understand. Where are the users? Where are the services they want to access? How are the users organized geographically? By geography I mean physical location on whatever scale is relevant. This book's primary focus is on Local Area Network (LAN) design, so I will generally assume that most of the users are in the same building or in connected building complexes. But if there are remote users, then this must be identified at the start as well. This could quite easily spawn a second project to build a Wide Area Network (WAN), a remote-access solution, or perhaps a Metropolitan Area Network (MAN). However, these sorts of designs are beyond the scope of this book.

One of the keys to understanding the local area geography is establishing how the users are grouped. Do people in the same area all work with the same resources? Do they need access to the same servers? Are the users of some resources scattered throughout the building? The answers to these questions will help to define the Virtual LAN (VLAN) architecture. If everybody in each area is part of a self-contained work group, then the network could be built with only enough bandwidth between groups to support whatever small amounts of interaction they have. But, at the opposite extreme, there are organizations in which all communication is to a centralized group of resources with little or no communication within a user area. Of course, in most real organizations, there is most likely a mixture of these extremes with some common resources, some local resources, and some group-to-group traffic.

Installed Base

The next major business requirement to determine is the installed base. What technology exists today? Why does it need to be changed? How much of the existing infrastructure must remain?

It would be extremely unusual to find a completely new organization that is very large, has no existing technology today, and needs it tomorrow. Even if you did find one, chances are that the problem of implementing this new technology has been broken down among various groups. So the new network design will need to fit in with whatever the other groups need for their servers and applications.

Installed base can cause several different types of constraints. There are geographical constraints, such as the location and accessibility of the computer rooms and LAN rooms. There may be existing legacy network technology that has to be supported. Or it may be too difficult, inconvenient, or expensive to replace the existing cable plant or other existing services.

Constraints from an existing installed base of equipment can be among the most difficult and frustrating parts of a network design, so it is critical to establish them as thoroughly and as early as possible.

Bandwidth

Now that you understand what you're connecting and to where, you need to figure out how much traffic to expect. This will give the bandwidth requirements. Unfortunately, this often winds up being pure guesswork. But if you can establish that there are 50 users in the accounting department who each use an average of 10kbps in their connections to the mainframe throughout the day, plus one big file transfer at 5:00 P.M., then you have some very useful information. If you know further that this file transfer is 5 gigabytes and it has to be completed by 5:30, then you have another excellent constraint.

The idea is to get as much information as possible about all of the major traffic patterns and how much volume they involve. What are the expected average rates at the peak periods of the day (which is usually the start and end of the day for most 9–5 type operations)? Are there standard file transfers? If so, how big are they, and how quickly must they complete? Try to get this sort of information for each geographical area because it will tell you not only how to size the trunks, but also how to interconnect the areas most effectively.

In the end it is a good idea to allow for a large amount of growth. Only once have I seen a network where the customer insisted that it would get smaller over time. And even that one got larger before it got smaller. Always assume growth. If possible, try to obtain business-related growth projections. There may be plans to expand a particular department and eliminate another. Knowing this ahead of time will allow the designer to make important money-saving decisions.

Security

Last among the top-level business requirements is security. What are the security requirements? This is even important in networks that are not connected to anything else, like the Internet or other shared networks. For example, in many organizations the servers in the Payroll Department are considered sensitive, and access is restricted. In investment banks, there may be regulations that require the trading groups to be separate from corporate financing groups. The regulatory organizations tend to get annoyed when people make money on stock markets using secret insider information.

The relationship between security and geography requirements may make it necessary to implement special encryption or firewall measures, so these have to be understood before a single piece of equipment is ordered.

Philosophical and Policy Requirements

Besides the business requirements, there could be philosophical requirements. There may be a corporate philosophy that dictates that all servers must be in a central computer room. Not all organizations require this, but many do. It makes server maintenance and backups much easier if this is the case. But it also dictates that the network must be able to carry all of the traffic to and from remote user areas.

There may be a corporate philosophy that, to facilitate moves, adds, and changes, any PC can be picked up and moved anywhere else and not require reconfiguration.

Some organizations insist that all user files be stored on a file server so that they can be backed up. Make sure that you have a complete list of all such philosophical requirements, as well as the business requirements, before starting.

OSI Protocol Stack Model

No book on networking would be complete without discussing the Open System Interconnection (OSI) model. This book is more interested in the lower layers of the protocol stack. One of the central goals of network design is to build reliable networks for applications to use. So a good design starts at the bottom of the stack, letting the upper layers ride peacefully on a stable architecture. Software people take a completely different view of the network. They tend to be most concerned about the upper layers, from Layer 7 down to about Layer 4 or 5. Network designers are most concerned with Layers 1 through 4 or 5. Software people don't care much about cabling, as long as it doesn't lose their data. Network designers don't care much about the data segment of a packet, as long as the packet meets the standard specifications.

This fact alone explains much of my bias in focusing on the lower parts of the stack. There are excellent books on network programming that talk in detail about the upper layers of the stack. That is largely beyond the scope of this book, however.

The Seven Layers

The OSI model is a useful way of thinking about networking. It's important not to confuse it with reality, of course. The most commonly used networking protocols, such as TCP/IP, don't completely match the model. But it is still a useful model. Table 1-1 shows this simple model in its usual form.

Table 1-1. The OSI model

Layer	Name	Uses	Examples
7	Application	User and application data	The reason for having a network in the first place
6	Presentation	Data formatting, encryption, character encoding	ASCII versus EBCDIC, software encryption of a data stream
5	Session	Negotiates and maintains connections	Name and address correlation, software flow control
4	Transport	End-to-end packet sequencing and reliability	UDP, TCP, SPX
3	Network	Routing, flow control, translation between different media types	IP, IPX
2	Data Link (MAC)	Basic framing of packets, error detection, transmission control	Ethernet packets, including collision mechanisms
1	Physical	Electrical and optical media, signaling and properties	Cabling, the electrical or optical pulses sent through the cabling

Layer 1

The Physical Layer is at the bottom. This includes the parts of the network that you can see, such as cables, patch panels, jacks, and optical fibers. Specifications for the Physical Layer have to do with the differences between categories of cables, the wavelength properties of optical fibers, the length restrictions, and electrical specifications. This is extremely important stuff, but most network designers only think about it briefly when they do the cable plant.

Other physical-layer issues, such as laser intensity, wavelength characteristics, attenuation, and so on, are important to engineers who design the equipment and cables. But for the network design they appear only in decisions to match the specifications of different pieces of hardware and cabling.

Layer 2

The Data Link Layer is where things start to get a bit more abstract, so some examples might help. This layer is where the difference between Ethernet, Fast Ethernet, and Token Ring exists. It includes all of the specifications about how to build a packet. It describes how the different nodes on this network avoid contention using collisions or token passing or perhaps some other algorithm. For broadcast media (as opposed to point-to-point media where you know that if you send out a packet, it can only be received by one other device), it defines how to actually specify for which device or devices the packet is destined.

Before going on, let me point out the ways that these first two layers are both connected and separable. For example, you have a certain physical layer, such as Category 5 twisted pair cabling. Then, when you decide to run Ethernet over this physical medium, you are constrained to use a particular type of signaling that works with this medium. It is called 10BaseT. There are other types of Ethernet signaling, such as 10Base2. In this case, though, you would have to use coaxial cable designed to have 50 Ω (ohm) characteristic impedance. But, over this twisted pair cabling, you could just as easily run Token Ring. Or, if you are working with Token Ring, you could choose instead to use Type 3 shielded cabling.

The point is that Ethernet means a particular way of forming packets and a particular way of avoiding contention (collisions). It can run over many different types of physical media. Going up the protocol stack, the same is true at each layer. You can run TCP/IP over Ethernet, or over Token Ring, ATM, or FDDI, or over point-to-point circuits of various descriptions. At each layer there is a set of specifications on how to get to the layer below. You can think of this specification as being the line between the layers of the stack. So the line between the Physical Layer and the Data Link Layer includes 10BaseT, 100BaseFx, and so forth.

Strictly speaking, these distinctions are described in sublayers of the standard OSI model. The IEEE provides detailed specifications of these protocols.

Layer 3

The Network Layer includes the IP part of TCP/IP. This is where the IP address lives. The Network Layer specifies how to get from one data-link region to another. This is called routing. See the next section on "Routing Versus Bridging" for a more detailed description of what routing means.

There are several other Network Layer protocols besides IP. One of the most popular for LANs is called IPX, which forms the basis of the Novell Netware NOS (Network Operating System). However, IPX can also be used by other systems including Microsoft Windows and Linux.

As an aside on the subject of the OSI model, it is quite common to use both IP and IPX simultaneously on the same network, over the same physical-layer equipment. But what's particularly interesting is that they don't have to use the same Data Link Layer protocol for their framing. Usually IP packets are framed using the Ethernet II data link layer. Meanwhile, IPX usually uses IEEE 802.2 with 802.3 Ethernet framing. There are several subtle differences between Ethernet II and 802.2, and it would certainly not be possible to run an IP network using both simultaneously on the same segment. But it is quite common to configure all of the devices on the network to expect their IP frames in one format and IPX in a different format.

Layer 4

At Layer 4, things become still more abstract. The IP protocol has two main transport-layer extensions, called TCP and UDP. TCP, or Transmission Control Protocol, is a connection-oriented protocol. This means that it forms end-to-end sessions between two devices. It then takes care of maintaining this session, keeping packets in order and resending them if they get lost in the network. For this reason, TCP is not useful for one-to-many or many-to-many communication. But it is perfect for building applications that require a user to log in and maintain a connection of any kind. A TCP session has to begin with a session negotiation that sets up a number of communications parameters such as packet size. At the end, it has to be torn down again.

UDP, or User Datagram Protocol, is connectionless. It is used for applications that just send one packet at a time without requiring a response. It is also used by applications that want to maintain their own connection, rather than using TCP. This can be useful if a server needs to support a large number of clients because maintaining connections with TCP can be resource-intensive on the server. In effect, each UDP packet is a complete session. UDP is also useful for multicast type applications or for applications where the data is time sensitive, so retransmitting a packet is worse than dropping it.

TCP, being a connection-oriented protocol, is inherently reliable. It ensures that all data sent from one end to the other gets to its destination intact and in the right order. UDP, on the other hand, is inherently unreliable. This doesn't mean it's bad; it just means that the application has to make sure that it has received all of the data it needs.

The other important thing that happens at Layer 4 is the differentiation between different application streams. In both TCP and UDP (as well as in IPX/SPX at the same layer) there is a concept called a port. This is really nothing more than a number. But it is a number that represents an application. For an application to work, there has to be not only something to send information, but also something on the other end to listen. So a server will typically have a program running that listens for incoming packets on a particular port (that is, packets that have the appropriate number in the port-number part of the packet).

The network also cares about port numbers because it is an easy way to differentiate between different applications. The port number can be used to set priorities so that important applications can pass through the network more easily. Or the network can reject packets based on port number (usually for security reasons, but sometimes just to clean up artificially for ill-behaved application chatter).

Layer 5

Layer 5 is not used in every protocol. It is where instructions for pacing and load balancing of different clients will occur, as well as where sessions are established. As I mentioned previously, the TCP protocol handles session establishment at Layer 4, and the UDP protocol doesn't really have sessions at all.

To make matters more confusing, the TCP/IP telnet and FTP protocols, for example, tend to handle the session maintenance as Layer 7 application data, without a separate Session Management layer. These protocols use Layer 4 to make the connection and then handle elements such as username and password verification as application information.

Some protocols such as SNA can use a real Session Layer that operates independently from the Transport Layer. This ability to separate the layers, to run the same Session Layer protocol over a number of possible Transport Layers, or to build applications that have different options for session control, is what makes it a distinct layer.

Layer 6

The Presentation Layer, Layer 6, is also not universally used. In some cases, a data stream between two devices may be encrypted, and this is commonly handled at Layer 6. But encryption can also be done in some systems at Layer 2, which is generally more secure and where it can be combined with data compression.

One common usae of Layer 6 is in an FTP file transfer. It is possible to have the protocol interpret the data as either 7-bit or 8-bit characters. Similarly, some terminal-emulation systems use ASCII characters, while others use EBCDIC encoding for the data in the application payload of the packet. Again, this is a Layer 6 concept, but it might not be implemented as a distinct part of the application protocol. In many cases, conversions like these are actually made by the application and then inserted directly into Layer 4 packets. That is to say, a lot of what people tend to think of as Layer 6 concepts are not really distinct protocols. Rather, they are implementation options that are applied at Layers 4 and 7.

Layer 7

And, finally, Layer 7 is called the Application Layer. This is where the contents of your email message or database query live. The Application Layer is really the point of having a network in the first place. The network needs to get information efficiently from one place to another. The Application Layer contains that information. Maybe it needs to be chopped up into several packets, maybe it needs to be translated into some sort of special encoding scheme, encrypted and forwarded through 17 different types of boxes before it reaches the destination. But ultimately the information gets there. This information belongs to Layer 7.

Where the OSI Model Breaks Down

In a sense, the model doesn't break down. It's more accurate to say that it isn't always strictly followed. And there are a lot of places where it is almost completely abandoned. Many of these examples involve concepts of tunneling.

A tunnel is a protocol within a protocol. One of the most frequent examples is a Virtual Private Network, or VPN. VPNs are often used to make secure connections through untrusted networks such as the Internet. Taking this example, suppose the users of a corporate LAN need to access some important internal application from out on the Internet. The information in the database is too sensitive to make it accessible from the Internet where anybody could get it. So the users have to make an encrypted VPN connection from their computers at home.

They first open a TCP connection from their home computers to the VPN server through the corporate firewall. This prompts them for usernames and passwords, and they log in. At this point everything seems to follow the OSI model. But then, through this TCP session, the network passes a special VPN protocol that allows users to access the internal LAN as if they were connected locally (although slower). They obtain a new IP address for this internal connection and work normally. In fact, they also can pass IPX traffic through their VPN to connect to the corporate file server. So the VPN is acting as if it were a Layer 2 protocol because it is carrying Layer 3 protocols. But in fact it's a Layer 6 protocol.

Now, suppose the users' own Internet connection is made via a DSL connection. One of the most popular ways to implement DSL in North America is to emulate an Ethernet segment, a Layer 2 protocol. But the connection over this Ethernet segment is made using PPPoE (PPP over Ethernet), a Layer 3 protocol that carries PPP, a Layer 2 protocol.

To summarize, there is a Layer 1 physical connection to the DSL provider. Over that the users run Ethernet emulations (Layer 2). On top of the Ethernet is PPPoE, another Layer 2 protocol.* Over that they run IP to communicate with the Internet at Layer 3. Then, using this IP stack, they connect to the VPN server with a special Layer 4 connection authenticated at Layer 5 and encrypted at Layer 6. Over this is new Ethernet emulation (back to Layer 2). The users can then run their normal applications (Layers 3–7) on top of this new Layer 2. And, if you wanted to be really weird, you could start over with another PPPoE session.

Things get very confusing if you try to map them too closely to the OSI model. But, as you can see from the previous example, it is still useful to think about the various protocols by function and the layers that represent those functions.

Routing Versus Bridging

Chapter 3 will discuss the design implications of the differences between routing and bridging. The discussion of the OSI model here makes it a good place to define them and talk about their technical differences.

I will use the terms "bridging" and "switching" interchangeably throughout this book. This is because early manufacturers of multiport fast bridges wanted to make it clear that their products were distinct from earlier products. The earlier products, called "bridges," were used primarily for isolation and repeating functions; the newer products tended to focus on reducing latency and increasing throughput across a network. Technically, they perform the same basic network functions. But these vendors wanted to make sure that consumers understood that their products were different from the earlier devices: so they gave them a different name.

To make matters more confusing, it has become fashionable to talk about "Layer 3 switches." These are essentially just routers. But, in general, they are special-function routers that route between like media, which allows certain speed optimizations. So, where you might use a Layer 3 switch to route between two VLANs, both built on Fast Ethernet, you would never use one to control access to a WAN. You probably would want to think very carefully before using a Layer 3 switch to regulate traffic between a Token Ring and an Ethernet.

Routing means sending packets from one Layer 3 network region to another using Layer 3 addressing information. These two Layer 3 regions could use different Layer 1 or 2 protocols. For example, one may be Ethernet and the other ATM. So part of the routing process requires taking the Layer 3 packet out of the Ethernet frame in

---

* PPPoE is a particularly interesting protocol when studied on the OSI stack because it looks like Layer 3 protocol to the Ethernet protocol on top of which it sits. But it presents a standard Layer 2 PPP interface to the IP protocol that lives above it on the stack.

which it was received, deciding where to send it, then creating ATM cells to carry this packet. Because ATM uses a cell size that is much smaller than the Ethernet packet size, the router has to chop up the Layer 3 packet and wrap each fragment in an ATM cell before sending it. When receiving from the ATM side, it has to wait until it receives all of the ATM cells that form one Layer 3 packet, reassemble the fragments in the correct order, and wrap it up in an Ethernet frame before sending it on. This allows easy transfer of data between LAN and WAN or between different LAN types.

Technically, bridging has some overlap into the Network Layer as well, because it specifies how the broadcast domains that are part of the Data Link Layer can interact with one another. But the special difference between routing and bridging is that in routing the Data Link properties don't need to have anything in common. It is easy to route IP from Ethernet to Token Ring without needing to consider anything but the IP addresses of both ends. But in bridging, the MAC (Media Access Control) addresses from one side of the bridge are maintained as the frame crosses over to the other side.

It is possible to bridge from Ethernet to Token Ring, for example. But the Token Ring devices must believe that they are talking to another Token Ring device. So the bridge has to generate a fake Token Ring MAC address for each Ethernet device, and a fake Ethernet MAC address for each Token Ring device taking part in the bridge.

With routing, though, there is only one MAC address visible, that of the router itself. Each device knows that it has to communicate with all off-segment devices through that address.

So routing scales much better than bridging when large numbers of devices need to communicate with one another. But the drawback is that the extra work of translating from one data-link layer to another means that the router has to read in every packet, decide where to send it, reformat it for the new medium, and then send it along.

With switching, however, it is possible to read in just enough of the packet to figure out where it needs to go and then start sending it out before it has all been received. This is called cut-through switching. Store-and-forward switching, in which the entire packet is read before forwarding, is also common. But the bottom line is that switching is generally faster than routing.

Layer 3 switching is sort of a hybrid. If you know that you are switching between like media, then the only things you need to change when you pass the packet along are the source and destination MAC addresses (and the checksum will also need to be corrected). This is considerably less work than the general media-independent problem of routing. So these Layer 3 switches are usually faster than a general-purpose router.

The other advantage of a Layer 3 switch over a router is that it can often be implemented as a special card in a Layer 2 switch. This means that it is able to do its work while touching only the backplane of the switch. Because the switch backplane doesn't need to go very far, and because it usually runs a proprietary high-speed protocol, it is able to run at extremely high speeds. So it is as if you were able to connect your router, not to a 100-Mbps Fast Ethernet or even to 1000Mbps Gigabit Ethernet, but to a medium many times faster than the fastest readily available LAN technologies. And this is done without having to pay a lot of extra money for the high speed access.

Chapter 3 will discuss how to use these sorts of devices effectively.

Top-Down Design Philosophy

Once the actual requirements are understood, the design work can begin, and it should always start at the top. Earlier in this chapter I described the standard seven-layer OSI protocol model. The top layer in this model is the Application Layer. That is where one has to start when designing a network. The network exists to support applications. The applications exist to fulfill business requirements.

The trick is that the network will almost certainly outlive some of these applications. The organization will implement new applications, and they will likely have new network requirements. They will form new business units, and new departments will replace old ones. A good network design is sufficiently flexible to support these sorts of changes without requiring wholesale redesign. This is why an experienced network designer will generally add certain philosophical requirements to the business requirements that have already been determined.

The network needs to be scalable, manageable, and reliable. Methods for achieving each of these topics will be examined in considerable detail throughout this book. It should be obvious why they are all important, but let me briefly touch on some of the benefits of imposing these as requirements in a network design.

Making a design scalable automatically dismisses design possibilities where switches for different workgroups are either interconnected with a mesh or cascaded one after another in a long string. Scalability will generally lead to hierarchical designs with a Core where all intergroup traffic aggregates.

Manageability implies that you want to see what is going on throughout the network easily. It will also demand simple, rational addressing schemes. Some types of technology are either unmanageable or difficult to manage. You probably wouldn't want to eliminate these outright because they may be cost effective. But you probably don't want to put them in key parts of the network.

Reliability is usually the result of combining a simple, scalable, manageable architecture with the business throughput and traffic-flow requirements. But it also implies that the network designer will study the design carefully to eliminate key single points of failure.

There are other important philosophical principles that may guide a network design. A common one is that, except for specific security exclusions, any user should be able to access any other part of the network. This will help ensure that, when new services are deployed, the network will not need to be redesigned.

Another common design philosophy says that only network devices perform network functions. In other words, never use a server as a bridge or a router. It's often possible to set up a server with multiple interface cards, but this philosophy will steer you away from doing such things. Generally speaking, a server has enough work to do already without having the resources act as some kind of gateway. It will be almost invariably slower and less reliable at these functions than a special-purpose network device.

If your network uses TCP/IP, will you use registered or unregistered IP addresses? This used to be a hotly debated subject, but these days it is becoming clear that there is very little to lose by implementing a network with unregistered addresses, as long as you have some registered addresses available for address-translation purposes.

Perhaps the most important philosophical decisions have to do with what networking standards will be employed. Will they be open standards that will allow easy interoperability among different vendors' equipment? Or will they be proprietary to one vendor, hopefully delivering better performance at a lower price? It is wise to be very careful before implementing any proprietary protocols on your network because it can make it exceedingly difficult to integrate other equipment later. It is always possible that somebody will come along with a new technology that is vastly better than anything currently on the market. If you want to implement this new technology, you may find that the existing proprietary protocols will force a complete redesign of the network.

CHAPTER 2
Elements of Reliability

Reliability is what separates a well-designed network from a bad one. Anybody can slap together a bunch of connections that will be reasonably reliable some of the time. Frequently, networks evolve gradually, growing into lumbering beasts that require continuous nursing to keep them operating. So, if you want to design a good network, it is critical to understand the features that can make it more or less reliable.

As discussed in Chapter 1, the network is built for business reasons. So reliability only makes sense in the context of meeting those business requirements. As I said earlier, by "business" I don't just mean money. Many networks are built for educational or research reasons. Some networks are operated as a public service. But in all cases, the network should be built for clearly defined reasons that justify the money being spent. So that is what reliability must be measured against.

Defining Reliability

There are two main components to my definition of reliability. The first is fault tolerance. This means that devices can break down without affecting service. In practice, you might never see any failures in your key network devices. But if there is no inherent fault tolerance to protect against such failures, then the network is taking a great risk at the business' expense.

The second key component to reliability is more a matter of performance and capacity than of fault tolerance. The network must meet its peak load requirements sufficiently to support the business requirements. At its heaviest times, the network still has to work. So peak load performance must be included in the concept of network reliability.

It is important to note that the network must be more reliable than any device attached to it. If the user can't get to the server, the application will not work—no matter how good the software or how stable the server. In general, a network will support many users and many servers. So it is critically important that the network be more reliable than the best server on it.

Suppose, for example, that a network has one server and many workstations. This was the standard network design when mainframes ruled the earth. In this case, the network is useless without a server. Many companies would install backup systems in case key parts of their mainframe failed. But this sort of backup system is not worth the expense if the thing that fails most often is connection to the workstations.

Now, jump to the modern age of two- and three-tiered client-server architectures. In this world there are many servers supporting many applications. They are still connected to the user workstations by a single network, though. So this network has become the single most important technological element in the company. If a server fails, it may have a serious effect on the business. The business response to this risk is to provide a redundant server of some kind. But if the network fails, then several servers may become inaccessible. In effect, the stability of the network is as important as the combined importance of all business applications.

Failure Is a Reliability Issue

In most cases, it's easiest to think about reliability in terms of how frequently the network fails to meet the business requirements, and how badly it fails. For the time being, I won't restrict this discussion to simple metrics like availability because this neglects two important ways that a network can fail to meet business requirements.

First, there are failures that are very short in duration, but which interrupt key applications for much longer periods. Second, a network can fail to meet important business requirements without ever becoming unavailable. For example, if a key application is sensitive to latency, then a slow network will be considered unreliable even if it never breaks.

In the first case, some applications and protocols are extremely sensitive to short failures. Sometimes a short failure can mean that an elaborate session setup must be repeated. In worse cases, a short failure can leave a session hung on the server. When this happens, the session must be reset by either automatic or manual procedures, resulting in considerable delays and user frustration. The worst situation is when that brief network outage causes loss of critical application data. Perhaps a stock trade will fail to execute, or the confirmation will go missing, causing it to be resubmitted and executed a second time. Either way, the short network outage could cost millions of dollars. At the very least, it will cause user aggravation and loss of productivity.

Availability is not a useful metric in these cases. A short but critical outage would not affect overall availability by very much, but it is nonetheless a serious problem.

Lost productivity is often called a *soft expense*. This is really an accounting issue. The costs are real, and they can severely affect corporate profits. For example, suppose a thousand people are paid an average of $20/hour. If there is a network glitch of some sort that sends them all to the coffee room for 15 minutes, then that glitch just cost the company at least $5,000 (not counting the cost of the coffee). In fact, these people are supposed to be creating net profit for the company when they are working. So it is quite likely that there is an additional impact in lost revenue, which could be considerably larger. If spending $5,000 to $10,000 could have prevented this brief outage, it would almost certainly have been worth the expense. If the outage happens repeatedly, then multiply this amount of money by the failure frequency. Brief outages can be extremely expensive.

Performance Is a Reliability Issue

The network exists to transport data from one place to another. If it is unable to transport the volume of data required, or if it doesn't transfer that data quickly enough, then it doesn't meet the business requirements. It is always important to distinguish between these two factors. The first is called *bandwidth*, and the second *latency*.

Simply put, bandwidth is the amount of data that the network can transmit per unit time. Latency, on the other hand, is the length of time it takes to send that data from end to end. The best analogy for these is to think of transporting real physical "stuff."

Suppose a company wants to send grain from New York to Paris. They could put a few bushels on the Concorde and get it there very quickly (low latency, low bandwidth, and high cost per unit). Or they could fill a cargo ship with millions of bushels, and it will be there next week (high latency, high bandwidth, and low cost per unit). Latency and bandwidth are not always linked this way. But the trade-off with cost is fairly typical. Speeding things up costs money. Any improvement in bandwidth or latency that doesn't cost more is generally just done without further thought.

Also note that the Concorde is not infinitely fast, and the cargo ship doesn't have infinite capacity. Similarly, the best network technology will always have limitations. Sometimes you just can't get any better than what you already have.

Here the main concern should be with fulfilling the business requirements. If they absolutely have to get a small amount of grain to Paris in a few hours, and the urgency outweighs any expense, they would certainly choose the Concorde option. But, it is more likely that they have to deliver a very large amount cost effectively. So they would choose the significantly slower ship. And that's the point here. The business requirements and not the technology determine what is the best way.

If the business requirements say that the network has to pass so many bytes of data between 9:00 A.M. and 5:00 P.M., and the network is not able to do this, then it is not reliable. It does not fulfill its objectives. The network could pass all of the required data, but during the peak periods, that data has to be *buffered*. This means that there is so much data already passing through the network that some packets are stored temporarily in the memory of some device while they wait for an opening.

This is similar to trying to get onto a very busy highway. Sometimes you have to wait on the on-ramp for a space in the stream of traffic to slip your car into. The result is that it will take longer to get to your destination. The general congestion on the highway will likely also mean that you can't go as fast. The highway is still working, but it isn't getting you where you want to go as fast as you want to get there.

If this happens in a network, it may be just annoying, or it may cause application timeouts and lost data, just as if there were a physical failure. Although it hasn't failed, the network is still considered unreliable because it does not reliably deliver the required volume of data in the required time. Put another way, it is unreliable because the users cannot do their jobs.

Another important point in considering reliability is the difference between similar failures at different points in the network. If a highway used by only a few cars each day gets washed away by bad weather, the chances are that this will not have a serious impact on the region. But if the one major bridge connecting two densely populated regions were to collapse, it would be devastating. In this case one would have to ask why there was only one bridge in the region. There are similar conclusions when looking at critical network links.

This is the key to my definition of reliability. I mean what the end users mean when they say they can't rely on the network to get their jobs done. Unfortunately, this doesn't provide a useful way of measuring anything. Many people have tried to establish metrics based on the number of complaints or on user responses to questionnaires. But the results are terribly unreliable. So, in practice, the network architect needs to establish a model of the user requirements (most likely a different model for each user group) and determine how well these requirements are met.

Usually, this model can be relatively simple. It will include things like:

- What end-to-end latency can the users tolerate for each application?
- What are the throughput (bandwidth) requirements for each application (sustain and burst)?
- What length of outage can the users tolerate for each application?

These factors can all be measured, in principle. The issue of reliability can then be separated from subjective factors that affect a user's perception of reliability.

Redundancy

An obvious technique for improving reliability is to duplicate key pieces of equipment, as in the example of the heavily used bridge between two densely populated areas. The analogy shows two potential benefits to building a second bridge. First, if the first bridge is damaged or needs maintenance, the second bridge will still be there to support the traffic. Second, if the roads leading to these bridges are well planned, then it should be possible to balance their traffic loads. This will improve congestion problems on these major routes.

Exactly the same is true of key network devices. If you duplicate the device, you can eliminate single points of failure. Using redundancy can effectively double through-put in these key parts of the network. But, just as in the highway example, neither benefit is assured. Duplicating the one device that never fails and never needs maintenance won't improve anything. And throughput is only increased if the redundant equipment is able to load-share with the primary equipment.

These two points are also clear when talking about the car bridge. It may be difficult to justify spending large amounts of money on a second bridge just because the first one might one day be flooded out, unless the danger of this failure is obvious and pressing. Bridges are expensive to build. Besides, if high water affects the first bridge, it might affect the second bridge as well. In short, you have to understand your expected failure modes before you start spending money to protect against them.

Similarly, if the access roads to the second bridge are poorly designed, it could be that nobody will use it. If it is awkward to get there, people will balance the extra time required to cross the heavily congested first bridge against the extra time to get to the under-used second bridge.

Finally, if the first bridge is almost never seriously congested, then the financial commitment to build a second one is only justified if there is good reason to believe that it will be needed soon.

All of these points apply to networks as well. If a network is considered unreliable, then implementing redundancy may help, but only if it is done carefully. If there is a congestion problem, then a redundant path may help, but only if some sort of load balancing is implemented between the old and new paths. If the problem is due to component failure, then the redundancy should focus on backing up those components that are expected to fail. If it is being built to handle future growth, then the growth patterns have to be clearly understood to ensure that the enhancements are made where they are most needed.

Redundancy also helps with maintenance. If there is backup equipment in a network, then the primary components can be taken offline without affecting the flow of traffic. This can be particularly useful for upgrading or modifying network hardware and software.

Guidelines for Implementing Redundancy

Clearly some careful thought is required to implement redundancy usefully. There are a number of general guidelines to help with this, but I will also discuss instances where it might be a good idea to ignore these guidelines.

The first rule of thumb is to duplicate all Core equipment, but don't back up a backup.[*] Figures 2-1 and 2-2 show a typical small part of a large LAN without and with redundancy, respectively. In Figure 2-2 the Core concentrator and the router have both been duplicated. There is even a second NIC installed in each of the servers. What has been accomplished in doing this?

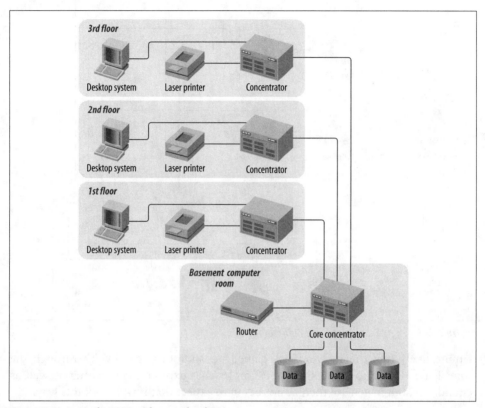

Figure 2-1. A simple LAN without redundancy

For the time being, I will leave this example completely generic. The LAN protocols are not specified. The most common example would involve some flavor of Ethernet. In this case the backup links between concentrators will all be in a hot standby mode (using Spanning Tree). This is similar to saying that the second highway bridge is closed unless the first one fails. So there is no extra throughput between the concentrators on the user floors and the concentrators in the computer room. Similarly, the routers may or may not have load-sharing capability between the two paths. So it

---

[*] As I will discuss later, there are actually cases where it is useful to back up a backup. If there are good reasons to expect multiple failures, or if the consequences of such a multiple failure would be catastrophic, it is worth considering. However, later in this chapter I show mathematically why it is rarely necessary.

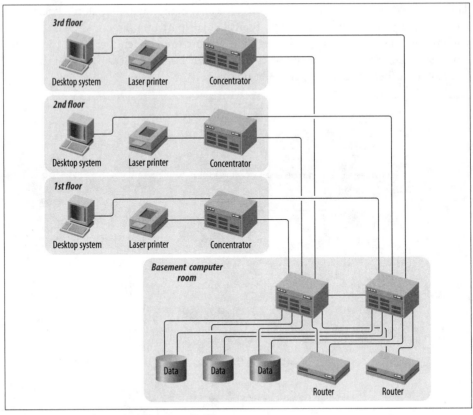

Figure 2-2. A simple LAN with Core redundancy

is quite likely that the network has gained no additional bandwidth through the Core. Later, I go into some specific examples that explore load sharing as well as redundancy, but in general there is no reason to expect that it will work this way.

In fact, for all the additional complexity in this example, the only obvious improvement is that the Core concentrator has been eliminated as a single point of failure. This may be an important improvement. But it could also prove to be a lot of money for no noticeable benefit. And if the switchover from the primary to secondary Core concentrators is a slow or manual process, the network may see only a slight improvement in overall reliability. You would have to understand your expected failure modes before you could tell how useful this upgrade has been.

This example looks like it should have been a good idea, but maybe it wasn't. Where did it go wrong? Well, the first mistake was in assuming that the problem could be solved simply by throwing gear at it. In truth, there are far too many subtleties to take a simple approach like this. One can't just look at physical connectivity. Most importantly, be very careful about jumping to conclusions. You must first clearly understand the problem you are trying to solve.

Redundancy by Protocol Layer

Consider this same network in more detail. Besides having a physical drawing, there has to be a network-layer drawing. This means that I have to get rid of some of the generality. But specific examples are often useful in demonstrating general principles.

Figure 2-3 shows the same network at Layer 3. I will assume that everything is Ethernet or Fast Ethernet. I will also assume a TCP/IP network. The simplest nontrivial example has two user VLANs and one server VLAN.

I talk about VLANs, routers, and concentrators in considerable detail in Chatpers 3 and 4. But for now it is sufficient to know that a VLAN is a logical region of the network that can be spread across many different devices. At the network layer (the layer where IP addresses are used to contact devices), VLANs are composed of groups of devices that are all part of the same subnet (assuming IP networking for now). Getting a packet from one VLAN to another is the same, then, as sending it from one IP subnet to another. So the traffic needs to pass through a router.

There are two groups of users, divided into two VLANs. These users may be anywhere on the three floors. All of the servers, however, are on a separate server VLAN. So, every time a user workstation needs to communicate with a server, it has to send the packet first to the router, which then forwards the packet over to the server.

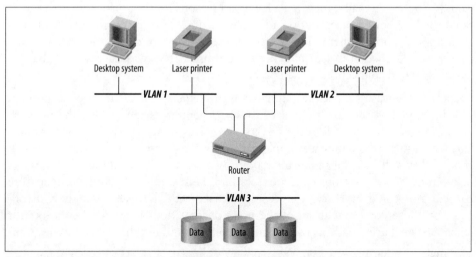

Figure 2-3. A simple LAN with no redundancy—network-layer view

Notice in Figure 2-3 how different the diagram looks at the network layer than it did at the physical layer. It is the same network, but looked at in another complementary way. There are many different ways to implement the same physical network logically. This subject will be discussed in depth later in this book because exploiting this flexibility is what network design is all about.

In Figure 2-3 there are two user VLANs and one server VLAN. These two user segments are spread throughout the three physical floors in Figures 2-1 and 2-2. So the users shown in Figure 2-3 could be anywhere in the building. The server VLAN exists only in the basement and only supports the servers. In theory there is no reason why this VLAN could not also be distributed among all of the concentrators, as the user VLANs were. But in this example, assume that the servers have been given their own VLAN.

Data has to pass through the router to get from one VLAN to another. In the physical-layer diagram (Figure 2-1), the router looks almost like just another server. It is much harder to see why it should have a backup. But in the network-layer diagram (Figure 2-3), it becomes the focal point of the whole network. Here is it clear that this router handles all intersegment traffic. Since the example assumes that the servers are all on separate segments from the users, essentially all application traffic except printing will pass through that router.

At the network layer the router is a single point of failure, just as the concentrator was at the physical layer. If either of these devices stops working, it will disable the entire network. This is why, in Figure 2-2, I replaced both the router and the concentrator.

I also made some other changes. I didn't duplicate the concentrators on the floors for the users, but I did duplicate the trunks connecting them to the basement. Why would I do this? Actually, there are a few good reasons for this. First, because I duplicated the backbone concentrators in the basement, I need to connect the floor concentrators to both of them. This way, if there is a failure of one of the backbone concentrators, it won't isolate an entire floor of users. This was the reasoning behind having a second connection to each of the servers.

Suppose there wasn't a backup interface on the servers, but the Core concentrators still duplicated as shown. If either of these concentrators then failed, the network would lose contact with all of the servers that were connected to that concentrator. Since all of this redundancy was implemented for these servers, it wouldn't do much good if they still had the same single point of failure. In the same way, the trunks between the Core and floor concentrators have been duplicated so that either Core concentrator could break without losing contact with the users. But the network could still lose contact with all of the users on that floor if the local concentrator failed. So why have I made just the trunks redundant and not the local concentrators?

The answer is that I'm not trying to make the network perfect, just better. There is a finite probability that any element anywhere in the network might fail. Before introducing redundancy, the network could lose connectivity to the entire floor if any of a long list of elements failed: the backbone concentrator, the floor concentrator, the fiber transceivers on either end of the trunk, the fiber itself. After the change, only a failure of the floor concentrator will bring down the whole floor. The section "Mean time between failures" will show some detailed calculations that prove this. But it is fairly intuitive that the fewer things that can fail, the fewer things that will fail.

Every failure has some cost associated with it, and every failure has some probability of occurring. These are the factors that must be balanced against the added expense required to protect against a failure. For example, it might be worthwhile to protect your network against an extremely rare failure mode if the consequences are sufficiently costly (or hazardous). It is also often worthwhile to spend more on redundancy than a single failure will cost, particularly if that failure mode occurs with relative frequency.

Conversely, it might be extremely expensive to protect against a common but inconsequential failure mode. This is the reasoning behind not bothering to back up the connections between end-user devices and their local hubs. Yes, these sorts of connections fail relatively frequently, but there are easy workarounds. And the alternatives tend to be prohibitively expensive.

Multiple Simultaneous Failures

The probability of a network device failing is so small that it usually isn't necessary to protect against multiple simultaneous failures. As I said earlier, most designers generally don't bother to back up a backup. The section "Mean time between failures" later in this chapter will talk more about this. But in some cases the network is so critically important that it contains several layers of redundancy.

A network to control the life-support system in a space station might fall into this category. Or, for more down-to-earth examples, a network for controlling and monitoring a nuclear reactor, or a critical patient care system in a hospital, or for certain military applications, would require extra attention to redundancy because a failure could kill people. In these cases the first step is to eliminate key single points of failure and then to start looking for multiple failure situations.

You'd be tempted to look at anything that can possibly break and make sure that it has a backup. In a network of any size or complexity, this will probably prove impossible. At some pragmatic level, the designer would have to say that any two or three or four devices could fail simultaneously.

This statement should be based on combining failure probabilities rather than guessing, though. What is the net gain in reliability by going to another level of redundancy? What is the net increase in cost? Answering these questions tells the designer if the additional redundancy is warranted.

Complexity and Manageability

When implementing redundancy, you should ask whether the additional complexity makes the network significantly harder to manage. Harder to manage usually has the unfortunate consequence of reducing reliability. So, at a certain point, it is quite likely that adding another level of redundancy could make the overall reliability worse.

In this example the network has been greatly improved at the cost of an extra concentrator and an extra router, plus some additional cards and fibers. This is the other key point to any discussion of redundancy. By its very definition, redundancy means having extra equipment and, therefore, extra expense. Ultimately, the cost must balance against benefit. The key is to use these techniques where they are needed most.

Returning to the reasons for not backing up the floor concentrator, the designer has to figure out how to put in a backup, how much this would cost, and what the benefit would be. In some cases they might put in a full duplicate system, as in the Core of the network in the example. This would require putting a second interface card into every workstation. Do these workstations support two network cards? How does failover work between them? With popular low-cost workstation technology, it is often not feasible to do this. Another option might be to just split the users between two concentrators. This way, the worst failure would only affect half the users on the biggest floor.

This wouldn't actually be considered redundancy, since a failure of either floor concentrator would still knock out a number of users completely. But it is an improvement if it reduces the probability of failure per person. It may also be an improvement if there is a congestion problem either within the concentrator or on the trunk to the Core.

Redundancy is clearly an important way of improving reliability in a network, particularly reliability against failures. But this redundancy has to go where it will count the most.

Redundancy may not resolve a congestion problem, for example. If congestion is the problem, sophisticated load-balancing schemes may be called for. This will be discussed in more detail in subsequent chapters.

But if fault tolerance is the issue, then redundancy is a good way to approach the solution. In general it is best to start at the Core (I will discuss the advantages to hierarchical network topologies later), where failures have the most severe consequences.

Automated Fault Recovery

One of the keys to making redundancy work for fault-tolerance problems is the mechanism for switching to the backup. As a general rule, the faster and more transparent the transition, the better. The only exceptions are when an automatic switchover is not physically possible, or where security considerations outweigh fault-tolerance requirements.

The previous section talked about two levels of redundancy. There was a redundant router and a redundant concentrator. If the first Core concentrator failed, the floor concentrators would find the second one by means of the Spanning Tree protocol, which is described in some detail in Chapter 3. Different hardware vendors have different clever ways of implementing Spanning Tree, which I will talk more about later, but in general it is a quick and efficient way of switching off broken links in favor of working ones. If something fails (a Core concentrator or a trunk, for example), then the backup link is automatically turned on to try to restore the path.

Now, consider the redundancy involving the Core router. Somehow the backup router has to take over when the primary fails. There are generally two ways to handle this switchover. Either the backup router can "become" the primary somehow, or the end devices can make the switch. Since it is a router, it is addressed by means of an IP address (I am still talking about a pure TCP/IP network in this example, but the general principles are applicable to many other protocols).

So, if the end devices (the workstations and servers) are going to make the switch, then they must somehow decide to use the backup router's IP address instead of the primary router's IP address. Conversely, if the switch is to be handled by the routers, then the backup router has to somehow adopt the IP address of the primary.

The end stations may realize that the primary router is not available and change their internal routing tables to point to a second router. But in general this is not terribly reliable. Some types of end devices can update IP routing tables by taking part in a dynamic routing protocol such as Routing Information Protocol (RIP). This mechanism typically takes several minutes to complete.

Another way of dealing with this situation at the end device is to specify the default gateway as the device itself. This method is discussed in detail in Chapter 5. It counts on a mechanism called *proxy ARP* to deal with routing. In this case the second router would simply start responding to the requests that the first router previously handled.

There are many problems with this method. One of the worst is that it generally takes several minutes for an end station to remove the old ARP entries from its cache before trying the second router.

It is also possible to switch to the backup router manually by changing settings on the end devices. This is clearly a massive and laborious task that no organization would want to go through very often.

Each of these options is slow. Perhaps more importantly, different types of end devices implement these features differently. That's a nice way of saying that it won't work at all on some devices and it will be terribly slow on others. This leads to a general principle for automated fault recovery.

Always let network equipment perform network functions

Wherever possible, the workings of the network should be hidden from the end device. There are many different types of end devices, all with varying levels of sophistication and complexity. It is not reasonable to expect some specialized, embedded system machine for data collection to have the same sophisticated capabilities as a high-end general-purpose server. Further, the network equipment is in a much better position to know what is actually happening in the network.

But the most important reason to let the network devices handle automated fault recovery is speed. The real goal is to improve reliability. And the goal of reliability is best served by hiding failures from the end devices. After all, the best kind of disaster is one that nobody notices. If the network can "heal" around the problem before anything times out and without losing any data, then to the applications and users it is as if it never happened.

When designing redundancy, automated fault recovery should be one of the primary considerations. Whatever redundancy a designer builds into the network, it should be capable of turning itself on automatically. So whenever considering redundancy, you should work with the fault-tolerance features of the equipment.

Intrinsic versus external automation

There are two main ways that automated fault-recovery systems can be implemented. I will generically refer to these as *intrinsic* and *external*. By intrinsic systems, I mean that the network equipment itself has software or hardware to make the transition to the backup mode. External, on the other hand, means that some other system must engage the alternate pathways or equipment.

An example of an external fault-recovery system would be a network-management system that polls a router every few seconds to see if it is available. Then, upon discovering a problem, it will run a script to reconfigure another router automatically to take over the functions of the first router. This example makes it clear that an automated external system is better than a manual process. But it would be much more reliable if the secondary router itself could automatically step in as a replacement.

There are several reasons why an intrinsic fault-tolerance system is preferable to an external one. First, it is not practical for a network-management system to poll a large number of devices with a high enough frequency to handle transitions without users noticing. Even if it is possible for one or two devices, it certainly isn't for more. In short, this type of scheme does not scale well.

Second, because the network-management box is most likely somewhere else in the network, it is extremely difficult for it to get a detailed picture of the problem quickly. Consequently, there is a relatively high risk of incorrectly diagnosing the problem and taking inappropriate action to repair it. For example, suppose the system is intended to reconfigure a backup router to have the same IP address as a primary router if the network-management system is unable to contact the primary. It is possible to lose contact with this router temporarily because of an unrelated problem in the network infrastructure between the management station and the router being monitored. Then the network-management system might step in and activate the backup while the primary is still present, thereby causing addressing conflicts in the network.

The third reason to caution against external fault-tolerance systems is that the external system itself may be unreliable. I mentioned earlier that the network must be more reliable than any device on it. If this high level of reliability is based on this lower requirement, it may not be helping much.

So it is best to have automatic and intrinsic fault-recovery systems. It is best if these systems are able to "heal" the network around faults transparently (that is, so that the users and applications don't ever know there was a problem). But these sound like rather theoretical ideas. Let's look briefly at some specific examples.

Examples of automated fault recovery

Consider the redundant router shown in Figures 2-2 and 2-4. Suppose that one of the user workstations shown in the diagram is communicating with one of the servers. So packets from the workstation are intended for the IP address of the server. But at Layer 2 the destination address in these packets is the Ethernet MAC address of the primary router. This router is the default gateway for the VLAN. So it receives all packets with destination addresses not on the subnet associated with this VLAN, and it forwards them to the appropriate destination VLAN.

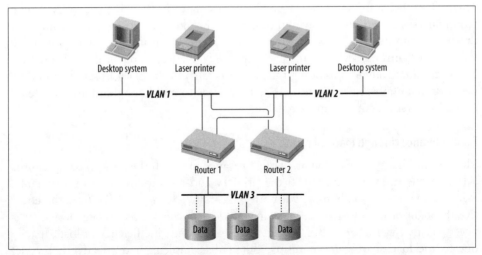

Figure 2-4. A simple LAN with redundancy—network-layer view

Now, suppose that this primary router's power supply has failed. Smoke is billowing out of the back, and it can no longer send or receive anything. It's gone. Meanwhile, the secondary router has been chattering back and forth with the primary, asking it whether it is working. It has been responding dutifully that it feels fine and is able to continue forwarding packets. But as soon as the power supply failed, it stopped responding to these queries. After a couple of repeated queries, the secondary router decides that it must step in to save the day. It suddenly adopts the Ethernet MAC address and the IP address of the primary on all of the ports that they have in common. Chapter 3 will discuss the details of how these high-availability protocols work.

The workstation has been trying to talk to the server while all of this is happening. It has sent packets, but it hasn't seen any responses. So it has resent them. Every one of these packets has a destination Ethernet MAC address pointing to the primary router and a destination IP address pointing to the server. For a few seconds while the secondary router confirmed that it was really appropriate to take over, these packets were simply lost. But most applications can handle the occasional lost packet without a problem. If they couldn't, then ordinary Ethernet collisions would be devastating.

As soon as the secondary router takes over, the workstation suddenly finds that everything is working again. It resends any lost packets, and the conversation picks up where it left off. To the users and the application, if the problem was noticed at all, it just looks like there was a brief slow-down.

The same picture is happening on the server side of this router, which has been trying to send packets to the workstation's IP address via the Ethernet MAC address of the router on its side. So, when the backup router took over, it had to adopt the primary router's addresses on all ports. When I pick up the discussion of these Layer 3 recovery mechanisms in Chapter 3, I talk about how to ensure that all of the router's functions on all of its ports are protected.

This is how I like my fault tolerance. As I show later in this chapter, every time a redundant system automatically and transparently takes over in case of a problem, it drastically improves the network's effective reliability. But if there aren't automatic failover mechanisms, then it really just improves the effective repair time. There may be significant advantages to doing this, but it is fairly clear that it is better to build a network that almost never appears to fail than it is to build one that fails but is easy to fix. The first is definitely more reliable.

Fault tolerance through load balancing

There is another type of automatic fault tolerance in which the backup equipment is active during normal operation. If the primary and backup are set up for dynamic load sharing, then usually they will both pass traffic. So most of the time the effective throughput is almost twice what it would be in the nonredundant design. It is never exactly twice as good because there is always some inefficiency or lost capacity due to the load-sharing mechanisms. But if it is implemented effectively, the net throughput is significantly better.

In this sort of load-balancing fault-tolerance setup, there is no real primary and backup system. Both are primary, and both are backup. So either can fail, and the other will just take up the slack. When this happens, there is an effective drop in network capacity. Users and applications may notice this change as slower response time. So when working with this model, one generally ensures that either path alone has sufficient capacity to support the entire load.

The principal advantage to implementing fault tolerance by means of load balancing is that it provides excess capacity during normal operation. But another less obvious advantage is that by having the backup equipment active at all times, one avoids the embarrassing situation of discovering a faulty backup only during a failure of the primary system. A hot backup system could fail just as easily as the primary system. It is possible to have a backup fail without being noticed because it is not in use. Then if the primary system fails, there is no backup. In fact, this is worse than having no backup because it has the illusion of reliability, creating false confidence.

One final advantage is that the money spent on extra capacity results in tangible benefits even during normal operation. This can help with the task of securing money for network infrastructure. It is much easier to convince people of the value of an investment if they can see a real improvement day to day. Arguments based on reducing probability of failure can seem a little academic and, consequently, a little less persuasive than showing improved performance.

So dynamic load-balancing fault tolerance is generally preferable where it is practical. But it is not always practical. Remember the highway example. Suppose there are two bridges over a river and a clever set of access roads so that both bridges are used equally. In normal operation, this is an ideal setup. But now suppose that one of these bridges is damaged by bad weather. If half of the cars are still trying to use this bridge and one-by-one are plunging into the water, then there is a rather serious problem.

This sounds silly with cars and roads, but it happens regularly with networks. If the load-balancing mechanism is not sensitive to the failure, then the network can wind up dropping every other packet. The result to the applications is slow and unreliable performance. It is generally worse than an outright failure because, in that case, people would give up on the applications and focus on fixing the broken component. But if every other packet is getting lost, it may be difficult to isolate the problem. At least when it breaks outright, you know what you have.

More than that, implementing the secondary system has doubled the number of components that can each cause a network failure. This directly reduces the reliability of the network because it necessarily increases the probability of failure.

Further, if this setup was *believed* to improve reliability, then it has provided an illusion of safety and a false sense of confidence in the architecture. These are dangerous misconceptions.

So, where dynamic load balancing for fault tolerance is not practical, it is better to have a system that automatically switches to backup when a set of clearly defined symptoms are observed. Preferably, this decision to switch to backup is made intrinsically by the equipment itself rather than by any external systems or processes.

If this sort of system is employed as a fault-tolerance mechanism, it is important to monitor the utilization. It is common for network traffic to grow over time. So if a backup trunk is carrying some of the production load, it is possible to reach a point where it can no longer support the entire load in a failure situation. In this case the gradual buildup of traffic means that the system reaches a point where it is no longer redundant.

If this occurs, traffic will usually still flow during a failure, but there will be severe congestion on these links. This will generally result in degraded performance throughout the network.

Avoid manual fault-recovery systems

It is universally true that automatic recovery processes are better than manual processes. There is far too much uncertainty in manual procedures. Differences in levels of experience and expertise in the network-operations staff can mean that sometimes the manual procedures work brilliantly. Sometimes the same procedure can fail catastrophically because of incorrect problem determination or execution. Almost invariably, human-rooted procedures take longer both to start and to complete than automatic processes.

There are only two valid reasons to use a manual recovery process. Either there is no cost-effective way to implement a reliable automatic system, or there are significant security concerns with an automatic system.

In the first case, it is generally wise to re-evaluate the larger design to understand why automatic features of the equipment are not applicable or are too expensive. Redesigning other elements could allow application of automatic fault recovery. But presence of key pieces of older equipment might also make automation impossible. In this case it would be wise to look at upgrading to more modern network technology.

The security reasons for manual processes are more difficult to discuss. But they come down to manually ensuring that the system taking over the primary function is legitimate. For example, a concern might be that an imposter device will attempt to assert itself as a new primary router, redirecting sensitive data for espionage reasons. Or a dial backup type system might be unwilling to accept connections from remote sites unless they are manually authenticated, thus ensuring that this backup is not used to gain unauthorized access to the network.

Usually there are encryption and authentication schemes associated with these sorts of automated processes to protect against exactly these concerns. In some cases the data is considered too sensitive to trust with these built-in security precautions. So, in these cases a business decision has to be made about which is more important, reliability or security.

Isolating Single Points of Failure

One often hears the term *single point of failure* tossed around. In a network of any size or complexity, it would be extremely unusual to find a single device that, if it failed, would break the entire network. But it is not unusual to find devices that control large parts of the network. A Core router will handle a great deal of intersegment traffic. Similarly, a switch or concentrator may support many devices. So, when I talk about single points of failure, I mean any network element that, if it failed, would have consequences affecting several things. Further, for there to be a single point of failure, there must be no backup system. If a single point of failure breaks, it takes out communication with a section of the network.

Clearly single points of failure are one of the keys to network stability. It is not the only one, and too much effort spent on eliminating single points of failure can lead to levels of complexity that also cause instability. So it is important to be careful with this sort of analysis. It can't be the only consideration.

I discuss other factors contributing to stability later, but for now I want to focus on this one. What makes one single point of failure more severe than another depends on the network. It will depend on how many users are affected, what applications are affected, and how important those users and applications are to the organization at that specific point in history. Losing contact with an application that is only used one day per year doesn't matter much unless it happens on that one day. While it's certainly not true that everybody in an organization is of equal value to the organization (or they'd all make the same amount of money), the number of people affected by a failure is clearly an important factor.

In general it isn't possible to say definitively which failure points are the most important. And it isn't always practical to eliminate them all. In Figure 2-2, two single points of failure at the Core of the network were eliminated by adding redundant equipment. But the concentrators on each floor were not made redundant. If one of these concentrators fails, the network will still lose connection to all of the users on that floor.

The simplest way to qualitatively analyze stability is to draw out a complete picture of the network and look at every network device one by one. In the previous section, both the physical- and network-layer diagrams were necessary to see all of the key points in the network, and the same is true here. In the preceding simple example, the router's critical function in the network was not immediately obvious from the physical-layer diagram. In a more complicated network the dependencies could be even less clear.

Look at each box in both of your drawings and ask what happens if this device fails. You may want to look at both drawings at the same time, referring back and forth between them. If the answer is that another device takes over for it, then you can forget about this device for the time being and move on to the next device. Similarly, if the device you are looking at exists purely as a standby, then you can skip it. What remains at the end are all of the places where something can go seriously wrong. In the process, remember to include the connections themselves. Fiber optic cable can go "cloudy," and any cable can be accidentally cut. Consider, for example, what would happen if somebody accidentally cut through an entire fiber conduit. It happens. Many network designers make a point of running their redundant connections through separate conduits.

For each of the remaining elements, it is useful to ask qualitatively how serious a problem it is if it fails. What is affected? How many users are unable to do their jobs? In many cases you will find that some people are unable to run some applications. How important is this to the organization? Rate these problem spots.

Doing this, it should quickly become apparent where the most glaring trouble spots are in your network. In effect you are doing the calculations of the next section "by eye." This tends to assume that the Mean Time Between Failure (MTBF) values for all network elements are similar. That may not be accurate if you are comparing a small workgroup hub to a large backbone switch. But, at the same time, chances are that the backbone switch is a much more critical device, in that it probably supports more traffic and more users.

As was shown in the previous section, the more of these key failure zones that can be eliminated, the better the overall stability of the network.

Consider an example network. Figures 2-5 and 2-6 show the Layer 1/2 and Layer 3/4 views of the same fictitious network. There are many problems with this network, making it a good example for analysis. But clearly there has been some effort at improving the stability. The engineers who run this imaginary network have twinned the switches carrying the router-to-router VLANs, "Core A" and "Core B." And they have built all of the user VLANs, the server VLAN, and the WAN with redundant connections as well. But there are still several serious problems.

Look at the "touchdown"* Ethernet segment in Figure 2-6. Clearly there is a single point of failure in each of the two firewalls. But perhaps this company's Internet usage and the connections to its partner firms are considered of lower importance to other Core parts of the network. So this may be all right. But they have made an effort to make the connections to the touchdown segment redundant, attaching it to both Router A and Router B.

Look at the same part of the network in Figure 2-5. The touchdown segment is carried entirely on one Ethernet hub. So the probability of failure for their Internet access, for example, is actually higher than the probability of failure for the firewall.

---

* This is a relatively common technique for connecting external networks into a LAN. It will be covered in more detail in Chapter 3.

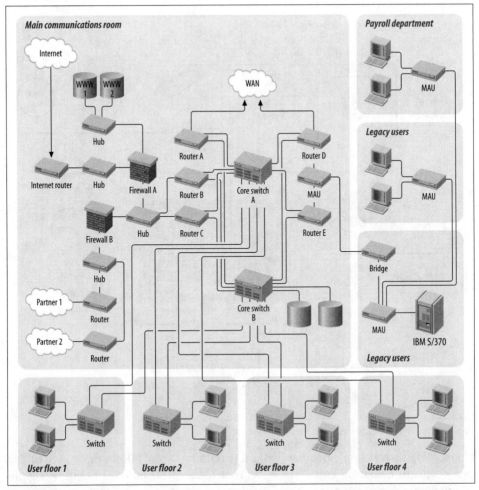

Figure 2-5. Physical-layer view of a rather poor LAN

At the Core of the network, care has been taken to include two main switches, Core switch A and Core switch B. But then both of the main application servers were connected to switch B. This means that much of the advantage of redundancy has been lost.

Now skip over to the right-hand sides of these diagrams. Figure 2-6 shows that the bridge that interconnects all of the Token Rings is a single point of failure. But there are two connections for Routers D and E. Now look at Figure 2-5.

Making two router connections seems to have been an almost wasted effort. After leaving the routers, all the traffic passes through a single Token Ring MAU, through a single fiber transceiver, through a single pair of fiber strands, through another single fiber transceiver, and then to a single bridge. These are all single points of failure.

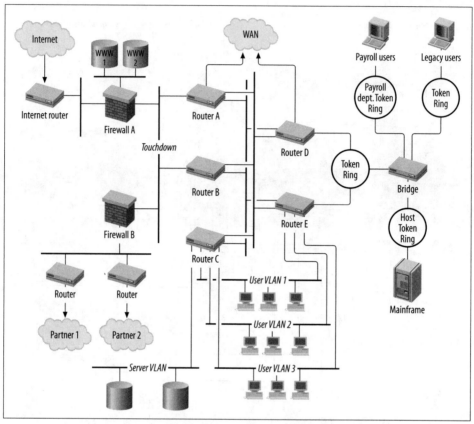

Figure 2-6. Network-layer view of a rather poor LAN

Connecting several single points of failure together in serial allows the failure of any one device to break the entire chain. So clearly the probability of failure is significantly higher than it has to be.

If you are dealing with a high-availability application where certain outages would be serious disasters, then the process of finding danger spots becomes more difficult. In these cases, it is best to break down the network into zones and deal with them separately. I discuss how to build network zones in the discussion of topology in Chapter 3. This concept makes isolating your problems much easier. The idea is to have a few well-controlled points where one network zone touches the next one. Then, as long as there is fault tolerance in the interconnections, you can analyze the zones more or less in isolation.

To deal with multiple failure situations, you can follow a strategy similar to the one described in the previous case, which was looking only for single points of failure. Except that this time it will be necessary to make several passes through. On the first pass, you will look at every network element and decide what will happen if it fails.

In a high-availability network, the answer to each of these questions should be that there is a redundant system to take over for the failed element automatically.

Next you will systematically look at each device and assume that it has already failed. Then go through the remainder of the network and analyze what would happen for each element if it failed in the absence of that first failed element. This process sounds time consuming, but it is not quite as bad as it sounds.

Suppose there are 100 elements to consider in this zone. Remember to include all connections as elements that can fail as well, so the number will usually be fairly high. The initial analysis has already established that any one element can fail in isolation without breaking the network. Now start by looking at element number 1, and supposing it has failed, decide what happens if element number 2 fails. And continue this process through to element 100. On the next pass you start by assuming that element number 2 has failed. This time you don't need to consider what happens if element number 1 fails, because you did that in the last pass. So each pass through the list is one shorter than the last one.

In practice, this sort of qualitative analysis usually takes many hours to complete. But it is a worthwhile exercise, as it will uncover many hidden problems if done carefully. Most of the time it will be obvious that there is no problem with the second element failing, since it is backed up by another element unrelated to the first failure. In fact, it is often worth doing this exercise in a less mission-critical network because it will show how vulnerabilities are connected.

But, as I mentioned earlier in passing, just eliminating the single points of failure does not guarantee a stable network. The sheer complexity of the result can itself be a source of instability for several reasons. First and most important, the more complex the network is, the greater the chance that a human will misunderstand it and inadvertently break it. But also, the more complex a network, the more paths there will be to get from point A to point B. As a result, the automated fault-recovery systems and automated routing systems will have a considerably harder time in finding the best path. Consequently, they will tend to take much longer in converging and may try to recalculate the paths through the network repeatedly. The result is a frustratingly slow and unreliable network despite the absence of single points of failure.

Predicting Your Most Common Failures

I have talked about implementing redundancy where it is most needed. But so far I have only given general comments about where that might be. I've mentioned duplicating systems "in the Core" and at "single points of failure," but the methods have been mostly qualitative and approximate. As a network designer, you need to know where to look for problems and where to spend money on solutions. This requires more rigorous techniques.

There is an analytical technique based on MTBF that provides a relatively precise way of numerically estimating probabilities of failure for not only individual components in a network, but also for whole sections of networks. I will demonstrate this technique. I will also discuss some more qualitative methods for finding potential problem spots.

Mean time between failures

One of the most important numbers your equipment manufacturer quotes in the specification sheet is the Mean Time Between Failures (MTBF). But this value is frequently misunderstood and misused. So I will discuss the concept a little bit before going on.

This number just represents a statistical likelihood. It means that half (because it's a statistical "mean") of all equipment of this type will no longer be functioning after this length of time. It does not mean that sudden and catastrophic failure will occur at the stroke of midnight. Failure can happen at any time. But just giving an average without saying anything about the shape of the curve makes it difficult to work with.

Figure 2-7 shows some possible versions of what the curve might look like. These curves plot the number of device failures as a function of time. There are N total devices, so at time MTBF, there are N/2 devices remaining.

The thick solid line represents a very ideal world where almost all of the gear survives right up until moments before the MTBF. Of course, the price for this is that a large number of devices then all fail at the same time.

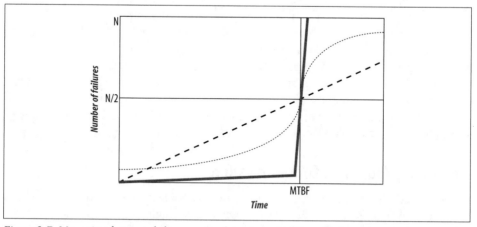

Figure 2-7. Mean time between failures, as it relates to probability of failure per unit of time

The dashed line, on the other hand, shows a sort of worst-case curve, in which the same number of devices fail every day. This is probably not a realistic approximation either because there are a lot of devices that either don't work when you open the box or fail soon after. Then age will take a toll later as gear gradually burns out through heavy use. The dotted curve represents a more realistic curve.

But the interesting thing is that, when you look at these curves, it's clear that the dashed line isn't such a bad approximation after all. It's going to be close. And up until the MTBF time, it will tend to overestimate the probability of failure. It's always a good idea to overestimate when it comes to probability of failure, because the worst you can do is end up with an unusually stable and reliable network. It's also going to be the easiest to do calculations with.

So the dashed line is the one I use for finding the most common failure modes. The slope of this line gives the failure rate, the number of failures per unit time, and because it is a straight line, the approximation assumes a constant failure rate. A little arithmetic shows that the line rises by $N/2$ in a distance of MTBF, so the slope is $N/(2 \times \text{MTBF})$. So, if the MTBF is 10 years, then you will expect to see 5% of your devices fail every year, on average. If the MTBF is 20 years, then the value drops to 2.5%. Most network-equipment manufacturers quote an MTBF in this range.

If you had only one device, then a 5% per year failure rate is probably quite acceptable. You may not care about redundancy. But this book is concerned with large-scale networks, networks with hundreds or thousands of devices. At 5% per year, out of a network of 1000 devices, you will expect to see 50 failures per year. That's almost one per week.

The important point to draw from this is that the more devices you have, the greater the chances are that one of them will fail. So, the more single points of failure in the network, the greater the probability of a catastrophic failure.

Multiple simultaneous failures

So the MTBF gives, in effect, a probability of failure per unit time. To find the probability for simultaneous failures, you need a way of combining these probabilities. I have already described the method of simply adding probabilities to find the aggregate failure rate. But this is a different problem. The important question here is the probability of exactly two or three or four simultaneous failures.

The naïve approach to combining probabilities would be to say that the probability of two simultaneous failures is twice the probability of one. This would be close to true for very small values, but not quite right. To see this, imagine a coin toss experiment. The probability of heads is 50%. The probability of flipping the coin 3 times and getting 2 heads is not 100%. And it certainly isn't equal to the probability of flipping the coin 100 times and getting 2 heads.

Now suppose that it is an unfair coin that has a probability P of coming up heads. In fact, it's an extremely unfair coin. P is going to be less than 1%. Later I adapt this simple probability to be a probability of failure per unit time, as it is needed for combining these MTBF values. But first I need the probability, $_kP_n$, of tossing the coin n times and getting heads k times. The derivation of this formula is shown in the Appendix.

$$_kP_n = \frac{n! \cdot P^k(1-P)^{n-k}}{k! \cdot (n-k)!}$$

For network MTBF, the interesting values are related to number of failures per unit time. If the MTBF value is M, then you can expect $N/(2 \times M)$ failures out of a set of N per unit time. If $N = 1$, then this is the probability per unit time of a particular unit failing. But you can't just plug this into the formula for $_kP_n$. Why not? Look at the formula. It contains a factor that looks like $(1-P)^{n-k}$. The number 1 has no units. So the number P can't have units either, or the formula is adding apples to oranges.

So it is necessary to convert this probability per unit time to a net probability. The easiest way to do this is to decide on a relevant time unit and just multiply it. This time unit shouldn't be too short or too long. The probability of having two failures in the same microsecond is very small indeed. And the probability of having two failures in the same year is going to be relatively large, but it is quite likely that the first problem has been fixed before the second one occurs.

This is the key to finding the right length of time. How long does it take, on average, to fix the problem? Note that this is not the length of time for the backup to kick in, because the result is going to show how appropriate that backup is. If the backup fails before the primary unit has been fixed, then that's still a multiple-failure situation. So the best unit is the length of time required to fix the primary fault.

For this I like to use one day. Sometimes it takes longer than one day to fix a major problem; sometimes a problem can be fixed in a few hours. But a one-day period is reasonable because, in most networks, a day with more than one major-device failure is an exceedingly busy day. And when there are multiple device failures in one day, there is usually a lot of reporting to senior management required. In any case, it generally takes several hours to repair or replace a failed device, so a one-day period for the time unit seems appropriate. At worst, it will overestimate the failure rates slightly, and it's always better to overestimate.

I will denote thie MTBF per-day value by the letter M. So the probability of one particular device failing in a given day is $P = 1/2M$.

So, substituting into the probability formula gives:

$$_kP_n = \frac{n! \cdot (2m-1)^{n-k}}{k! \cdot (n-k)! \cdot (2m)}$$

where $m = M/1$ day.

This formula gives the probability that, in a network of n devices, each with an MTBF value of M, there will be k failures in one day. Figure 2-8 is a graph of the probabilities for some representative values. Notice that for most of the values plotted, it is quite rare to have any failures at all. But for a network of 1000 nodes, each with a 100,000-hour MTBF, there will be failures on about 1 day in 10. If that same network had 10,000 nodes in it, the analysis predicts that only 30% of all days will have no failures. 36% of days would have some device fail, and about 1 day in 5 would see 2 or more failures. Even the smaller network with only 1000 nodes would have days with 2 failures 0.6% of the time. That amounts to just over 2 days per year. So it will happen.

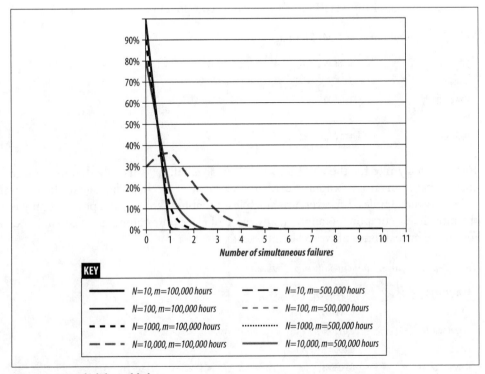

Figure 2-8. Probability of failure

Generally you want to work out these probabilities for your whole network. You should plan your network for a level of redundancy that the business can handle. Personally, I don't like to deal with multiple failures in a single day, so I plan my networks so that these bad days are expected much less than once every year. But you need to determine what your business and your network-management team can handle.

Combining MTBF values

In general, in a multivendor network, there will be many different MTBF values. In fact, many vendors quote distinct MTBF values for every component of a modular device. They do this because how you combine these values to find the number relevant to your network depends greatly on how you decide to use the device.

This section will describe how to combine the values. I start by looking at how to combine the MTBF values for a single device and then move on to how to combine these values for various elements making up a network. A common technique for this sort of estimation says that the chain is as strong as its weakest link. But this is not actually a very good rule, as can be seen with a simple example.

Suppose you have a generic device. Maybe it's a router. Maybe it's a switch of some sort. It doesn't really matter for this example. Table 2-1 shows some fairly typical made-up values for the MTBFs of these various components.

Table 2-1. Typical component MTBF values

Component	Hours
Chassis	2,000,000
Power supply	100,000
Processor	200,000
Network card	150,000

It is extremely rare for the chassis to fail. If it does fail, it is usually due to damage such as bent pins from swapping cards too aggressively or heat damage to the backplane. Power supplies, however, are much less reliable. Typically the power supply is the most likely component failure in any piece of electronic equipment. See Table 2-2 for failure probabilities of typical components.

Table 2-2. Typical component-failure probabilities

Component	Probability
Chassis	0.0006%
Power supply	0.0120%
Processor	0.0060%
Network card	0.0080%

So, this generic device has a chassis, two power supplies (for redundancy), a processor module, and two network modules. There is no redundancy for the processor or for the network modules. What is the aggregate MTBF for the device? This could involve any failure to any component. But the twist is that, if one of the power supplies fails, the other will take over for it.

First these MTBF values have to be converted to probabilities of failure per day. Recall that the formula for this is just $1/(2m)$, where $m = \text{MTBF}/1\text{ day}$.

First combine the probabilities for the two power supplies failing simultaneously. That would be two simultaneous failures out of a set of two. This is just $_2P_2 = P^2$ in the joint probability formula. The square of 0.0120% is a very small number, $1.44 \times 10^{-6}\%$. So clearly the decision to use redundant power supplies has significantly improved the weakest link in this system.

Any of the remaining components can fail independently and count as a device failure, so you can just add these probabilities to get the net probability.

$$Pnet = 0.0006\% + 1.44 \cdot 10^{-6}\% + 0.0060\% + 2 \cdot (0.0080\%)$$
$$= 0.02260144\%$$

You can now convert this back to an aggregate MTBF for the device. Since $P = 1/(2m)$, $m = 1/(2P)$. So, in this case, $m = 53,100$ hours.

As you can see, the weakest-link rule is quite wrong. It would have said that you could neglect the power supplies because they are redundant (and it would have been right in saying that). Then it would have picked out the network card's 150,000-hour MTBF value.

The trouble with this is that it completely neglects the fact that there are several elements here, any of which can fail. The chances of getting into a car accident are exceedingly small. Most people only have a few in their entire lives. And yet, in a large city there are accidents every day. It's the same with networks. The more components you have, the more likely something will fail.

To take this example slightly further, let's try to understand why many hardware vendors offer the capability of redundant processor modules. In this case the net probability is:

$$Pnet = 0.0006\% + (0.0120\%)^2 + (0.0060\%)^2 + 2 \cdot (0.0080\%)$$
$$= 0.01660\%$$

which corresponds to an aggregate MTBF for the device of 72,300 hours. So, duplicating the processor module has improved the net MTBF for the device by 36%.

There is one final example to look at before moving on to calculating MTBF values for an entire network. Often, particularly for power supplies, devices employ what is called "N+1" redundancy. This means that there is one extra power supply in the box. Suppose the device needs only 3 power supplies to work. Then you might install a fourth power supply for redundancy. For a complete failure, you need to lose 2 of the 4 power supplies. To calculate the probability for this, use the formula derived in the previous section:

$$_kP_n = \frac{n! \cdot (2m-1)^{n-k}}{k! \cdot (n-k)! \cdot (2m)^n}$$

with $k = 2$ and $n = 4$.

$$\begin{aligned}
_2P_4 &= \frac{4 \cdot (2m-1)^2}{2! \cdot (2)! \cdot (2m)^4} \\
&= \frac{6(2m-1)^2}{(2m)^4} \\
&= 0.000000015\%
\end{aligned}$$

Recall that the single power-supply failure probability was 0.0120%. For two fully redundant power supplies the probability is $(0.0120\%)^2 = 0.00000144\%$. So it becomes clear that N+1 redundancy in these small numbers provides a large benefit and is a cost-effective strategy.

The net probability of failure for the entire device (with dual processors, as in the previous example) would become:

$$\begin{aligned}
Pnet &= 0.0006\% + 0.000000015\% + (0.0060\%)^2 + 2 \cdot (0.0080\%) \\
&= 0.000166\%
\end{aligned}$$

which is effectively the same as the previous example with full redundancy for the power supplies.

As a quick aside, consider how N+1 redundancy works for larger values of N. How much can the situation be improved by adding one extra hot standby? In other words, I want to compare the probability for one failure out of N with the probability for two simultaneous failures:

$$_2P_n = \frac{n(n-1) \cdot (2m-1)^{n-2}}{2(2m)^n} \sim n^2/(8m^2)$$

and:

$$_1P_n = \frac{n \cdot (2m-1)^{n-1}}{2(2m)^n} \sim n/(2m)$$

So $_2P_n / _1P_n \sim n/4m$. This means that as long as N is much smaller than 4 times the MTBF in days, the approximation should be reasonable. But, for example, if the MTBF were 100 days, then it would be a very bad idea to use N+1 redundancy for 25 components. In fact, it would probably be wise to look at N+2 or better redundancy long before this point.

The same prescription can be used for calculating the probability of failure for an entire network. Consider the network shown in Figures 2-1 and 2-2. How much has the network's net MTBF improved by making the Core redundant? Note, however, that there are failures in this more general case that do not wipe out the entire network. For example, if any of the floor concentrators fails, it will affect only the users on that floor. However, it is still useful to do this sort of calculation because it gives an impression of how useful it has been to add the redundancy.

Calculating the MTBF for only the Core could well miss the possibility that the worst problems do not lie in the Core. In any case, it is worthwhile understanding how often to expect problems in the entire network.

Table 2-3 presents some representative fiction about the MTBF values for the individual components in the network. Note that I have included the fiber runs between the floors, but I assume that the fiber transceivers are built into the concentrators, and are included in the MTBF for the device. Also note that for simplicity, I use the same model of device for the floor and Core concentrators. This would probably not be true in general.

Table 2-3. Example component-failure probabilities

Component	Hours	Probability
Concentrator	150,000	0.0080%
Fiber connection	1,000,000	0.0012%
Router	200,000	0.0060%

Adding up the net probability for the network without redundancy gives:

$$Pnet = 4 \cdot (0.0080\%) + 3 \cdot (0.0012\%) + 0.0060\%$$
$$= 0.0416\%$$

So the net MTBF is 28,846 hours. And, with redundancy:

$$Pnet = 3 \cdot (0.0080\%) + 6 \cdot (0.0012\%) + (0.0080\%)^2 + (0.0060\%)^2$$
$$= 0.0312\%$$

which gives a net MTBF of 38,460 hours. This is a 33% improvement in MTBF, or a 25% improvement in *Pnet*. So implementing redundancy has helped significantly. Looking specifically at the terms, one can easily see that the terms for the Core are now very small. The bulk of the failures are expected to occur on the floor concentrators now. Interestingly, this was true even before introducing the Core redundancy. But, clearly, the redundancy in the Core has radically improved things overall.

This way of looking at reliability provides another particularly useful tool: it shows where to focus efforts in order to improve overall network reliability further.

It could be that there are only 3 users on the first floor and 50 on the second. In some sense, the failure of the second floor is more important. So it may be useful to produce a weighted failure rate per user. To do this, look at each device and how many users are affected if it fails. Then, in the calculation of *Pnet*, multiply the number of users by the probability. When you do this, the number is no longer a probability, and you can no longer convert it back to an MTBF. You can only use it as a relative tool for evaluating how useful the change you propose to make will be. See Table 2-4 for user failure probabilities for sample components.

Table 2-4. Example component-failure probabilities by user

Component	Hours	Probability	Users
First floor concentrator	150,000	0.0080%	3
First floor fiber connection	1,000,000	0.0012%	3
Second floor concentrator	150,000	0.0080%	50
Fiber connection	1,000,000	0.0012%	50
Third floor concentrator	150,000	0.0080%	17
Third floor fiber connection	1,000,000	0.0012%	17
Backbone concentrator	150,000	0.0080%	70
Router	200,000	0.0060%	70

So adding up the weighted probability for the nonredundant case gives:

$$Wnet = 3 \cdot (0.0080\%) + 3 \cdot (0.0012\%) + 50 \cdot (0.0080\%) + 50 \cdot (0.0012\%)$$
$$+ 17 \cdot (0.0080\%) + 17 \cdot (0.0012\%) + 70 \cdot (0.0080\%) + 70 \cdot (0.0060\%)$$
$$= 1.624\%$$

I have changed the symbol from *Pnet* to *Wnet*. This is to remind you that this is not a real probability anymore. It is just a tool for comparison.

Now let's look at the redundant case:

$$Wnet = 3 \cdot (0.0080\%) + 2 \cdot 3 \cdot (0.0012\%) + 50 \cdot (0.0080\%) + 2 \cdot 50 \cdot (0.0012\%)$$
$$+ 17 \cdot (0.0080\%) + 2 \cdot 17 \cdot (0.0012\%) + 70 \cdot (0.0080\%)^2 + 70 \cdot (0.0060\%)^2$$
$$= 0.728\%$$

This shows that the changes have improved the per-user reliability by better than a factor of 2. It also shows that doing any better than this will mean doing something for the people on the second floor, because the terms corresponding to them make up more than 2/3 of the total value of *Wnet*.

But perhaps network engineering is on the first floor and marketing or bond trading is on the second. In this case, losing the 50 users on the second floor could be a net benefit to the company, but losing the 3 network engineers would be a disaster. If this is the case, you may want to use another weighting scheme, based on the relative importance of the users affected. Remember, though, that these weighted values are no longer probabilities. Weighting the different terms destroys what mathematicians call normalization. This means that these *W* values will not sum to 1. So you can't use the numbers where you would use probabilities, for example, in calculating MTBF.

Failure Modes

Until I have talked about the various standard network topologies, it will be difficult to have an in-depth discussion of failure modes. But I can still talk about failure modes in general. Obviously, the worst failure mode is a single point of failure for the entire network. But, as the previous section showed, the overall stability of the network may be governed by less obvious factors.

At the same time, this proves that any place where you can implement redundancy in a network drastically improves the stability for that component. In theory it would be nice to be able to do detailed calculations as earlier. Then you could look for the points where the weighted failure rates are highest. But in a large network this is often not practical. There may be thousands of components to consider. So this is where the simpler qualitative method described earlier is useful.

What the quantitative analysis of the last section shows, though, is that it is a serious problem every time you have a failure that can affect a large number of users. Even worse, it showed that the probability of failure grows quickly with each additional possible point of failure. The qualitative analysis just finds the problem spots; it doesn't make it clear what the consequences are. Having one single point of failure in your network that affects a large number of users is not always such a serious problem, particularly if that failure never happens. But the more points like this that you have, the more likely it is that these failures will happen.

Suppose you have a network with 100,000 elements that can fail. This may sound like a high number, but in practice it isn't out of the ordinary for a large-scale LAN. Remember that the word "element" includes every hub, switch, cable, fiber, card in every network device, and even your patch panels.

If the average MTBF for these 100,000 elements is 100,000 hours (which is probably a little low), then on net you can expect about one element per day to break. Even if there is redundancy, the elements will still break and need to be replaced: it just won't affect production traffic. Most of these failures will affect very small numbers of users. But the point is that, the larger your network, the more you need to understand what can go wrong, and the more you will need to design around these failure modes.

So far I have only discussed so-called hard failures. In fact, most LAN problems aren't the result of hard failures. There are many kinds of failures that happen even when the network hardware is still operating. These problems fall into a few general categories: congestion, traffic anomalies, software problems, and human error.

Congestion

Congestion is the most obvious sort of soft problem on a network. Everybody has experienced a situation where the network simply cannot handle all of the traffic that is passing through it. Some packets are dropped; others are delayed.

In dealing with congestion, it is important to understand your traffic flows. In Figure 2-5, user traffic from the various user floors flows primarily to the Internet, the application servers, and the mainframe. But there is very little floor-to-floor traffic. This allows you to look for the bottlenecks where there might not be enough bandwidth. In this example all traffic flows through the two Core VLANs. Is there sufficient capacity there to deal with all of the traffic?

Congestion is what happens when traffic hits a bottleneck in the network. If there is simply not enough downstream capacity to carry all of the incoming traffic, then some of it has to be dropped. But before dropping packets, most network equipment will attempt to buffer them.

Buffering basically means that the packets are temporarily stored in the network device's memory in the hopes that the incoming burst will relent. The usual example is a bucket with a hole in the bottom. If you pour water into the bucket, gradually it will drain out through the bottom.

Suppose first that the amount you pour in is less that the total capacity of the bucket. In this case the water will gradually drain out. The bucket has changed a sudden burst of water into a gradual trickle.

On the other hand, you could just continue pouring water until the bucket overflows. An overflow of data means that packets have to be dropped, there simply isn't enough memory to keep them all. The solution may be just to get a bigger bucket. But if the incoming stream is relentless, then it doesn't matter how big the bucket is: it will never be able to drain in a controlled manner.

This is similar to what happens in a network when too much data hits a bottleneck. If the burst is short, the chances are good that the network will be able to cope with it easily. But a relentless flow that exceeds the capacity of a network link means that a lot of packets simply can't be delivered and have to be dropped.

Some network protocols deal well with congestion. Some connection-based protocols such as TCP have the ability to detect that some packets have been dropped. This allows them to back off and send at a slower rate, usually settling just below the peak capacity of the network. But other protocols cannot detect congestion, and instead they wind up losing data.

Lost data can actually make the congestion problem worse. In many applications, if the data is not received within a specified time period, or if only some of it is received, then it will be sent again. This is clearly a good idea if you are the application. But if you are the network, it has the effect of making a bad problem worse.

Ultimately, if data is just not getting through at all for some applications, they can time out. This means that the applications decide that they can't get their jobs done, so they disconnect themselves. If many applications disconnect, it can allow the congestion to dissipate somewhat. But often the applications or their users will instead attempt to reconnect. And again, this connection-setup traffic can add to the congestion problem.

Congestion is typically encountered on a network anywhere that connections from many devices or groups of devices converge. So, the first common place to see congestion is on the local Ethernet or Token Ring segment. If many devices all want to use the network at the same time, then the Data Link protocol provides a method (collisions for Ethernet, token passing for Token Ring) for regulating traffic. This means that some devices will have to wait.

Worse congestion problems can occur at points in the network where traffic from many segments converges. In LANs this happens primarily at trunks. In networks that include some WAN elements, it is common to see congestion at the point where LAN traffic reaches the WAN.

The ability to control congestion through the Core of a large-scale LAN is one of the most important features of a good design. This requires a combination of careful monitoring and a scalable design that makes it easy to move or expand bottlenecks. In many networks congestion problems are also mitigated using a traffic-prioritization system. This issue is discussed in detail in Chapter 10.

Unlike several of the other design decisions I have discussed, congestion is an ongoing issue. At some point there will be a new application, a new server. An old one will be removed. People will change the way they use existing services, and that will change the traffic patterns as well. So there must be ongoing performance monitoring to ensure that performance problems don't creep up on a network.

Traffic Anomalies

By traffic anomalies, I mean that otherwise legitimate packets on the network have somehow caused a problem. This is distinct from congestion, which refers only to loading problems. This category includes broadcast storms and any time a packet has confused a piece of equipment. Another example is a server sending out an erroneous dynamic routing packet or ICMP packet that caused a router to become confused about the topology of the network. These issues will be discussed more in Chapter 6.

But perhaps the most common and severe examples are where automatic fault-recovery systems, such as Spanning Tree at Layer 2, or dynamic routing protocols, such as Open Shorted Path First (OSPF) at Layer 3, become confused. This is usually referred to as a convergence problem. The result can be routing loops, or just slow unreliable response across the network.

The most common reason for convergence problems at either Layer 2 or 3 is complexity. Try to make it easy for these processes by understanding what they do. The more paths available, the harder it becomes to find the best path. The more neighbors, the worse the problem of finding the best one to pass a particular packet to.

A broadcast storm is a special type of problem. It gets mentioned frequently, and a lot of switch manufacturers include features for limiting broadcast storms. But what is it really? Well, a broadcast packet is a perfectly legitimate type of packet that is sent to every other station on the same network segment or VLAN. The most common example of a broadcast is an IP ARP packet. This is where a station knows the IP address of a device, but not the MAC address. To address the Layer 2 destination part of the frame properly, it needs the MAC address. So it sends out a request to everybody on the local network asking for this information, and the station that owns (or is responsible for forwarding) this IP address responds.

But there are many other types of broadcasts. A storm usually happens when one device sends out a broadcast and another tries to be helpful by forwarding that broadcast back onto the network. If several devices all behave the same way, then they see the rebroadcasts from one another and rebroadcast them again. The LAN is instantly choked with broadcasts.

The way a switch attempts to resolve this sort of problem usually involves a simple mechanism of counting the number of broadcast packets per second. If it exceeds a certain threshold, it starts throwing them away so that they can't choke off the network. But clearly the problem hasn't gone away. The broadcast storm is just being kept in check until it dies down on its own.

Containment is the key to traffic anomalies. Broadcast storms cannot cross out of a broadcast domain (which usually means a VLAN, but not necessarily). OSPF convergence problems can be dealt with most easily by making the areas small and simple in structure. Similarly, Spanning Tree problems are generally caused by too many interconnections. So in all cases, keeping the region of interest small and simple helps enormously.

This doesn't mean that the network has to be small, but it does support the hierarchical design models I discuss later in this book.

Software Problems

Software problems are a polite term for bugs in the network equipment. It happens. Sometimes a router or switch will simply hang, or sometimes it will start to misbehave in some peculiar way.

Routers and switches are extremely complex specialized computers. So software bugs are a fact of life. But most network equipment is remarkably bug-free. It is not uncommon to encounter a bug or two during initial implementation phases of a network. But a network that avoids using too many novel features and relies on mature products from reputable vendors is generally going to see very few bugs.

Design flaws are much more common than bugs. Bugs that affect Core pieces of code, like standard IP routing or OSPF, are rare in mature products. More rare still are bugs that cannot be worked around by means of simple design changes.

Human Error

Unfortunately, the most common sort of network problem is where somebody changed something, either deliberately or accidentally, and it had unforeseen consequences. There are so many different ways to shoot oneself in the foot that I won't bother to detail them here. Even if I did, no doubt tomorrow we'd all go out and find new ones.

There are design decisions that can limit human error. The most important of these is to work on simplicity. The easier it is to understand how the network is supposed to work, the less likely that somebody will misunderstand it. Specifically, it is best to make the design in simple, easily understood building blocks. Wherever possible, these blocks should be as similar as possible. One of the best features of the otherwise poor design shown in Figure 2-5 is that it has an identical setup for all of the user floors. Therefore, a new technician doesn't need to remember special tricks for each area; they are all the same.

The best rule of thumb in deciding whether a design is sufficiently simple is to imagine that something has failed in the middle of the night and somebody is on the phone in a panic wanting answers about how to fix it. If most of the network is designed using a few simple, easily remembered rules, the chances are good that you'll be able to figure out what they need to know. You want to be able to do it without having to race to the site to find your spreadsheets and drawings.

CHAPTER 3

Design Types

A large-scale network design is composed of several common building blocks. Every LAN, of whatever size, has to have an Access system by which the end stations connect to the network. There are several inexpensive options for LAN connections, such as Ethernet and Token Ring. As a philosophical principle, the network should be built using basic commonly available technology. The design shouldn't have to reinvent any wheels just to allow the machines to talk to one another.

So, just as basic commonly available technologies exist for connecting end stations to LANs, there are common methods for interconnecting LAN segments. Once again, these technologies and methods should involve the most inexpensive yet reliable methods. But in this stage of interconnecting, aggregating, and distributing traffic between these various LAN segments, the designer runs into some serious hidden problems.

There may be thousands of ways to connect things, but most of these methods result in some kind of reliability problems. This book intends to establish general methodologies for designing networks so that designers can avoid these sorts of problems.

Basic Topologies

There are four basic topologies used to interconnect devices: bus, ring, star, and mesh. In a large-scale LAN design, the ultimate goal includes a number of these segments. Figures 3-1 to 3-4 show these four basic topologies.

Basic Concepts

Before getting into the solutions, I want to spend a little bit of time making sure that the potential problems are clear. What are the real goals of the network design? What are the options? Ultimately, I want to help point you toward general approaches that can save a lot of worry down the road.

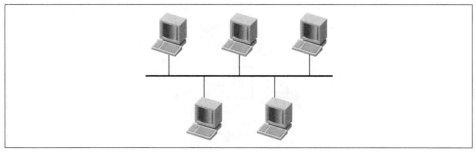

Figure 3-1. Bus topology

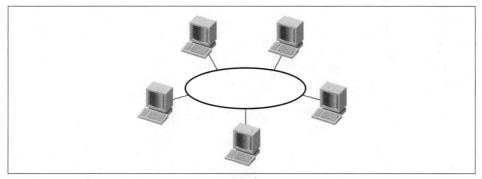

Figure 3-2. Ring topology

The main goal is to build an infrastructure that allows end devices to communicate with one another. That sounds simple enough. But what is an end device? I don't include network devices when I talk about end devices. This fact sounds pedantic, but it's important. A network device is one that cares about the lower layers of the protocol stack. It exists to facilitate the flow of traffic between end devices. End devices are the devices that care about Layer 7. End devices run applications, request data from one another, present information to humans, or control machinery; most importantly, end devices should never perform network functions.

Why do I make this point? I believe that a number of common practices on networks are dangerous or at least misguided, and they should be stopped. Here are some examples of cases in which end devices are permitted to perform network functions (such as bridging or routing) at the expense of network stability:

- File servers with two LAN NIC cards, configured to bridge between the two interfaces
- Application servers with one or more WAN cards in them that allow bridging or routing
- Servers with any number of NIC cards taking part in dynamic routing protocols such as RIP or OSPF

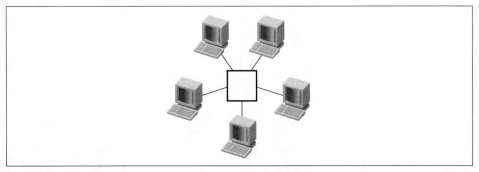

Figure 3-3. Star topology

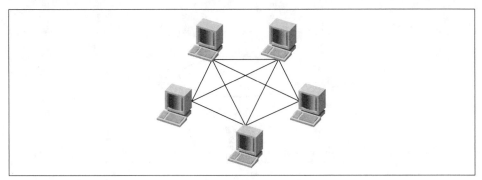

Figure 3-4. Mesh topology

In each of these cases (which I am quite sure will get me in trouble with certain vendors), an end device is permitted to perform network functions. No file or application server should ever act as a router or a bridge. If you want a router or a bridge, buy a real one and put it in. Note that I am not talking about devices that just happen to have a PC form factor or use a standard PC CPU. For example, a dedicated firewall device with a specialized secure operating system is a network device. As long as you refrain from using it as a workstation or a server, you're fine. But in no case should a file or application server act as a bridge or a router.

The concern is that any device that is not dedicated to performing network functions should not be permitted. Furthermore, with the exception of highly specialized security devices such as firewalls and similar gateways, using any general-purpose computing device in a network function is a bad idea. So, even if you only use the Linux PC as a router, and that's the only thing it does, it is still going to be less reliable and probably more expensive than using a device designed from the outset as a router. I don't like home-rolled network equipment. Real routers and switches are not very expensive, and trying to build your own is not going to save you any money in the long run, no matter how good of a programmer you are. At some point in the distant future, somebody else will inevitably have to deal with it and will fail to understand the unique system.

The same thing is true in reverse. Network devices should not perform Layer 7 functions. No router should run an email server. No firewall should be a web or email server. Sometimes you will run applications on your network devices, but they are never Layer 7 functions. For example, running a DHCP server from a router might be expedient. Or, having a web server on a router is often worthwhile if it is used only for the purposes of managing the router itself in performing its network functions. Having a Network Time Protocol (NTP) server running on your network equipment, with all other devices synchronizing their clocks to "the network" is also useful. But these are all very specific exceptions, and none of them are really user applications.

Failing to separate network functions from application functions creates so many problems that it is hard to list them. Here are a few of the most compelling:

- Generally, network engineers are not properly trained to deal with application issues. In most organizations, there are staff members who are better equipped to manage applications and servers. These people can't do their jobs properly if the network staff controls the resources. For example, if the corporate web site is housed inside of the corporate firewall, how effectively will the web mistress work with it? What if a bug is in the web server? Upgrading code could mean taking the whole Internet connection offline.

  The same situation is true of devices that include email functions such as POP servers with network functions. Such devices, if also central components of the network, make maintenance on the email server extremely difficult.

- Running applications is hard work. Running network functions is also hard work. Doing both at the same time often creates serious memory and CPU resource problems. These problems tend to occur during the most busy peak periods of the day, thereby breaking not just the application, but the entire network when it is most needed.

- I've already indicated that the network must be more reliable than any end device. If the network is an end device, then it presents an inherent reliability problem.

- If an end device takes part in a dynamic routing protocol such as RIP or OSPF, and it is either misconfigured or suffers a software bug, then that one end device can disrupt traffic for the entire network. This is why no end device should ever be permitted to take part in these protocols. There are much more reliable ways of achieving redundancy, which I will discuss throughout this book.

- Finally, it is common for file servers with multiple NICs to be configured for bridging. Having multiple NICs can be very useful—it might allow the server to exist simultaneously on several segments, or it might allow the server to handle significantly more traffic. But if these NICs are also permitted to bridge or route traffic between them, they can easily create network loops that disrupt traffic flows. These bridging and routing functions should always be disabled on servers. Consult your server vendor for information on how to ensure that these functions are disabled.

With respect to running dynamic routing protocols on an end device, a device might passively listen to a routing protocol (particularly RIP) but not send out routing information. This situation is certainly less dangerous than allowing the end device to affect network routing tables, but it is still not a good idea; in a well-designed network, no end device should ever need to care how the network routes its packets. It should simply forward them to a default gateway and forget about them. Part of the problem here is that RIP in particular can take a long time to update after a failure. In general, allowing the network to take full responsibility for traffic flow is more reliable.

Bus topology

In a bus topology, there is a single communication medium, which I often call "the wire." It actually doesn't need to be a physical piece of wire, but a wire is a useful image. In fact, 10Base2 Ethernet looks exactly like Figure 3-1, with a long 50 Ω (50 ohm characteristic impedance) coaxial cable connecting all of the devices. Because of the analogy with 10Base2, it is customary to draw an Ethernet segment like this, with a straight line intersected at various points by the connections (sometimes called "taps") to the various devices. In the drawing, this line (the wire, or bus) extends beyond the last device at each end to symbolize the fact that the bus must be terminated electrically at both ends.

On a bus, any device can communicate directly with any other device and all devices see these messages. This is called a "unicast."[*] Similarly, any device can send a single signal intended for all other devices on the wire. This is a "broadcast."

If every device sees every signal sent by all other devices, then it's pretty clear that there's nothing fancy about a broadcast. To get point-to-point unicast communication going, however, there has to be some sort of address that identifies each device uniquely. This is called the MAC address.

There also has to be some sort of mechanism to ensure that all devices don't try to transmit at the same time. In Ethernet the collision detection algorithm (CSMA/CD), which I will talk about more in Chapter 4, prevents such a problem. The other network standard that employs this basic topology is called "token bus," which works by passing a virtual "token" among the devices. Only the device that holds the token is allowed to transmit. The term "token bus" is not used much anymore, so I will not cover it in detail in this book.

---

[*] This odd word, "unicast," comes from the word "broadcast." A broadcast is sent to everybody, a "mulitcast" is sent to several recipients, and a "unicast" is sent to just one recipient.

There are a few common failure modes in a bus topology. It is possible to have cable break in the middle, thereby isolating the two sides from each other. If one side holds the router that allows devices on the segment to get off, then the devices on the other side are effectively stranded. More serious problems can result if routers are on both sides of the break.

The other problem that often develops in bus architectures is loss of one of the bus termination devices. In the case of 10Base2, this termination was a small electrical resister that cancelled echoes from the open end of the wire. If this terminator was damaged or removed, then every signal sent down the wire was met by a reflected signal. The result was noise and a seriously degraded performance.

Both of these problems are avoided partially by using a central concentrator device such as a hub or a switch. In fact, new Ethernet segments are usually deployed by using such a device.

Ring topology

The second basic segment architecture is a *simple ring*. The most common example of the simple ring architecture is Token Ring. SONET and FDDI are based on double ring architectures.

In Token Ring, each device has an upstream and a downstream neighbor. If one device wants to send a packet to another device on the same ring, it sends that packet to its downstream neighbor, who forwards it to its downstream neighbor, and so on until it reaches the destination. Chapter 4 describes the Token Ring protocol in more detail.

Token Ring relies on the fact that it is a ring. If a device sends a frame on the network, it expects to see that frame coming around again. If it was received correctly, then this is noted in the frame. Thus, the ring topology allows a simple verification that the information has reached its destination.

The closed ring also facilitates token passing and ensures that the network is used efficiently. Thus, a broken ring is a serious problem, although not as serious as a broken bus, since the Token Ring protocol has a detailed set of procedures for dealing with physical problems such as this.

It might look like each device taking part in the Token Ring acts as a bridge, forwarding each frame from its upstream neighbor to the downstream neighbor. But this is not really accurate, since the network interface cards in each device passes the Layer 2 frames along, regardless of their content. Even if the frame is intended for the local device, it still must pass along a copy, although it will change a bit in the header to indicate that it has been received.

FDDI uses another ring architecture that gets around this broken ring problem in a rather clever way. In FDDI, two rings run at all times. The tokens on these two rings travel in opposite directions, so the upstream neighbor on one ring is the downstream neighbor on the other. However, in normal operation, only one of these rings is used. The second ring acts as a backup in case of a failure, such as a broken ring.

Figure 3-5 shows what happens when the rings break. If the connection between devices A and B breaks, then the devices know about it immediately because there is two-way communication between them, and they have now lost contact with one another. They respond by closing the ring. Now when device A receives a token from device E on the clockwise-rotating ring, instead of sending it on to B, it turns around and sends it back to E on the counterclockwise-rotating ring. The token doesn't get lost because the rings have healed around the fault. The same thing happens if one of the devices taking part in the FDDI ring disappears.

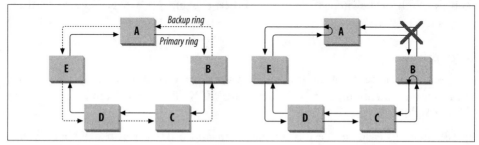

Figure 3-5. Fault tolerance of a dual-ring architecture

Star topology

In practice, most Ethernet and Token Ring LANs are implemented in a star topology. This implementation means that a central device connects to all of devices. All devices communicate with one another by passing packets first to this central device.

In one option for a star topology, the central device aggregates the traffic from every device and broadcasts it back out to all other devices, letting them decide for themselves packet by packet what they should pay attention to. This is called a *hub*. Alternatively, the central device could act as a *switch* and selectively send traffic only where it is intended to go.

The star topology is often called *hub and spoke*, as an analogy to a bicycle wheel. This term can be misleading because sometimes the hub is a hub and sometimes it's a switch of some kind. So I prefer the term *star*.

Most modern LANs are built as stars, regardless of their underlying technology. There are many reasons for this. It's certainly easier to upgrade a network by upgrading only the device in the closet, without having to change the expensive cabling to every desk. It's also much easier to make fast switching equipment in a small self-contained box than it would be to distribute the networking technology throughout the work area.

Even when Token Ring and Ethernet are implemented using a star topology, they still obey their own rules internally. For example, a Token Ring MAU transmits frames to each port in succession, waiting each time until it receives the frame back from the port before transmitting it to the next port. In Ethernet, however, the hub simultaneously transmits the frame to all ports.

The prevalence of star topology networks has made it possible to build general-purpose structured cable plants. The cable plant is the set of cables and patch panels that connect all user workspaces to the aggregation point at the center of the star.

With a structured cable plant of Category 5 cabling and IBDN patch panels, it's relatively easy, for example, to switch from Token Ring to Ethernet or from Ethernet to Fast Ethernet. Executing a change like this means installing the new equipment in the wiring closet, connecting it to the rest of the network in parallel with the existing infrastructure, and then changing the workstations one by one. As each workstation is changed, the corresponding cable in the wiring closet is moved to the new switching equipment.

Chapter 4 discusses structured cable plants in more detail.

When it comes to fault tolerance, however, star topologies also have their problems. The central aggregation device is a single point of failure. There are many strategies for reducing this risk, however. The selection and implementation of these strategies are central to a good network design.

Mesh Topology

A mesh topology is, in some ways, the most obvious way to interconnect devices. A meshed network can be either *fully meshed* or *partially meshed*. In a fully meshed network, every device is connected directly to every other device with no intervening devices. A partial mesh, on the other hand, has each device directly connected to several, but not necessarily all of the other devices.

Clearly, defining a partial mesh precisely is a bit more difficult. Essentially, any network could be described as a partial mesh with this definition. Usually, a mesh describes a network of multiple point-to-point connections that can each send and receive in either direction. This definition excludes descriptions of both the ring and bus topologies because the ring circulates data in only one direction and the bus is not point-to-point.

Since a mesh has every device connected to every other device with nothing in between, the latency on this sort of network is extremely low. So why aren't mesh networks used more? The short answer is that mesh networks are not very efficient.

Consider a fully meshed network with N devices. Each device has to have $(N-1)$ connections to get to every other device. Counting all connections, the first device has $(N-1)$ links. The second device also has $(N-1)$ links, but the one back to the first device has already been counted, so that leaves (N–2). Similarly there are (N–3) new links for the third device, all the way down to (N–N = 0) for the last device (because all of its links were already counted). The easiest way to see how to add these devices up is to write it in a matrix, as shown in Table 3-1.

Table 3-1. Connections in a meshed network

	1	2	3	4	...	N
1	x	1	1	1		1
2		x	1	1		1
3			x	1		1
4				x		1
...					...	...
N						x

An "x" runs all the way down the diagonal of the matrix because no device talks to itself. The total number of boxes in the matrix is just N^2. The number of entries along the diagonal is N, so there are (N^2–N) links. But only the upper half of the matrix is important because each link is only counted once (the link from a → b is included, but not b → a, because that would be double counting). Since there is exactly the same number above the diagonal as below, the total number of links is just $N(N$–1$)/2$.

Making a fully meshed network with 5 devices requires 5(5-1)/2 = 10 links. That doesn't sound so bad, but what happens if this number is increased to 10 devices? 10(9)/2 = 45 links. By the time you get to a small office LAN with 100 devices, you need 100(99)/2 = 4950 links.

Furthermore, if each of these links is a physical connection, then each of the 100 devices in that small office LAN needs 99 interfaces. It is possible to make all those links *virtual*—for example, with an ATM network. But doing so just moves the problem and makes it a resource issue on the ATM switching infrastructure, which has to keep track of every virtual circuit.

The other reason why meshed networks are not particularly efficient is that not every device needs to talk to every other device all of the time. So, in fact, most of those links will be idle most of the time.

In conclusion, a meshed topology is not very practical for anything but very small networks. In the standard jargon, it doesn't scale well.

Scalability

This discussion has just looked at certain basic network topologies. These concepts apply to small parts of networks, to workgroups, or to other local groupings. None of the basic topologies mentioned is particularly useful for larger numbers of users, however. A mesh topology doesn't scale well because the number of links and ports required grow too quickly with the number of devices. But ring and bus architectures also don't scale particularly well.

Everybody seems to have a different rule about how many devices can safely connect to the same Ethernet segment. The number really depends on the traffic requirements of each station. An Ethernet segment can obviously support a large number of devices if they all use the network lightly. But in a Token Ring network, even devices that never talk must take the token and pass it along. At some point, the time required to pass the token all the way around the ring becomes so high that it starts to cause timeouts. The number of ring members required to achieve this state is extremely high, though. Other types of problems generally appear first.

Both Ethernet and Token Ring networks have theoretical upper limits to how much information can pass through them per second. Ethernet has a nominal upper limit of 10Mbps (100Mbps for Fast Ethernet and 1000Mbps for Gigabit Ethernet), while 4, 16, and 100Mbps Token Ring specifications are available. Clearly, one can't exceed these nominal limitations. It actually turns out that the practical limits are much lower, though, particularly for Ethernet.

The collision rate governs throughput on an Ethernet network. Thus, the various rules that people impose to set the maximum number of devices in a particular collision domain (i.e., a single Ethernet segment) are really attempts to limit collision rates. There is no generally reliable rule to decide how many devices can go on one segment.

This fact is easy to deduce from a little calculation. Suppose you have an Ethernet segment with N devices. Each device has a certain probability, P, of wanting to use the network at any given moment. The probability of having k simultaneous events is:

$$_kP_N = \frac{N!P^k(1-P)^{N-k}}{k!(N-k)!}$$

Thus, for two devices, both wanting to talk at the same time, $k = 2$.

$$_2P_N = (1/2)N(N-1)P^2(1-P)^{N-2}$$

$$\sim (1/2)N^2P^2$$

Taking this equation a step further to work out real numbers is more difficult because it would require a detailed discussion of collision back-off algorithms. One would also have to be very careful about how P was calculated, as a collision is only counted when two devices actually send packets simultaneously. Usually, one sends first and the second device simply buffers its packet and waits until the wire is free. But the most important result is already here. The probability that two devices want to talk at the same time is proportioned to N^2, where N is the number of devices on the segment.

Interestingly, the probability goes like P^2. P is the probability that a particular device will want to use the network (in a suitable unit of time, such as the MTU divided by the nominal peak bandwidth). This probability is clearly going to be proportional to the average utilization of each device. The probability $_2P_N$ is essentially the probability that a device will have to wait to transmit because another device is already transmitting. Since the probability of having to wait is proportional to P^2, a small increase in the average utilization per device can result in a relatively large increase in the collision rate. But the real scaling problem is because of the factor of N^2, which rises very quickly with the number of devices.

This is why there are so many different rules for how many devices to put on an Ethernet segment. The number depends on the average utilization per device. A small increase in this utilization can result in a large increase in the collision rate, so it is not safe to trust these general rules.

Remember that collision rates cause the effective throughput on an Ethernet segment to be significantly smaller than the nominal peak. You will never get a 10Mbps throughput on a shared 10BaseT hub. You will never get 100Mbps on a Fast Ethernet hub, either. In fact, if there are more than 2 or 3 devices you probably can't get close to that nominal peak rate. Typically, the best you will be able to get on a shared Ethernet segment is somewhere between 30 to 50%. Sometimes you can do better, but only if the number of talking devices is very small. This is true for both Ethernet and Fast Ethernet hubs, but it is not true for switches.

Each port on an Ethernet switch is a separate collision domain. If every device is connected to its own switch port, then they are all on their own collision domains. Now they can all talk at the same time, and the switch will make sure that everything gets through.

Token Ring, on the other hand, has a much simpler way of avoiding contention. If two devices want to talk at the same time, they have to wait their respective turns. If another device is inserted into the ring, then everybody has to wait slightly longer. The average amount of time that each device has to wait is roughly proportional to the number of devices on the ring, N. This result is much better than N^2.

Also note that in Ethernet, the collision rate goes up proportionally to the square of the average utilization of each device. In Token Ring, the average wait time between each device's transmission bursts is the corresponding rate limiting factor. This factor scales roughly to the average per device utilization, not its square.[*]

As a result, a Token Ring "segment" can hold more devices than an Ethernet segment before contention becomes a serious problem. It's also much safer to rely on

---

[*] Some people say that Token Ring is deterministic because of this property, meaning that you can readily calculate how the traffic from a group of devices will aggregate on the entire ring. But you can do similar calculations for Ethernet if you understand how to combine probabilities and how the collision mechanisms work. It's just a harder calculation. Since everything is measured statistically anyway, having a deterministic model for your network is actually not much of an advantage.

general rules for how many devices to put on a ring. Even with Token Ring, there is an upper limit of how many devices can take part in a particular segment. Efficiency usually demands that you break up your rings through a bridge or a switch, exactly the same as for Ethernet.

You have seen that all of the basic LAN building blocks have different types of scaling problems. A 16Mbps Token Ring can hold more devices than a 10Mbps Ethernet segment, but in both cases there is a practical upper limit to how many devices you can put on the network before you start having performance problems. I have already alluded to one practical solution that allows us to continue growing our network beyond these relatively small limitations: switches.

You can connect a large number of Ethernet segments or Token Rings with a central switch. This switch will create a single point of failure, as I discussed in the previous chapter, but it will also move the problem up only a level. Now, instead of having a limit of N devices per segment, there is a limit of N devices times the number of ports on the switch. Expanding beyond this new upper limit is going to create a new problem.

Solving this new problem is what this whole book is about.

Reliability Mechanisms

Before moving on to larger-scale topologies, it is important to review some of the systems for automated fault recovery that are used in large networks. Just inserting backup switches and routers connected with backup links is not enough. The network has to be able to detect problems quickly with its primary paths and activate the backup devices and links.

There are two main methods for doing this, and most large-scale networks use both. You can detect and repair the fault at either Layer 2 or at Layer 3. The Layer 2 mechanism employs a special IEEE standard called Spanning Tree. As an IEEE standard, Spanning Tree is applicable across a wide range of Layer 2 networks, including the commonly used Ethernet and Token Ring protocols.

Conversely, there are many different ways of detecting and working around faults at Layer 3. Selecting among these different possibilities depends on what the Layer 3 protocols on the network are and on the scope of the fault tolerance. There are purely local mechanisms as well as global ones.

Spanning Tree

Spanning Tree, also called STP or IEEE 802.1d, is a Layer 2 protocol that is designed to accomplish two important tasks. It eliminates loops and it activates redundant links for automated fault recovery. Figure 3-6 shows a simple bridged network that employs Spanning Tree for both of these purposes.

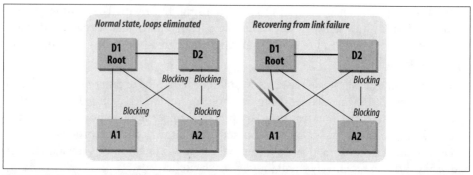

Figure 3-6. Spanning Tree is used to eliminate loops and activate backup links

Figure 3-6 has four switches. D1 and D2 are the central Distribution switches, while A1 and A2 are downstream Access switches that connect to end-device segments. The Spanning Tree priorities have been adjusted to give D1 the lowest value, making it the "Root Bridge."

Now, suppose D1 has a packet intended for a device on A1. It has several ways to get there. It can go directly, or it can go over to D2, which also has a link to A1. Or, it can go to A2, back to D2, and over to A1. The worst thing it could do is to go around in circles, which it can also do in this diagram. In fact, every device in the picture except the one containing the end device wants to helpfully forward the packet along to any other device that might be able to deliver it. This forwarding results in a big mess of loops. Spanning Tree removes this problem.

Spanning Tree eliminates loops

Each port taking part in Spanning Tree can be in one of five different states: blocking, forwarding, listening, learning, or disabled. Blocking means that Spanning Tree is preventing this port from forwarding packets. Each switch looks at its neighbors and inquires politely whether they are the Root Bridge or whether they can help it get to the Root Bridge. Only one Root Bridge is allowed in a broadcast domain, and that device is the logical center of the network. This is why the priorities have been set manually to force the network to elect D1 as the Root Bridge. D2 is configured to be the second choice in case D1 fails. You never want a switch that serves the end-device Access level of the network to be Root Bridge.

In this way, the network is always able to designate a Root Bridge. This device serves as the main Distribution point for all packets that a switch can't otherwise deliver itself. Every switch keeps track of the next hop that will take it to the Root Bridge. In effect, the network, with all of its redundant cross-connections, becomes a simple tree topology, which eliminates the loops.

Spanning Tree activates backup links and devices

Now suppose the link from A1 to D1 suddenly fails, as shown in the diagram. A1 knows it has lost its Root Bridge connection because it stops exchanging hello packets on that port. These packets exist purely for this reason—to keep checking that everything is working properly. When the link breaks for any reason, A1 remembers that it had another link to the Root Bridge via D2, and so it tentatively activates that port. It isn't certain yet that this way is correct, so it doesn't start forwarding data; instead, it goes into a "listening" state. This state allows it to start exchanging Spanning Tree information over this other port—to see if this is the right way.

Once A1 and D2 have established that they can use this link as a valid backup, both ports go into a *learning* state; they still do not forward data packets; they first must update their MAC address tables. Until the tables are updated, switch D2 doesn't know what devices are on A1. Then, once they have synchronized all of this information, both switches set this new port to a *forwarding* state, and the recovery process is complete.

In this picture, all switches are connected directly to the Root Bridge, D1. All links that do not lead to Rome are set to the blocking state, so A1 and A2 both block their links to D2. At the same time, D2 sets all the links it has that do not lead to D1 to blocking as well. The other links—the ones that do lead to the Root Bridge—are all set to their forwarding state.

The thick line connecting D1 and D2 is a higher bandwidth link. Suppose the thin lines are 100Mbps Ethernet links, while the thick line is a 1000Mbps Gigabit Ethernet link. Clearly the thick line is a better link to the Root Bridge than one of the slower links. So, the engineer sets the priority on this port so that, if there is a choice between what link to use, the switch always chooses the faster one.

Having a link between D1 and D2 is important. Imagine what would happen if it were not present and the link between A1 and D1 failed. A1 would discover the new path to the Root Bridge through D2, exactly as before. However, D2 doesn't have its own link directly to D1, so it must instead pass traffic through A2 to get to the Root Bridge. This means that traffic from A1 to the Root Bridge must follow the circuitous path—A1 to D2 to A2 to D1. In this simple example, the traffic passes through every switch in the network! This situation is clearly inefficient.

But wait—it gets worse. Now suppose a third switch, A3, is connected to both D1 and D2, and the link from A1 to D1 fails. A1 will again try to use D2 as its backup, but D2 now has two possible paths to the Root Bridge—one through A2 and the other through A3. It picks one of these links at random as the best path—say A2— and it blocks the other. Now, because of an unrelated failure elsewhere in the network, A2 has extra traffic load and A3 has no redundancy.

In the hierarchical network designs that this book recommends, the configuration with two redundant Core (or Distribution) switches connected to each of several Access switches will be common. Therefore, it is important to include a separate trunk connecting the two central switches each time this configuration is used.

It can take several seconds for conventional Spanning Tree to activate a backup link. This may not sound like a long time, but it can be a serious problem for some applications. Fortunately, trunk failures don't happen very often, but techniques for improving recovery time are available.

Spanning Tree has three adjustable timers that can be modified to make convergence faster. These times are called *hello*, *forward delay*, and *maximum age*. All bridges or switches taking part in Spanning Tree send out hello packets to their neighbors periodically, according to the hello timer. All neighboring devices must agree on this interval so that they all know when to expect the next hello packet. If the timers do not agree, it is possible to have an extremely unstable network, as the switch with the smaller timer value thinks that its trunks are continuously failing and recovering.

The forward delay timer determines how long the switch will wait in the listening and learning states before it sets a port to the forwarding state. The maximum age timer determines how long the switch should remember old information.

By reducing the hello and forward delay timers, you can improve your convergence time in a failure, but there are limits to how far you can push these numbers. The forward delay timer exists to prevent temporary loops from forming while a network tries to recover from a serious problem. The switch has to be certain that the new link is the right one before it starts to use it.

For example, suppose your Root Bridge fails. In this case, all switches must elect a new Root Bridge. In the example, the priorities are adjusted so that, if D1 fails, D2 becomes the Root Bridge. D2 has to realize that D1 has failed and has to alert every other device that it is now the Root Bridge. The forward delay timers on all of these switches have to be long enough to allow this process to complete.

Having a short hello interval is the easiest way to speed up the convergence of a Spanning Tree network. But even this process has to be done carefully. Remember that a packet is sent in both directions over all of your production trunks once every time interval. If the interval becomes too short, then link congestion and CPU loading problems can result. If hello packets are dropped for these reasons, Spanning Tree may assume that links have failed and try to find alternate paths.

The best set of Spanning Tree timers vary from network to network. By default, the values of the hello and forward delay timers will be approximately a few seconds each. The best way to determine the appropriate values is to start with the defaults and then try reducing them systematically. Then try deliberately failing links to verify that these settings result in a stable network. In most cases, the default parameters are very close to optimal. Since timer changes must be made on all devices, it is generally best to use the defaults unless there is a compelling requirement to improve convergence efficiency.

Some switch vendors have implemented additional Spanning Tree features that facilitate faster convergence and greater stability. Generally, these features work by allowing ports that are nominally in blocking states to behave as if they are in a perpetual learning state. This way, in the event of a simple failure, they can find the new path to the Root Bridge more quickly. Of course, in the case of a Root Bridge failure, the network still has to calculate a new topology, and this calculation is difficult to speed up.

Layer 3 Recovery Mechanisms

There are two main methods of implementing fault tolerance at Layer 3. You can either take advantage of the dynamic routing protocol to reroute traffic through the backup link or you can use an address-based redundancy scheme, such as HSRP (Hot Standby Router Protocol) or VRRP (Virtual Router Redundancy Protocol). The choice depends on the location.

I have already said that running a dynamic routing protocol on any end devices is a bad idea. If the problem is to allow end devices to stop using a failed default gateway on their LAN segment and use its backup instead, the dynamic routing protocol can't help. Instead, you need to use HSRP or VRRP. There is considerable similarity between these two protocols, which is why I mention them together. HSRP is a Cisco proprietary system defined in RFC 2281, and VRRP is an open standard defined in RFC 2338. In general, it is not a big problem to use the proprietary standard in this case because, if two routers are operating as a redundant pair, the chances are good that they are as nearly identical as possible; they will almost certainly be the same model type and probably have the same software and card options. This is one of the relatively rare cases in which the open standard doesn't matter very much.

Both of these protocols work by allowing end devices to send packets to a default gateway IP address that exists on both routers. However, end devices actually send their packets to the Layer 2 address associated with that default gateway IP address in their ARP cache. They don't use the default gateway address directly. When the backup router takes over for the primary router's default gateway functions, it must adopt both the IP address and the Layer 2 MAC address. Both VRRP and HSRP have quick and efficient methods of making this change. When one router fails, the other takes over and the end stations on that segment are not even aware that a problem has occurred.

On segments that do not have any end stations, particularly router-to-router segments, there is no need for HSRP or VRRP. In these cases, all devices can take part in the dynamic routing protocol (such as OSPF). In these places, using HSRP or VRRP is not a good idea because it has the potential to confuse the routing tables of the other routers on the segment. These routing protocols are very good at maintaining lists of alternative paths and picking the one that looks the best. If two paths have the same "cost," then most routers simply use both, alternating packets between them. If one router fails, the other routers quickly drop it out of their routing tables and start using the remaining path exclusively.

VLANs

VLAN is an acronym for "Virtual LAN." This name gives a good picture of what it is. A VLAN is, in effect, a *logical* LAN segment. But physically, it is spread throughout a larger network. The term VLAN also refers to a LAN port grouping within a single switch. If ports 1, 2, 5, and 12 are all part of the same broadcast grouping on an Ethernet switch, then this segment is also often called a VLAN. However, this designation is used mainly for simplicity when this switch is connected to another switch and they share this VLAN between them.

Figure 3-7 shows two switches connected by a trunk. Each switch has three VLANs. Switch A has VLAN 1, VLAN 2, and VLAN 3, while Switch B has VLAN 1, VLAN 2, and VLAN 4. Designating VLANs with numbers in this way is common. Ports 1, 2, 5, and 12 of Switch A are assigned to VLAN 1. On Switch B, VLAN 1 consists of ports 3, 5, and 7. Since these two switches are connected through a trunk, all seven ports can now communicate as if they were all part of the same LAN segment.

In an IP network, the ports from the same VLAN can all be part of the same IP subnet. In an IPX network, then they share the same IPX network number. Other ports on both switches are unable to communicate with any of these ports except through a router. They must all be on different IP or IPX networks.

Similarly, all ports assigned to VLAN 2 on Switch A are part of the same logical network as the VLAN 2 ports on Switch B. To make things a little more interesting, I have also included a VLAN 3 and a VLAN 4. VLAN 3 only appears on Switch A, while VLAN 4 is only visible on Switch B. Since these two VLANs are both entirely local to their respective switches, they do not use the trunk. If I were to define a new VLAN 3 on Switch B and assign a port to it, it could also use the trunk to allow the VLAN 3 ports on both sides to communicate.

So that's a VLAN; it's a simple but exceptionally powerful and useful concept. Like all powerful concepts, it can be used well or abused horribly.

The advent of VLAN technology was a mixed blessing to large-scale LANs. On the one hand, it has made it much easier to build a rational hierarchical network with a minimal number of components, which is very cost effective. On the other hand, VLANs make it easy to construct extremely bad network designs.

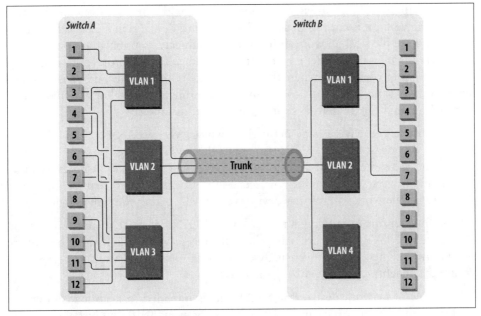

Figure 3-7. VLANs are shared through trunks

Avoid Spaghetti VLANs

The worst thing you can do in any network is build a random mess of spaghetti. With VLAN technology, you can create a completely rational and logical physical network of switches and trunks and then ruin it by superimposing an irrational VLAN design on top of it. You can assign one port on each of a hundred switches in a dozen different buildings to the same VLAN. All VLANs can exist everywhere simultaneously.

But why would this situation be bad? It sounds like it could be a great thing. You could have a highly integrated office real-estate plan so a working group or department may have members spread throughout the campus. Well, there are two main problems with this sort of topology. First, it's hard to manage and troubleshoot problems in such a network. Second, it leads to terrible problems with latency and trunk congestion.

Consider the first problem. Suppose you have to troubleshoot a problem in which two devices cannot communicate. The first step in such a problem is to figure out where these devices are in both a Layer 2 and a Layer 3 picture. Once you have located these devices, you try to figure out where things are broken. Is there an intermediate device that can get to one of these devices? Can other devices on the same IP subnet as one of the problem devices communicate with it? Can this third device communicate with the other end?

Those are the questions an engineer always starts with. In a network of spaghetti VLANs, however, it is entirely possible that this third device is in a completely different part of the physical network. If it can't communicate, you may have only proved that there is a physical problem. Is it part of the same physical problem or a different one? You have to determine where these devices are both logically and physically and figure out what trunks they use to communicate through. Unraveling the spaghetti of the VLANs can be extremely frustrating and time consuming.

Now, suppose you have a large network in which every VLAN is present on every switch. A broadcast from one device on one of these VLANs must be sent to all other devices on the same VLAN. That means that a broadcast has to go to every other switch and traverse every trunk. This scenerio is at least as inefficient as building a huge bridged network where every device is effectively part of the same single VLAN.

Lesson number one in building a network with VLANs is to use them sparingly and thoughtfully. VLAN is an extremely powerful concept with wide-ranging benefits to a network designer. But power usually comes with risks, and I want to help you to realize the benefits while minimizing these risks.

An old rule of network design, the 80/20 rule, is intended to keep loads down on routers. Some designers have used 60/40, 70/30, or even 90/10, but just about everybody has such a rule. It says that 80% of your traffic is local and only 20% need to cross the Core. Clearly, the less traffic that has to cross through the Core, the happier and less congested it will be, but making these sorts of rules isn't always practical. As network designers, we have very little control over how the applications are used, but we can exercise some direction. If most user traffic is destined for one central mainframe device, then there is no way we will ever be able to make such rules.

This rule is useful in VLAN construction, particularly in deciding which users will be in which VLAN groupings. But it is important to weigh this rule against the Spaghetti Factor. The point of the 80/20 rule is to try to reduce loading on the routers that direct your VLAN-to-VLAN traffic. In some organizations this is not practical, sometimes the only way to create well-segmented VLANs is by adding too many devices to the VLAN or by making every VLAN present on every switch. In such situations, remember that the point is to create a stable, reliable network; in a conflict, the 80/20 rule should be sacrificed before reliability and manageability.

Protocol-Based VLAN Systems

I need to talk about one other extremely serious VLAN-related trouble pit before moving on to specific VLAN topologies. There are really two main ways that a switch can color packets to associate them with a particular VLAN. The switch can say that every packet coming from any given switch port is automatically on only one VLAN. Or, alternatively, it can look at each packet and decide what VLAN to put it on based on what it sees.

Some switch vendors have implemented their VLAN technology with some clever protocol-dependent VLAN tagging features. Each time one type of packet (e.g., a particular application) is sent out, the switch assigns that packet to VLAN 1 and forwards it appropriately. Another packet, corresponding to a different application, would be forwarded as if it were on VLAN 2.

This feature sounds, on the surface, like it should be extremely useful and clever. It is definitely clever. But please use it with extreme caution. Many potential disasters are hiding in a feature this clever.

First, suppose that both protocols are IP-based. Then the network has a serious problem. How is it supposed to handle the IP addressing of these two VLANs? Which one will the default router for this IP address range take part in? It could be set up to take part in both. This way, the packets used by a particular application are shunted off onto a different VLAN so they can use higher speed trunks. But this leads to serious troubleshooting and fault-tolerance problems. So it should be avoided.

This sort of topology might be useful if a semitrusted external information vendor's server is to be placed on the network. Then, when workstations communicate with that server, the traffic is segregated from the rest of the network. This segregation could have important security benefits because this special server could then be prevented from taking part in the regular VLAN for these users. In other words, the protocol-based VLAN tagging feature is a sort of security filter. However, if you want a security filter, why not just use a filter? It is simpler conceptually to just implement a security filter on the one VLAN so packets from the vendor's switch port are treated specially.

Suppose you want to have your IP traffic all use one VLAN and have all other protocols use a different VLAN. This situation is actually more useful and sensible than the all-IP case. You might use some nonroutable protocol such as NetBEUI or a legacy LAT application. Then you could construct your network so everybody takes part in the same VLAN for the nonroutable traffic, but your IP traffic would be segregated. This is, in fact, the only time when I would recommend using this sort of feature.

You must be extremely careful when you try to troubleshoot this network. You have to remember that the nonroutable protocol is on a different VLAN than the IP traffic. So traditional troubleshooting tools such as *ping* and *traceroute* are not going to provide useful information on this other VLAN. A *ping* may work fine over the IP VLAN, but that has nothing to do with how the same network handles the NetBEUI VLAN. In general, this sort of feature should be considered dangerous and avoided unless there is absolutely no other way to accomplish the design goals. Even then it should be used with extreme care.

Usually, the best way to implement VLANs is by switch port. This way, each device is a member of only one VLAN, regardless of protocol. Overlaying several different logical topologies on the same network will always cause confusion later when troubleshooting unrelated network problems.

Toward Larger Topologies

Until now, this chapter looked at small-scale LAN structures and described some of the concepts, such as VLANs and reliability mechanisms, that allow designers to glue these small-scale concepts together into a large network. Now I'd like to move on to talk about how these basic building blocks are used to put together large-scale networks. To do this, I need to put many of these ideas into their historical context. New technology has allowed larger and more stable networks. It is useful to talk about the simpler creatures that evolved into more sophisticated modern networks. By reviewing how we got where we are, I hope to prevent you from making old mistakes or reinventing old wheels.

Collapsed Backbone

There are many ways to create larger networks from basic LAN segments. The simplest is to just interconnect several Ethernet segments or Token Rings via a single switch. This type of large-scale LAN architecture is called a *Collapsed Backbone*. Although it may sound like the painful result of a highway accident, the Collapsed Backbone topology gets its name from the concept of a network backbone that interconnects various segments.

In general, the backbone of the network can be either collapsed or distributed. I use the general term backbone to refer to a high-capacity part of the network that collects traffic from many smaller segments. It can gather traffic from several remote LANs onto a network backbone that connects to a central computer room.

The network backbone concept also works well in more peer-to-peer networks where there is no central computer room, but there is communication among the various user LANs. Figure 3-8 shows a simple example of a traditional network backbone design. In the early days of LAN design there was no such thing as the collapsed backbone—it was itself just some sort of LAN.

Why collapse a backbone?

The various user LANs connect to some sort of shared medium that physically runs between the separate areas. This medium could be some flavor of Ethernet, in which case the little boxes making these connections could be bridges, switches, or repeaters of some kind. Or the backbone could be a completely distinct network technology

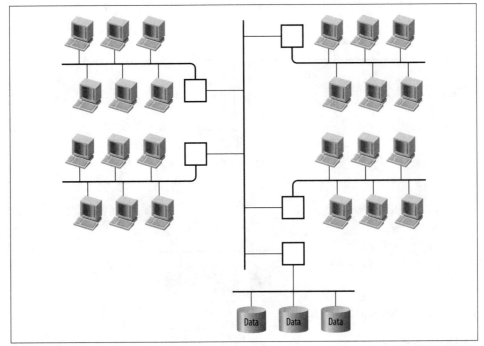

Figure 3-8. A simple network backbone technology

such as ATM or FDDI, in which case the little boxes must be capable of interconnecting and converting between these different network types.

Figure 3-9 shows the same diagram with a collapsed backbone. Here, some sort of central router or switch has long-haul connections to the various user areas. Typically, these connections would be fiber connections. Note that there is still a backbone, exactly the same as in the previous diagram, but here the backbone is contained inside the central concentrator device.

The two diagrams look essentially similar, but there is a huge potential performance advantage to the collapsed backbone design. The advantage exists because the central concentrator device is able to switch packets between its ports directly through its own high-speed backplane. In most cases, this means that the aggregate throughput of the network is over an order of magnitude higher.

The essential problem is that all network segments must share the bandwidth of the backbone for all traffic crossing it. But how much traffic is that? If the separate segments are relatively autonomous, with their own file and application servers, there may be very little reason to send a packet through the backbone. But, in most large LAN environments, at least one central computer room contains the most heavily used servers. If everybody shares these servers, then they also share the backbone. Where will the bottleneck occur?

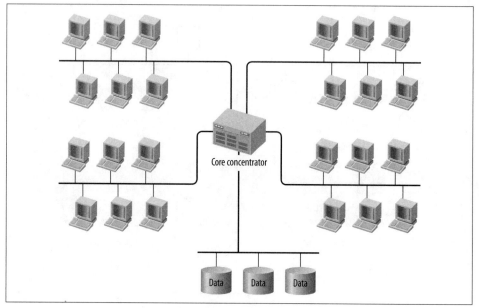

Figure 3-9. A collapsed backbone technology

Backbone capacity

In the diagram shown, bottleneck is actually a bit of a moot point because there is only one central server segment. If all traffic crossing the backbone goes either to or from that one segment, then it's fairly clear that all you need to do is control backbone contention a little bit better than on the server segment and the bottleneck will happen in the computer room. But this is not the usual case. Drawing the central server segment with all of those servers directly connected to a Fast Ethernet switch at full duplex would be more realistic. With just three such servers (as in the drawing), the peak theoretical loading on the backbone will be 600Mbps (100Mbps for Fast Ethernet times two for full duplex times three servers).

Clearly that number is a maximum theoretical burst. In the following section I will discuss how to appropriately size such trunk connections. The important point here is that it is very easy to get into situations in which backbone contention is a serious issue.

This is where the collapsed backbone concept shows its strength. If that central concentrator is any commonly available Fast Ethernet switch from any vendor, it will have well over 1000Mbps of aggregate throughput. The backplane of the switch has become the backbone of the network, which provides an extremely cost effective way of achieving high throughput on a network backbone. The other wonderful advantage to this design is that it will generally have significantly lower latency from end to end because the network can take advantage of the high-speed port-to-port packet switching functions of the central switch.

In Figure 3-8, each user segment connects to the backbone via some sort of Access device. The device may be an Ethernet repeater, a bridge, or perhaps even a router. The important thing is that any packet passing from one segment to another must pass through one of these devices to get onto the backbone and through another to get off. With the collapsed backbone design, there is only one hop. The extra latency may or may not be an issue, depending on the other network tolerances, but it is worth noting that each extra hop takes its toll.

Backbone redundancy

The biggest problem with this collapsed backbone design should already be clear. The central collapse point is also a single point of failure for the entire network. Figure 3-10 shows the easiest way around this problem, but forces me to be more specific about what protocols and technology the example network uses.

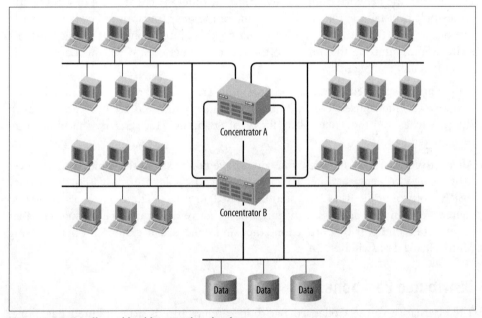

Figure 3-10. A collapsed backbone with redundancy

The most common way to collapse a LAN backbone is through a layer 2 Ethernet switch. So let's suppose that each user segment is either Ethernet or Fast Ethernet (or perhaps a combination of the two). The central device is a multiport Fast Ethernet switch with an aggregate backplane speed of, say, 1Gbps (this number is much lower than what is currently available in backbone switches from any of the major vendors, but it's high enough for the example). Each user LAN segment connects to these central switches using two fiber optic Fast Ethernet connections, one to each switch.

Then the two switches can be configured to use the Spanning Tree protocol. This configuration allows one switch to act as primary and the other as backup. On a port-by-port basis, it is able to ensure that each user LAN segment is connected to only one of the two switches at a time. Note that a switch-to-switch connection is indicated in the diagram as well. This connection is provided in case LAN segment 1 is active on Switch A and segment 2 is active on Switch B. If this happens, there needs to be a way to cross over from one switch to the other.

There are several important redundancy considerations. First, it may seem more complicated to use port-by-port redundancy rather than redundancy from one whole switch to the other. After all, it means that there will probably be complicated switch-to-switch communication, and seems to require the switch-to-switch link that wasn't previously required. But this is actually an important advantage. It means that the switch can suffer a failure affecting any one port without having to flip the entire backbone of the network from one switch to the other. There are a lot of ways to suffer a single port failure. One could lose one of the fiber transceivers, or have a cut in one of our fiber bundles, or even have a hardware failure in one port or one card of a switch. So minimizing the impact to the rest of the network when this happens will result in a more stable network.

This example specified Ethernet and Spanning Tree, but there are other possibilities. If all LAN segments used Token Ring, for example, you could use two central Token Ring switches and the Token Ring flavor of Spanning Tree. Exactly the same comments would apply.

Alternatively, for an IP network you could have done exactly the same thing at Layer 3 by using two central routers. In this case, you could use the Cisco proprietary HSRP protocol or the RFC 2338 standard VRRP protocol. These protocols allow two routers to own this address, but only one is active at a time. The result provides exactly the same port-by-port redundancy and collapsed backbone properties using routers instead of switches.

Distributed Backbone

The alternative to the Collapsed Backbone architecture is a Distributed Backbone. Later in this chapter, I describe the concept of hierarchical network design. At that point, the implementation of distributed backbone structures will become clearer. For now, I need to discuss some general principles.

A Distributed Backbone just indicates more than one collapse point. It literally distributes the backbone functions across a number of devices. In a network of any size, it would be extremely unusual to have a true single collapsed backbone. A large network with a single collapsed backbone would have a terrible single point of failure. It would also probably suffer from serious congestion problems if all inter-segment traffic had to cross through one point. Even if that collapse point had extremely high capacity, it would probably be difficult to get a high enough port density for it to be useful in a large network.

All practical large-scale networks use some sort of distributed backbone. Moving the backbone functions outside of a single chassis introduces two main problems: trunk capacity and fault tolerance.

Trunk capacity

Suppose you want to distribute your backbone-switching functions among two or more large switches. The central question is how much capacity should you provide to the trunk? By a trunk I mean any high-speed connection that carries traffic for many end-device segments. In this book, I often use the term trunk to refer specifically to a connection that carries several VLANs. I want to consider the more general case here.

A naïve approach would be simply to add up the total burst capacity of all segments feeding this trunk. If you had, for example, 5 Fast Ethernet (100Mbps half-duplex) LAN segments flowing into one trunk, then you would need 500Mbps of trunk capacity. But this scenerio presents a serious problem. How do you practically and inexpensively get this much bandwidth? Do you really have to go to a Gigabit Ethernet or an ATM just because you're trying to run a few trunks? Even load sharing isn't much of an option because you would need as many Fast Ethernet trunks as you have segments, so why use trunks at all in that case?

Needless to say, this approach is not very useful. You have two options for more efficient ways to think about trunk sizing. You could either develop some generally useful rules of thumb, or you could give up completely and just keep throwing bandwidth at it until the congestion goes away. You could actually take a rigorous approach to this second idea by using simulation tools. In the end, you will always have to monitor your trunks for congestion and increase their capacity when you start to get into trouble. A few good rules would give a useful starting point. Trunks should have more capacity than the average utilization. The only question is how much of a peak can the network deal with. Congestion on these trunk links is not a disaster in itself. Later in this book I talk about prioritization schemes to ensure that the important data gets through no matter how heavy the flow is. But there needs to be enough capacity for the normal peak periods, and this capacity needs to be balanced against cost because the higher speed technologies are significantly more expensive to implement.

The key to this discussion is the fact that all end segments are not statistically expected to peak at once. Most of the time, there will be an average load associated with all of them. Every once in a while, one or (at most) two experience a burst to full capacity. The basic rule for sizing trunks is to make sure that they have enough capacity for two end (shared) segments to peak at the same time plus 25% of capacity for all the remaining end segments. If the trunk has full-duplex transmission, consider the directions separately.

For an example, look at Figure 3-8. A central trunk connects four user segments with a server segment. First assume that this is a half-duplex trunk and that all end segments are 10Mbps Ethernet segments. Then the rule says to allow for two times 10Mbps plus 25% of three times 10Mbps, which works out to be 27.5Mbps. It would be completely safe to use a Fast Ethernet trunk in this case.

If the trunk technology is capable of full-duplex transmission, then you need to consider the two directions separately. Suppose that all traffic is between the users and the servers, with little or no user segment to user segment communication. This situation will help to establish the directions. For the user-to-server direction, there are four 10Mbps Ethernet segments. If two of these segments burst to capacity at the same time, the other two reach 25% of their capacity, and the trunk load will be 25Mbps in this direction. In the other direction, there is only one segment, so if it bursts to capacity, then it will have only 10Mbps in the return direction. As a side benefit, this activity shows that upgrading the server segment to full-duplex Fast Ethernet doesn't force an upgrade on the full-duplex Fast Ethernet backbone.

But this rule doesn't work very well for LANs that have every PC connected to a full-duplex Fast Ethernet port of its own. The rule allows two PCs to burst simultaneously and add 25Mbps to the trunk for every other PC on the network. 50 PCs connected in this way would need a full-duplex trunk with 1.4Gbps in either direction. This doesn't make much sense.

Individual workstations do not behave like nice statistical collections of workstations. The problem is not in assuming that two will burst simultaneously, but rather in the 25% of capacity for the rest. When workstations are connected to a switch like this, the typical utilization per port looks like silence interspersed with short hard bursts. A completely different sort of rule is necessary to express this sort of behavior.

A simple way to say it is that some smal percentage of the workstations will operate at capacity, while the rest do nothing. The actual percentage value unfortunately changes radically depending on the organization and even on the department. A graphic design group that spends its time sending large graphic image files might have a relatively high number. A group that only uses the network for printing the occasional one-page document will have a much smaller number. A general rule requires a reasonable mid-point number that is useful for Distribution trunks in a large network. A fairly safe number for this purpose is 5%. This percentage may be a little on the high side for many networks, so you can consider reducing it to 2.5%. Bear in mind that the smaller this number is, the less capacity for expansion allowed in your network.

Consider another example to demonstrate this rule. Suppose the end-segments in the network shown in Figure 3-8 have switched full-duplex Fast Ethernet to every desk. Suppose that 25 workstations are in each of the four groups. Then, for the user to server traffic, the trunk should allow for 5% of these $4 \times 25 = 100$ workstations to burst to their full 100Mbps capacity simultaneously. Thus, the trunk will operate at 500Mbps in at least this direction. Gigabit Ethernet or ATM can achieve these bandwidths, as can various vendor-proprietary Ethernet multiplexing technologies.

But wait, there's a twist in this example. So far, the discussion has assumed that all traffic is between the users and the servers. So what good does it do if the network can burst to 500Mbps on the trunk for traffic destined for the server segment, if the server segment can't deal with this much traffic? If 5 or more servers are all connected similarly to full-duplex Fast Ethernet switch ports, then this is possible. But the burst would have to be conveniently balanced among these servers. In this case, because traffic patterns are known very precisely, it is possible to reduce the trunk capacity to save money. The point is that this rule is just a starting point. You should always re-evaluate according to your own network conditions. Also note that the rule doesn't apply at all on the server side because you should always expect the servers to work the network very hard.

Trunk fault tolerance

A trunk, like any other part of the network, can fail. If it happens to carry all traffic from some part of the network at the time, though, it could be disastrous. Since trunk failures are potentially serious, it is always wise to include some sort of redundancy in every trunk. In fact, in most organizations I have seen personally, trunk failure is more common than hardware failure on key network equipment. This information is anecdotal, and I have no statistics on it, but it makes sense that delicate strands of optical fiber stretching long distances might be more vulnerable than a tank-like Ethernet switch chassis. If that switch is located in a locked room while the fiber has to run through a conduit shared with other building tenants, there's an even stronger reason to worry about the fiber. In some cases, it is physically damaged while technicians are doing other work. But even if fiber is never touched and the conduit remains sealed forever, eventually it degrades due to a host of environmental hazards, such as background radiation.

All of this information is intended to scare the reader into worrying about trunk failures. In most network designs, the trunks are the first things I would want to provide redundancy for. There are many ways to do so. The actual redundancy mechanism depends on trunk type. If the trunk is itself a multiplexed collection of links (like Cisco's EtherChannel or Nortel's MultiLink Trunking), then redundancy is inherent in the design. In this case, it would be wise to employ an N+1 redundancy system. This means that the trunk capacity should be sized as discussed in the previous section, and then increased by one extra link. This way, there is still sufficient capacity if any one link fails.

However, if a single fiber pair carries the trunk, then the only useful way to add redundancy is by running a second full-capacity trunk link. Since one of the main concerns is environmental or physical damage to the fiber, putting this second link through a different conduit makes sense.

The only remaining question is whether to make the backup trunk link a hot standby or to have it actively share the load with the primary link. And the answer, unfortunately, depends on what you can get with the technology you're using. In general, if you can do it, load sharing is better for two reasons:

- In case you inadvertently underestimate your trunk capacity requirements, or in case those requirements grow over time, load sharing gives you extra bandwidth all the time.
- If the primary can fail, so can the backup. The difference is that you notice when the primary fails, and you don't necessarily know when the backup fails. If traffic goes through it all the time, then you'll usually know pretty quickly that you've had a failure of your backup link.

Switching Versus Routing

In the discussion of backbone designs, I mentioned that the same general design topologies are applicable to both Layer 2 and Layer 3 implementations. Thus, at many points the designer can choose to either bridge or route. There are philosophical reasons for choosing one or the other in many cases, but there are also several practical reasons for favoring either switching (bridging) or routing implementations.

Ancient history

The old rule for designing large-scale LANs was "bridge on campus, route off campus." There were good reasons for this rule, but many of these reasons are less relevant today than they once were. Figure 3-11 shows an example of a LAN designed using this rule. It consists of a number of separate Ethernet-based work groups, all interconnected via an FDDI ring. I don't call this an "old-style" design to disparage it. In its day, this was cutting-edge technology. Although I modify the basic rule later in this chapter, the general design concept points out some important principles of network design that are still applicable.

Suppose that the network protocol in this diagram was TCP/IP. The entire campus, then, would have been addressed from the same large address range, such as a Class B or Class A. In fact, because all of these segments were bridged together, there would have been no technical requirement to break down the user segments into their own specific address ranges. The whole campus looked like one gigantic common flat network at the IP layer.

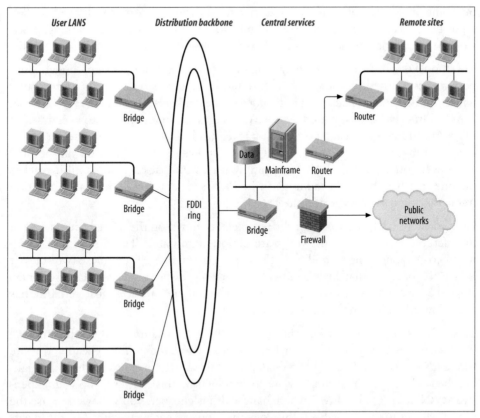

User LANS   Distribution backbone   Central services   Remote sites

Bridge

Bridge

FDDI ring

Router

Data

Mainframe Router

Bridge

Bridge

Firewall

Public networks

Bridge

Bridge

Figure 3-11. Old-style "bridge on campus, route off campus" design

In practice, however, most network administrators would have broken down their larger address range into subranges, and allocated these subranges to different user LAN segments. This allocation would be done purely for administrative reasons and to make troubleshooting easier.

In this old-style design, if someone on one of the user LAN segments wants to access the central database, they first look up the IP address (probably using DNS). They then send out an ARP (Address Resolution Protocol) packet to find the Ethernet MAC address associated with this IP address. This ARP packet goes out through the bridge and onto the FDDI backbone ring. Every other bridge on the ring forwards this packet onto its local segment. Eventually, the packet reaches the database server, which responds appropriately.

This approach immediately points out one of the important limitations of this design principle. Broadcast packets (like the ARP packet in the example) are sent to every distant corner of the network. This may be fine if there is very little broadcast traffic, but some broadcasts, like ARP, are a Core part of the network protocol. Every station sends broadcasts. There are necessarily limits to how big one can make a bridged network before routine broadcast traffic starts to choke off production application traffic.

This model does a nice job of segregating the regular application traffic, though. Suppose a user on the left side of the picture talks to a server on the right with regular unicast packets. Each packet on both sides of the conversation contains the Ethernet MAC address of the destination device. All bridges are smart enough to keep track of the MAC addresses on each port. So, a packet heading for the database server enters the FDDI ring because the user's local bridge knows to find that MAC via the ring. Then every other bridge on the ring simply leaves the packet alone until it reaches the one that has that MAC address on its LAN segment. Thus, normal application traffic takes an efficient direct route.

Now consider traffic destined for the remote site shown on the far right-hand side of the picture. Two rules of networks are almost immutable. The first is that bandwidth costs money; the second is that distance costs money. From these two rules, it is safe to conclude that high bandwidth over long distances costs a lot of money. Whatever technology is used to connect to the remote site, it almost certainly has much lower bandwidth than any LAN element.

This point is important because the rule was "bridge on campus, route off campus." In other words, it says that you should bridge where bandwidth is cheap and route where it's expensive. Bridging allows all broadcast chatter to go everywhere throughout the bridged area. You simply want to avoid letting this chatter tie up your expensive WAN links. On the LAN, where bandwidth is cheaper, you will want to use the fastest, cheapest, most reliable technology that you can get away with. At least in earlier times, that meant bridging.

A bridge is generally going to be faster than a router because the decisions it makes are much simpler. The manipulations it does to packets as they pass through it are much simpler as well. In the example, these bridges interconnect Ethernet and FDDI segments, so the Layer 2 information in the packets needs to be rewritten. This is a simpler change, though, than what a router needs to do with the same packet.

Modernizing the old rule

This old rule has merit, but it needs to be modernized. It is still a good idea to keep broadcast traffic off of the WAN, for exactly the same reasons that it was important 10 to 15 years ago. However, two current trends in networking are leading network designers away from universally bridging throughout a campus. First, many more devices are being connected to the network than there ever were in the past. Second, certain changes in network technology have changed the way things scale.

Let me explain what I mean by this second point. In the old-style network of Figure 3-11, user workstations were connected to shared 10Mbps Ethernet segments. All segments were interconnected via a 100Mbps FDDI ring. If you have a dozen active devices sharing a 10Mbps Ethernet segment, the collision overhead limits the total throughput on the segment to somewhere between 3 and 5Mbps in practice. So each of these dozen devices can use a steady state bandwidth of a few hundred kbps and a burst capacity of a fewMbps.

Today it is common to connect end devices directly to 100Mbps Fast Ethernet switch ports, and backbone speeds are several Gbps. Thus, each station has access to a steady state bandwidth of 100Mbps sending and receiving simultaneously. Each station is therefore able to use 200Mbps of backbone capacity, with the lack of local contention increasing the tendency for routine traffic to burst from very low to very high instantaneous loads. This is almost a factor of 1000 higher than in the older style of network, but our backbone speed has only increased by a factor of between 10 and 100.

In other words, each station is now able to make a much larger impact on the functioning of the network as a whole. This is why traffic prioritization and shaping (flattening out the bursts) have become so much more critical in network design. If more cars are on the road, there is a limit to how much the flow rate can be improved by just increasing the number of lanes. New methods of traffic control are needed as well.

Hierarchical Design

What's really valuable about the old-style design shown in Figure 3-11 is that it leads to the useful and practical concept of hierarchical network design. Figure 3-12 and 3-13 show what a hierarchical network design is and how it works. At this point, however, whether this network is basically bridged or routed is still questionable.

Figure 3-12 is a conceptual drawing of the hierarchical design model. There are three main levels, the Core, Distribution, and Access. These terms are widely used. End stations are connected at the Access level. You will sometimes see a drawing like this in which central servers are connected at the Core. If end node devices are connected at the Core, then the model is not strictly hierarchical. It may be some sort of hybrid. Or, more likely, the diagram could be an application-oriented diagram rather than a network diagram.

Figure 3-12 shows how connections are made. End devices connect at the outside edges of the diagram. They are connected to the Access Level of the network. This level exists primarily to give a place for these end devices to connect to the network. At the center of the diagram is the Core Level, which performs the main traffic switching functions, directing packets from one part of the network to another. The Distribution Level exists to connect the Access and Core Levels.

The name "Distribution Level" is appropriate for a couple of reasons. First, this level is what allows the network to spread out the distributed backbone. Second, the Distribution Level distributes data from the Core out to the Access Levels of the network.

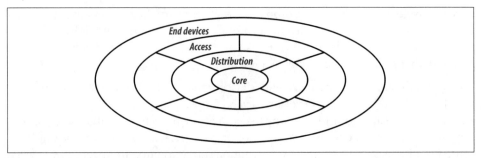

Figure 3-12. Hierarchical network-design concept

The basic idea is to separate the different functions of the network and hopefully make them more efficient. What does a network do? It directs traffic (Core), it conveys packets from one place to another (Distribution), and it provides connection points for end devices (Access). In a small network these functions could all be performed in one box, or even a simple piece of wire. But the larger the network, the more these component functions have to be separated for efficiency.

There are usually important cost advantages to using a hierarchical model. For example, the Access Level needs to give a high port density with a low cost per port. At the Core Level, it is more important to have high throughput devices with a few high-speed ports. Expecting one type of device to fill both of these categories isn't always reasonable.

Figure 3-13 shows a more specific example of how to think about hierarchical design models. In the middle is the Distribution Level, which carries traffic between the various Access groups and the Core. Two new ideas here were not shown in Figure 3-12. The first is the addition of some redundancy; the second is the implication that not all traffic needs to cross the Core.

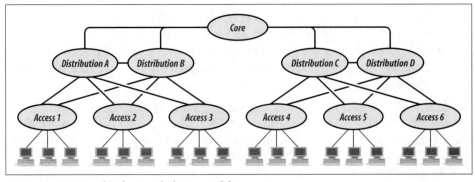

Figure 3-13. Hierarchical network-design model

Each of the Access Level devices is connected to two devices at the Distribution Level. This connection immediately improves the network throughput and reliability. Doing this has effectively eliminated the Distribution Level devices as single points of failure. For example, if Distribution "cloud" A broke then all three of the Access groups using it can switch over to Distribution "cloud" B transparently.

I am deliberately leaving the contents of these clouds vague for the moment. Notice that I have included a connection between Distribution clouds A and B so that the Core connection for either can break and traffic will simply shift over to the other.

Now consider the traffic patterns. Suppose an end device connected to Access cloud 1 wants to talk to another end device in the same cloud. There is no need for the packets to even reach the Distribution Level. Similarly, if that same device wants to talk to an end node connected to Access cloud 2, it doesn't need to use the Core. The packets just go through Distribution clouds A and B to get from Access cloud 1 to Access cloud 2. It needs to cross the Core only when the packet needs to go further afield, to another Access cloud that is not connected to the same Distribution cloud.

This principle is important because, if used carefully, it can drastically reduce the amount of traffic that needs to cross the Core. Because everybody shares the Core, the design principle needs to be used as efficiently as possible.

Recall the 80/20 rule that I mentioned earlier in this chapter. This rule is particularly applicable to the Distribution Level. If certain groups of users tend to use the same resources, then it makes sense to group them together with these resources. It's best to group into the same VLAN. But putting them into the same Distribution groups also saves traffic through the Core. In most large companies, separate business divisions have their own applications and their own servers. Try to consider these relationships when deciding how to divide your Distribution and Access groups.

To look more deeply into the various clouds shown in Figure 3-13, I need to first tell you where the network routes and where it uses bridging or switching.

Routing Strategies

Relaxing the "bridge on campus, route off campus" rule opens up the question of where to use routers. Designers could use them at every level of the LAN, including the Access Level, if they wanted to. Or, they could use them just at the Distribution Level and use switches in the Core and Access Levels. How do they decide what's right?

Well, you need to start by remembering what routers do. A router is a device that connects two or more different Layer 3 addressing regions. So, by the same token, routers break up Layer 2 broadcast domains. A router is also a convenient place to implement filtering, since it has to look much further into the packet than a switch does.

There are also negative aspects of routers. Every packet passing through a router has to be examined in much more detail than the same packet passing through a switch. The Layer 2 MAC addresses and framing have to be rewritten for every packet. Thus, latency through a router is necessarily going to be higher than through a switch.

Furthermore, Layer 3 dynamic routing protocols such as OSPF, RIP, and EIGRP must all be considered every time a router is installed. The designer has to ensure that the dynamic routing protocol will be stable and will converge quickly and accurately whenever the state of a network connection changes. The more routers in a network, the more difficult this process becomes.

Because of these negative aspects of routing, I would happily bridge the whole LAN if I could get away with it, but I've already discussed the inherent problems in this strategy. What else can be done?

When the requirements include filtering for security, the answer is easy; use a router. If a sensitive part of the network needs to be separated from the rest (for example, the Payroll Department or the Corporate Finance Department of a brokerage company), the designer should make sure that it's behind a router.

For the rest of the network, the routers are used only for breaking up broadcast domains. The improved congestion control properties from installing routers have to be balanced against the extra latency that they introduce. At the same time, you have to be careful of how you implement your dynamic routing protocols.

One-armed routers and Layer 3 switches

One way of implementing a router into the Core of a network is to use a so-called *one-armed router*. This picturesque term refers to a router that connects to several logical networks via a single physical interface. One clever modern way of accomplishing this feat is by making the router a card in a Layer 2 switch. This card, called a *Layer 3 switch*, then makes a single physical connection to the shared backplane of the switch. This backplane is generally an extremely high-speed proprietary medium. Attaching the router directly to it resolves several problems simultaneously.

First, you don't need to pay a huge amount of money to install a super high-speed network media module in the switch just to run the connection out to an external router. Instead, you can bring the router directly to the backplane of the switch. Second, the high bandwidth available on the backplane drastically reduces congestion problems that often plague one-armed router constructions. Third, because the Layer 3 switch module only has to form packets for the proprietary backplane of the switch, it is able to drastically reduce overhead required when routing between different media types. It only needs to know one Layer 2 protocol, which is the proprietary protocol used internally on the backplane.

It is possible to make a one-armed router act as a Layer 3 switch and achieve many of the same benefits. The single port on the router can be configured to support several VLANs, looking like a trunk connection to the switch. If this router-to-switch connection is sufficiently fast, such as a Gigabit or ATM link, then it is almost the same as a Layer 3 switch. Specifically, it has the benefit of being able to flip packets between different VLANs all using the same Layer 2 protocol.

This construction can be a useful way of getting the benefits of a Layer 3 switch when using equipment that doesn't support integrated Layer 3 switching, or for which the performance of these switches is poor. However, I would expect to see better performance from an integrated Layer 3 switch that is able to access the higher capacity backplane directly.

Using a construction in which several different Layer 3 networks converge on a single point makes sense. In a network like the one in Figure 3-11, putting a one-armed router on the FDDI backbone would have been fairly common. Then the various bridged Ethernet segments shown could be on different IP subnets. The FDDI interface on the router would also have an address from each of the various subnets. Although this scenerio was not uncommon, there are several deficiencies in a network built this way.

Network designers put routers into networks to separate broadcast domains. If they are just going to bridge everything together and have a single one-armed router in the middle, then they haven't separated the broadcast domains. Furthermore, they've made the network one step worse because they have introduced a new, artificial single point of failure for the entire network.

The same criticism is not necessarily true for Layer 3 switches, though. If the network consists of many VLANs, then the trunks between the switches ensure that all VLANs are visible on the backplane of the switch. Thus, the Layer 3 switch will not only route, but will also flip the packets between the various VLANs. This step can be done very efficiently, and the problem of failure to segregate the broadcast domains largely disappears (however, as I will discuss later in this chapter, it is possible to make bad design decisions for the VLAN structure that will negate this advantage).

The question remains, where should you use these sorts of devices? One obvious answer is the Core Level of the network. At the Core you have the greatest need for speed, and the greatest potential number of converging VLANs. But this second point is only true if you have no (or few) routers in the Access and Distribution Levels of the network. Figure 3-14 shows a hierarchical LAN design in which all VLANs converge on the Core of the network. In the two Core switches at the center, a pair of Layer 3 switches handles all routing for the network. Everything is redundant at the Core and Distribution Levels.

In this picture, there are four Access switches for each pair of Distribution switches. A total of four user LANs converge on the Core switches from above, and another four converge from below. Now the designer has to make important decisions about how to handle the VLAN trunks, which affect how routing is handled in the Core. There are many options. One option is to simply make everything one large VLAN, in which case there is no need to route anything. Or, one could make several small VLANs, all of which are visible everywhere in the network. Once again, this means that there is very little advantage to having the routers because all (bridged) VLANs must send their local traffic through the entire network anyway.

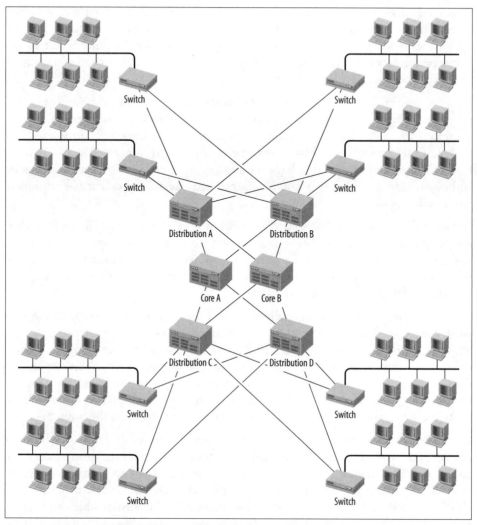

Figure 3-14. Hierarchical LAN with central routing

Always bear in mind that one of the key points in putting in routers is to limit the chances of broadcast traffic from one part of the network causing congestion some-place else. A VLAN is a broadcast domain, so you might think that making lots of VLANs results in small broadcast domains and eliminates your broadcast problems. This is only partially true, however. Remember that each trunk probably contains several VLANs. If an Access Level trunk circuit holds all VLANs for the entire network, it has to carry all of the broadcast packets. The effect is the same as if you had done no VLAN segregation at all, only with more inherent latency.

In Figure 3-14, I assume that I have been able to reduce the traffic so that the upper two Distribution switches carry completely different VLANs than the lower two. The only way to get between them is through the Layer 3 switches contained in the two Core switches. These Layer 3 switches also have to handle the inter-VLAN routing within each of these two groups of VLANs. Figure 3-15 shows the same picture at the Network Layer. In this case, it is easy to see the pivotal role played by the Layer 3 switch. For symmetry, I have shown four VLANs for both the upper and lower pair of Distribution switches (see Figure 3-14). However, as I will discuss later in this chapter, there is no need for the VLANs to correspond to the physical Access switches.

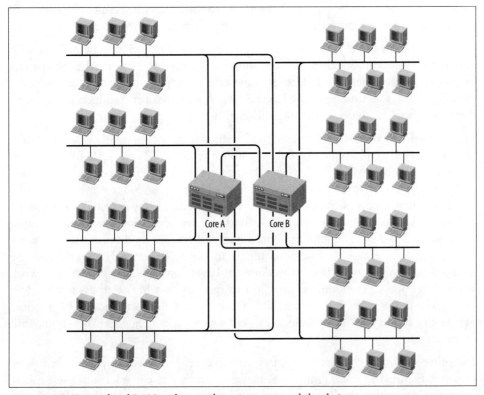

Figure 3-15. Hierarchical LAN with central routing—network-level view

The important thing to note from Figure 3-15 is that a total of eight VLANs converge on the redundant pair of Layer 3 switches. It is not possible for traffic to cross from any VLAN to another without passing through one of them. Obviously, redundancy is an important concern, as I will discuss in a moment. But there's another important feature. Because all off-segment traffic for each segment must pass through these devices, they tend to become serious network bottlenecks if congestion is not controlled carefully. The fact that they are connected directly to the backplane of the two Core switches starts to look like a necessity. This relatively small example collapses eight separate full-duplex 100Mbps feeds from the various Access switches.

Redundancy

Another key feature shown in Figure 3-14 is redundancy. The two Core switches are completely redundant. If all of the traffic aggregates onto a single router that handles the whole enterprise, then that's one colossal single point of failure. With some manufacturers, you have the option of putting a redundant Layer 3 switch module in the same chassis. This option is certainly an improvement, as I showed in the previous chapter. It's still necessary to do all of the MTBF calculations to figure out how much of an improvement it gives, though, and to show how the result compares with having a completely separate chassis plugged into different power circuits.

Unfortunately, I can't do this calculation for every possible switch type because vendors implement new switches with awe-inspiring regularity. You need to watch out for devices with which the failure of some other component, such as a controller module, affects functioning of the Layer 3 switch module or its redundancy options. Every switch seems to do these things differently.

The bottom line is that, to achieve good redundancy with a single chassis device, there can be no single points of failure within the device. Typical MTBF values for the chassis of most switches is sufficiently long not to be a serious concern. If you are going to implement a single-chassis solution, however, it has to have redundant Layer 3 switch modules, redundant power (N+1 redundancy is usually sufficient), and redundant connections to all Distribution Level devices. It may also require redundant CPU modules, but in some designs the CPU module is used only for reconfiguring otherwise autonomous media modules. Be careful, though, because such a design might mean that redundancy of Layer 3 switch modules will not work in the event of a CPU module failure. In this case, the net MTBF needs to be calculated. Even in this case, I am talking about a multiple failure situation (CPU module plus one of the Layer 3 switch modules), for which the aggregate MTBF should still be quite high.

The other solution, which is conceptually simpler, is to use two separate chassis, as shown in Figure 3-14 and Figure 3-15. However, in this case you have to use a router redundancy protocol to allow one of these devices to take over for the other. In the most common (and most stable) configuration, end devices send all of their off-segment traffic to a default gateway. In the one-armed router model, this default gateway is the same physical device for all of the segments. To make the module in the second switch chassis become the active default gateway for all segments, it has to somehow adopt the same IP address.

This adoption is most easily accomplished by means of either the Cisco proprietary HSRP protocol or the open standard VRRP protocol.

Router-to-router segments. When two or more routers or Layer 3 switches function between the same set of LAN segments, it is common to implement an additional segment just for the routers. This construction is shown in Figure 3-16.

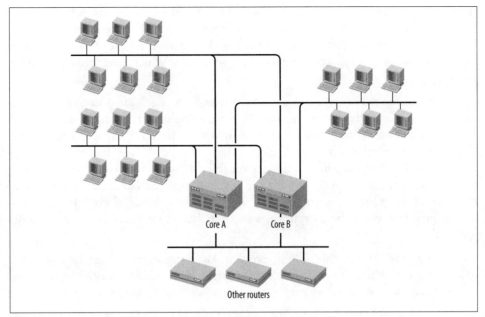

Figure 3-16. Implementation of a router-to-router segment

The diagram shows three user LAN segments connecting to the two routers called Core A and Core B. These two routers also interconnect using the special router-to-router segment. If other routers are in this location, then they would be connected here as well. These other devices might be WAN routers or other special function routers like tunnel termination points for X.25 or SDLC sessions, for example.

The router-to-router segment serves two main purposes. First, and most obvious, if special function routers are at this location, it provides a place to connect them where they will not suffer interference from user LAN traffic. In many cases, these legacy protocols exist because the applications using them are extremely critical to business. Routine word processing and low priority LAN traffic should not be allowed to disrupt the more important tunneled traffic, so it needs to go on its own segment. And, conversely, end-user devices don't need to see dynamic routing traffic.

To see the second reason, however, suppose that these other devices are not present and the network consists of the two Core routers and three user segments. Now suppose the first Ethernet connection on Core A breaks. HSRP or VRRP kicks in promptly, making Core B the default gateway for this segment. Core A is still the default gateway for the other two segments, though. Now consider the flow of traffic between Segment 1 and Segment 2.

A user on Segment 1 sends a packet to its default gateway, Core B. Core B forwards this packet out its port for Segment 2 and the user on this segment receives it. The response, however, takes a very different route. This packet goes to the default gateway for Segment 2, which is Core A, but Core A doesn't have an active port on Segment 1 because it's broken. It has to somehow send this packet over to Core B. I'll presume for the moment that there is a good dynamic routing protocol, so the two routers know how to get to one another and know which ports are functioning properly.

Core A sends the packet through one of the user LAN segments over to the Core B router. From there, it is sent out and received by the right user. So, there are two possibilities in this case. Either the packet was forwarded back out on Segment 2 to get over to the other router, or it was sent across on segment three. If it went via Segment 2, then that packet had to appear on this LAN segment twice, which could have a serious affect on overall congestion. If it went via segment three, then it potentially causes congestion on a completely unrelated user segment where it has no business being. This could be a security issue, but it is more likely just a congestion problem.

The easiest way around this sort of problem is to implement a special router-to-router segment. The routing protocols must then be carefully adjusted so that this segment is always preferred whenever one router needs to access the other.

Some network designers consider this problem aesthetic and ignore it. If all router ports are connected to high-bandwidth full-duplex switch ports, then the problem is much less dangerous. Another thing to remember is how VLAN trunks might be loaded in failure situations. For example, if the router-to-router segment is carried in the same physical trunk as the user segments, then it doesn't prevent congestion.

Physical diversity. As long as I'm talking about router redundancy, I need to mention a special side topic because it can be quite dangerous. On the surface it sounds like putting those two routers in different physical locations would be a good idea. For example, they might be in different rooms, on different floors, or even in different buildings. This arrangement could save the network in the case of a fire or large-scale power problem. But it could also make some simpler types of problems much worse.

To see why, look at Figure 3-16 and suppose that the left half of the picture including router Core A and two user segments are all in one building and everything else is in another building. Now, suppose that you have a relatively simple and common problem—a fiber cut between the two buildings. I'll go one step further and assume that both routers have some other form of connection back to a central network. Perhaps this is actually part of the Distribution level of a larger network, for example. The problem still exists without this added twist, but I think this example makes it a little easier to see it.

When the fiber was cut, VRRP or HSRP kicked in and made sure that all three segments still have a default gateway, so all inbound traffic from the user LAN segments will be delivered properly. The problem is with the return path. Look at the ports for LAN segment number 1. Both routers Core A and Core B have valid connections to this segment, but only one of them actually contains the particular user expecting this packet. Which one is right?

In many cases, if the central router has two paths available with the same cost, it just alternates packets between the two. The first one gets to the correct destination. The second one goes to the other router—the one that has a valid connection to the segment that has the right IP address but just doesn't have this user on it because the connection between the two sides is broken. So the packet is just tossed off into the ether and lost forever.

Different routers implement this in different ways. For example, some routers work based on *flows*. A flow is a single session. This concept is important to Quality of Service, so it is discussed in detail in Chapter 8. In this case, the router handles each flow separately, routing all packets belonging to a particular session through the same path.

This just means that some sessions will work and others will try to follow the path that is broken. Also, for applications that do not use a Layer 4 connection, such as those built using UDP, it is not possible to divide applications into unique flows. In these cases, some of the packets will be randomly lost.

This will happen for all of the user segments. So a measure that was intended to give better reliability in a rare failure mode has actually reduced the reliability in a more common failure mode.

If you really want to use physical diversity in this way, it has to be combined with path redundancy. Instead of running all of your LAN segments through the same fiber conduit so they could all break together, you could have another fiber conduit. In this second conduit, you would run redundant connections for all segments. Then, to complete the picture, you would use Layer 2 switches with Spanning Tree to switch to the backup fiber in case the primary breaks.

Figure 3-17 shows how this concept might work. In this figure, I've only drawn one of the segments for simplicity. The thick dashed lines represent the backup fiber pairs, which go through the second conduit. For symmetry, I've also included a backup connection from Switch A to the user segment, even though this segment is within the same building. The connection between Switch A and Switch B is required for Spanning Tree to work properly, as I discussed earlier in this chapter.

The Core A and Core B routers are assumed to be directly connected to their respective switches, so you don't need to worry about extra redundancy in these connections. Spanning Tree is configured on Switches A and B so that when the primary fiber stops working, the secondary one is automatically engaged. The same procedure would be followed on all other segments, including the router-to-router segment, if applicable.

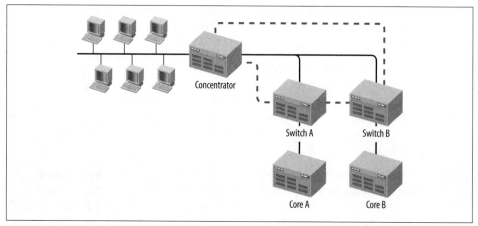

Figure 3-17. Physical diversity the safe way

In this picture the local floor connection is shown as a concentrator. The actual technology is irrelevant, however. It could be a hub, or a switch, or even a piece of 10Base2 cable connected to the fiber pairs by means of transceivers.

Filtering

There are three reasons why you might want to implement filtering on a router:

- Security
- Clean up for ill-behaved applications
- Policy-based routing

If you really want hard security on an IP network, you should probably be looking at a proper firewall rather than a router. But, in many cases, you just want a little security. In an IPX network, a router may be the only practical option for implementing security precautions.

You can do several different types of security-based filtering on a router:

- Filtering based on source or destination IP address
- Filtering based on UDP or TCP port number
- Filtering based on who started the session
- Filtering based on full IPX address or the external network number

The decision about which combination of these different filters to use depends on what you're trying to accomplish. So, I want to look at some different examples and see how different filter rules might apply.

Filtering for security. It is fairly common, particularly in financial companies, to have an external information vendor such as a news or stock quote service. The vendor's service involves putting a box on the client's internal LAN to allow them to access real-time information. The security problem is obvious: the external vendor theoretically has full access to the client LAN. Since financial companies usually have strict rules about access to their internal networks, they need to provide a mechanism that allows the information vendor's box to see only the genuine application data that it is supposed to see.

Assume that the vendor's special application server is hidden on a special segment behind a router. Now what sorts of filters can be implemented on this router?

The first type of filter, based on source or destination address, is probably not going to be useful here. There could be many internal users of this service, and you don't want to have to rewrite your filter rules every time somebody new wants access. It doesn't do any good to filter based on the address of the server because that's the only device on the special segment anyway.

The second type of filter, based on TCP or UDP port number, on the other hand, should be quite useful here. Since the application probably uses a designated port number (or perhaps a range), this could be a good way to identify the application packets.

The third type of filter is only useful if the application is TCP-based. If it is UDP-based, then the router cannot discern a session, so it can't tell who started the conversation. If it is TCP-based, and if the application starts with the user logging in (which is common), then this filter will help you to prevent the vendor's box from being used to initiate an attack on the client LAN.

What you really want is to combine the second and third filter types. You can do this on a Cisco router just adding the "established" keyword to an Access list for the required TCP port number.

The other example concerns the IPX filter. It's fairly common to have a special Novell server for sensitive data like personnel and payroll records, or other secret information. The payroll server makes a good example. The company might have this server on the Human Resources segment and use standard Novell authentication systems to ensure that only authorized people can see secret files.

But the organization may be concerned that these measures are not sufficient to prevent people from trying to give themselves a special pay bonus. To help prevent this, you can keep this server on a special segment and configure the router to disallow any access from off-segment. The trouble is that members of the Human Resources staff still need to get to the other corporate Novell servers. The CEO or other high-ranking corporate officials that it is supposed to seemight need access to the Human Resources server. So you can build a special filter that allows only the CEO's full IPX address (which includes the workstation's MAC address) to connect to the full IPX network number (including internal and external network numbers) of the server. Then you can allow all other internal network numbers to leave the segment. Consult your router vendor's documentation for information about constructing IPX filters.

Filtering for application control. Some applications do not behave in a friendly manner on a large network. An application might try to do any number of unfriendly things. For example, it might try to register with a server on the Internet. Or, it might send out SNMP packets to try and figure out the topology of the network. Sometimes a server tries to probe the client to see what other applications or protocols it supports. From there, the list branches out to the truly bizarre forms of bad behavior that I'd rather not list for fear of giving somebody ideas.

The trouble with most of these forms of bad behavior is that, if you have several hundred workstations all connecting simultaneously, it can cause a lot of irrelevant chatter on your network. If you don't have the spare capacity, this chatter can be dangerous. The SNMP example is particularly bad because a number of applications seem to think that they should have the right to poll every router on the network. In general, you don't want your servers to know or care what the underlying network structure looks like. It can actually become a dangerous problem because SNMP queries on network gear often use excessive CPU and memory resources on the devices. If several servers try to gather the same information at the same time, it can seriously hamper network performance. I have seen this problem cripple the Core of a mission-critical network during the start-of-day peak.

If you suspect that you have a problem like this, you need to use a protocol analyzer to get a good picture of what the unwanted information looks like. You also need to prove experimentally that this information is really unwanted. Some applications may just work in mysterious ways.

Once you have established what the unwanted data looks like and where it's coming from, then you can start to filter it out. Usually, it's best to put the filters close to the offending server (hopefully it's the server and not the client that is to blame) to help contain the unwanted traffic.

Policy-based routing. Policy-based routing is a Cisco term. Some other vendors' routers have similar capabilities, but I have to admit I learned this stuff first while using Cisco gear, so I still think in Cisco terms. This term means that the router is able to make routing or prioritization decisions based on whether a particular packet matches predefined characteristics. Perhaps it is a source or destination IP address, or perhaps a TCP, a UDP port number, or a packet size. By whatever mechanism, you define rules for what happens when the router receives packets of this type.

The rule may specify that you tag the packet with a special priority code so that every other device in the network will know that this packet is important and will forward it first (or last, or whatever). Or, the rule may be that certain types of packets use the high-speed trunk, while others use the low-speed trunk.

This last case, in which a routing decision is made based on the policy, is what gives the concept its name. It warrants special comment, though. In general, it is extremely dangerous to do this kind of thing for three reasons. First, it can interfere with redundancy mechanisms. Second, it makes troubleshooting unnecessarily difficult. (The low-priority ping packet gets through, but the application doesn't work. Is it the server or the high-priority trunk that's down?) Third, it has a nasty tendency to run up the CPU on your router (although this tendency is less likely in IOS Version 12 and higher because of support for FastSwitching of policy-based routing). Yes, it will work, but it's an extremely bad idea in most real world networks. Having said this, however, using the same feature to tag packets for priority works extremely well.

One final comment on filtering on a router: it's important to watch your CPU utilization. Modern routers tend to try to offload most routing decisions onto hardware associated with the port itself, so most packets never have to hit the CPU. This situation results in much faster and more efficient routers. But, depending on the router and the specific type of filter you are implementing, you may be forcing a lot of the processing back to the CPU. The result could be that your powerful expensive router is no longer able to handle even modest traffic volumes. So, when implementing filters, always take care to understand what it will do to the processing flow through the router. Often the best way to do this is simply to mock up the change in a lab and see what happens to your CPU statistics.

Switching and Bridging Strategies

In a LAN, every connection that isn't routed must be either bridged or repeated. I won't discuss repeaters much in this book. In modern LAN technology, there is rarely a good reason to use them. In nearly all cases, a switch is a better choice, both for cost and functionality. For that matter, conventional bridges are also increasingly rare, having been replaced by switches.

Of course, these comments are mostly semantics. People still use hubs. And what is a hub but a multi-port repeater? People still use switches, which are really multi-port bridges.

If you are dealing with a portion of a LAN that is all logically connected at Layer 3, then you have two main choices for our Layer 2. You can use a hub or a switch. This is true regardless of whether the LAN technology used at Layer 2 is Ethernet, Fast Ethernet, or Token Ring. It is also true for Gigabit Ethernet, although in this case I question the usefulness of Gigabit Ethernet hubs, preferring switches in all cases. Fortunately, it appears that the market agrees with me, as I am not aware of any major network hardware vendor who has implemented the hub part of the Gigabit Ethernet specification.

So I'll start by discussing where to use hubs and where to use switches in an Ethernet or Token Ring environment.

Switches have three main advantages over hubs:

- Higher throughput
- The ability to communicate at full-duplex (Ethernet)
- Better control over multicast traffic

There are two disadvantages to weigh against these advantages:

- Switches are more expensive
- It is much easier to use diagnostic tools such as protocol analyzers on a hub than a switch

A hub (sometimes called Media Attachment Unit [MAU] in Token Ring literature) is basically a way of sharing the network's Layer 2 medium. This sharing necessarily has overhead. In Ethernet, the overhead comes in the form of collisions. In Token Ring, it appears as token passing latency. In both cases, the system for deciding who gets to speak next takes a toll.

If you replace the hub with a switch instead, then this overhead essentially disappears. There are only two devices on the segment (or ring)—the end device and the switch itself. If it is a Token Ring switch, then every end device gets, in effect, its own token. There is never any waiting for the token, so each device can use the entire 16Mbps capacity of the ring.

If it is an Ethernet switch, on the other hand, the only times you should expect to see collisions are when both the switch and the end device try to talk at once. Even this small collision rate can be eliminated if you go to full-duplex Ethernet. On a large shared Ethernet segment, you can only practically achieve between 30% and 50% of the capacity because of the collision overhead. On a half-duplex switch this jumps well over 90% of capacity for every device and 100% for full-duplex switching. Thus, the net throughput of a switch is considerably higher than a hub with the same number of ports, for both Token Ring and Ethernet.

Most Fast Ethernet and many Token Ring switches can operate in a full-duplex mode. This means that they can send and receive simultaneously without collisions. Obviously this mode only works when a single end device is attached to each switch port. You can't have a full-duplex connection to a hub. Using a full-duplex switch has the effect of theoretically more than doubling the throughput to each device. It more than doubles because a half-duplex port still loses some capacity due to collisions. This advantage is most significant on servers, where it is not unusual to have a high volume of traffic both sending and receiving.

Containing broadcasts

Broadcasts are an integral part of many network protocols including TCP/IP and IPX. However, having too many broadcasts on a network can cause serious problems. The most obvious problem is simply bandwidth utilization. However, it is important to remember that broadcasts are delivered to every end device. Because these broadcast packets are addressed generically, the network interface cards of these end devices cannot tell whether they are important. So they are all passed up the protocol stack to be examined by the main CPU of the end device. Having a lot of broadcasts on a LAN segment can cause CPU loading problems on end devices, even when they are not actively using the network. Thus, broadcasts must be controlled.

A bridge or switch is supposed to forward broadcasts. This is, in fact, one of the most fundamental differences between bridging and routing. Forwarding broadcasts allows devices that are part of the same Layer 3 network to communicate easily. All global information on the network is shared.

A hub can't stop a broadcast without breaking the Layer 2 protocol. Those broadcast packets have to circulate, and stopping one would also throw a wrench into the congestion control mechanism (token passing or collisions). A switch or bridge, however, can choose which packets it forwards.

Normally, the way a switch or bridge makes this decision is by looking at its MAC address table. If the packet has a destination MAC address that the switch knows is on a particular port, then it sends the packet out that port. If the packet has an unknown destination address or if it has a broadcast or multicast destination address, then the switch needs to send it out to every port.

If the network is very large, then the number of packets that need to go out every port can become a problem. Usually, in most networks, the broadcast volume is a relatively small fraction of the total number of packets. Pathological conditions called "broadcast storms" (see the discussion in the previous chapter) can make this broadcast volume suddenly high, though. If these conditions occur frequently, then serious performance problems may occur on the network.

Controlling broadcasts is one of the main reasons why network designers have historically gone from bridged to routed networks. With many modern switches, it is possible to push this decision further because of broadcast control mechanisms available on these devices. Usually, the broadcast control mechanism works by simply monitoring how frequently broadcast packets are seen on a port or on the switch as a whole. When the broadcast volume rises above this high-water mark, the switch starts to throw away broadcast packets.

Clearly, this threshold level has to be high enough that the network rarely loses an important broadcast packet (such as an ARP packet). It also has to be low enough so it doesn't interfere with the normal functioning of the network.

This way of treating broadcast storms is reasonably effective. It doesn't prevent them, of course; there will still be storms of packets. But this kind of simple measure ensures that they don't represent a serious traffic performance problem on the network.

There is an interesting trade-off in the place where the decision is made to start throwing away packets. If the decision is made on a whole switch that happens to be in a broadcast-heavy network, then throttling for broadcast storms can actually interfere with normal network operation. On the other hand, just looking at the per-port broadcast volumes ignores the possibility that the storm has been caused by the interaction between several different devices.

One of the most difficult types of broadcast storms to control starts with a single device sending out a broadcast packet. Then one or more other devices on the network receive this packet and respond to it by either sending out a new broadcast (such as an ARP for the originator's IP address) or forwarding the original broadcast back onto the network. A good example is the old RWHO protocol, which broadcasts periodically.

Some IP stack implementations like to send an ARP packet in response to a broadcast packet from an unknown source. This way, they are able to keep a more complete ARP cache. A large number of different devices that respond like this simultaneously, can choke the network for an instant. RWHO is still run on many network print servers by default for historical reasons (although I will never understand why it is still needed). This problem is actually rather common, and it can be extremely serious if the timeout in the ARP cache is shorter than the interval between RWHO broadcasts.

In this case, the per-port monitoring is not effective at stopping the storm. The storm originates with a single broadcast packet, which is the one that really should be stopped, but it is the response that causes the problem, and that response comes from everywhere.

The moral of this story is that just because you implement broadcast storm controls on your switches doesn't mean that you won't have broadcast storms. However, if you have such controls in place, you will be able to prevent this storm from migrating to another switch. The second switch will see an incoming storm on its trunk port and will block it. The problem is at least partially contained.

Redundancy in bridged networks

Redundancy in bridged networks is important for exactly the same reasons as in routed networks. The only differences are in the methods and protocols for redundancy. Just as in the router case, the first step is to install a second switch that is capable of taking over if the first fails. Thus, it needs an automatic mechanism for this to work effectively.

The most commonly employed fault recovery mechanism in bridged networks is the Spanning Tree protocol. The other type of fault recovery system that I mentioned earlier in the case of trunks is a multiplexed arrangement of individual connections. That type of system works well for trunks, but is very difficult to use to make the switches themselves redundant. It is difficult because the individual connection lines must connect between two specific endpoints. If you have a Distribution level switch connecting to a Core switch, you can use this type of system.

For good redundancy, you should have the Distribution switches connected to two Core switches. If the multiplexed bundle of links is split between two switches, then the packets can be sent in two different ways. Some trunk mechanisms treat the bundle in parallel and break up each packet into small fragments, which are each sent through different links and reassembled at the other side. Other multilink solutions, such as Cisco's Fast EtherChannel, ensure that each packet is sent through a single link intact. In this case, the extra capacity is achieved by distributing packets among the various links in the bundle.

In any case, splitting one bundle among two different switches makes it much harder for the switches to effectively manage the bandwidth. It is generally simplest to think of the bundle as a single logical trunk and connect it between the two end point switches. Just avoid splitting the bundles.

Filtering

Most organizations do little or no filtering on their switches. For most networks, this is the right amount. It is generally much easier to filter on routers than switches. However, in some cases it is more effective to filter on the switches. In general, the same reasons for filtering on routers also apply here:

- Security
- Cleaning up for ill-behaved applications

The other reason I listed in the router case, policy-based routing, could theoretically apply here as well. But that sort of facility should be used sparingly at best, and where it is used, routers are a more natural place for it, so I do not include it here.

Security filtering is usually handled on switches in two ways. Many vendors offer some sort of port-level security, in which only a specified MAC address is permitted to connect to a particular port. The second type of security filtering typically restricts packets according to their contents, usually allowing only packets with certain source MAC addresses to communicate with sensitive devices.

Port-level MAC address security features allow the switch (or hub, since this feature is also available on some hubs) to lock out any devices except the one specified. If a particular workstation is supposed to be connected to a particular port, then only that workstation will function on that port. If another device is connected, it will have a different MAC address and the switch (or hub) will disable the port, requiring manual intervention.

This sort of feature is provided to prevent people from putting unauthorized equipment on the network. It is not perfect because many types of devices can use a manually configured MAC address instead of their burned-in-address (BIA). But it is a useful measure if this sort of problem is a concern. Note, however, that there is significant administrative overhead comes in maintaining the table of which MAC addresses are permitted on which ports throughout a large network. Generally, I wouldn't use this feature unless a compelling security concern warranted it.

In the second type of security filtering, you instruct the switch to look at the packet before transmitting it. If a sensitive server, for example, is only permitted to communicate with a small list of other MAC addresses, then this information could be programmed into the switch. Not all switches allow this sort of functionality, and it can be difficult to maintain such a switch. Once again, this feature should only be used if there is a strong overriding security concern.

I have already talked about certain broadcast storm problems. These problems are commonly handled with a simple volume filter. In some cases, it may be worthwhile to use a more specific filter. For example, I was once responsible for a network that suffered from the RWHO problem mentioned earlier. I was able to write a special purpose filter to restrict these packets on the switch. As for the security-based filtering, it was also a huge administrative problem. This sort of filtering should be used sparingly, and only where absolutely necessary. Bear in mind that switch manufacturers know this, so they tend not to provide extensive filtering capabilities.

VLAN-Based Topologies

Now that I have discussed how not to use VLANs, I'd like to turn to more positive matters. VLANs are typically used in bridged sections of a LAN, but they give two important advantages over older bridging techniques. First, they allow much more efficient use of trunk links. The ability to combine several segments into one trunk without having to first bridge these segments together allows you to use far fewer physical resources (ports and fiber or copper connections). Second, a VLAN-based architecture built on top of a rational hierarchical structure allows great flexibility in expanding or modifying the network without having to fundamentally change the Core.

Here are a few good ways of employing VLANs in a hierarchical network design. Figure 3-18 shows a rather typical VLAN topology. In this picture, several different segments are visible on the various Access Level switches. These VLANs are collected on the two redundant Distribution Level switches. At the Core, two redundant routers handle the VLAN to VLAN routing.

Although this diagram is a vastly simplified version of what you might find in a real large-scale LAN, it demonstrates some important features for VLAN topologies. First consider the trunk design.

Trunk design

Each Access Level switch has two trunk connections to redundant Distribution switches. This switch provides excellent fault tolerance. For the purposes of this discussion, let's assume that the trunks are configured so that only one trunk is active at a time. The primary trunk must fail completely before the secondary trunk becomes active. This fault tolerance scheme is fairly typical for trunks. Each Access switch has

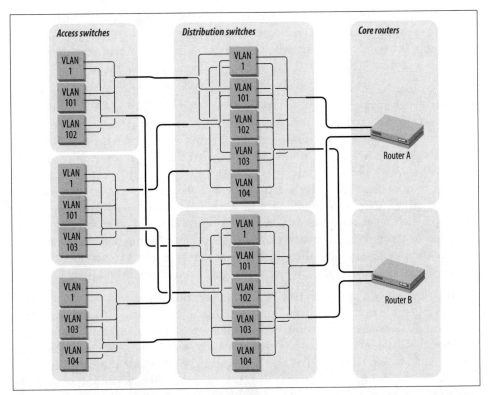

Figure 3-18. VLANs in a hierarchical network design

two trunk connections to provide complete redundancy. Notice that if you had to run a separate link for every VLAN, you would need six links for redundant connections to each Access switch. Worse still, if you added another VLAN on this Access switch, you would need two more ports and two more fiber connections. With the design shown in Figure 3-18 you can keep adding more VLANs to the existing trunks until you start to get congestion problems.

Figure 3-18 has five different VLANs. VLAN 1, the management VLAN, is present on all switches. I will talk about network management considerations in more detail later in this book, but for now I will just point out that separating your management traffic from your business traffic is a good idea. With this sort of VLAN structure, putting the management segment for all switches on the same VLAN is very convenient. In any case, one can generally expect management traffic requirements to be much smaller than for business application traffic.

VLAN 1 is used for network management because some low-end switches require their management IP address to be associated with VLAN 1. Since the VLAN naming convention is globally relevant over large portions of the network, it's a good idea to use VLAN 1 for management on all switches just in case it's required on a device somewhere in the region.

The other four VLANs are all user segments of various types. I have arbitrarily put two such user segments on each Access switch. The actual number of VLANs you should support on each Access switch depends on geography and port density. In general, it is a good idea to keep it fairly low for efficiency on your trunks.

Notice no user VLANs appears on all Access switches. VLAN 101 appears on the first two switches, but is not present on the third. Similarly, VLAN 102 is only configured on the first switch. This configuration is important because of the way it affects trunk utilization. The trunks serving the first Access switch carry no broadcast traffic from VLAN 103 or 104, so that spaghetti VLANs can be avoided. If I had not done this, I would have quickly wound up with Spaghetti VLANs. Remember that one of the main reasons for segregating our traffic is to break up the broadcast traffic. If all VLANs are present on all switches, then all broadcasts traverse all trunks. In such a network, the only benefit to using VLANs is that the end devices don't see as many broadcast packets. VLANs can provide much greater benefits if they are used more carefully, though. Network designers use VLANs for efficiency, so they should not throw that efficiency away on a Spaghetti VLAN topology.

The Distribution switches collect all VLANs. In general, this sort of two-point redundancy is a good idea at the Distribution Level, but there will usually be several pairs of Distribution switches collecting VLANs for large groups of Access switches. For example, this diagram might just show the first two Distribution switches, which collect the first 4 user VLANs (plus the management VLAN) for the first 12 Access switches (of which I have shown only 3). Then the next pair of Distribution switches might collect the next 6 user VLANs for the next 8 Access switches, and so forth. Each group of switches will have a VLAN 1 for management. This VLAN 1 may or may not be the same VLAN 1 throughout the network, but it can be simpler to handle routing if it is.

Trunking through a router

The previous example had the routers at the Core. This location turns out to be one of the most natural places for them in a VLAN-based network design. Suppose, for example, that you wanted to put your routers at the Access Level. Then you necessarily route between user VLANs, so it becomes harder to bridge different user segments via VLANs. The same is true to a lesser extent if you wanted to put the routers at the Distribution Level.

It's more difficult, but possible, to have the same VLAN existing on two different sides of a router. Figure 3-19 shows one way to accomplish this feat. This picture shows three switches interconnected by three different routers. Switch A holds VLAN 102, Switch B holds VLAN 103, and Switch C holds VLAN 104. VLAN 102 has IP address 10.1.102.0, VLAN 103 has 10.1.103.0, and VLAN 104 has 10.1.104.0. So, as long as the three routers know how to route to these three IP addresses, everything will work fine.

But there is a problem with VLAN 101. This VLAN, which has IP address `10.1.101.0`, is present behind all routers. So if a device on VLAN 101 on Switch A wants to communicate with another device on VLAN 101 on Switch B, the packet will hit Router A and won't know where to forward this packet. After all, the IP address range `10.1.101.0` is directly connected to one of its Ethernet ports. The IP address range is broken up behind different routers. Even the VLAN tagging information present on the other three VLANs disappears as soon as it hits the routers.

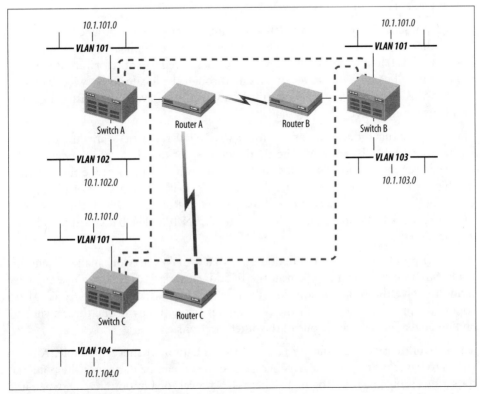

Figure 3-19. A VLAN split by routers

Routers are Layer 3 devices and they forward packets based on Layer 3 protocol information. VLAN information is fundamentally a Layer 2 concept. Thus, the only way to get around this problem is to configure a bridge or a tunnel that emulates Layer 2 between the various routers or switches (it could be done either as a router-to-router tunnel, or a switch-to-switch, or even switch-to-router bridge group). Then, when the device on VLAN 101 on Switch A sends a packet to the device on VLAN 101 on Switch B, the packet enters the tunnel and is transmitted to both Switch B and Switch C automatically. In short, the network has to bypass the routers.

There are many problems with this sort of solution. It is inherently more complicated because of the extra step of setting up tunnels or bridge groups. The designer has to be extremely careful that whatever fault tolerance systems he has in place supports the tunnel or bridge group transparently. As I have mentioned previously, having an IP subnet broken across two routers is disastrous.

There is also potentially much extra traffic crossing these links. Suppose a device on Switch C, VLAN 104, wants to communicate with a device on Switch A, VLAN 101. The packet first goes to Router C, where it is forwarded to the local Switch C instance of VLAN 101. Then the switch bridges the packet over to Switch A. This packet passes through Router C twice.

Now suppose a device on VLAN 101 on Switch A sends out a broadcast packet to every other device on VLAN 101. This packet has to be duplicated and sent out to both Switches B and C (hopefully they will be configured to not reforward the packet again or it will cause a mess), again passing through the local router twice. The network in this simple picture has effectively doubled whatever broadcast congestion problems it might have otherwise had.

Now suppose that a device on any of these VLAN 101 segments wants to send out a packet to a VLAN 102 device. The destination is not on the local segment, so the source device must send this packet to the default router. But there are three routers on this segment—which one is the default? In fact, it could be any of them, so a device on Switch A may need to send its packets to Router B, which then forwards the packet back to Router A to be delivered to VLAN 102. The backward path is just as convoluted.

The other problem with this configuration is that it makes network management difficult. Suppose there is a problem in the IP address range 10.1.101.0. The engineer trying to solve the problem still doesn't have any idea where that device is. There could be a problem with any of the three routers or with any of the three switches, and it could affect devices in one of the other locations.

The network designer should try to avoid this situation whenever possible. A good rule is to never try to split a VLAN across a router. It can be done, but the potential for serious problems is far too high. There is, however, one important case when it is unavoidable: when some external network vendor provides the intermediate routed network. The two sides of the same VLAN could be in different buildings on the opposite sides of a city, for example. If the link supplied by the network vendor is provided through a routed network, then there may be no other option but to use such an approach.

Trunks

So far I've talked about trunk links like they had some sort of magical properties, but there is really nothing particularly special about them. A trunk can be any sort of physical medium. Generally, it should support relatively high bandwidth to be effective, but the actual medium could be just about anything. The most common technology used in trunks is Fast Ethernet, although Gigabit Ethernet is increasingly popular. ATM links are also used frequently. FDDI used to be fairly common, but it is being replaced as a trunk technology because Fast and Gigabit Ethernet systems are cheaper and faster.

What makes a trunk link special is the fact that it carries several distinct VLANs simultaneously. This is done by an extremely simple technique. Each packet crossing through the trunk looks exactly like a normal packet, but it has a couple of extra bytes called the VLAN tag, added to the Layer 2 header information. The tag's precise format and contents depend on the specific trunk protocol.

Trunks are useful because they allow the network designer to economize greatly on switch-to-switch links. If you had to carry three different VLANs (a modest and reasonable number) from an Access switch to a pair of redundant Distribution switches without using trunks, you would need at least six links. But if you did use trunks, you could achieve full redundancy with only two links. Better still, if you suddenly had to set up a new VLAN on that Access switch, you could do it all in software. There is no need to run another pair of uplink fibers to the Distribution switches.

To work as a trunk connecting two switches, both ends must know that the link in question is intended to be a trunk. They must also agree on the trunk protocol (which specifies the VLAN tagging format). This protocol usually has to be configured manually. But then, by default, most switches treat this link as a common trunk for all the VLANs this switch knows about. Some switches allow you to separately specify which VLANs use which trunks. In some ways, this specification is contrary to the spirit of trunks. But it can be a simple method for balancing the loading of your trunks, and in particular a method to divide up the broadcast traffic.

Generally, the trunks connect Access Level switches to Distribution Level switches in hierarchical network designs. Then there may or may not be further trunks connecting Distribution to Core Levels, depending on where the routers are. Extending trunks between two Access Level devices is not usually recommended; one usually wants to keep the relationship between the different levels as clear and clean as possible. Access devices that act as Distribution devices can make troubleshooting network problems difficult.

Trunk protocols. There is an IEEE standard trunk protocol, called 802.1Q. Because this standard was developed and released in 1998, after the requirement for such a protocol appeared, a handful of vendor-proprietary trunk protocols also exist. One of the most common is Cisco's ISL protocol, but several other proprietary trunk protocols are on the market.

ISL and 802.1Q share many similarities. Both protocols feature a generic VLAN header that can support several different standard LAN types. A trunk can contain many different VLANs, each of which can run many different Layer 3 protocols.

Other proprietary trunk protocols have other nice features as well. The Cabletron SmartTrunk system was relatively popular at one time because of its automated fault-recovery and load-sharing properties.

However, I recommend using the open standard wherever possible. All major manufacturers now implement 802.1Q, so there is very little reason to use the proprietary trunk solutions any longer, and I don't recommend doing so. The unique nature of trunking makes it one of the most important areas for using open standards.

Most networks have distinctly different requirements at their Access Level than in the Core or Distribution Levels. Consequently, it is quite likely that the switches at these different levels could come from different vendors. Since the hierarchical design model has most of its trunks running between these different levels and only a small number within a level, there is a good chance that you will have to connect a trunk between switches made by different vendors.

The difference between a regular Ethernet frame and an 802.1Q tagged frame is shown in Figure 3-20. Four extra octets (8-bit bytes) are added to the frame just before the length/type field. To ensure that this tagged frame isn't mistaken for a normal Ethernet frame, the "tag type" field is always the easily identified sequence "81-00" (that is, the first byte is 81 in hex and the second is 00 in hex). Then the remaining two bytes specify the VLAN information. For compactness, these two bytes are broken down into three fields of different bit lengths.

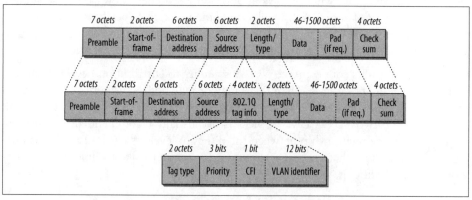

Figure 3-20. Q VLAN tagging format compared with normal Ethernet framing

The priority field is a three-bit number, also called "Class of Service" in some literature. Because it has three bits, this field can have values from 0 to 7. I will talk more about prioritization later in this book. But for now it's important only to note that Class of Service is a MAC-level priority, so it is not the same thing as the higher layer QoS concepts such as the TOS (Type of Service) or DSCP (Distributed Services Control Point) fields in the IP packet header. Putting this new Class of Service field in Layer 2 makes it easier for Layer 2 devices such as switches to use it.

Also note that the priority field is independent from the VLAN identifier field. It is possible to classify priorities on a trunk so that one VLAN has precedence over another and that a particular application on one VLAN has precedence over another application on a different VLAN. This concept will be important when you start to encounter congestion on your trunks.

The one-bit CFI field is the "Canonical Format Indicator." This field is set to 1 if a RIF (Routing Information Field) is in the Data segment of the frame, and 0 if there isn't. A RIF is a piece of information that allows a device to request a particular path through a bridged network. The CFI field makes it easier for switching devices to deal with RIF data by saving them the time of looking for this data when it isn't present.

And then comes the 12-bit VLAN identifier field. Having 12 bits, it could theoretically handle up to 4,094 different VLANs (since there is no VLAN zero and VLAN 4,095 is reserved). But I urge caution in configuring VLAN numbers greater than 1000 because of intervendor compatibility problems. The problem is that some switch vendors implement VLANs internally using their own native proprietary systems and then merely translate to 802.1Q. Some of these internal schemes have trouble with VLAN numbers greater than 1000. Worse still, some early VLAN schemes could only support a few hundred VLAN numbers, so don't assume that it will work until you've tried it.

Always remember that if you share VLAN numbers across a large Distribution Area, every switch in this area must agree on VLAN numbers. This is rarely a serious problem because a Distribution Area containing more than a few hundred VLANs would suffer from serious efficiency problems anyway.

Trunk redundancy. All of our discussion of trunks so far in this chapter has assumed that you will run redundant trunk links everywhere, but, in fact, there are two different ways to handle trunk redundancy. You can use Spanning Tree to keep one entire trunk dormant until there is a failure on its partner. Or, you can run both trunks simultaneously and consider all of the individual VLANs running through them to be distinct virtual links. Then you can run Spanning Tree separately for each VLAN.

In fact, it is not possible to run Spanning Tree separately for each VLAN when using 802.1Q, but it is possible with other trunk protocols, such as Cisco's ISL.

The per-VLAN option is considerably more complex, but it can sometimes be useful. Consider, for example, the network shown in Figure 3-18. The first Access switch has trunk connections to both Distribution switches. Suppose the upstream connections to VLAN 101 on the first Distribution switch were to break. In this case, you would want to use the second trunk, which goes to the second Distribution switch.

This scenario is actually relatively easy to get around. All you need is a trunk link between the Distribution switches. Then the first Distribution switch acquires its lost connection to VLAN 101 via the second Distribution switch through this trunk link.

In fact, it is extremely difficult to come up with examples where this is not the case. In general, since I always prefer simplicity to complexity, I prefer to use Spanning Tree on whole trunks rather than more individual VLANs within a trunk. Further, because many switches do not support running Spanning Tree for individual VLANs, compatibility helps to dictate the best methods as well.

However, this example brings up an important issue. If you run Spanning Tree on the individual VLANs in a network, you should not run it on the trunk as a whole. Conversely, if you run it on the trunk, you should disable it on the individual VLANs. It is very easy to generate serious loop problems by using a mixture of the two approaches.

When considering trunk redundancy, it is important to think through what will happen when a trunk breaks. A good hierarchical design with Spanning Tree should have very few problems recovering from a fault. One thing to beware of is a failure that breaks a Layer 3 network.

Figure 3-21 shows a network that has two routers for redundancy. These networks both serve the same IP subnet and the same IPX network. Assume that they have an automated system for IP redundancy such as VRRP or HSRP. No such system is required for IPX, so if the primary router on the segment fails, the other one will take over.

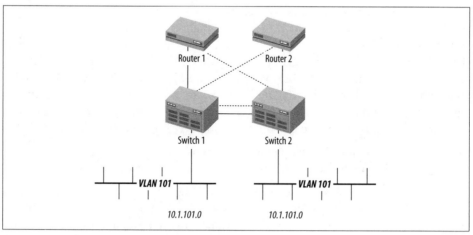

Figure 3-21. When a trunk breaks, it must not fragment a Layer 3 network

The same VLAN, number 101, which has IP address 10.1.101.0, exists on both switches. Then, for diversity, the first router connects to the first switch and the second router connects to the second switch.

This design is seriously flawed. Consider what happens when the trunk connecting the two switches fails. Suddenly two distinct unconnected LAN segments have the same IP address range and the same IPX network number. Now both routers provide valid routes to these networks. Thus, no communication will work properly to either segment. This is almost exactly the same problem I described earlier with two routers on the same LAN segment, but here you can see that it happens with VLANs as well.

How does one resolve this problem? A couple of different approaches are available. One method connects both routers to both switches, as shown by the addition of the dashed lines in Figure 3-21. This solution is not always practical, depending on the capabilities of the routers, since it implies that both routers have multiple interfaces on the same network.

In fact, the simplest solution is to just run a second trunk between the two switches, as shown with the dotted line. Then you can simply rely on Spanning Tree to activate this link if the primary fails. Furthermore, if you suffer a complete failure of one entire switch, then you lose half of your workstations, but at least the other half continues to work. A failure of one router allows the other to take over transparently, so this is the most acceptable solution.

However, in a good hierarchical design, this sort of problem is less likely to arise because each Access switch connects to two different Distribution switches. Thus, the network would need to have multiple simultaneous trunk failures to get into this sort of problem.

Trunks on servers. Some types of servers support VLAN trunks directly so that you can have a single server with simultaneous presence on several different VLANs, as shown in Figure 3-22.

This is certainly an interesting thing to do, but it's important to understand why you would want to do this before trying it. There are different ways to achieve similar results. For example, many servers support multiple network interface cards (NIC). Installing two NICs in a server and connecting them to different VLANs via different switch ports has the benefit of simpler configurations on both the switch and the server and provides higher net throughput. Alternatively, if you can't afford to use multiple physical ports for whatever reason, then you could just as easily put the server behind a router and let the traffic route to all of the different user segments.

However, this strategy is cost-effective in some cases. For example, if the trunk connection is a Gigabit Ethernet link, it might be significantly less expensive than deploying a router solution, as routers with high-speed interfaces tend to be very expensive. At the same time, Gigabit Ethernet ports on switches can be costly. This strategy may be a convenient way of deploying a server for multiple user VLANs.

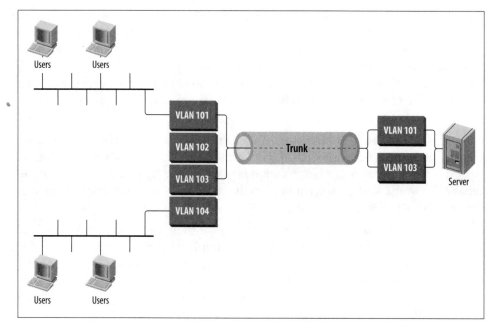

Figure 3-22. Some servers connect directly to trunk links to access several VLANs simultaneously

However, this method does not scale very well. If there will be many such servers, it would likely be less expensive in the long run to build a specialized high-speed server segment behind a router. Because it is a trunk link, the different VLANs will also compete with one another for server bandwidth on this link.

In previous chapters I made the point that only network devices should perform network functions. Therefore, I don't like connecting an end device to multiple VLANs, whether it is through a single port or through multiple ports. An end device should have a single connection to the network unless there is a compelling reason to do something more complicated.

VLAN Distribution Areas

One of the key concepts in building a VLAN-based network is the VLAN Distribution Area. Many networks have only one VLAN Distribution Area, but having only one in extremely large networks is not practical. It may be useful to break up the Distribution Areas of a network to improve efficiency. Figure 3-23 shows what I mean by a Distribution Area. This example is unrealistically symmetrical but the symmetry is not relevant to the concept.

In this diagram, four Access switches are connected to each pair of Distribution switches; Access switches A1, A2, A3 and A4 all connect to Distribution switches D1 and D2. Similarly, the next four Access switches connect to the next two Distribution switches, and so on. The central routing Core of the network allows the VLANs that appear on these various switches to connect to one another.

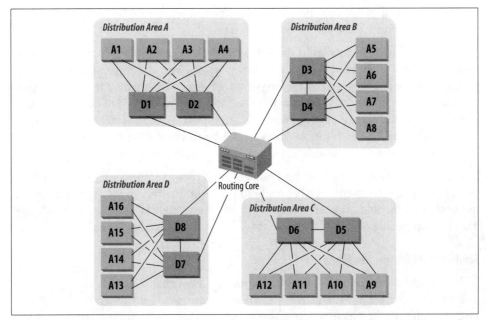

Figure 3-23. Distribution Areas

The four VLAN Distribution Areas in this picture are arbitrarily named A, B, C, and D. There is really no need to name your Distribution Areas, but it might help to rationalize the scheme if you do so. The essential idea is that the VLAN scheme is broken up so that there is no connection between the VLANs of different areas.

Why would you want to break up the scheme this way? Well, there are two main advantages to this approach. First, you may need to reuse certain VLAN numbers. This might happen because certain VLAN numbers such as VLAN 1, which is often reserved for network management purposes, are special. Or, it may happen simply because of limitations on VLAN numbering schemes on some hardware. For example, some types of switches only allow VLAN numbers up to 1000 or 1005, despite the theoretical limit of 4094 in 802.1Q.

The second and more compelling reason for breaking up your VLAN Distribution Areas is to simplify your Spanning Tree configuration. The network shown in Figure 3-23 has four different Root Bridges. All traffic has to pass through the Root Bridge in Spanning Tree networks. This situation can result in wildly inefficient traffic patterns. Breaking up your hierarchical design, as in this example, allows you to control your traffic patterns so that all packets between Core and Access Levels take the most direct path.

The disadvantage to building a network this way is that it makes it harder to share VLANs throughout the larger network. For example, since no trunks exist between Distribution Areas A and B, sharing VLANs between these areas is not possible. It is critically important that you thoroughly understand what VLANs need to go where when constructing a VLAN Distribution system.

In most cases, it is best to build these Distribution Areas geographically. It is quite rare to find an organization that does not physically group employees performing related tasks. If there is a need for easy information sharing over the network, then chances are that this need exists for physical proximity as well. This is not true universally, of course, but most organizations attempt to group themselves this way. A logical way to build Distribution Areas would be to build on a campus LAN, or by groups of floors in a large building.

The other nice feature about using Distribution Areas in this way is that it tends to prevent propagation of the VLAN Spaghetti problem. It tends to force the network to use both a reasonable number of VLANs in an area as well as prevent too much geographical spreading of VLANs.

Sizing VLAN Distribution Areas

Although technical and theoretical limitations on how many VLANs one can define in a VLAN Distribution Area exist, practical limitations are considerably lower. The Distribution switches have to see all of these VLANs, as do the routers that allow VLAN-to-VLAN connections. If the connection to the router is done by means of trunk connections, then the router has to have a logical interface for every VLAN.

Every additional VLAN in a Distribution Area requires additional CPU and memory resources in the Distribution (and possibly also the Core) Level of the network. Since every vendor implements these features differently, establishing solid rules for the maximum number of VLANs in a VLAN Distribution Area is not possible. A dozen VLANs are not likely to cause any problems, but a thousand is probably a bad idea. The two places you need to be concerned about are the routers that handle VLAN-to-VLAN connections and the Distribution switches (particularly the Root Bridge) that have to handle all the individual VLANs.

On Cisco routers, the usual rule for a safe upper limit to the number of logical interfaces is somewhere between 50 and 200, depending on the type of router and the amount of processing required. If the router (or Layer 3 switch) has to do a lot of filtering or has to look at more than just the destination address of each packet, then the number of VLANs should be reduced radically.

Remember that these numbers, while just general orders of magnitude, are for the entire router. If the router is used to interconnect several different Distribution Areas, then the number of VLANs in each area should be kept low to allow the router to function effectively.

The same arguments apply to the switches themselves. If the Distribution switches act strictly as switches, without needing to do any filtering, prioritization or other CPU intensive activities, they should be able to handle more VLANs. The more additional work the switch needs to do, the fewer VLANs it should have to carry.

In many cases, the governing factor for how many VLANs to allow in a Distribution Area is actually the backplane bandwidth of the Root Bridge (which should be the primary Distribution switch for the area) and the aggregate downstream bandwidth used by the trunks to the Access switches. There is a single Root Bridge through which all off-segment packets for a VLAN must pass.

Earlier in this chapter, I said that a good rule for trunk aggregation is to assume that 5% of the devices on the network will burst simultaneously. If you apply this limit to the backplane of the Root Bridge, then you should get an extreme upper limit to how many devices should be supported by a single Distribution Area, independent of the number of VLANs used.

Typical modern switch backplane speeds are between 10 and 50Gbps. If all workstations are connected to Fast Ethernet ports, then this switch can support somewhere between 10,000 (for the 10Gbps backplane) and 50,000 (for the 50Gbps backplane) workstations. Because the aggregate backplane speed includes all possible directions, I have included a factor of 2 to account for both sending and receiving by the bursting workstations.

Clearly, these numbers are vast overestimates for several reasons. First, these nominal aggregate backplane speeds are measured under optimal conditions and ideal traffic flow patterns that are almost certainly not realized in a live network. Second, this switch may have to do a lot of work filtering, tagging, and prioritizing traffic, as well as its primary switching functions. So it probably doesn't have the CPU capacity to handle this much traffic, even if its backplane does. Third, you should always keep a little bit of power in reserve for those rare moments when the network is abnormally busy. Fourth, related to the third point, you should always allow room for growth.

A reasonably safe hands-waving estimate for the maximum number of workstations that should go into a Distribution Area is somewhere on the order of 1000. If every VLAN supports 50 workstations, it would probably be a good idea to keep the number of VLANs in each Distribution Area at around 20.

As the backplane speeds of these switches increases, generally so do the attachments speeds of devices. The reader may have access to switches with backplane speeds of several hundred Gbps that were not available when this book was written. If the reader also has a number of devices connected using Gigabit (or the emerging 10Gbps Ethernet Standard), then the factors still come out about the same.

Implementing Reliability

Reliability in a network comes primarily from careful design work—the result of the right mixture of simplicity and redundancy. Too much redundancy in either equipment or connections results in complexity, which makes a network harder to maintain and more likely to break in strange, unexpected ways, having too many links also makes it hard for the dynamic routing protocols to find the best paths through the network, which results in instability as well. Of course, you need some redundancy to eliminate your key single points of failure. However, you should never sacrifice the simplicity in your overall concept of the network.

Coupled with this concept is the issue of scaling. The concept of the network should be clear enough that adding new parts or eliminating old ones should not change it fundamentally. Scaling becomes a reliability issue because every network grows and changes over time. You should ensure that something that once worked will continue to work.

Throughout this chapter, I show example networks that have every Distribution Area connected through two Distribution switches, with every Access switch connected to both. Every Core or Distribution router has a backup. Every trunk link has a secondary link. These backup connections are never *ad hoc*; they are part of the global plan of the network. If a particular structure is used in the Distribution Level of the network, then it is used similarly in every Distribution Area. This modular construction scheme makes the network much easier to manage and easier to grow, migrate, and change.

Wherever you use backup links and backup devices, you must have automated fault recovery systems. There is little point in implementing a secondary device that does not automatically take over when the primary fails. Once again, simplicity of concept is the rule in the fault recovery system.

It is best to use as few automated fault recovery systems as possible. Spanning Tree is able to swing traffic to backup trunk links when the primary trunks fail, but the same configuration can also bring a backup switch on line if the primary switch fails. There is no need in this case to implement more complex strategies that might treat these two problems separately.

Multiple Connections

Not every device can have a backup. In most cases, it is neither cost effective nor technically practical to back up the Access Level of the network. Most end devices can only effectively use one network connection. Any system of redundancy at the Access Level ultimately reaches a single point of failure somewhere. Since one of the primary design goals is simplicity, it is best to acknowledge that one cannot readily implement redundancy in the Access Level and should instead work on ensuring the reliability of the rest of the network.

Looking back at Figure 3-23, each Access switch has two trunks, one to each of two redundant Distribution switches. With this configuration, you can lose any trunk connection, or even one of the Distribution switches, without affecting user traffic through the network.

In this picture, both Distribution switches also have redundant connections to the network Core, but the Core itself is not shown in detail. It is not shown because, up to this point, the network design is fairly generic. Later in this chapter, I will discuss the different options for locations of routers in a large-scale LAN. They can be in the Core, in the Distribution Level, or in both. The appropriate types of connections for these different design types are slightly different.

The key to working with backup links, switches, and routers is in the automated fault recovery system used. Since a Distribution Area is essentially a set of parallel broadcast domains, the best way to implement redundancy is to use Spanning Tree.

I mentioned earlier in this chapter that to use Spanning Tree effectively, the two Distribution switches must have a trunk connection between them. Another way of looking at this is by our simplicity requirement. The Spanning Tree Protocol needs to have a Root Bridge, which is the main switch for a Distribution Area through which all traffic must pass. Simplicity tells you that you should have every other switch in the Distribution Area connected as directly as possible to this Root Bridge. If possible, the Root Bridge should have a single trunk connection to every other switch in the area. Then, the backup Root Bridge switch also must have a direct trunk connection to the primary. Similarly, every other switch in the area needs a direct trunk to the backup Root Bridge in case the primary fails.

There are inherent scaling problems with directly connecting every switch to both of the two Distribution switches, which will always limit the number of switches in a Distribution Area, as I have already discussed. Keeping your Distribution Areas relatively small and modular will be good for overall network performance anyway.

Router-to-router redundancy has different requirements for multiple connections than the switch-to-switch case I was just discussing. The dynamic routing protocols for IP operate completely differently from the Spanning Tree Protocol. Instead of shutting down redundant links, IP routing protocols seek only to rate the different path options and select the most appropriate at the time. If one path goes away, another is selected from the list of possibilities.

Again, simplicity is the watchword for IP dynamic routing protocols. Every router in an OSPF area must maintain information about all of its neighboring routers (the ones with which it shares a direct link), and routing table information about every other device in the area. It is important to keep the topology of an area as simple as possible. The simplest schemes connect everything redundantly, but with as few connections as possible.

Large-Scale LAN Topologies

There are three main options for large-scale topology. If you want to use VLANs, and their benefits should be clear by now, then you need to have routers to interconnect them. Your options basically come down to where to put these routers. You can put them in the Core or in the Distribution Level, or you put them in both. It is usually best to avoid putting routers at the Access Level of a LAN, but for very large networks it is easy to see that you get much better scaling properties if you include routers in the Distribution Level.

Routers in the Core Level

Perhaps the simplest and most obvious way to build a large-scale hierarchical network is to use a model like that shown in Figure 3-24. In this diagram, several different Distribution Areas are connected via a central Routing Core consisting of two routers. All Distribution Areas are redundantly connected to both Core Routers from both Distribution switches.

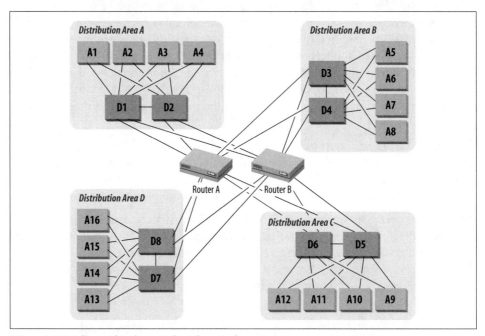

Figure 3-24. A hierarchical network with central routing

The result of all these redundant connections is that any device in the Core or Distribution Levels can fail without affecting network operation. Each Distribution Area has redundant Distribution switches, either of which can act as a Root Bridge for this area. Both Distribution switches have connections to both of the two Core routers. If either Core Router fails, you have complete redundancy.

The best part of the redundancy in this network is its simplicity. There are only two central routers (there may be additional routers connecting to remote sites, as I will discuss shortly), and either can quickly take over all central routing functions in case the other fails. Because of the way that these routers are connected to one another and to all Distribution switches, they can both be used simultaneously. However, the extent to which these routers share the load depends on how the dynamic routing protocols are configured.

The limitation to this design is the capacity of one of the Core Routers. You must configure these two routers so that either is able to support the entire network load in case the other fails. So Figure 3-25 shows a simple way of overcoming this limitation. It still has a central routing Core, but now there are four routers in the Core. Each pair of routers is responsible only for a small part of the network.

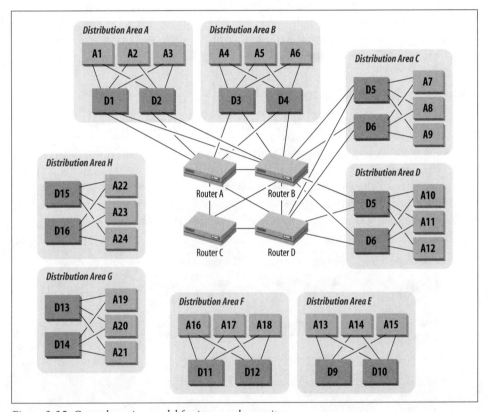

Figure 3-25. Central routing model for increased capacity

There are many different ways to connect such a Core. Figure 3-25 shows a Core with four routers that are interconnected with a full mesh. I have already indicated that a full mesh does not scale well, so if the network will need further expansion, full mesh would not be a good option. Figure 3-26 shows a similar network but with six central routers connected to one another by a pair of central switches.

Note that there need be no VLANs defined on these two switches. Both switches S1 and S2 have connections to all six routers. A natural way to define the IP segments on these switches is to have one switch carry one subnet and the other carry a different subnet. Then if either switch fails, the dynamic routing protocol takes care of moving all traffic to the second switch.

In this sort of configuration, it is generally useful to make the routers act in tandem. Assuming that Distribution Areas consist of two Distribution switches and several Access switches, you would connect both switches to both routers in this pair, and you can connect several Distribution Areas to each pair of routers. The actual numbers depend on the capacity of the routers. All connections will be fully redundant. Then only the Distribution switches that are part of this group of Distribution Areas will connect to this pair of routers. The next group of Distribution Areas will connect to the next pair of Core Routers.

Routers in the Distribution Level

There are two ways to bring the routers into the Distribution Level. One is to simply extend the concept shown in Figure 3-26 and arbitrarily proclaim that the two central switches S1 and S2 are now the Core and the routers are all in the Distribution Level. The distinction between "Core" and "Distribution" Levels is somewhat vague and depends partially on where you draw the lines. One problem with this way of drawing the lines is that these routers interconnect different Distribution Areas, so it is a little tenuous to claim that they are part of the Distribution Level.

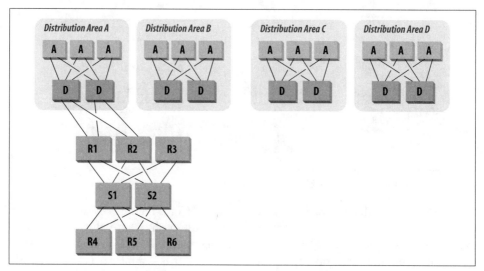

Figure 3-26. Central routing and switching

The second way of bringing routers into the Distribution Level is to have one (or preferably two, for redundancy) router for each Distribution Area. This option is shown in Figure 3-27.

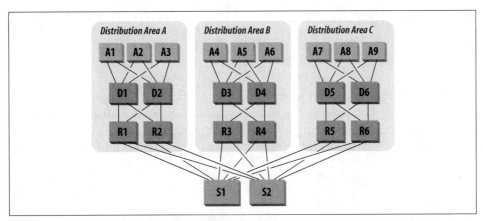

Figure 3-27. Distributed routing and central switching

One advantage to this approach is that it provides a very natural application of Layer 3 switching. Each Distribution switch could contain a Layer 3 switching module. This way, you can provide efficient VLAN-to-VLAN communication within each Distribution Area. You would then construct two additional VLANs on each Distribution switch that would connect to the two central switches.

In this sort of model, where routing functions are downloaded to the Distribution Level, another sort of efficiency can be used. Since how you decide which VLANs comprise a VLAN Distribution Area is somewhat arbitrary, you can deliberately choose your areas to limit traffic through the Core. This may not always be practical, particularly if the Distribution Areas are selected for geographical reasons. If it can be done, though, it may radically improve the network performance through the Core.

Routers in Both the Core and Distribution Levels

It's pretty clear that the network shown in Figure 3-27 has good scaling properties, but there are limits to even this model. In Chapter 6, I will discuss the IP dynamic routing protocol called OSPF. This protocol allows IP routers to keep one another informed about how best to reach the networks they are responsible for. There are other dynamic routing protocols but OSPF is an open standard and an industry norm. The comments that follow turn out to be applicable to most of the alternatives as well.

In Figure 3-27, all of the routers talk directly to one another through the Core switches. In any dynamic routing protocol, every router must know about all of its neighboring routers. It maintains a large table of these neighbor relationships and has to keep it continuously up to date. The more neighbors it has, the harder this job becomes, with similar scaling properties to a fully meshed network. The usual rule is that you never want more than 50 routers in one OSPF area. There are exceptions to this rule, as I will discuss in the section on OSPF, but it is never wise to push it too far.

If you want no more than 50 routers in your Core, then you can have no more than 25 VLAN Distribution Areas, since there are two routers in each area. With a capacity of over a thousand users in each Distribution Area, this is a limit that only large organizations will hit. However, it turns out that it isn't terribly difficult to overcome.

All you need to do is create a hybrid of the two solutions, with routers in the Core and Distribution Layers. Each Core router will handle several Distribution routers to allow excellent scaling properties. Figure 3-28 shows an example of how this hybrid might work. In this figure, the two Core routers that serve the Distribution Areas shown are the OSPF Area Border Routers (ABR) for these Distribution Areas.

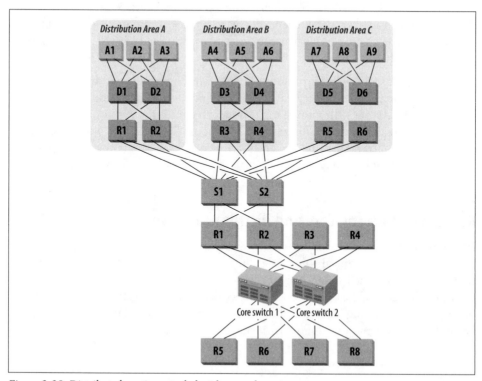

Figure 3-28. Distributed routing coupled with central routing

There are two other key advantages to this sort of design. First, it makes it extremely easy to spread the Distribution Areas geographically. In fact, you could even make your Core spread physically throughout a campus area, or even across several cities. However, doing so is generally not a good plan. The Core in this case represents our OSPF area 0 (a concept that I will explain in Chapter 6). There can be performance and reliability problems in a network that has its area 0 dispersed over wide area links. These problems can be overcome with careful tuning of OSPF parameters, but it leads to a network Core that has to be monitored very closely. A broken link in the Core could have disastrous consequences.

It is actually simpler to have the Core in a single geographical location and to bring the links to the various Distribution Areas via WAN links.

That point leads to the second advantage. It is very easy to integrate a large WAN into this sort of design, as I will show in the next section.

Connecting Remote Sites

In all but rare exceptions, if you want to get data to remote locations, it is best to route it. Bridging over WAN links should never be the first choice. Thus, the question becomes, where do you connect the routers for these remote sites into your LAN?

There are three possible types of WAN links that you might be interested in connecting. There might be a few geographically remote sites connecting into your LAN, or you might want to attach a more elaborate branch network. The third option involves connecting to external networks such as the public Internet.

In both of the internal cases, it is best to put these connections on routers, and in both cases you should put these routers as close to the Core as possible. Exactly where you connect them depends on where your other routers are. In the external case, the connection should almost certainly be behind a firewall. The question you need to answer here is where to put the firewall.

For internal networks, including both WANs of minor and major proportions, you have to share dynamic routing information with the existing routers. I assume throughout this discussion that this dynamic routing protocol is OSPF, but again, the comments apply generally to most dynamic routing protocols.

The main difference between the case of the small and large WAN is just one of numbers. A WAN of any size should never be part of the network's OSPF area 0. For a single external site, you might be able to get away with it, so I will briefly discuss the single site case.

The easiest way to treat a single external site is to think of it as a VLAN Distribution Area of its own. If it is a sufficiently important external site, then you might want to allow multiple routers and multiple WAN links. A smaller site might be connected with only a single link, probably with dial backup.

There will be a router on the remote site with some sort of WAN circuit connecting it to a router on the main site. One simple way of connecting this router on the main site is to treat it as just another VLAN router. For the case where routers are connected only in the Core, the easiest method is to connect this WAN router to the Core routers as if it were one of them.

It is generally not a good idea to use the LAN Core router as a WAN router. The requirements for LAN Core routers are different from the requirements for a WAN router. The LAN Core router has to handle a lot of VLANs and has to move packets between similar media as quickly as possible. The WAN router has to buffer data and act as a point of junction between LAN and WAN. It is likely that this role will force you to use different router models, perhaps even from different vendors for these two functions.

In the cases in which the VLAN routers are moved into the Distribution Level, it becomes easier to connect the WAN routers. Then, for either a single-site or a multiple-site WAN, you would connect them as shown in Figure 3-29.

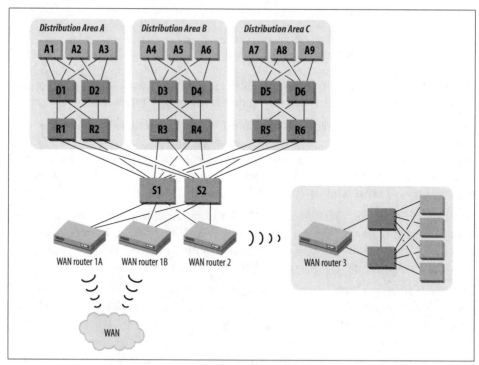

Figure 3-29. Connecting to remote networks in the Distributed Routing model

This diagram shows both a single-site and a multiple-site WAN. For the single-site WAN, I assume that the remote site is sufficiently complex to require its own hierarchical network. If it were smaller, then a single switch might be sufficient.

For the multiple-site WAN, the entire cloud is connected to two routers for redundancy. Both routers connect to the LAN Core switches. These new WAN Access routers become members of the OSPF area 0. In the multiple-site case, there will be too many downstream routers to put them all into area 0. This means that the router at the main site must be an OSPF area Border Router. Again, I will explain this concept in more detail in Chapter 6.

The other common way of connecting remote sites uses a WAN Touchdown segment. This segment is simply a separate router-to-router LAN segment or VLAN that only connects WAN routers, as shown in Figure 3-30. In this picture, the Touchdown Segment is created by two redundant routers that connect into the network Core. These routers may be part of the Core, or they may be Distribution Level routers; it all depends on the type of large-scale topology being used.

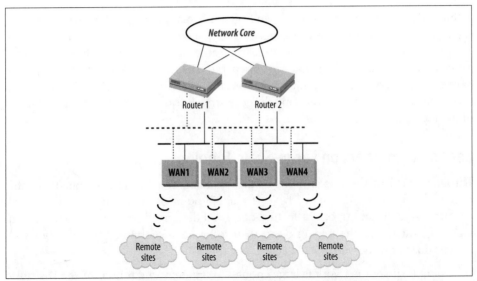

Figure 3-30. Connecting to remote networks with a WAN Touchdown Segment

The segment itself is a single VLAN that may be implemented on more than one switch or hub. A single segment like this has an inherent lack of redundancy. However, it can easily be improved by doubling the segment as indicated by the dotted lines.

The Touchdown Segment model for connecting WAN routers to a LAN is a fairly common technique. It has several advantages over connecting the WAN directly to the Core of the network due to the segment being separated from anything internal by means of routers.

First, if there is a requirement for security filtering, then this is a safer method for connecting the WAN. The remote sites may be less trustworthy than the internal network, or they may even be connections to an information vendor's site. In these cases, it is easy to offer basic security support by implementing filtering on the two routers that connect the Touchdown segment or segments to the main network.

Second, WAN links are inherently less reliable than LAN links. It may be desirable to protect the internal network from the effects of unstable links by using these routers as a sort of buffer zone. One of the problems with using a dynamic routing protocol is that flapping links cause all other routers in the area to repeatedly update their routing tables to reflect each change of state. One way to protect against this updating is by using the two routers that connect to the Core as a transition point in the routing protocol. You could run a different routing protocol on the Touchdown segments than you do in the Core, or you could use Border Gateway Protocol (BGP, another routing protocol) on these routers to separate the Touchdown segment's routing protocol from the internal network's routing protocol. BGP will be discussed in Chapter 6.

A third advantage to using Touchdown Segments this way is that it provides an easy expansion method for better scaling. If the Touchdown Segments become congested, building additional segments in the same pattern is relatively easy. If you were connecting each WAN router as a separate Distribution Area, then you would have to think very carefully about its connections to the Core each time. However, with Touchdown Segments, it is much more straightforward to expand the architectural model.

General Comments on Large-Scale Topology

Throughout all of these examples, I have assumed considerable symmetry in the large-scale topology. Although I haven't made a point of discussing this topic until now, it is actually an important feature of a good design. It's important to decide on a global strategy for the network and then follow it. Combining different types of designs doesn't work well.

For example, if your network is large enough to require using routers at the Distribution Level, then all Distribution Areas should have routers. It is certainly reasonable to have a migration plan to do this one area at a time, but this phase is transitional. In the target design, the network should follow consistent rules.

There will always be portions of the network that need to be treated as exceptions. It is generally a good idea to devise a standard method for dealing with exceptions, as I did with the remote sites considered in the previous section. If a few special VLANs require filtering, then they should all be treated with the same technique.

A theme that will repeat throughout this book is simplicity of concept. The benchmark for the appropriate level of simplicity is that an engineer familiar with the network in general should be able to troubleshoot problems on the network without documentation. This rule may sound arbitrary, but any engineer who has been awakened to diagnose network problems over the phone in the middle of the night will immediately recognize its value.

Another key advantage to this level of simplicity is that it allows new staff to learn the system quickly. Building a network that only one genius can understand is a terrible mistake. Sooner or later this genius will grow tired of taking trouble calls and will want to train a successor. Furthermore, a simple network design can also be handed over easily to relatively junior operations staff to manage. This feature has obvious advantages for maintainability, and maintainability is an important key to reliability.

Local Area Network Technologies

This chapter focuses on the selection of appropriate LAN technologies for a network. Many options are available. At the more traditional end of the LAN technology spectrum, we have various flavors of Ethernet and Token Ring. Competing with these technologies are some very interesting modern alternatives such as ATM and wireless networking. Each of these different technologies has its strengths and weaknesses. Some are strikingly effective in certain situations, while awkward and difficult in others.

Selecting Appropriate LAN Technology

You should consider four main factors when selecting a LAN technology:

- Cost efficiency
- Installed base
- Maintainability
- Performance

Cost Efficiency

One of my central assumptions throughout this book is that the network is built for some business reason. It may not directly involve making money, but there must be some benefit to having the network that justifies the expense of building it. Clearly, the benefit is never infinite, so as network designers, we have a responsibility to build a network that meets the requirements for the lowest possible cost.

This problem is particularly important in the selection of network technologies. The classic example is that Token Ring cards for PCs are more expensive than the equivalent Ethernet cards. This fact alone has explained why so many organizations have undergone expensive changes in their LAN infrastructure to use more cost-effective options. As discussed previously, Token Ring has many performance benefits over

Ethernet. But if the cost of Ethernet is low enough and the cost of Token Ring is high enough, then you can engineer around the performance benefits to build an Ethernet network that is at least as good as Token Ring, but less expensive. Or, you may decide to spend more money on Token Ring and get better performance.

Similarly, you could get a high-performance network by running Gigabit Ethernet to every desk. But the cost of doing this would be orders of magnitude higher than the same network using Fast Ethernet. There may still be valid business reasons for wanting to build the faster network. However, it is more likely that a hybrid of the two approaches would meet all of the business requirements with a much more attractive budget.

In general, faster technology is more expensive. This is not universally true, however. Fast Ethernet equipment has become nearly ubiquitous, making the cost of building a Fast Ethernet network similar to the cost of building a regular 10Mbps Ethernet. This is even truer of the 4Mbps and 16Mbps Token Ring—it is now difficult to find Token Ring equipment that doesn't support both standards.

The other important cost/performance decision in both Ethernet- and Token Ring–based networks is the granularity of shared and switched segments. The finest granularity network has a switch port for every end device, which has significant performance benefits—particularly because it allows full-duplex operation. However, switch ports are generally more expensive than hub ports. A more cost-effective solution might involve a hybrid network in which some important end devices are directly attached to switch ports, while others are grouped in small numbers on hubs.

Another important economy involves the use of unmanageable Access devices. Small workgroup hubs and switches with no management capabilities are available for remarkably low prices. In the same vein, it is still possible to build an old-fashioned 10Base2 network, using a long piece of coax cable (often called "thin-net"), for almost nothing.

These inexpensive Access options definitely have their place. They may be ideal for the home or small office LAN. They can also be used to increase the effective port density of the network's Access Level by allowing small groups of users to share ports, as shown in Figure 4-1. This figure shows a Distribution Area containing two Distribution switches and three Access switches. Workgroup hubs and workgroup switches are connectd to these Access switches. Some users are connected through the workgroup devices and some are connected directly to the Access switches. Note that I have shown some of these workgroup devices with dual attachments to the Access switches to provide extra redundancy.

This approach works well, but two main structural disadvantages should be considered. First, even if the end devices are able to connect to a workgroup switch at full-duplex Fast Ethernet speeds, they are still constrained by the uplink speed to the

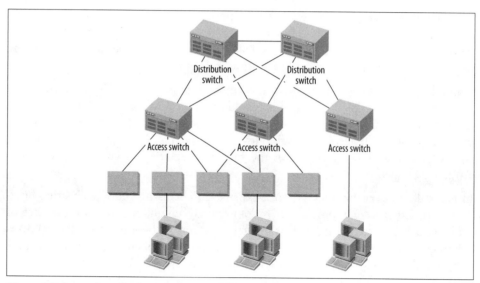

Figure 4-1. Increasing effective port density of the LAN Access Level with unmanageable devices

Access switch. If the Access switch is also Fast Ethernet, then remember that these end devices must share that link. This option may or may not be acceptable, given the application traffic patterns.

The second disadvantage is the increased probability of failure. The diagram shows that some of the workgroup devices have dual connections to the Access switches, and having these connections is a good way of helping to reduce the net probability of failure. However, workgroup devices are generally not built for the same level of serious use as the chassis switches that I prefer for the Access switches. Specifically, they often have external power supplies of similar quality to those used for low-end consumer electronics.

Augmenting the network's Access Level with workgroup hubs or switches (or passive MAUs in Token Ring networks) is sometimes a reasonable way to reduce costs. Giving up manageability can be dangerous, though, or at least inconvenient. Connecting end devices directly to Access switches allows control over their VLAN membership. Connecting these devices through an intermediate workgroup hub or switch, however, generally means that every device on the workgroup hub or switch must be part of the same VLAN. This requirement affects flexibility.

A more serious problem is the loss of fault management information. An unmanageable workgroup hub or switch cannot tell you when one of the devices misbehaves or when a cable is faulty. It can't tell you when its power supply is overheating. You might be able to get some information about an ill-behaved device somewhere on a workgroup hub by looking at the more complete management information on the Access switch. It can be difficult to narrow down which device is in trouble, though.

Most seriously, if there are problems with one or more devices connected to a workgroup switch, then the only noticeable result will be performance problems for the other devices in that workgroup. The workgroup switch will not pass bad frames to the Access switch,* and it can't complain about the bad frames it receives from its end devices. It is possible to have a serious problem that simply will never be seen unless the users are diligent about complaining.

Installed Base

Installed base is another facet of cost effectiveness. The chances are slim that you are building a new network from scratch. In most cases, there is existing equipment, existing applications, servers, and a cable plant. A significantly cheaper alternative network technology may be available. If migrating to that means that you have to absorb a high cost in changing your installed base, then simply staying with the existing technology may be more cost-effective.

For example, a large company may make extensive use of native Token Ring protocols to connect to legacy mainframe equipment. Token Ring equipment is more expensive than Ethernet equipment, but after factoring in the cost of replacing the mainframe, rewriting the applications to use TCP/IP, and changing every end device to use this new application, they probably won't want to make the change.

This is where it is useful to have a long-term strategic information technology vision for the entire organization. If you have a long-term goal to phase out these legacy applications, then you need to build a network that can accommodate a phased-in migration to the target technology. Perhaps you will migrate the Core of the network from Token Ring to Fast and Gigabit Ethernet with TCP/IP routing and use DLSw to tunnel the native Token Ring protocols. Then, when the new servers and applications are available, you can migrate user devices in relatively small groups.

An installed base doesn't need to cripple a network, but it can limit your design options temporarily.

Maintainability

One of the biggest potential hidden costs in a network is maintenance. I have mentioned how using unmanageable workgroup devices in the Access Level of the network can make it harder to find problems. I previously mentioned that the design principle of simplicity makes network maintenance easier. Remember that these are not just annoyance factors for the engineer who gets stuck with the ultimate responsibility for running the network. There are costs are associated with these issues.

---

* It is customary to use the word "frame" when talking about the Layer 2 view of a chunk of data and the "packet" at Layer 3.

The trouble is that quantifying these costs can be extremely difficult. How can you tell, for example, that cutting a particular corner will result in needing an extra staff member to keep the network going? Only experience can tell you what the hidden costs are. In general, since your design goals are centered on reliability, the more corners you cut, the less reliable the results will be. Lower reliability generally translates into higher maintenance costs.

Performance

And this topic brings us to performance considerations. You always want to build the fastest and best network you can for the money. Of course, by "best," I mean that the network best fulfills the business application requirements. A brilliant network with unbelievable throughput and low latency is useless if it doesn't support the applications for which it was built.

I mention performance last because it is far too easy to get absorbed in abstract issues of technology improvement. You always have to bear in mind that a network is built for a business reason. It has a budget that is based on how much money this business goal is worth to the organization. If you spend more on building and maintaining the network than it is worth to the organization, either through money saved or revenue earned, then the network actually hurts the organization more than it helps.

Within these limitations, your goal is to build the best network that you can. That also implies that you have to select technology that is appropriate to what you want to accomplish. Part of a LAN may serve an environment where cabling is impossible, so wireless technology could be a natural fit. But wireless technology tends to offer relatively poor bandwidth and latency compared to a similar network built with Fast Ethernet. When selecting appropriate technology, you have to be sensitive to these trade-offs and understand the strengths and weaknesses of the different options available to you.

Ethernet and Fast Ethernet

Ethernet is a bus topology LAN technology with a collision-based mechanism for dealing with contention. Physically, there are several different options for implementing an Ethernet network. I am generally including Fast Ethernet in these comments because the similarities between Ethernet and Fast Ethernet are strong. I will explicitly note where the comments do not apply to both.

Physical implementations of Ethernet and Fast Ethernet are generally determined by their IEEE designations. For 10Mbps standard Ethernet, the most common option today is 10BaseT. This option uses standard twisted pair cabling, such as Category 5 (although 10BaseT also works well over Category 3 cable plants). Other options include 10Base2 and 10Base5, which implement the LAN bus with an extended cable.

In 10Base2 (also called "thin-net"), the cable is an inexpensive 50Ω impedance coaxial cable that is terminated at both ends with an impedance-matching resistor. Devices connect to the wire by means of T-junction connectors along the length of the cable. Some end devices are equipped with 10Base2 connectors, but a transceiver is frequently required. I will discuss transceivers later in this section.

10Base5 (also called "thick-net") is less common these days because it is difficult to maintain and considerably more expensive than higher speed options. This system uses a thick coaxial cable with considerably longer distance limitations than 10Base2 (500 meters for 10Base5 versus 185 meters for 10Base2). Devices connect to the wire using a "vampire tap," which uses a retractable spike to connect to the wire in the middle of the cable. A transceiver is then required to connect this tap connector to the end device.

It is safe to consider both 10Base2 and 10Base5 as essentially obsolete technology, but they are still in use in some older networks, which is why I mention them here.

Besides copper-based Ethernet technologies, several different fiber optic systems are grouped together under the general IEEE title of 10BaseF. The most common 10Mbps fiber optic Ethernet standard is 10BaseFL. Other options exist, such as 10BaseFB and 10BaseFP. The term FOIRL (Fiber Optic Inter-Repeater Link) is often used generically to describe any 10BaseF transceiver, although technically, FOIRL describes an earlier standard.

Since the same fiber optic cabling is capable of transmitting Gigabit Ethernet, there is seldom much point in installing new 10BaseF systems. It is still used primarily in places where the distance limitations on copper Ethernet standards make it necessary to use fiber optic cable, which has much longer distance capabilities. The dominant flavors of Fast Ethernet are 100BaseTX, which runs over standard Category 5 twisted pair cabling, and 100BaseFX, which uses a fiber optic cable.

Designations such as 10BaseT may appear mysterious and arbitrary, but they have simple logic. The first part of the designation refers to the theoretical peak bandwidth—in this case, it is 10Mbps. For 100BaseT, it is 100Mbps. The word "Base" signifies *baseband* rather than *broadband* signaling. Baseband simply means that there is just one carrier frequency. Broadband, on the other hand, can multiplex several different signals on the same medium by transmitting them with different carrier frequencies.

The last part is used inconsistently. The "2" in 10Base2 means 200 meters for the maximum distance of a segment, while the "5" in 10Base5 stands for 500 meters. When twisted pair standards such as 10BaseT came along, the developers probably felt that designating the type of medium was more important. Instead of calling the new twisted pair Ethernet standard 10Base1 to show that it has a 100-meter distance limit, it was called 10BaseT to designate that it operates over twisted pair cabling. Similarly, when the fiber optic standards were developed, the letter "F" was adopted to designate this different cabling standard.

The naming standards start to get a little strange when we get to names like 100VG-AnyLAN (actually, 100VG-AnyLAN isn't really Ethernet at all, because it doesn't use collisions to control contention). If the reader wants more details on these standards and the naming conventions, it is best to look at the reference section of this book to find other books that focus more specifically on these matters.

Ethernet Framing Standards

Figure 4-2 shows the standard 802.3 Ethernet frame structure. Several standard fields are defined, and they must all be present in some form.

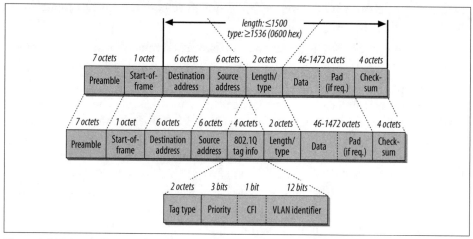

Figure 4-2. Ethernet framing formats, including 802.1Q VLAN tagging

The frame starts with a "preamble." The preamble consists of a string of seven bytes of the binary pattern "10101010" to indicate that the device is about to start sending a frame. Then the eighth byte, called the "start of frame delimiter," is nearly the same as the preamble except for the last bit: "10101011". The preamble and the start of frame delimiter are not included in the frame length counter. Once you get past the preamble and start of frame delimiter, you get into the interesting parts of the Ethernet frame. Three important fields are in the frame header: the source and destination MAC addresses and the length/type field.

All Ethernet MAC addresses are 6 bytes long. Every network interface card (NIC) has a globally unique address "burned-in" to it. It is possible to override this burned-in address (BIA) to create a locally administered address (LAA). However, there are also more special-purpose MAC addresses, such as multicast and broadcast addresses. I will discuss these special-purpose addresses later in this book.

The destination MAC address is always first. This gives the network devices every possible advantage in forwarding packets as quickly as possible. Modern high-speed networking equipment is able to read the frame as it is received. Since the network usually only need to look at where the packet is going, if the destination address is first, it is often possible to start directing the frame to the appropriate destination port just from this information.

The source MAC address comes next. This is the address of the device that sent the frame. Note that it is not necessarily the originator of the packet. If the packet came from an intermediate device such as a router, then the source address will be that of the router. This address is included mostly for the benefit of the recipient device, which needs to know where to send its responses. If the return path needs to pass through a router, then the router's address needs to be here.

The third important field in the Ethernet frame header is the multipurpose "length/type" field (also called Ethertype). This 2-byte number could either be a length or a type. The only way to tell the difference is that the maximum valid length is 1500 bytes.[*] If the value in this field is less than or equal to 1500, it is interpreted as a length.

Similarly, anything larger than 1500 must be a type. Just to be absolutely certain, there is a small gap to the nearest "round" number in hexadecimal, 0600, which is 1536 in decimal. The actual values in the type field represent different protocols, and the IEEE keeps track of these values. An up-to-date list of assigned values is available online from the IEEE web site at *http://standards.ieee.org/regauth/ethertype/type-pub.html*. This list includes a very large number of companies that have registered particular Ethernet protocol types, although only a handful of types are commonly seen in most production LANs.

Novell reserves Ethernet types 8137 and 8138 for IPX. Type 8137 designates an older version of IPX that is not widely used anymore, while 8138 is the most typical for modern IPX installations. Apple's Ethernet protocol uses type code 809B. The Banyan Network Operating System uses 0BAD and 0BAF, and 8191 is reserved for Net-BEUI, which is frequently used for PC file-sharing systems. The most common type field values are 0800, used for frames containing standard IP packets, and 0806, used for IP ARP packets.

In most LANs, IPX uses the length rather than the type. If you look at a protocol analyzer, you will probably see all of the IPX frames with a length/type value of something less than 05DC (the hex value of the decimal number 1500).

TCP/IP, on the other hand, almost universally uses the type rather than length. The reason for the difference is largely historical. The type interpretation is used by an earlier standard for defining Ethernet frames, called Ethernet II. The length interpretation, on the other hand, is the method employed by the newer IEEE 802.3 standard.

---

[*] Note that this length is the size of the packet's data segment. If you include the MAC header's 6-byte source and destination addresses, the length/type field itself, and the 4-byte checksum at the end of the packet, the maximum Ethernet frame length is 1518 bytes. The 8-byte Ethernet preamble is not included when people talk about frame sizes.

It should be obvious why it is more efficient to use the type field as a type rather than as a length. If any one protocol prefers to use its length, then that protocol has effectively trampled over 1500 possible type codes. Furthermore, it is much more efficient if the protocol stacks of both the end and network devices don't have to read into the data portion of the frame before they can figure out what type of packet it is. Not every device cares about every protocol (particularly when the packets are received as broadcasts), so knowing whether they should bother decoding any given packet is useful. But there are other benefits to this system.

For protocols that use the 802.3 standard, it is necessary to use another method for identifying the type. Using this method is done by adding Sub-Network Access Protocol (SNAP) information to the packet. SNAP is part of the LLC (Logical Link Control) sublayer of the Data Link Layer. It is defined as an extension to the 802.2 standard. The presence of a type rather than a length value in the "length/type" field automatically tells the receiving station to look for LLC information later in the packet.

This process may sound complicated, but it allows greater flexibility in the protocol. Rather than a single type field, 802.2 allows the creation of an arbitrary Protocol Data Unit (PDU), which can be used to contain a huge variety of extensions to the protocol. This LLC PDU information is tacked on to the start of the data portion of the packet, immediately after the standard Ethernet header information. In effect, it looks like another type of header, placed after the MAC header.

Also note that the 802.2 LLC sublayer is not unique to Ethernet. Exactly the same SNAP PDU that defines IPX in an Ethernet frame can be used to define IPX in a Token Ring frame.

SNAP is just one simple example of this type of a PDU. Inside the SNAP PDU is a field that defines that protocol type.

At the end of every 802.3 Ethernet frame is a 4-byte checksum called Frame Check Sequence (FCS). This checksum is a relatively simple method of ensuring that the packet was not damaged as it crossed through the network. Generally, one doesn't expect to see very many checksum errors in a stable Ethernet network. Those that are seen are usually caused by other problems, such as late collisions. However, when random electrical problems are on a link, these checksums are useful in finding them.

This checksum is calculated on the entire Ethernet frame from the Destination Address right up to the Data (and possible padding). If the payload protocol contains another checksum, it provides an extra layer of certainty. When there are checksum failures, it can also be used to investigate which layers of the protocol see the problem. For example, if the Ethernet level FCS field is good, but the TCP checksum is bad, then the problem must have existed before the packet hit this part of the network.

The same 802.3 Ethernet frame used for 10Mbps Ethernet is also used for 100Mbps, Gigabit, and 10 Gigabit Ethernet. The same MAC multicast and broadcast addresses are used by all of these standards. The use of these addresses makes life much easier for the network designer because it means that you can freely mix these different standards to fit your immediate needs.

For example, you can have Gigabit Ethernet trunks connecting your Distribution switch to your Access switches. Then you can have 100Mbps Fast Ethernet links to some workstations, and even step down to workgroup hubs of standard half-duplex 10BaseT for the less active user workstations. Throughout this complex hybrid of media types, the same Ethernet frames can be transmitted without change.

Ethernet addresses

Every 6-byte Ethernet address is divided into two parts. The first three bytes represent the vendor, and the rest are allocated by that vendor in whatever method is appropriate. The first half of the address is called the vendor Organizationally Unique Identifier (OUI) value. Again, an up-to-date list of OUI values is available on-line from the IEEE at *http://standards.ieee.org/regauth/oui/oui.txt*.

One of the OUI codes for Compaq is 00-80-5F. With this OUI, they are able to define MAC addresses for their equipment by specifying the last three octets by whatever system is most meaningful. One example might be 00-80-5F-12-34-56.

Only the vendor who owns a particular OUI may generate MAC addresses in that range. Every device has a unique MAC address, but they are really the so-called BIA. Many devices have the capability to override the BIA with a user-defined MAC address, called an LAA. This capability can be useful if one device has to masquerade as a second device. In Chapter 3, I discussed the HSRP and VRRP protocols that use this sort of MAC address masquerading to facilitate automated fault recovery.

Some protocols, such as DECNET, can generate MAC addresses dynamically. This generation can cause confusion when looking at a protocol analyzer on the segment because, for example, the MAC used for DECNET would be different from the MAC used by the same device for TCP/IP. In the case of DECNET, this problem is relatively easy to spot because DECNET addresses always use an OUI value of AA-00-04.

This situation can lead to problems for network segments that have DECNET and TCP/IP operating together. Some devices confuse the two MAC addresses. For example, if a router has DECNET enabled suddenly, it may opt to use the new DEC-NET MAC for its IP packets as well, ignoring IP packets destined for its BIA. Whether this problem occurs depends on the router implementation.

There are two other important classes of Ethernet MAC addresses: the broadcast and multicast addresses.

A standard broadcast address of FF-FF-FF-FF-FF-FF is used by all Ethernet protocols to indicate a packet that should be delivered to every other device in the broadcast domain. When a device sends out a broadcast packet, it usually either advertises itself as a service of some kind or looks for a network resource.

A good example of using a broadcast to look for a network resource is the IP ARP packet. In an ARP packet, the requesting device specifies its own IP and MAC addresses and the IP address for which it is looking. Then it sets the Layer 2 destination to FF-FF-FF-FF-FF-FF and sends it out. This way, the packet gets sent to every other device in the local address range, and hopefully the owner of the requested IP address will respond. In some cases, a router might respond by Proxy ARP for a downstream device. The two devices can then hold their conversation in private without bothering everybody else on the LAN.

And a typical example of a service advertisement is the Novell Service Advertisement Protocol (SAP). In this case, the server periodically sends SAP packets to every device on the network, telling potential LAN clients about what sorts of services the server offers. The SAP may say, for example, that this server offers file-sharing services, printing, or time, database, or other application services. In a large LAN with many servers, SAP can represent a lot of traffic. I discuss IPX SAP issues in more detail in Chapter 7.

Multicast packets are intended for groups of users, but not necessarily the entire network. To help achieve this feat, another group of what might be called "multicast OUIs" is defined. For example, the IP multicast standard specifies the address range from 01-00-5E-00-00-00 to 01-00-5E-7F-FF-FF for all IP multicast traffic.

There is a simple rule for multicast MAC addresses: the lowest bit in the first octet of any multicast MAC address is always 1. The way 802.3 specifies byte ordering of information in the frame header, this is the first bit received. The IEEE has been careful to ensure that every standard vendor OUI has this bit equal to 0.

It is possible, therefore, to convert any standard vendor OUI to a multicast OUI by simply flipping this bit from a 0 to a 1. For example, Cisco has the OUI 00-00-0c, which allows Cisco to define multicast MAC addresses that begin with 01-00-0c.

I talk more about multicast IP networking in Chapter 10.

Collision Detection

Ethernet is always specified with strict distance limitations. These distance limitations are carefully calculated so that the first bit of the preamble can reach all parts of the network before the last bit of data is transmitted, even for the smallest possible frame size.

When a device wants to send a packet, it first listens to verify that nothing else is currently transmitting. This verification is called the "carrier sense" phase. If the line is quiet, it starts to send its frame. Meanwhile, another device may also want to send data, and it does the same thing. If the network is built within Ethernet specifications, the second device sees the frame coming from the first device before it has finished sending its own. It will realize that it has suffered a collision, and will send a "jamming" pattern to ensure that the first device knows that its packet has been damaged. The first device, meanwhile, has seen the start of the second device's packet, and it too sends the jamming pattern.

This procedure is normal when a collision is encountered. Then both devices wait for a random short time interval called the "backoff" interval before trying again. This time interval must be random because if both devices waited the same amount of time, then they would just collide again as soon as the backoff interval had expired. This whole system is called Carrier Sense Multiple Access/Collision Detection (CSMA/CD). It is fundamental to all multiple-access Ethernet systems.

A "late collision" means that the collision process has been followed, but that one of the devices was past the minimum frame size for the medium when it saw the colliding frame. This collision is a bad sign because it either means that the second device does not follow Ethernet rules for collision detection or that it is too far away to see the frame in time. Either way, late collisions usually indicate a serious problem because the time required to inject a whole packet into the Ethernet segment is less than the time required to have it hit the farthest point on that network. A collision can happen to a packet in flight, but the sender will not know about it, and therefore won't be able to retransmit the lost data. This is why late collisions should always be taken seriously.

There is an important difference between a collision and simply having to wait to transmit. When a device wants to send data, it first listens to the wire to see if another device is already talking. If the line is busy, it waits until the current packet is finished. After the current packet is completely sent, the device waits a standard Inter-Frame Gap Time to make sure that the line is really free before it tries to send its packet. A collision only happens if another device also sends a packet at the same time.

The critical difference is that, while a device waits to talk, the network is fully utilized. When two packets collide, no information is transmitted. I make this distinction because some devices report statistics on packets that have been delayed or "deferred," as well as packet collisions. The mere presence of either deferred packets or collisions is not a sign of problems. The packets or collisions are both perfectly normal aspects of Ethernet that we expect to see all the time. What you don't want to see is a high ratio of collisions to packets sent. This ratio is a very accurate measure of network efficiency.

Note, however, that switched full-duplex access is a completely different matter. In fact, collision detection doesn't exist in full-duplex operation. When a network segment operates in full-duplex mode, only two devices are on that segment. One of these devices is usually a switch. Because it is full-duplex, both devices can send and receive at the same time without contention, so there can never be a collision. This feature makes full-duplex much simpler to implement and gives much better performance.

In full-duplex operation, each device sends a frame whenever it has a frame to send, with two small caveats. First, a standard time interval called the Inter-Frame Gap Time must elapse after the last frame is sent and before the next one. This relatively short time period required by the protocol ensures that the start of the next frame is properly distinguished from the last one.

Note that one relatively common Ethernet problem occurs when a half-duplex device is connected to a full-duplex switch, or vice versa. This is normally not a problem, since most devices are set up by default to automatically detect and negotiate the best duplex settings. However, sometimes the negotiation process fails to work properly, particularly when the equipment comes from different vendors. It is also possible to statically configure most Ethernet equipment to use either duplex setting exclusively. This configuration represents a good solution to the problem of improper negotiation, but it also makes it possible to configure a conflict.

The problem with this particular conflict is that, in most cases, the connection still works, but the full-duplex device ignores collision information. The result is that the half-duplex device sees large numbers of late collisions.

A special addition was made to the 802.3 standard when full-duplex modes of operation became available. The problem with being able to talk all the time is that you might exceed your partner's capacity to listen. Buffers can fill up, particularly if upstream bottlenecks prevent the data from being passed along as it is received. Without collisions to offer a natural mechanism for forcing a backoff, a new mechanism had to be added to the protocol. This mechanism is the PAUSE frame.

The PAUSE frame is a short instruction that simply tells the other device that it must stop sending anything for a specified short period of time. The time interval is a number from 0 to 65,535, which measures time in units of "pause quanta." One pause quantum is the time it takes to send 512 bits. Fast Ethernet is able to transmit 100Mbps serially, so the time to transmit one bit is 0.01 μs (microseconds). The maximum total pause duration in Fast Ethernet, then, is .35 seconds.

Because Gigabit Ethernet uses 10-bit rather than 8-bit encoding at Layer 1, the maximum pause time actually drops by a little more than a factor of 10.

There are several interesting features of this PAUSE frame. It is always sent to the multicast address 01-80-C2-00-00-01, and it is the only defined member of a new class of MAC Control packets. Perhaps future versions of 802.3 will require other types of control messages. In general, the PAUSE looks like a regular 802.3 frame, except that the value in the length/type field is 88-08. The data segment of the frame contains the two-byte Control Opcode type, followed by the value of the pause time variable and sufficient padding of zeros to make the frame reach the required length. Since this is the only defined Control message, it has a Control Opcode of 00-01.

Hubs, Bridges, and Switches

I have already discussed hubs, bridges, and switches in earlier chapters. Here I will focus on design issues of the various options.

A hub is a way of allowing devices to share a collision domain, while a switch is a way of separating collision domains. All other things being equal, the smaller the collision domains are, the better the overall network performance will be. Clearly, if you could afford to do it, you'd rather put every single workstation on its own switch port. However, this solution is not always practical.

Much of the literature on Ethernet discusses the so-called 5-4-3 Repeater rule. This rule is at best a loose approximation of IEEE standards. It also represents a completely outdated way of looking at Ethernet segment combinations that I don't support. I favor a simpler rule, for which I'll make up the name the 1 Repeater rule. My simplified rule says that every time I use a hub, I will connect it directly to a switch. Cascading hubs and repeaters one after another is dangerous and is never necessary in a modern, well-designed network. The only time I will break my 1 Repeater rule is when I need to use transceivers that are also technically repeaters. In this case, it is acceptable to connect a hub to a switch by means of a pair of transceivers, one at each end.

In any case, I never recommend connecting one hub directly to another hub. Hubs should only connect back to the Access switches (or Distribution switches, in a very small network). Even in a small office or home network, cascading multiple hubs together results in instability and poor performance. In large networks, it has the added problem of making troubleshooting far more difficult than it needs to be.

These comments apply to both 10 and 100Mbps Ethernet configurations.

In a network of any size, manageability of Access devices becomes increasingly important. It doesn't matter whether the Access devices are hubs or switches. What matters is that the network manager can easily tell when end devices have problems. Approaching the same problem from the other direction, the network manager also needs to be able to find individual devices by MAC address wherever they are on the network.

These goals are relatively easy to achieve by just using manageable hubs and switches and having good network management software. Chapter 9 discusses how to build a manageable network in more detail. A key requirement will always be that Access devices have to be manageable.

The only place where unmanageable Access devices are acceptable is in networks too small to be managed proactively. In a home or small office network there probably will not be a dedicated system monitoring the few network devices, and the small number of devices actually makes it less necessary to monitor them. As discussed in Chapter 2, the probability of any one device failing is relatively small. It only becomes a serious issue when there are so many devices on the network that one can statistically expect to see something fail fairly often. Fault isolation in small networks is rather simple when there are very few possible failure points.

In small networks, manageable hubs and switches do not actually provide much real benefit. Since unmanageable devices are usually significantly less expensive, it makes sense to use them here. In any network large enough to warrant full-time network staff, though, it is best to have network management functionality on all network devices.

In some bridged protocols, such as some IBM LLC protocols, the number of bridge hops can become extremely important. Thus, it is important to know where all bridges in the network are. A network could have an unmanaged bridge that the network engineer may not know about.

This is the case for all of the so-called 10/100 hubs. These devices are hubs in the standard sense of the word, except that they have the added feature of being able to autosense whether the devices connecting to them are capable of 100Mbps Fast Ethernet speeds. If the device is Fast Ethernet capable, then the hub operates as a 100BaseT hub.

Obviously, it is not possible to run a hub with a mixture of 10BaseT and 100BaseT ports. The two protocols are electrically different at the physical layer. Thus, these devices are actually made up of two hubs—one for 10BaseT and the other for 100BaseT. Whenever a new device is connected to a port on this hub, it automatically senses which Ethernet standard is appropriate. In the case of NICs that are also able to operate in either mode, the autonegotiation process tries to pick the fastest speed available. There are some cases of vendor incompatibility problems in this autonegotiation process, so it is possible to get the slower connection.

When the autonegotiation process decides to use the 10BaseT standard, the hub connects the port internally to its 10BaseT hub circuitry. When it finds Fast Ethernet capability, it uses the faster 100BaseT internal hub circuits. To allow these two sides of the hub to communicate internally, a bridge contained inside the hub interconnects the two hubs at the logical link layer.

Transceivers

A transceiver is a specialized device used to interconnect two different physical media types. The term is just a contraction of "transmitter" and "receiver," which, unfortunately, is no longer as meaningful a name as it originally was.

Some of the earliest transceiver implementations were the devices that converted the media-independent Attachment Unit Interface (AUI) port that was common on a NIC to whatever medium was required. For example, some transceivers that converted AUI were 10Base2, 10Base5, 10BaseT, and 10BaseF. The advantage with this scheme was that users could buy a simple generic Ethernet card and use whatever type of transceiver was appropriate to their requirements.

However, with the advent of Fast Ethernet, this solution became less practical. There is a media-independent interface defined for Fast Ethernet, called simply Media Independent Interface (MII). However, this interface has not enjoyed widespread acceptance, and MII transceivers are rare and expensive. It is more common to find Fast Ethernet devices implemented with a built-in transceiver; they present only a RJ45 or a fiber optic connector.

In these cases, if you want to convert from, say, RJ45 to fiber connections, you would have to use another type of transceiver. This media conversion device is actually two transceivers in one box. It is a 100BaseT transceiver on the RJ45 side and is a 100BaseFX transceiver on the fiber optic side. Between these two transceivers is a repeater. This may sound like an academic distinction, but it can be important. Some repeaters act more like switches, since they can operate at full-duplex; but most do not.

Suppose you want to connect the 100BaseT ports on two devices, such as a trunk link, between two switches. However, these devices are physically separated by more than 100 meters—perhaps they are on different floors. You can connect them easily by using a fiber optic connection. Connect an RJ45-to-fiber Fast Ethernet transceiver to both ends and connect the fiber between the two.

In this environment, unless the two transceivers are both capable of operating at full-duplex, the trunk link must be configured as half-duplex at both ends.

Token Ring

Token Ring is a ring topology LAN technology with a token-passing mechanism for eliminating contention. There are actually two standards for Token Ring. It was originally developed by engineers at IBM who created the initial specification. Subsequently, the IEEE took on the responsibility of making an industry standard Token Ring specification, under the designation 802.5. There are slight differences between the two standards, but they interoperate without any issues. One of these minor differences is that the IEEE reduced the maximum number of devices on a ring from 260 to 250 for Type 1 shielded cabling. The maximum number of devices for a ring built with Category 5 unshielded twisted pair cabling (UTP) is only 72, however.

Figure 4-3 shows the formats for both an empty token and a frame that carries user data. Several features are remarkably similar to Ethernet and some are quite different. For example, the maximum Ethernet frame is 1518 octets long, while the maximum Token Ring frame size can be as much as 4550 octets in a 4Mbps ring, or 18,200 for a 16Mbps ring. In general, the Token Ring frame size is governed by the ring's hold-time parameter, which governs how long any one device is permitted to have the token.

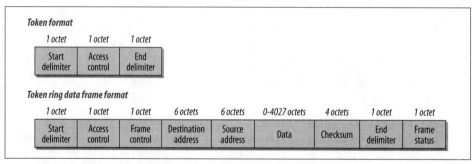

Figure 4-3. Token Ring frame formats

Both Ethernet and Token Ring use 6-byte addresses. This fact makes bridging between the two much easier. However, there is one significant twist. Token Ring orders its bytes so that the most significant bit comes first, while Ethernet does exactly the opposite. If you bridge Ethernet and Token Ring segments together, you have to translate the addresses from one format to the other by changing the bit ordering.

A quick side note on the subject of Ethernet to Token Ring bridging is that there are in fact two different options for running LLC2 on Ethernet. The most common method is to simply use 802.3 format frames. The second option that appears in some installations is the so-called 80d5 format. This strange name refers to the Ethernet type code for the Ethernet II style frames. I have seen some overly helpful LLC2 server software that uses both frame types. This software tends to cause serious confusion on the bridge and should be avoided.

In general, bridging works well between Ethernet and Token Ring networks, but it is important to be careful of Maximum Transmission Unit (MTU) and watch out for these address translation issues. This warning implies, in turn, that it is possible to create a bridge between two Token Ring segments through an intermediate Fast or Gigabit Ethernet segment. If this is the goal, it would usually be more practical to use a TCP/IP tunnel protocol such as DLSw. This protocol would then allow the Token Ring MTU to be preserved through the Ethernet leg of the connection.

There are two common standards for Token Ring; one operates at 4Mbps and the other at 16Mbps. A high-speed standard also operates at 100Mbps. But, unlike the 4 and 16Mbps standards, the 100Mbps version has not seen widespread use to date.

In most cases, running the same equipment at either 4 or 16Mbps is possible. This possibility is useful, since it allows the network to use the lowest common technology. But there is an unfortunate converse to this property: once a ring has started operating at either speed, introducing a new device at the other speed can cause serious problems for the entire ring.

The *token* in Token Ring refers to the way that the ring avoids packet collision problems. There is a simple token packet that contains no user information. This packet is passed from station to station around the ring from an upstream to downstream neighbor. If a device has something to send, it waits until it gets the token. Then it replaces the token packet with a data packet, which it sends to its downstream neighbor instead of the token. The first two fields of this data packet look similar to the original token packet, except for one bit (the token bit) that indicates that data will follow.

This device then continues to transmit data until it either runs out of data to send or until it sends a predefined maximum number of bytes. The data can be sent either as one packet or it can be broken up into several separate packets, which can be useful if the device is talking to many other devices. Once it is done talking, it places a new token on the ring so that other devices will have an opportunity to talk as well. This method ensures that every device gets to participate fairly.

The packets that are sent this way all pass from the sender to its downstream neighbor, which forwards them on to the next downstream neighbor, and so forth, until they reach all the way back around the ring to the original sender. The sender is then responsible for removing the frames from the ring (which is called "stripping"). Once these frames are removed from the ring, the sender replaces a token onto the ring so the next device can talk.

Another interesting feature that is available in the 16Mbps Token Ring (but not in the 4Mbps standard) is Early Token Release (ETR). In this case, the sender doesn't wait until it has seen its own frames finish circulating around the ring. Instead, it puts the token back onto the ring for the next device as soon as it has finished its transmission. This placement makes the ring much more efficient. What's particularly useful about ETR is that not all devices on the ring need to support it. In fact, it should be fairly obvious that the whole ring benefits from improved throughput if even a few devices can do this.

The most common problem that arises in Token Ring topologies is a broken ring. If, for whatever reason, the ring is not closed, then the packets never get back to their starting point. As I just described, the normal token-release mechanism depends on the source device receiving the frames it has sent before it passes the empty token along for another device to use. A broken ring is a serious problem.

The ring deals with a break by sending around a *beacon* packet. The device that is immediately downstream from the break alerts the rest of the ring by sending this special type of frame. The beacon frame contains the Layer 2 MAC address of the upstream neighbor that has lost its connection. In this way the *failure domain*, the area in which the break has occurred, is identified. This identification allows the ring to go into its reconfiguration procedure.

A particular device on the ring is designated as the *ring monitor*. This device is responsible for putting new tokens onto the ring when they are lost. In a broken ring situation, the monitor device is able to keep communication working. However, this situation is considerably less efficient than having a properly closed ring.

Token Ring has, in general, seen significantly less industry acceptance than Ethernet, despite having some useful advantages. There are important exceptions, particularly in mainframe environments, where Token Ring is more popular, but Ethernet is definitely more popular. With the advent of higher speed versions of 802.3, the industry preference for Ethernet appears to be growing.

The main reason for this gap in acceptance is simply the implementation cost. Token Ring hubs and switches cost more than Ethernet hubs and switches. However, the largest portion of the cost difference comes from the higher prices of Token Ring NICs and the cost of the Token Ring chipsets used by these cards.

The development of 100Mbps Fast Ethernet finally eliminated the bandwidth advantages of Token Ring. By the time the new 100Mbps Token Ring devices were available, Gigabit Ethernet was also coming out. Although Token Ring has not reached any theoretical limitations, it seems unlikely that a Gigabit Token Ring standard will be available before the 10 Gigabit Ethernet makes it obsolete.

The result is that Token Ring tends to be used primarily in organizations with large legacy mainframe environments that make extensive use of Token Ring and protocols such as LLC2. In organizations with modern mainframes, there is a trend toward adopting TCP/IP as the protocol of preference and toward the installation of Gigabit Ethernet modules into the mainframes or their front-end processors.

MAUs, Bridges, and Switches

One of the most popular methods for connecting devices to a Token Ring is the Multistation Access Unit (MAU). This unit is traditionally an unmanaged device, with the classic example being the IBM 8228. The 8228 requires no external power. Rather, the individual end devices provide the power for the MAU to operate. When no device is connected to a port, a relay switch disconnects it from the ring. Then, when a device connects, it provides power to this relay and is inserted into the ring electrically.

At either end of the MAU are ports labeled "Ring-In" (RI) and "Ring-Out" (RO). These ports are provided to allow several MAU devices to be chained together into a larger ring. The RI port from one MAU is connected to the RO port of the next, and so on around the ring until the RO port of the first MAU is connected back to the RI port of the last to close the ring. These RI and RO ports are not equipped with the same sort of relay switching as the regular device ports, so they can only be used for interconnecting MAUs.

The IBM 8228 uses IBM UDC connectors (also called "hermaphroditic" connectors because they are both male and female), which are usually used with IBM Type 1 shielded cabling. However, there are also RJ45 MAU units from both IBM and other manufacturers. Generally, the RJ45 units require external power like Ethernet hubs. Other than this, no real functional differences exist between these two types of MAUs.

A managed Token Ring hub is also sometimes called a Controlled Access Unit (CAU). This hub generally operates in a similar manner, except that it becomes possible to monitor utilization and error statistics on individual ports, and activate or deactivate ports individually. Some of these hubs have the ability to assign individual ports to different physical rings internally, similar to an Ethernet VLAN.

Token Ring switching is really nothing more than Token Ring bridging, just like in Ethernet. Also as in Ethernet networks, Token Ring switches are becoming a popular method of connecting important end devices to the network. In effect, the switch becomes a multiport bridge that interconnects a large number of different rings.

Typically, source-route bridging is used in Token Ring networks. Besides the simple bridging functions that allow a separate token on each port, source-route bridging allows devices to find the optimal path through the network. They find this path by means of Routing Information Field (RIF) data that is added to packets as they travel through the network.

When a device wants to find a particular MAC somewhere on the network, it sends out an "explorer" packet. This broadcast frame finds its way throughout the whole network, hopefully to the desired destination. Along the way, the explorer packet picks the RIF information that describes the path it took. The destination device then responds using the shortest path.

As with Ethernet switches, Token Ring switches are able to implement VLANs. This is done in exactly the same way as on Ethernet. All ports that are part of the same VLAN are bridged. Meanwhile, distinct VLANs do not communicate directly, but must instead communicate through a router.

Each port on a Token Ring switch is a distinct ring, regardless of VLAN membership. This situation is analogous to Ethernet, where each port is a distinct collision domain, regardless of VLAN membership. Two ports that are members of the same VLAN have a bridge connecting them, while ports from distinct VLANs do not. As in Ethernet, when individual end devices are connected to a switch directly, it is possible to use a full-duplex version of the protocol allowing simultaneous sending and receiving of packets. This full-duplex version of Token Ring requires that the end device have Direct Token Ring (DTR) capabilities. DTR is not part of the 802.5 standard, but is nonetheless a widely implemented feature.

Gigabit and 10 Gigabit Ethernet

At Layer 2, Gigabit Ethernet looks exactly like 10Mbps and 100Mbps Ethernet. They all apply the same 802.3 standards for framing and addressing. This similarity is convenient because it means that interconnecting Ethernet segments of these different types is simple. At Layer 1, however, the electrical signaling standards for Gigabit Ethernet are completely different.

The first set of Gigabit IEEE standards was specifically geared toward a fiber optic implementation. Naturally, the first Gigabit devices on the market all used fiber optic connectors. However, shortly thereafter, an addendum was released that included specifications for running Gigabit Ethernet over Category 5 unshielded twisted pair (UTP) cabling. Gigabit Ethernet over Category 5 cabling is called 1000BaseT. It allows for distances of up to 100 meters, similar to the 100BaseT and 10BaseT standards. This is convenient because it means that Gigabit Ethernet should, in principle, be able to operate over the same cable plant as an existing Fast Ethernet implementation.

However, there is one important caveat to this Category 5 implementation of Gigabit Ethernet, as I discuss later in this chapter. The original specifications for Category 5 cable plants did not specify signal reflection properties of connectors, which turn out to be important in Gigabit. Thus, older Category 5 cabling may not work properly with Gigabit Ethernet.

The physical layer differences between even fiber optic implementations of Fast Ethernet and Gigabit Ethernet go well beyond merely changing the clock rate. The most important issue is the use of 8B10B encoding. At its lowest level, Gigabit Ethernet uses a 10-bit byte; at these extremely high speeds, it can be difficult to accurately distinguish between bits. Thus, 10-bit patterns have been selected to represent the 8-bit octets. The specific 10-bit patterns are chosen for their transmission reliability. There is 25% of extra overhead in encoding this way, but the improvement in reliability compensates for this additional overhead.

To make implementation details easier, the Gigabit Ethernet group has defined a natural transition point in their protocol stack called the Gigabit Media Independent Interface (GMII). This sublayer is similar in concept to the Fast Ethernet MII and the standard Ethernet AUI interface. Each case specifies a point that is technically in the middle of Layer 1. Everything above this point is generic to all different implementations of the protocol. This way, only the hardware and the protocols below the dividing point need to change when a new physical layer is defined.

Most Gigabit Ethernet hardware uses either a physical fiber optic or an RJ45 connector. However, it is possible to implement a Gigabit Ethernet interface on a device using a generic GMII connector. Then the network designer could simply connect the appropriate GMII transceiver.

Gigabit to the Desk

Now that Gigabit Ethernet is available over Category 5 cabling, putting Gigabit NICs into servers and workstations has become technically viable. The market is also already seeing price competition between NIC vendors, which drives down the costs of running Gigabit to the desktop.

I recommend using full-duplex switched connections for connecting end devices directly to Gigabit Ethernet networks; there would be little real advantage to running a shared half-duplex Gigabit network over running a switched full-duplex Fast Ethernet network. In any Ethernet environment with several devices sharing a collision domain, the effective throughput is typically 30 to 40% of the total capacity, so you can expect to get something on the order of 300–400Mbps total aggregate capacity out of a shared Gigabit hub. Each individual device on this hub would get some small fraction of this total on average. So, for a small network with 5 Gigabit devices sharing a hub, you would expect each device to have access to an average of 60–80Mbps. The peaks for each device are, of course, much higher than this, but it is reasonable to expect that devices being considered for Gigabit Accesses will be heavily used—at least in the near future.

One can already achieve a higher average utilization using simple switched Fast Ethernet. Because the cost of Fast Ethernet is still much lower than Gigabit Ethernet for both the NICs and network devices, it is not cost-effective to use Gigabit Ethernet this way.

Consequently, if an organization has end devices that are important enough and used heavily enough to warrant connecting to the network at Gigabit speeds, it makes sense to use full-duplex switched connections. As it turns out, the marketplace appears to have already made this decision, as Gigabit hubs are not made by any major vendor, while there are several vendors selling Gigabit switches.

In a unanimous decision, the IEEE 802.3 committee on 10 Gigabit Ethernet has decided not to bother implementing anything but a full-duplex version of the new protocol. So, although the standard is not yet complete as of the time of writing this book, we already know a few things about what it will look like. We know that there will be no such thing as a 10 Gigabit hub and that there will be no defined collision mechanism. This is a good thing. It seems that the market has already decided that the Gigabit standard is most useful in a switched full-duplex mode. Most organizations using Gigabit Ethernet use it as a trunk or backbone technology or attach only a small number of important servers at Gigabit speeds.

It is important to remember that this is similar to how Fast Ethernet started out. In the future, some organizations may have large numbers of Gigabit end user devices.

Adoption of the new high-speed protocol as a standard for end devices has been a little slow, mostly because of the time lag between the fiber and copper standards for delivering the medium. However, now that a version of Gigabit Ethernet that works over Category 5 cabling has been finalized and hardware vendors are releasing equipment based on the standard, there should be more use of the high-speed protocol.

The lack of a half-duplex version for 10 Gigabit Ethernet means that, when it is available, it will probably not be quickly extended to the desktop. It is not yet completely clear what sort of twisted pair copper cabling the 10 Gigabit standard will eventually use. Category 5 cable is certainly reaching its limitations with Gigabit Ethernet. However, the emerging Category 6 standard has not yet been fully embraced by the 10 Gigabit working groups, which are naturally focused on optical fiber implementations.

The bottom line is that it will be many years before you can expect to see 10 Gigabit Ethernet extended to the desktop. At the very least it will require new cable plants for most organizations, unless they happen to have optical fiber running to their desks.

I envision Gigabit and 10 Gigabit Ethernet as backbone and trunk technologies. Given the trunk aggregation rules discussed in Chapter 3, it is clear that if an organization makes extensive use of Fast Ethernet today, then it needs an inexpensive fast trunk technology. These new Gigabit and 10 Gigabit standards are ideally suited to this purpose.

Gigabit as a Backbone Protocol

One of the most positive features of Gigabit Ethernet trunks is their ability to use a common 802.3 framing throughout all levels of the network. This is important because the same VLAN tags and MAC addresses are shared throughout any Distribution Area. You don't want to have to rewrite or tunnel these pieces of information for three reasons.

First, each step introduces latency. Second, you sometimes want to put a protocol analyzer on a trunk to see what passes through it. If you can't readily distinguish the VLAN associated with a frame and if you can't easily identify the source and destination devices, it can be difficult to tell if you have a problem. Most modern protocol analyzers are able to read into a packet to help with this problem, but it can still be difficult to see what's going on, depending on the types of tunneling employed.

The third advantage to using the same 802.3 frame at each stage of a packet's journey through the network is that it ensures consistency in the treatment of its priority. As I mentioned previously, the Class of Service (CoS) field is associated with the VLAN tag. Knowing this allows the network to have a consistent logical identifier for the prioritization scheme to use at each hop up until the packet hits a router. At the router, of course, a higher layer identifier (such as the IP TOS or DSCP field) has to carry the information, since the packet will lose its Layer 2 information as it crosses through the router.

I consider Gigabit and 10 Gigabit Ethernet naturally suited to trunk links in large-scale LANs. Interestingly, much of the current discussion regarding these standards involves their use in larger Metropolitan Area Network (MANs) and Wide Area Networks (WANs) as well. As it is currently common to see MAN and WAN networks implemented using ATM and delivered to the customer premises as an Ethernet or Fast Ethernet port, it does seem natural to extend this delivery to Gigabit speeds as well. Certainly this extension would give efficient near-capacity access to the current highest-speed ATM link technologies. It might turn out to be a good low-cost delivery mechanism for these links. However, any more detailed discussion of WAN technologies or speculation on yet unwritten standards is beyond the scope of this book.

ATM

At one time, ATM looked like it was going to take over the entire networking world. With highly successful WAN implementations coupled with LAN Emulation (LANE), it looked like ATM would be able to provide inexpensive end-to-end solutions. However, the emergence of Gigabit and 10 Gigabit Ethernet standards appear to make this less likely. Implementing a LAN with end-to-end 802.3 framing is certainly easier than building a distinct Distribution and Core level network that merely emulates 802.3 at the edges of the Access Level.

However, for WAN carriers, particularly telephone companies that are concerned with carrying voice, data, and perhaps even video information over the same network, ATM is still the natural choice. There is no 802.3 implementation that is as efficient over long distances as ATM. The small ATM cell size makes it perfect for carrying real-time voice and video information with minimal latency.

There are two real problems with using ATM in a large LAN. The first problem is the additional overhead of the various LAN Emulation servers required for either LANE or Multiple Protocol Over ATM (MPOA) implementations. The second serious drawback is the high cost-to-bandwidth ratios. The fastest commonly available ATM modules for LAN switching are OC-12, and some vendors also make OC-48 modules. The wire speed for OC-12 is only 622Mbps, OC-48 runs at 2.48Gbps (2488Mbps), as compared to 1000Mbps for Gigabit Ethernet. The OC-12 modules are generally more expensive than Gigabit Ethernet and offer less bandwidth. Currently, only fiber optic implementations are available for either OC-12 or OC-48, which is generally more expensive than twisted pair implementations of Gigabit Ethernet.

OC-192, which has a wire speed of 10Gbps, is still a viable option for high-speed LAN backbones if speed is the primary objective. With 10 Gigabit Ethernet just around the corner, it is unlikely that the additional expense of implementing an ATM LAN backbone will be justified in the long run. Furthermore, current OC-192 products tend to be deliberately targeted toward WAN and MAN service providers, so support for LAN Emulation implementations is weak.

If you want high-speed LAN infrastructure, ATM is probably not the most cost-effective way to get it. However, because many sites still have some ATM infrastructure, and because some networks require the highest speeds available, I will spend a little bit of time discussing ATM's properties.

ATM uses a completely different design philosophy than Ethernet or Token Ring. An ATM network is composed of a number of switches interconnected by high-speed (usually fiber optic) links. The native ATM packet is called a "cell." Each cell consists of a 5-octet header and a 48-octet payload, as shown in Figure 4-4. The small size of these cells ensures that latency passing through the network is minimized. This minimization is critical for real-time communications such as voice or video. Furthermore, by making every cell exactly the same size, the work of the switches becomes much easier. All cells are switched according to the information in the cell header. Once a connection is established, the switch always knows exactly what the bit offset is to find every piece of information it needs to do this switching, thereby minimizing the amount of work it has to do.

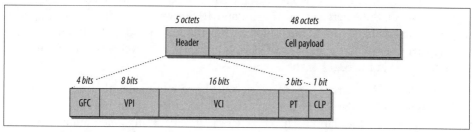

Figure 4-4. ATM cell format

The key to taking advantage of these efficiencies lies in the creation of Virtual Circuits (VCs)through the ATM network. A VC can be either a Permanent Virtual Circuit (PVC) or a temporary Switch Virtual Circuit (SVC). Once a VC is created, however, the end point switches know it by a Virtual Path Identifier (VPI) and a Virtual Channel Identifier (VCI). Each Virtual Path can theoretically contain as many as 65,536 Virtual Channels. A switch can address up to 256 different Virtual Paths.

PVCs are commonly used in WAN applications, allowing the virtual creation of high-speed long-haul links through existing ATM clouds. SVCs, on the other hand, have many different sorts of applications and are frequently seen in LANE-type situations.

Figure 4-4 shows a User-Network Interface (UNI) cell. This cell is what one would most commonly expect to see at the edges of a LAN, as it is used to connect between a switch and an end device (in this case, the end device could also be a router). There is, however, another cell format called Network-Network Interface (NNI) that is used to connect switches to one another. For private networks, there is another cell format defined for Private Network-Network Interface (PNNI) as well. However, describing switch-to-switch interactions in ATM networks is beyond the scope of this book.

ATM was designed as a fast, scalable, low-latency network protocol for transporting a variety of real-time data types. One of the most common applications is found in Telephony applications. Most modern telephone networks are now built using ATM fabric because of its efficient resource utilization and relatively low cost for high-speed long-distance links. It is also commonly used in wide-area data networks for the same reasons. However, in both cases, the network service provider frequently hides the ATM network from the customer and presents some sort of emulated service instead. For example, most modern Frame Relay WAN links are actually provided over an ATM network fabric.

Several different so-called Adaptation Layers are defined for ATM. Data communication uses ATM Adaptation Layer 5 (AAL5), which defines how the ATM cell payload is used to carry packet-type data. Similarly, AAL1 is used for emulating legacy circuit technology such as T1 or E1 circuits with Constant Bit Rate (CBR) Quality of Service characteristics. AAL2 is intended for transmitting packetized audio and video information with a variable bit rate (VBR). AAL3 and 4 are generally merged as AAL3/4, which is similar to AAL2, except that it includes no facility for keeping timing information intact across the network.

Quality of Service is built into the ATM protocol. Several standard methods for delivering packets are defined according to how much bandwidth needs to be reserved for each Virtual Channel or Path. This is called the bit rate, so you can have CBR, in which no bursting is assumed. The channel is always run as if it contains a steady stream of data. Running it this way is useful for emulating analog services. However, it is wasteful of network bandwidth if you are able to packetize your data—allowing bursts when you need them and letting the network go quiet when you don't need them. To allow these options, ATM defines VBR and UBR.

VBR has two options, real-time and non-real-time. The real-time option is generally used for applications that are particularly sensitive to latency, such as video. The non–real time option is more frequently used for data communications. UBR, on the other hand, handles all packets on a "best efforts basis."

The last category is Available Bit Rate (ABR). ABR is an adaptive system in which the end nodes are able to take advantage of extra bandwidth. When the network is short of resources, it can ask the end devices to slow down. This method of handling bandwidth resources is often used in LANE applications.

ATM LAN Services

ATM is typically used in a LAN in one of four different ways. The earliest ATM LAN applications were usually built using the standard defined in IETF RFC 1483. This standard specifies a method for bridging standard LAN protocols such as Ethernet and Token Ring over an ATM network. Usually, this type of system is used with a set of ATM PVC links. The standard needs only to define how packets from the various LAN protocols are chopped up into small ATM cells and carried through the network.

RFC 1483 is an effective way of extending a LAN bridge across a WAN, and it is also useful as a LAN backbone. If you have a LAN that has an ATM-based Core or Distribution level, then it is simple to use RFC 1483 encapsulation for your various trunk links. All you need to do is to build a set of ATM PVC links between the various Distribution switches and use these PVCs as the trunks.

Some vendors of ATM equipment have clever proprietary systems for maintaining PVCs through an ATM network. These systems allow the ATM network to contain a number of different physical paths between the two end points. When a network link or node fails, then the other ATM switches detect the failure and reroute the PVCs through another physical path. Thus, rerouting provides excellent fault tolerance capabilities.

Another common early technique for using ATM in the LAN is defined in RFC 1577 and updated in RFC 2225. This technique is called "Classical IP and ARP over ATM. " Classical IP provided an effective method for connecting end devices to an ATM network directly. But it has the serious drawback that it is specific to the IP protocol. Thus, it does not work with any other common LAN protocols such as IPX or NetBEUI. In effect, it views ATM as just another Layer 2 protocol, similar to Ethernet or Token Ring. As such, it has to use a new form of ARP, called ATMARP, to allow ATM-attached IP devices to find one another.

ATMARP is handled by the creation of a new server. Since ATM is always connection-based, and you don't necessarily want to create a lot of VCs every time you need a physical address, an ARP cache server with a well-known ATM address is included in each IP subnet area.

Because of the high cost per interface of using ATM, most installations using RFC 1577 do so only on a handful of important servers. These servers are then directly connected to ATM switches. This connection lets these servers tap directly into the LAN backbone. However, Gigabit Ethernet is currently a more natural and cost-effective way to implement this sort of high-speed server farm. Thus, Classical IP is becoming less common than it once was.

The remaining two ATM LAN systems are closely related. The first is LANE, and the second Multiple Protocol Over ATM (MPOA). MPOA contains a set of improvements and upgrades over LANE, but otherwise the two systems are functionally similar. In both cases, end devices are connected to standard LAN equipment, usually Ethernet or Token Ring. The LAN switches include ATM connections as well as LAN connections. The trunk links are made up of ATM connections between these LAN switches.

Rather than using VLANs and 802.1Q tagging, ATM LANE and MPOA use Emulated LANs (ELANs). This service allows the ATM network to bridge the standard Ethernet or Token Ring LAN traffic, creating connections as required.

The biggest difference between an Ethernet or Token Ring LAN and an ATM network is that the ATM network is connection oriented. This means that every conversation passing through an ATM network must use a virtual circuit. This virtual circuit can be either permanent (PVC) or temporary (SVC), but a connection must be built and maintained for the conversation to work. Ethernet and Token Ring, on the other hand, allow any device to communicate with any other device whenever they feel like it. All that is needed is the destination device's MAC address, and a packet can be sent to it directly.

Emulating a LAN using ATM requires sophisticated call setup procedures. The ATM network has to be able to keep track of all LAN MAC addresses and use this information to quickly create new SVCs between the appropriate switches whenever two devices want to talk. The ATM network also has to monitor these SVCs to make sure that the calls are torn down when they are no longer required.

Each device that connects directly to the ATM cloud is called LAN Emulation Client (LEC). The LEC is usually a LAN switch with an ATM interface, but it could be a native ATM device such as a server with an ATM interface. Each LEC can talk to any other LEC that is in the same ELAN.

Every ELAN must have two special servers called the a LAN Emulation Server (LES) and Broadcast and Unknown Server (BUS). As the name suggests, the BUS is responsible for handling the LAN broadcasts and for resolving unknown MAC addresses. The LES is what the LEC talks to first whenever it wants to start a conversation with another LEC. The LES then begins the process of setting up the SVC required for the conversation.

There is also a universal server called the LAN Emulation Configuration Server (LECS) that is common to all ELANs on the entire ATM network. This server keeps track of which ELAN each LEC belongs to. Every time a new LEC is activated, it has to ask the LECS for information about its ELAN and for help in finding the appropriate LES and BUS servers. As such, the LECS is a critical device to the entire network, but it actually is not used very often.

Most LANE and MPOA implementations offer clever methods for switching to redundant backup LES, BUS, and LECS servers. Usually, these servers are themselves contained in the management modules of the ATM switches. These servers are critical network devices, so it is wise to have them housed inside of network equipment. Whatever the physical configuration, they absolutely must have fully redundant backups capable of restoring all functionality quickly in the event of a failure. In one LANE installation I know of, a LECS failure required several minutes to switch over to the backup. Although the network was still operational during this period, a failure that occurred during a peak period, such as the start of the business day when calls are first being set up throughout the network, would be disastrous.

There is significant additional complexity involved in building redundancy for LES, BUS, and LECS servers. The network designer must ensure that failover from primary to backup is acceptably fast. This issue has proven to be a serious hidden problem with many ATM-based LANs, and is yet another reason for using Gigabit Ethernet instead.

FDDI

Fiber Distributed Data Interface (FDDI), like ATM, was once a good choice for LAN backbones because of higher available speeds. But, just as with ATM, it appears to have been supplanted by the advent of high-speed Ethernet technology. In general, I don't advise implementing new FDDI networks without a compelling and unique requirement. However, it is important to understand FDDI because many networks still contain FDDI elements. If a network designer wants to upgrade a LAN infrastructure that contains FDDI components, she needs to understand how it works. It is likely that legacy FDDI installations are in critical parts of the network.

FDDI is a fiber optic–based networking protocol that uses two counter-rotating rings. I discussed it briefly in the previous chapter and showed how its clever fault tolerance system works. Since the protocol allows data transmission at 100Mbps, it was once useful as a network backbone. It has also been used effectively to create server farms close to the network Core Level. However, Fast Ethernet and 100Mbps Token Ring have effectively killed FDDI, and Gigabit Ethernet has rendered it obsolete. We still sometimes see legacy FDDI equipment supporting server farms. There are also some older implementations of network disk arrays and server clusters using FDDI that are still in operation.

You can build an FDDI network in two ways. The simple method is to connect fiber patch cords directly between the various ring components. Each device connects to the next, all the way around the ring. It is also possible to use an FDDI switch and construct a star topology. In this latter case, the ring becomes naturally full-duplex and closely resembles a switched Token Ring construction. Of course, it is possible to combine the two approaches, using the central switch as a multiport FDDI bridge.

Perhaps the simplest way to execute a phased removal of an FDDI backbone is to first bridge the FDDI ring to a Gigabit Ethernet switch. Then the FDDI devices can be migrated to the Ethernet switch one at a time. This way, there is no need to readdress the devices. This is important particularly in the case of server farms because readdressing servers may require changing configurations on a potentially large number of client devices.

Wireless

Over the last few years, wireless networking has seen a huge increase in public acceptance and in use. It is still considerably more expensive, less reliable, and slower than conventional wire-based networks. However, in many cases, wireless is the most convenient method for delivering network services.

Two main standards are currently used for wireless local area communications: 802.11 and Bluetooth. In their most popular current implementations, both protocols use the 2.4 GHz ISM and 5 GHz UNII bands. (ISM stands for Industrial, Scientific, and Medical, and UNII for Unlicensed National Information Infrastructure.) These bands are reserved sets of frequencies that can be used without a license.

Despite having the same frequencies and similar throughput capabilities, these two protocols are not compatible with one another. Thus, it is important to understand the strengths and weaknesses of both.

Bluetooth (whose underlying protocol is currently being standardized by the IEEE under the 802.15 designation) was created as a wireless method for replacing serial, parallel, and USB-type cables. It also includes a LAN specification, but even this specification is based on an underlying serial cable emulation. Thus, the LAN links created with Bluetooth always use point-to-point protocol (PPP), which is a logical link protocol frequently used over modem-type links.

The 802.11 standard, on the other hand, is intended purely as a wireless LAN protocol. As such, its logical link protocol is similar to Ethernet. In fact, it uses Carrier Sense Multiple Access/Collision Avoidance (CSMA/CA), as opposed to Ethernet's CSMA/CD, avoiding collisions because the radio medium does not allow for reliable collision detection.

In general, the topology of a wireless LAN involves a number of wireless devices connecting to a central Access point device. It is also possible to build an *ad hoc* peer-to-peer network. However, this book is about large-scale LANs, so it is most concerned with how this sort of technology would be used in such a LAN.

Figure 4-5 shows how a wireless LAN might work in the context of a larger network. Every device taking part in the wireless network has its own radio receiver and transmitter built into it. It uses this radio to connect to an Access point device. The Access point is effectively a wireless hub. In fact, in many ways, it behaves exactly like an Ethernet hub.

Like a hub, the Access point provides a central connection point. Also like a hub, it allows all connecting devices to share a common pool of network bandwidth. The more devices you connect to a single Access point, the smaller the share of the bandwidth each receives. This is one of the two important considerations in deciding how many Access points will be required. The other important question is how much physical area must be covered.

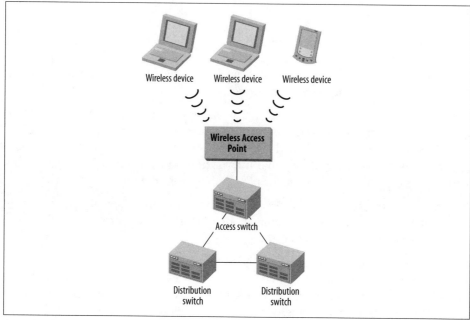

Figure 4-5. A simple wireless LAN

Before building a wireless LAN, the first question is what the wireless network will actually be used for. Will it be used to deliver standard LAN services to stationary devices, such as desks or factory assembly line stations? This might be the case because traditional LAN cabling can be awkward, expensive, or dangerous to deliver in some settings. Another place where wireless technology is useful is in highly mobile networks. For example, it might be necessary to communicate with a mobile robotic device that could be anywhere on a factory floor. Or, people might be walking around the floor of a warehouse with laptop computers for inventory checking.

The mobility of the wireless devices turns out to be extremely important. Since the greatest distance one can cover with a wireless LAN is about 100 meters, it is often necessary to have several different Access points throughout the work area and to allow devices to "roam" from one area to another. In 802.11, the area served by each Access point is called a Basic Service Set (BSS). The collection of BSS "cells" is called an Extended Service Set (ESS). These concepts are illustrated in Figure 4-6.

Roaming is a key concept in wireless communications and is mentioned in the 802.11 specification. However, the specification does not include standards for roaming protocols that allow devices to freely move from one BSS to another or from one ESS to another. The only way to accomplish this movement with current technology is by means of vendor proprietary roaming protocols and software. If roaming is a requirement, then it is important to ensure that all of the wireless communications equipment comes from the same vendor (to ensure interoperability).

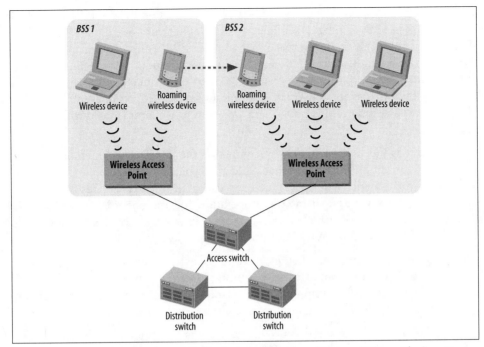

Figure 4-6. Roaming in a wireless LAN (device moves from one Access point to another)

It is possible to use either Bluetooth or 802.11 to construct a wireless LAN replacement. In general, 802.11 is the better choice for several reasons. First, Bluetooth devices generally operate at much lower power, and consequently have less range. Typical ranges quoted by manufacturers are 10 meters, compared with 100 meters for 802.11. Second, the nominal throughput with an 802.11 system is generally much better than for Bluetooth. Bluetooth LAN bandwidths are typically between 1 and 2Mbps, the same as the original 802.11 systems. However, the newer 802.11b specification allows speeds of up to 11Mbps, and 802.11a can run at over 70Mbps.

Furthermore, because Bluetooth is intended primarily as a way of replacing short cables to peripheral devices, these bandwidths are completely adequate and appropriate to this purpose. Thus, we will probably see future development of still higher-speed versions of 802.11 than for Bluetooth. However, just as with the upgrade from 100Mbps to 1000Mbps Ethernet, each new 802.11 specification will likely have physical layers that are different from previous versions. Indeed, this is already the case with the upgrade to 802.11b. As with these 802.3 examples, upgrading to the newer standard is usually relatively easy to accomplish, while switching from one standard to another (for example, Token Ring to Ethernet or, worse still, ATM to Gigabit Ethernet) can be costly and difficult.

Another new version of 802.11, called 802.11a, operates on the 5 GHz band. The 5 GHz band has a larger range of frequencies available than does the 2.4 GHz band. This fact, coupled with innovative physical coding schemes, means that 802.11a LANs will have bandwidths of at least 54Mbps. One vendor even claims to have a dual-channel mode that will operate at a theoretical maximum bandwidth of 108Mbps, although more conservative estimates say that it can deliver 72Mbps. At the time of the writing of this book there are not yet any commercial products using this technology, but they are expected shortly.

Finally, there is the issue of security in comparing the 802.11 and Bluetooth wireless systems. Because of the shorter ranges and the typical sorts of applications, Bluetooth does not actually require as much sophisticated security as does 802.11. In a true wireless LAN with larger ranges of operation and the potential for much more sensitive applications, security becomes extremely important. For this reason, 802.11 includes a specification for Wired Equivalent Privacy (WEP).

Unfortunately, a group from Berkeley recently analyzed the actual cryptographic properties of WEP and found it badly wanting.[*] In their report, they made several key recommendations for improving 802.11 security and included some network design ideas for limiting an organization's exposure.

First, a little bit of background is necessary. WEP is an optional method for implementing security in a wireless LAN. It can be turned on or off by the network administrator. When it is activated, every packet sent through the wireless medium is encrypted using an RC4 keystream. RC4 is a method of creating long, pseudorandom sequences of characters, and it is generally considered highly secure.

In 802.11, a common starting string (called the Initial Vector) is known by all end devices and by the central Access point. In fact, implementing an 802.11 network with a different Initial Vector (IV) for every device is possible, but not commonly done. The problem is that several types of attacks, which I will not describe here, can allow some or all the packets encrypted this way to be decrypted. The longer an attacker listens to the network, the better the decryption becomes.

This attack is not trivial. It requires a deliberate and concerted effort over the course of a few days to get enough information to decrypt all of the packets sent over a wireless LAN reliably. However, it is possible to do it, and it would be very difficult, if not impossible, to detect the intrusion. As network designers, we must take the possibility seriously.

---

[*] See the paper "Intercepting Mobile Communications: The Insecurity of 802.11" by Borisov, Goldberg, and Wagner, published in the proceedings of the Seventh Annual International Conference on Mobile Computing and Networking, July 16-21, 2001.

Furthermore, the attacks described in the article are not all purely passive "listening" attacks. It is also possible to circumvent Access security in WEP and connect devices to the 802.11 network. Since the LAN is wireless, people in the building across the street could potentially gain active access to your corporate network without ever leaving their office.

There are two ways to approach these security problems. You can either wait until the WEP improvements mentioned in the article have been adopted and implemented, or you can consider the wireless LAN insecure and not trustworthy from the outset. It all depends on how urgent the requirement for wireless communications is to the organization. If you can wait for the protocol improvements, it would probably be better to do so.

If it is necessary to build a wireless portion to a corporate LAN, then the most secure way of doing so with current technology is to put the actual Access point on the outside of a firewall, similar to how Internet connections are made. The article mentioned previously recommends putting the wireless Access point outside of the Internet firewall, but this solution is not ideal because it potentially exposes workstations and the wireless Access point itself to Internet-based attacks. Furthermore, it presents IP addressing problems to organizations that do not possess large ranges of registered addresses. A better solution is to implement the wireless Access point behind a separate firewall.

With the Access point secured in this way, you then need to make the individual wireless connections secure through the firewall to the interior of the network. Making such selections secure is readily accomplished using standard Virtual Private Network (VPN) technology. Since VPN cryptography has been around for several years, it has finally reached a point at which it is relatively secure against all but the most concerted brute force attacks.

Figure 4-7 shows how wireless security might work. This drawing shows two distinct firewalls, one for the public Internet and the other for general untrusted devices. Many organizations have connections to external vendors and information suppliers. The information supplied by these vendors is business critical, but legitimate security concerns about exposing the internal network to external networks still exist. Thus, these external networks are called "untrusted," although a better term might be "semitrusted." This is an appropriate location for the wireless LAN connection.

Wireless users then connect to the Access point device located behind the firewall. Once they have authenticated appropriately with the Access point, using standard 802.11 authentication systems, they establish a VPN connection through the firewall to the secure internal network. This combination of security measures gives the wireless users as much security as any standard cable-based LAN connection.

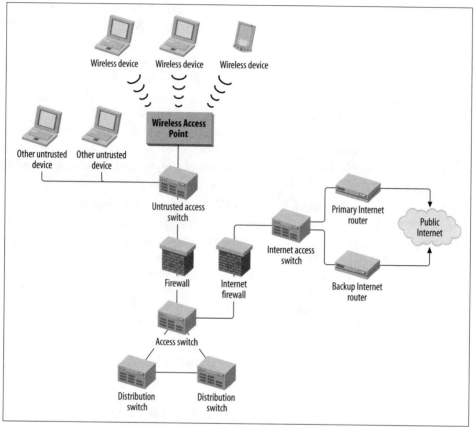

Figure 4-7. For security reasons, a wireless LAN should be connected through a firewall

Firewalls and Gateways

Each time I discuss firewalls in this book, I refer to IP examples. This is because, quite simply, there are no real firewalls for other protocols. It might be useful to have an IPX firewall that could handle IPX address translation and SAP proxy services, but I am aware of no such commercially available device. The reason for the large number of sophisticated IP firewalls is clearly connected to the growth of the Internet. The fact that every large organization needs an Internet connection has become a fact of life. This connection is simply not safe without a firewall, so there is extensive demand for IP firewalls. But the lack of public IPX or Appletalk networks, for example, has meant that there is very little demand for sophisticated firewalls for these protocols.

I have already mentioned that the difference between a bridge and a router is related to the OSI Layer where they operate. A bridge preserves Layer 2 information but can change Layer 1 properties. Put another way, a bridge terminates Layer 1 and continues a Layer 2 connection. A router preserves Layer 3 and changes Layer 2. It also terminates Layer 2 connections and allows Layer 3 to carry on. This distinction is important because there is considerable confusion in marketing literature about what firewalls and gateways are.

In a TCP/IP application, a router is one level of gateway device. More commonly, the word refers to an application gateway device that terminates the TCP session on one side and starts a new session on the other. It does not retain Layer 4 information like packet sequence numbers, but it does pass application data through, perhaps with reformatting. Therefore, an application gateway is a network device that operates above Layer 4.

This sort of gateway that runs the same protocol on both sides is sometimes also called a proxy host. One common application is a web proxy, which proxies HTTP connections. In this case, the proxy is done both for security reasons, allowing only one device to directly connect to the public Internet, and for efficiency. If the same web sites are visited repeatedly, the proxy host can cache the commonly viewed information. When a client device requests information from the web site that has recently been cached, it can receive it more quickly from the proxy server. This convenience has the added benefit of reducing traffic on the Internet access links.

However, some gateways also run different protocols on both sides. For example, it is relatively common to use gateways to access remote SNA services. If the workstations run a routable protocol, such as IP or IPX, they can connect to the SNA gateway device. This gateway then connects directly to the SNA host and converts the traffic in both directions.

A firewall is rarely so well defined. For instance, there are firewalls that are, in fact, little more than routers. They may do extensive packet filtering and they may even do network address translation (NAT) to change IP addresses. But their net effect is to change only Layer 3 information without necessarily terminating the Layer 4 session and establishing a new one on the other side. Some firewalls act as gateways, fully terminating each call and passing only application data through from one side to the other. Some firewalls also effectively operate as packet filtering bridges.

A firewall is a security device. It can only be defined in terms of the security it provides. An application gateway, however, is a network device with a specific network meaning. Because every firewall operates in a unique way, it is difficult to make general statements about them. Rather, it is best to evaluate specific security requirements and select a firewall that appropriately fills these requirements.

For large networks with serious security issues, I always recommend using a specially designed commercial firewall. I especially recommend it for firewalls protecting access to a public network such as the Internet. There are many ways to make a firewall, including commonly available software for the Linux operating system. These systems may work well enough for a small office or home network, but it is important to remember that network security is not simple. Building a highly secure firewall is not easy. Commercial firewall manufacturers frequently issue bug fixes and updates to correct recently discovered flaws and foil clever new attacks. It is unlikely that a homemade system will be kept up-to-date like this.

Similarly, it is not difficult to implement basic packet filtering on most commercial routers. This filtering may be sufficient for use with a semitrusted external network, such as that connecting to an external information vendor. But it is unlikely that this sort of safety measure will be adequate against a genuinely hostile environment like the Internet. If your network is valuable enough to protect with a firewall, it is valuable enough to protect with a proper firewall.

It is beyond the scope of this book to offer any particular guidance in selecting one commercial firewall over another. Essentially, all of them are good and offer excellent levels of security. However, they all have subtle differences that make some more useful in some environments than others. Furthermore, because several new security products come onto the market each year, it is best to simply evaluate security requirements at the time they arise and select the best currently available product.

However, remember that no firewall will make your network inherently secure and keep your data safe. At best, it will prevent interactive connections from the outside of your network to the inside. However, there are many ways to steal information and even more ways to corrupt information or to disrupt network services. Most of these methods do not involve interactive connections from an external network. I discuss security in more detail in Chapter 10.

Structured Cabling

One of the most important, yet least discussed, factors in building a successful LAN is a good cable plant. Of course, by cable I mean not only copper, but also fiber optic cabling. A good cable plant design considers several factors.

First, there is a difference between vertical and horizontal cable runs. In a simple high-rise office tower with one LAN room on each floor, the difference is relatively clear. Vertical cable runs interconnect the different floors, while horizontal cabling is used to connect users to the LAN Access equipment such as hubs or switches. In a more complicated real estate plan, the terms become a bit confusing because not all horizontal runs are parallel to the ground, and not all vertical cable runs are perpendicular to it.

By horizontal cable runs, I mean Access Level wiring. I only use this term to describe cables that connect end station equipment to Access hubs and switches. Vertical cabling, on the other hand, is never used for end stations. Rather, it is used to interconnect hubs and switches. In a hierarchical design, vertical cabling usually means cabling that connects Access Level hubs and switches to Distribution switches. Vertical cabling is also often used to connect Distribution to Core devices.

Horizontal Cabling

For the horizontal cable runs, the important considerations are:

- Type of cabling employed
- Number and type of connectors at each desk
- Number and type of connectors in each computer room rack
- Patch panel design
- Physical routing of cable

The gold standard for horizontal cabling is currently Category 5 (sometimes just called Cat5). This system was originally introduced to support 10BaseT networks, with all of the required growth capability for Fast Ethernet, which was not yet commonly available. It turns out that Category 5 is even able to support Gigabit Ethernet, so the investment in a Category 5 cable plant has been well worth the money.

One of the most fortuitous features of the Category 5 specifications for Fast and Gigabit Ethernet is that, like 10BaseT, they all specify a distance limitation of 100 meters. If the cable plant was built to respect this specification, it should theoretically be able to handle these speed upgrades.

Furthermore, Category 5 cabling can also support 4 and 16Mbps Token Ring standards with the same 100-meter distance limitation. And in all cases, the same standard RJ45 connector is used, so you can freely change your environment among any of the most popular LAN standards without needing to change your cabling. This fact is important because, although the cable itself may not be terribly expensive, the cost of rewiring an entire work area to support a new cabling standard is daunting.

However, the Category 5 standard has evolved slightly since it was introduced. To support Gigabit Ethernet, it became necessary to modify the standard, called Enhanced Category 5 or Category 5e. This enhanced standard includes limits on signal reflection properties and cross talk at junctions. While it is true that a good Category 5 cable plant supports Gigabit Ethernet, if the installation is more than a few years old, it may have trouble with Gigabit speeds. The compatibility can be tested easily by any certified cabling contractor. It is definitely a good idea to pretest any cable plant before assuming that it will support an upgrade from Fast to Gigabit Ethernet.

A new Category 6 standard is currently nearing the final stages of acceptance. Some organizations have rushed to implement the new standard in the hopes that it will provide further growth capabilities. But there have been a number of reported interoperability problems with the Category 6 cable systems, mostly caused by pushing ahead before the standard was completed. Furthermore, if these organizations implement Category 6 in the hopes that it will support similar future growth to 10 Gigabit Ethernet, they may be sorely disappointed. The 10 Gigabit Ethernet project is moving ahead quickly, but has not yet settled on any copper-based cabling standard. And it is possible that they will have to bypass Category 6 and jump directly to Category 7, which is also currently in development.

The current picture of the world of cabling standards is rather uncertain. There are no guarantees that any of today's cabling standards will support tomorrow's high-speed networking. The good news is that a good Enhanced Cat5 cable plant will readily support both 100Mbps Fast Ethernet and Gigabit Ethernet speeds.

One of the best cost-saving measures available when designing a horizontal cable plant is simply deciding how many LAN drops will be put at each user work area. In general terms, the cost of pulling one cable to a desk is the same as pulling several cables. This is because the cabling contractor simply bundles all wires together and pulls the bundle. The same amount of labor is required either way. In cabling jobs, the labor cost is commonly around 75% of the total cost. Doubling the number of LAN drops at each desk will likely increase the total cost by 25%. However, coming back to pull a new bundle of cables to every desk after the original job is done can be prohibitively expensive. It is better to slightly overestimate the number of LAN drops that will be required at each desk.

An organization that expects every user to have only one network device on his or her desk should probably consider pulling two LAN drops to each desk. This way, if several users suddenly need a second workstation or a printer, it is easily accommodated with minimal expense. Similarly, if it is known from the start that a lot of users will have two network devices on their desks, then pulling at least three LAN drops would be wise.

Some organizations, particularly investment banks with large computerized trading floors, opt to pull both fiber and copper cabling to every desk. This way, they know that they will be able to support future speed increases, even if the standards for copper cabling change. But this option is probably overkill for most office applications.

Another common cost-saving measure in horizontal cabling is combining LAN and telephone cable runs, terminating them all on the same termination block at the workstation. This measure is particularly useful if the telephone system uses the same wiring closet as the LAN does.

The same considerations apply to the cabling of server racks in the computer room. Some organizations take advantage of their raised computer room floor to do all of their server cabling in an ad hoc, as needed fashion. However, this can make trouble-shooting problems extremely difficult because there will be no reliable pattern associating particular racks with patch panels.

I generally recommend precabling every rack in the computer room in a rational pattern. Then, if additional cables are required, they can be pulled with minimal disruption. Remember that every time somebody works under the floor tiles, they risk disrupting power or network cables that are already present. For this reason, many organizations have strict rules prohibiting any such work during business hours. Thus, precabling the racks can result in significant time savings when connecting new systems.

Patch panels are critical to maintaining the required signal loss and reflection characteristics of LAN cabling systems. Generally, the horizontal runs that terminate under user desks are collected on patch panels in a wiring closet near the work area. The total distance limit on any twisted pair copper cable run should be kept below 100 meters because this length is the upper limit to most 802.3 and 802.5 specifications. This length restricts the service area of any given wiring closet.

The most common method for terminating the horizontal cable runs in the wiring closet is to use a patch panel of RJ45 connectors. This panel is called the *station field*, as shown in Figure 4-8. It was once common to also have a similar second patch panel called the *equipment field* that connected to LAN Access hubs or switches. However, with the advent of higher speed LAN technology, simply using the RJ45 connectors on the front of the Access equipment as the equipment field is usually preferable. You generally do not want to introduce an additional connection point, as it can result in too much signal loss and reflection.

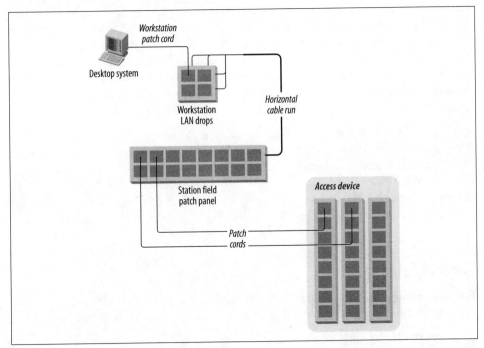

Figure 4-8. Typical horizontal cabling construction

Also, to reduce signal loss and reflection, it is generally preferable to run directly from the back of the station field patch panel to the user's desk, with no intermediate terminations or patch panels. Again, in earlier implementations, using an intermediate BIX style (that is, punch-down connectors with individual wires rather than RJ45 connector jacks) panel was relatively common, since this style gave the cabling contractor extra flexibility in running the cabling.

The patch cords, both at the user's desk and connecting from the station field to the Access equipment, must be compatible with the cabling specification used for the horizontal runs and the patch panels. This compatibility becomes particularly important in Gigabit applications where signal reflections and cross talk between wire pairs can destroy the signal. In fact, existing cable plant problems are almost invariably in the patches and terminations.

One last important thing to consider when designing a cable plant is the physical routing of the cables. For horizontal cabling, this routing generally means avoiding sources of electrical noise. Fluorescent lights are some of the worst noise sources in an office building, and they are often difficult to fully avoid. However, the noise radiated from any such source decreases rapidly with distance, so an extra few feet can make a huge difference.

Usually, it is better to pull horizontal LAN cabling through the floor or walls rather than the ceiling. In an open-concept office, using walls may be impossible, however. The relatively common practice of running cables through the ceiling and down into each user cubicle by means of a hollow pole is unattractive and tends to age poorly; over time the floor layout will inevitably change. If the LAN drops come up out of a panel in the floor, it is often easy to move cubicle walls by several feet in any direction. However, with the hollow pole systems, the pole generally has to line up perfectly with the cubicle wall. Even shifting the wall by a few inches can result in a mess of bizarre angles.

Some buildings were never designed for cabling through the floor. Some building designs use thick floors of solid concrete. The only way to run cable through the floor is actually to drill through to the false ceiling of the floor below and run the cables through those holes. Drilling holes through cement (called "coring") can be extremely expensive. In these cases, it may be necessary to run the horizontal cables through the ceiling and down hollow poles, but I recommend this option as a last resort.

Vertical Cabling

For vertical cabling the considerations are similar, except that you should never connect end stations directly to vertical cable runs. The important considerations are:

- Type of cabling employed
- Patch panel design
- Physical routing of cable

The distances involved in vertical runs are often larger than the distances used in horizontal runs. This is particularly true when talking about "vertical" runs between buildings. Consequently, for vertical cabling you generally want to use fiber optic cabling instead of copper, although there are still times where copper cabling is required between floors. Vertical copper cabling, often called "house pairs," is usually run in large bundles with 25 pairs of wires twisted together, which retain the Category 5 specifications. These cable bundles are normally terminated either on an Amphenol connector or on a BIX-style punch-down block. They can be used either for standard LAN protocols over shorter distances or for legacy serial standards such as X.25 or SDLC connections.

There are two main types of fiber optic cable—single mode and multimode. Multimode fiber is less expensive, and devices that use it have lower optical power requirements, making them less expensive. However, this lower power generally means that multimode fiber is useful only for shorter distances. Most vertical cable runs use multimode fiber optic cabling. For longer distance requirements the power of the injected signal has to increase, which usually requires single mode fiber cable.

The rule has historically been that multimode fiber is used for LANs and any short distance requirements while single mode is used by WAN and MAN service providers. This rule may need to be altered because of multimode distance restrictions on Gigabit Ethernet.

The current Gigabit Ethernet specification restricts multimode fiber cable runs to 500 meters. This length is enough to reach from the top to the bottom of the world's tallest office buildings, but it is not sufficient to cross even a modest-sized campus. Thus, some organizations will probably need to pull new single-mode fiber runs between buildings to allow them to take full advantage of Gigabit Ethernet trunks.

Fiber patch panels are similar in concept to patch panels for twisted pair cabling. Usually, a bundle of fibers is run from any given LAN wiring closet to a central Distribution LAN room. Multimode fiber comes in a variety of different bundles. The smallest bundles generally include only a single pair of fibers. As with horizontal LAN cabling, the main expense in pulling a bundle of fiber optic cable is in the labor, not the cable. Thus, it is usually wise to pull a larger bundle of fibers, even if there is no immediate requirement for more than one pair. Remember that fiber is almost always used in pairs, so it is easy to use up all available strands quickly when new requirements emerge.

The usual method for running vertical fiber cabling is to designate a few Distribution LAN rooms where the Distribution Level switches will be housed. Then all Access devices that use this Distribution Area will be housed in local wiring closets. You need to run at least one bundle of fibers from each local wiring close to the Distribution LAN room. Then you can simply use fiber patch cords to connect the Access equipment to the patch panel on one end and the Distribution equipment to the patch panel on the other end.

Fiber optic cabling is not susceptible to electrical interference. It is, however, far more susceptible to cutting and breaking than copper wire. You can use two common methods to help protect against these problems.

First, though the fiber bundles themselves are held together in a protective sheath, this sheath is not sufficient to protect the delicate fiber from damage. The bundles are usually passed through long metal conduits, which helps protect them against damage from accidental bumping or crushing.

Second, and most important to a stable LAN design, running two sets of fiber bundles through different conduits is a good idea. It is even better if these conduits follow completely different physical paths. For example, in many cases, vertical cabling runs through the elevator shafts of a building. The preference here would be to run two bundles through separate conduits located in different elevator shafts. This way, even if a fire or other similar disaster in the building destroys one physical path, it doesn't destroy your only way of connecting to a remote area.

In this case, you would also carefully construct your trunks so that you always run redundant pairs of trunks, one from each conduit. Then if you have a physical problem that damages one fiber bundle, Spanning Tree or some other mechanism will activate the backup trunk and there will be no service outage.

Another good reason to use physically separate fiber conduits is that fiber cable itself is susceptible to low levels of background radiation. If one conduit happens to pass through an area that has unusually high radiation (a radiology office, or perhaps some impurity in the concrete), then over time the fiber could become cloudy and start showing transmission errors. In this case, the other conduit will probably not have the same problem. Thus, you can simply switch over to the backup link.

CHAPTER 5

IP

The most common Layer 3, or network layer, protocols in use on LANs are Internet Protocol (IP), IPX, and AppleTalk. IP, sometimes called TCP/IP, is an open standard protocol that is defined and developed by an organization called the Internet Engineering Task Force (IETF). The standards that define IP are distributed in the form of Request for Comment (RFC) documents that are freely available from many sites on the Internet. IP, IPX, and AppleTalk are all routable protocols and thus effective for large-scale networking.

Nonroutable protocols such as NetBEUI, SNA, and the older LAT protocol pose serious scalability problems to a LAN because they require that all segments sharing resources be bridged together. Breaking up broadcast domains (network regions interconnected by repeaters or bridges) by using routable protocols leads to much more efficient networks.

There are other routable protocols in use on LANs, such as the Banyan Vines VIP protocol. Banyan Worldwide officially changed its name to ePresence Solutions in 2000 and dropped support for all Banyan products in 2001 to become a service-centered, rather than a product-centered, company. Thus, this protocol is effectively obsolete and should be avoided in any LAN architecture.

Sometimes you'll encounter a handful of other routable protocols, such as DECNET and OSI. DECNET was used primarily by equipment made by Digital Equipment Corporation. When that company broke up, most organizations that had used DEC-NET began to migrate away from it. It can still be found in some networks, however. OSI, on the other hand, is a general purpose routable protocol that was once championed as the next great thing in networking. But it never quite managed to secure a foothold in the networking marketplace.

Over the last several years, IP has been replacing these other protocols as the favorite option of many network designers. This growth of IP has been fueled by a number of factors, particularly the public Internet, which uses IP exclusively. Accompanying this growth has been a steady development of new features for IP. Features such as DHCP, VRRP/HSRP, multicast, and Quality of Service capabilities have effectively eliminated the technological advantages of some of these other protocols. Today, the only reason to consider other protocols is for compatibility with legacy applications.

I discuss IPX design issues in Chapter 7. IPX has some particularly interesting properties that affect how it is used in a LAN, and I still frequently encounter it in large LANs. AppleTalk, on the other hand, is a topic that would require an entire book of its own to do it justice. Its breadth puts it beyond the scope of this book.

IP is the protocol that the Internet uses, appropriately enough. Most comments I make in this section are specific to IPv4. A newer version, called IPv6 (or sometimes IPNG for "next generation"), is not yet in wide use. It seems likely that one day IPv6 will supplant the current IPv4 as the dominant version. I discuss IPv6 in more detail in Chapter 10.

IP-Addressing Basics

IP network addresses consist of 4 octets (8-bit bytes). The standard notation for this address is to express each octet as a decimal number from 0 to 255, separated by dots (dotted-decimal notation), for example, 10.212.15.101. Because groups of these IP addresses identify network segments, it must be possible to express ranges of addresses in a simple summary notation. Using a *netmask* expresses these ranges. The netmask is another 4-octet number that is also often expressed as decimal numbers separated by dots. However, it is actually easiest to understand the meaning of the netmask in its binary representation.

Each 1 bit in the netmask indicates that the corresponding bit in the IP address is part of the network address. Each 0 bit in the netmask similarly identifies a host part of the address. As shown in Figure 5-1, if the address 10.212.15.101 has a mask of 255.255.255.0, then the network portion of the address is 10.212.15.0 and the host portion is just the last 101.

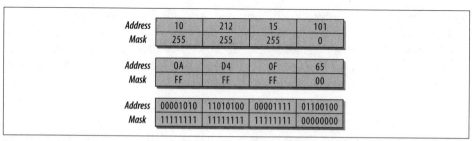

Figure 5-1. Netmask example showing addresses and masks in decimal, hexadecimal, and binary

The netmask can also create larger or smaller networks. If the mask is 255.0.0.0, then you can put a large number of hosts on a small number of networks. Similarly, a mask of 255.255.255.252 allows a very small number of hosts and potentially more networks. The smaller networks that can be created this way are called subnets. Depending on the mask, though, not all IP addresses are usable.

Consider the common example where the netmask is 255.255.255.0, and assume that the network address is 10.212.15.0. As a result, the first usable host address in this range is 10.212.15.1 and the last one is 10.212.15.254.

The general rule is that you cannot use addresses that have either all ones or all zeros in the binary expression of the host parts of their addresses because these addresses are reserved for local broadcast purposes. Consider a subnet with a mask of 255.255.255.252 whose address is 10.212.15.100. The first available address to use on this subnet is 10.212.15.101. The last one is 10.212.15.102. Thus, this network segment can only have two devices on it.

Table 5-1 shows the number of host addresses available for several commonly used netmask options.

Table 5-1. Commonly used subnet masks

Netmask	Host bits available	Number of hosts	Applications
255.255.255.255	0	1	Host mask
255.255.255.252	2	2	Point-to-point links
255.255.255.248	3	6	Small special-purpose segments
255.255.255.240	4	14	Small special-purpose segments
255.255.255.224	5	30	Medium-sized segments
255.255.255.192	6	62	Rarely used
255.255.255.128	7	126	Rarely used
255.255.255.0	8	254	General-purpose segments

Notice that the first entry in this table, the one with netmask 255.255.255.255, has a binary representation that is all ones. In effect, the entire address is a network address. Clearly, this leaves no room for host addresses, but that doesn't mean that you can't configure a host on this network; you just can't differentiate between the hosts that are within a particular network using this address. As long as only one host is in the network, there is no conflict.

How can there be a network with only one host? What will that host send its packets to in order to get to other networks? Paradoxically, this netmask can be quite useful; it is typically used as a loopback address, for example. This is a purely internal address within a host that can be used for special purposes such as management. It is also common to use a loopback address for tunnel terminations, since this loopback interface is always guaranteed to be active, even if the device itself is on a backup circuit. Loopback addresses are also often used in conjunction with dial backup applications.

The 192 and 128 masks are rarely used for subtle compatibility reasons. This has to do with the closely related concepts of multiple subnet broadcasting and address classes. These concepts are now considered optional parts of the IP Core standard. I discuss these issues later in this chapter.

At one time it was fashionable to use more complicated subnet masks. Instead of just using masks that had all ones up to a certain bit, usually in the last octet, some large networks used masks such as 255.255.255.56, for which the bit pattern in the last octet is 00111000. The idea of these masks was to provide a way to open up a smaller address range. For example, the engineer could start with a mask of 255.255.255.248 (11111000). She might initially assign a particular Ethernet segment the subnet 192. 168.1.16. Then, as that segment grows beyond the 6 available addresses, she could give it an additional block by just changing the subnet mask to 255.255.255.120 (01111000). The available range of addresses now includes 192.168.1.17-23 and 192. 168.1.144-150. The range from 17 to 23 is the addresses that have the 0 bit in the first position. The address 144-150 has a 1 in this bit position. Table 5-2 shows why this works.

Table 5-2. Subnetting "counting from the left"

First three octets	Last octet	Binary last octet	Comment
255.255.255.	120	0-1111-000	Mask
192.168.1.	16	0-0010-000	All zeros
192.168.1.	17	0-0010-001	First address available
192.168.1.	23	0-0010-111	Last address, first half
192.168.1.	144	1-0010-000	First address, last half
192.168.1.	150	1-0010-110	Last address available
192.168.1.	151	1-0010-111	All ones

This procedure of subnetting is called "counting from the left." While it is effective, it is not commonly used anymore for several reasons. First, how the range from 17–23 is connected to the range from 144–150 confuses most casual observers. This confusion will invariably make troubleshooting much more difficult than it needs to be. Second, if you really want to use this scheme, then you have to set the second range aside just in case you need it later. If you think you might need more addresses, though, why not just assign larger subnets in the first place? The third reason to avoid using this sort of scheme is that specifying a subnet mask by just counting the one-bits has become commonplace. So the mask 255.255.255.240 would be the 28-bit mask. It is common to specify the subnet 192.168.1.16 with this mask as 192.168.1.16/28. But 255.255.255.120 also has 28 bits of ones, so there is a risk of confusing these two networks.

Finally, this type of subnetting scheme clearly breaks one of network design's Core principles. It is inherently complicated and difficult to understand. Simplicity is always the best policy in network design.

Some networks may still use a counting-from-the-left subnetting scheme. This scheme is used because, once started, it would be difficult to get away from it without readdressing large numbers of end devices. However, I believe that this technique is not good, and I recommend migrating away from it if possible.

IP-Address Classes

IP defines four network classes called A, B, C, and D. Class A networks provide the largest number of addresses. Before subnetting is done, a Class A network has a mask of 255.0.0.0. Unsubnetted, it supports up to 16,777,214 host addresses. Of course, it would be extremely unusual to use a Class A address without subnetting. Similarly, Class B networks have a mask of 255.255.0.0 before subnetting. Continuing the pattern, Class C networks use 255.255.255.0 and Class D networks consist of only one address, 255.255.255.255.

Strictly speaking, Class only refers to the network mask before any subnetting is done. Sometimes people use the language loosely and call a subnet that has a mask of 255.255.255.0 a Class C subnet. That is not really what "class" means, however. There is actually a simple rule involving the first few bits of any IP address that determines what the class of a network is. If the first bit is a 0, which is to say that the first octet of the address has a value from 1 to 127, then it is a Class A address. If the first bit is 1 and the second bit is 0, then it is a Class B address. Class B addresses run from 128 to 191; Class C addresses have 1s in the first 2 bits and a 0 in the third bit, which includes everything from 192 to 223; Class D networks begin with 3 bits of 1s and a 0 in the fourth bit; a final group of Class E addresses includes everything else. Table 5-3 illustrates this.

Table 5-3. Classes of IP addresses

Class	Range of network addresses	Mask	Maximum number of host addresses per network	Number of networks
A	0.0.0.0–127.0.0.0	255.0.0.0	16,777,214	128
B	128.0.0.0–191.255.0.0	255.255.0.0	65,534	16,384
C	192.0.0.0–223.255.255.0	255.255.255.0	254	2,097,152
D	224.0.0.1–239.255.255.255	255.255.255.255	1	248,720,625
E	240.0.0.1–255.255.255.255	255.255.255.255	1	248,720,625

Note that some of these address ranges are reserved and will never be available for normal network addressing. For example, the networks 0.0.0.0 and 127.0.0.0 are reserved. The network 0.0.0.0 is used as a generic broadcast address and every host has a local loopback address of 127.0.0.1 by which it knows itself. In many routing protocols, the global default address is designated as 0.0.0.0 with a netmask of 0.0.0.0.

These entire ranges are set aside and not used for anything. The other important block of reserved addresses is the 224-239 range. Everything that starts with 224 through 239 is reserved for multicast addresses. An address starting with 255 in its first octet will probably not be assigned because of potential confusion with broadcast address conventions. Similarly, the entire range of Class E addresses is effectively unusable.

Originally, the classification scheme stopped with the last two classes taken together as Class D. The newer Class E range was developed to separate a distinct group of single-host addresses from the emerging multicast requirements.

Class is now considered an outdated concept. I have discussed it here because the word is still used. The various Internet authorities have stopped allocating IP addresses according to class, and all routing through the Internet uses Classless Inter-Domain Routing (CIDR). The currently preferred method for expressing the size of a network is to use the number of bits in the mask. For example, you would refer to the Class A address 10.0.0.0 as 10.0.0.0/8. If you grouped together the first two unregistered Class B networks, you would call the resulting range of addresses 172.16.0.0/15.

In CIDR, the IP address can be divided into host and network portions at any bit, but there are still some important addresses in this scheme. The address 0.0.0.0 is sometimes used as a source address. Any host can use it, particularly when the host doesn't know its own address (for example, during the first steps of a DHCP query). Similarly, it is possible to use an address in which the network part consists of all zeros and the host part is properly specified. Again, this address can only be used as a source address.

The address 255.255.255.255, which is all ones in binary, is used as a destination address in a local broadcast. In effect, it indicates all hosts on the local network. This address is also used frequently when a device doesn't know anything about its local network number, as in the first steps of a DHCP query.

Related to this issue is the address in which the host portion is all ones in binary and the network portion is a real subnet address. Again, this address can only be used as a destination address. In this case, the packet is intended for all hosts on a particular subnet. The CIDR specification also allows one to specify a broadcast destination address in which the main network address is a real address and the subnet address and the host portion of the address are all ones. This specification is intended as a broadcast to all hosts in all subnets. However, I have never seen this specification used in practice, and it seems less than useful, if not unwise.

As in the Class system, any address with the decimal number 127 in the first octet is reserved as a local loopback address. Even in CIDR, all Class D addresses are reserved for multicast purposes.

ARP and ICMP

Address Resolution Protocol (ARP) and Internet Control Message Protocol (ICMP) are both key low-level parts of the IP protocol that one encounters every day. ARP is how end devices on the same network segment learn the Layer 2 MAC addresses for one another. ICMP is used for a wide variety of different network control and management functions.

ARP

For a device to take part in a Layer 3 protocol such as IP, it has to be able to send and receive these packets through a Layer 2 medium. Suppose a device wants to communicate with another device on the same Ethernet segment. It knows the IP address for this destination device, but, in general, it doesn't know the Ethernet MAC address. The 802.3 protocol says that if this is going to be a point-to-point conversation, then the Ethernet frame must have valid source and destination addresses.

The conversation can't begin until these two devices discover one another's MAC addresses. And, of course, this problem isn't specific to Ethernet. The same problem exists on every Layer 2 network, whether it is Token Ring or ATM. You must have a valid Layer 2 destination address before you can send even the first packet.

This is the problem that ARP solves. For simplicity, I will restrict this discussion to Layer 2 network technology that supports broadcasting. ARP still exists for non-broadcast media such as ATM networks, but it becomes significantly more complicated in these cases.

The solution is remarkably simple. Every device on the network segment receives broadcasts. All one has to do is send out a broadcast packet called an ARP Request and look for the required destination IP address. If one of the devices receiving this packet is the owner of this IP address, it sends back an ARP Reply.

The body of the ARP Request packet contains both the sender and receiver IP and MAC addresses. Some information is, of course, duplicated in the Layer 2 frame header. Since the sender doesn't actually know the receiver's MAC address, it fills in the broadcast address FF:FF:FF:FF:FF:FF.

The ARP Reply then contains similar information. The sender and receiver fields are swapped and the missing MAC address is filled in.

When the first device receives the ARP Reply in response, it puts the information in its ARP Cache. This cache is simply a local table of IP and MAC addresses for all devices it has communicated with recently. This cache allows the first device to avoid another ARP exchange as long as the two devices are in contact. However, if a device is not heard from in a standard timeout period, it is removed from the table. This period is usually about 20 minutes, but individual devices can define it locally.

ICMP

The first kind of ICMP packet most people think of is a *ping*. The ping function is an echo request and response facility that allows one to test whether certain devices are reachable on the network. ICMP actually has a wide range of other uses, particularly for reporting network errors.

The ping function is relatively simple. One device sends an ICMP echo request packet to another. The receiving device then responds to this packet with an echo response. This response has many uses, particularly in network management. It is also frequently used by applications that want to verify that a server is available before starting a session. For network management, it provides a simple way to measure end-to-end latency in the network—by taking the time difference between sending the request and receiving the response packet.

ICMP packets also provide a way to report several important error conditions. For example, one fairly common error situation is to have a packet dropped because there is no route available to the destination.

Another important example is when an IP packet is too large to pass through a particular section of the network. Ordinarily, this is not a problem because the router simply breaks up the packet into fragments and passes it along. However, some applications set a flag in their packets to prevent them from being fragmented. In this case, the router has no choice but to drop the packet.

In each of these cases, the router that drops the packet alerts the source device of the problem by sending a special ICMP message. This message allows the application or the user to take appropriate action to fix the problem. In the case of the large packet, the router might simply try again using smaller packets, for example.

Another common and important type of ICMP message is the ICMP Redirect. The redirect is most frequently seen when two or more routers are on the same network segment as the end device. If these routers handle different sets of IP addresses, the end device could inadvertently send a packet to the wrong router. This is particularly common if one of the routers is configured as the default gateway for the end device.

When this happens, the first router simply forwards the packet over to the other router and sends an ICMP redirect message. This message tells the end device that it has delivered the packet, but that, for future reference, another router has a more direct path. The end device should then update its internal routing table to use this second router the next time it sends such a packet.

This issue is particularly important for the network designer to understand because some devices do not respond correctly to ICMP redirection. In these cases, it is often necessary to configure the routers to not send these messages and just to forward the packets. Otherwise, the segment can suffer from extra congestion due to all of the redirection messages—one for every application packet.

In general, I prefer to only have one router on any end device segment, configured as the default gateway for all end devices. As I've mentioned earlier, this router can be made redundant by adding a second router and using HSRP or VRRP. As far as the end devices are concerned, there is only one way off the segment. Network segments built this way should never see any ICMP Redirect messages.

Network Address Translation

One common feature of many firewalls is Network Address Translation (NAT). Many routers now offer NAT as an optional service. NAT can function in several different ways, but they all involve rewriting the source address in IP packets. NAT is also sometimes called address masquerading.

Figure 5-2 shows a typical NAT implementation. The protected internal network is on the inside of the firewall, to the left. The external network is to the right. Perhaps the most important feature here is that the IP addressing of the internal network is completely unregistered.

I will discuss IP addressing schemes shortly, but one common scheme involves using an open range of addresses that cannot be owned by any organization. These addresses are, in effect, public domain. Because of this, they can never be presented to a public network. Since any organization is allowed to use the IP address range 10.x.x.x, for example, then it is impossible for the public network to know which of the millions of sites using this range is the right one.

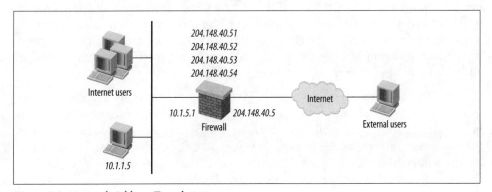

Figure 5-2. Network Address Translation

Figure 5-2 has the interior of the network using 10.x.x.x for its address range. This means that the firewall must rewrite every packet that passes through it so that the 10.x.x.x addresses on the inside are changed to legitimate addresses on the outside. A workstation on the inside of the firewall uses the IP address 10.1.1.5. The outside of the firewall has the legitimate registered address 204.148.40.5. For the example, assume that this organization has registered the entire range 204.148.40.x.

Every packet passing through the firewall from 10.1.1.5 must have its source address rewritten to something in the range 204.148.40.x. There are three common ways to do this. You can make every internal device appear with the same address as the outside of the firewall, 204.148.40.5. The second option is to create a range of legitimate addresses, such as 204.148.40.51, 52, 53, and 54. These addresses are then uniquely and permanently assigned to specific internal devices, so 10.1.1.5 will always appear on the outside of the firewall, 204.148.40.51, 10.1.1.6 will always appear as 204.148.40.52, and so forth.

The last commonly available option is to assign a pool of address such as 204.148.40.51-54, as in the previous example. This time, the addresses will be dynamically associated with internal devices. When one device wants to make a connection to the Internet, it gets whatever address is the next one available in the list. The next internal device gets the second address from the list, and so forth. This technique makes better use of the address resources than the previous example because an idle device returns its external address to the pool.

The most common method, however, is the first one, in which every internal device has the same IP address on the outside of the firewall. This situation makes the entire network look to the outside world as if it is a single, very busy device. Internally, the firewall must do a very difficult task, however. It must keep track of which of the many sessions are associated with which internal devices.

This method is considerably easier to use with TCP than with UDP-type services because the firewall can keep track of the different TCP sessions. With UDP, the firewall has to try to associate incoming packets with previous outgoing UDP packets. If a particular internal device sends out a UDP packet on a particular port number, then the firewall simply waits a short time for a response from that same external IP address and directs it to the originating internal device.

The problem becomes even harder for ICMP packets such as ping, though. The firewall has only the IP address of the external device to connect to the originating internal device. If several people all try to ping the same external device at the same time, it can be very difficult for the firewall to figure out which response packets to direct to which internal devices. To the outside world, all packets look like they came from the firewall itself; they all have the same source IP address.

Not only must the firewall rewrite the source address of every outgoing packet, but it must also rewrite the destination address of all incoming packets. If it doesn't know how to rewrite the address, then most firewalls take the safe approach—they assume that the incoming packet is unsolicited and drop it.

NAT can cause serious confusion in some places. Specifically, some applications include the IP address information somewhere inside the packet's data segment. One common example of this is SNMP. If one attempts to manage a network through a firewall, NAT can become extremely confusing.

The worst case comes when a network management service vendor tries to manage the networks of several different clients who all use the same IP address ranges. The vendor may try to use NAT to rewrite the addresses of the monitored client machines, but data contained inside the SNMP packets indicate the real source address, and the conflicting address ranges have to be removed by other means.

A worse example is seen in the applications of certain information service providers. Some of these applications work by means of TCP connections from the client workstation to the vendor's server. The TCP connection starts with a packet from the client workstation that passes through the firewall. As I discussed earlier, the packet's header contains four key pieces of information: the source and destination IP addresses and the source and destination TCP port numbers. The firewall rewrites the source address and often also rewrites the source TCP port. The server then responds with a packet addressed back to the modified source address (which is delivered to the firewall) and the modified source port. This information is rewritten by the firewall to the original values and directed back to the client workstation.

If the source IP address and port number are also contained within the data part of the packet, perhaps for some sort of authentication system, then the server has considerable room to be confused. It cannot communicate directly with the real source IP address indicated. The real source TCP port number is also of no use to it.

Unfortunately, there is no universal solution to this problem. Some firewalls are able to work around parts of the problem—for example, by maintaining the source TCP port number. But in the worst examples, the only way around the problem is to simply eliminate the firewall, eliminate NAT, and use a standard router with extensive packet filtering to implement the required security precautions.

Multiple Subnet Broadcast

On any individual subnet, you can issue a broadcast to every other device on the subnet by doing two things. First, on the data link layer (Layer 2), you set the MAC address to the appropriate broadcast address for that medium. For Ethernet and Token Ring, the broadcast address is FF-FF-FF-FF-FF-FF—that is, all bits are set to one. Note that this address is consistent with what I mentioned earlier when talking about multicast addresses on Ethernet. Any time the lowest order bit of the destination MAC address is set to one, the packet is either a multicast or broadcast. Then, on the IP layer, you just set the destination address of the packet to be the subnet address followed by all ones or all zeros for the host portion of the address.

In fact, the standard prefers using all ones for the broadcast addresses, but both are used in practice. If the subnet uses a mask of 255.255.255.0, as in 10.1.2.0, then the broadcast address for this subnet would be 10.1.2.255 (all ones, the preferred version) or 10.1.2.0 (all zeros). Similarly, if the mask were 255.255.255.240 for the subnet address 10.1.2.32, then the all-ones broadcast address would be 10.1.2.47. The addresses in this subnet that are available for hosts range from 10.1.2.33 to 10.1.2.46.

The IP standard defines another type of broadcast called the all-subnets broadcast, which is seldom used in practice. It is considered optional, but on most equipment it must be explicitly disabled if it is not required. The all-subnets broadcast is exactly what it sounds like. It allows a broadcast to be sent simultaneously to every subnet in a network. The address for the all-subnets broadcast is simply the broadcast address for the entire network address. The previous example had a subnet of 10.1.2.32 with a mask of 255.255.255.240. But this is a subnet of the Class A network 10.0.0.0. Thus, you can send an all-subnets broadcast by addressing a packet to 10.255.255.255.

If you were dealing with a subnetted Class C network such as 192.168.1.0, then you have a mask of 255.255.255.0 for the whole network. The subnets may have a mask of 255.255.255.224, for example. Then the subnets would be as shown in Table 5-4.

Table 5-4. Example subnets on a Class C network

Subnet	Binary representation of last octet	Comment
192.168.1.0	000-00000	All zeros in the network portion of the address
192.168.1.32	001-00000	First nonzero subnet
192.168.1.64	010-00000	
192.168.1.96	011-00000	
192.168.1.128	100-00000	
192.168.1.160	101-00000	
192.168.1.192	110-00000	
192.168.1.224	111-00000	All ones in the network portion of the address

This table should make the mechanics of subnetting clearer. Just as the all-zeros or all-ones addresses in each subnet are not used for host addresses, the all-zeros and all-ones subnet addresses are also problematic. Specifically, if you want to do any all-subnets broadcasting, you cannot use these networks. However, all-subnets broadcasting becomes ill-defined with CIDR.

If you look back at Table 5-1, it becomes clear why the subnet masks 255.255.255.192 and 255.255.255.128 are rarely used. The bit pattern for the number 192 is 11000000. If you subnet a Class C network, only the first two bits of the last octet are available for indicating subnets. If you don't use the all-zeros or all-ones subnets, you are left with only 01-000000 and 10-000000, which are 64 and 128, respectively. The situation is even worse if you want to use a mask of 255.255.255.128 on a Class C address because the bit pattern for 128 is 10000000, leaving you only one bit for selecting the subnet. This bit can be either one or zero, and that means it is always either all ones or all zeros, and therefore possibly reserved for broadcasts.

There are three important caveats to all of this. Because multiple subnet broadcasting is optional, you can still use the all-ones or all-zeros subnets if you just disable the feature on every router in the network. Since the routers are the only devices that care about propagating any packet between subnets, they are the only devices that need to be affected by this change.

The second caveat is that only subnets of Class C networks are covered here. If you subnet a Class A network, then you need ensure that you have a nonzero or nonone bit somewhere in the subnet address. However, this is a dangerous strategy. There have been a number of non-compliant IP implementations over the years, and the inability to distinguish properly between IP address classes is a bug that has appeared in some of these flawed implementations. In particular, some implementations assume that every subnet is a subnet of a Class C, regardless of the first octet in the address.

The third caveat is that you can use CIDR. As mentioned earlier, traffic passing through the Internet already assumes classless addressing. However, many organizations still use class-based addressing internally. If you enable classless routing, then the multiple subnet broadcast option also automatically disappears in most CIDR implementations because there is no longer any way to define a unique broadcast address for the entire network.* If the designer wants larger subnets, such as a 255.255.255.128, or even larger subnets, as in 255.255.254.0, it is best to explicitly disable the all-subnets broadcast feature and enable classless routing on all routers in the network.

On some types of routers, the command to disable multiple subnet broadcasting takes the approach of allowing the all-zeros subnet addresses. But it should be clear that this is another way of saying the same thing, since you can't have all-subnets broadcasting if you don't reserve the all-zeros and all-ones subnet addresses for that purpose.

---

* Note that the CIDR documents do not rule out an all-subnets broadcast. RFC 1700, when describing CIDR, states that all-subnets broadcasts still exist. However, it is not fully defined, and I am not aware of any working implementations or of any useful applications. Using multicast would probably be a better way to accomplish the same thing.

General IP Design Strategies

Until now, I have looked only at theoretical ideas about how subnetting works. Now I want to talk about how to use it in a real network. The first step, before anything else can be done, is to decide how many segments are required and how many devices these segments need to support. These estimates need only be rough ballpark estimates because a good designer always assumes that a network will grow in time. This estimate constrains what sort of IP-address range is required. Generally, the network should be built out of subnets of a larger network because you will want to take advantage of route summarization later. Simply allocating a new distinct Class C network for every user segment is not useful.

Unregistered Addresses

At one time, there was a hot debate about the use of unregistered addresses on large LANs. Many organizations developed internal policies that forbade the use of unregistered addresses on principle. Before the advent of firewalls with NAT, it would have been impossible to connect these networks to the public Internet (or even to build nonpublic shared Internets between collaborating organizations) without the IETF centrally controlling all IP address allocations.

This sort of policy had an unfortunate side effect that nearly destroyed the Internet. An IP address has only 4 octets, so there can be at most 4,294,967,295 devices. Four billion sounds like it should be enough, but remember that the first half of these addresses are allocated as Class A networks, of which only 128 are possible (and some are reserved, as mentioned above). The next quarter includes the 16,384 possible Class B addresses (and again, some of these are reserved). Thus, three quarters of the available address range is used up on just 16 thousand large companies, universities, and government agencies. The Internet has many millions of participants, though, and they all must have registered IP addresses. Clearly, it isn't a possible, practical, or responsible use of scarce resources to use registered addresses on internal corporate networks.

The alternative is using unregistered addresses, but you have to be careful with unregistered addresses. If you arbitrarily pick an address range for internal use, the chances are good that this range is already in use somewhere on the Internet. As long as you hide everything behind a firewall and use NAT to hide your unregistered address, you won't conflict openly with anything. But one day you want to exchange email with whoever actually owns this address range or even connect to their web site, it will not work.

There is an easy resolution to this problem: you just need to use addresses that you know are not in use and never will be. The IETF set aside several ranges of addresses for exactly this purpose, and they are documented in RFC 1918. The allowed ranges are shown in Table 5-5.

Table 5-5. RFC-allowed unregistered IP addresses

Class	Network	Mask	Comment
Class A	10.0.0.0	255.0.0.0	One large Class A network
Class B	172.16.0.0 through 172.31.0.0	255.255.0.0	16 Class B networks
Class C	192.168.0.0 through 192.168.255.0	255.255.255.0	255 Class C networks

Anybody is free to use these addresses for anything they like, as long as they don't connect them directly to the Internet. For a very small LAN, such as a home or small office, it makes sense to use one of the 192.168 addresses. In the author's home LAN, I use 192.168.1.0, for example, with a firewall to connect to the Internet. The Internet Service Provider (ISP) supplies a registered address for the outside interface of the firewall. For larger networks where a Class B is required, the organization is free to pick from any of the 16 indicated unregistered addresses. There is only one unregistered Class A network, so almost every large network in the world uses 10.0.0.0 for its internal addressing. This doesn't cause any problems unless these organizations need to communicate directly with one another without intervening firewalls, which sometimes happens, particularly when one organization provides some sort of network service to another, as might occur with information service providers, network-management service providers, and corporate mergers. When conflicts like this occur, the best way to get around them is to carve off separate sections of the network interconnected by firewalls performing NAT.

IP Addressing Schemes

A successful IP addressing scheme operates on two levels. It works on a global level, allowing related groups of devices to share common ranges of addresses. It also works on a local level, ensuring that addresses are available for all local devices, without wasting addresses.

The global issue assumes that you can break up the large network into connected regions. Having done so, you should summarize routing information between these regions. To make route summarization work in the final network, you need a routing protocol that is able to do this work for you. Thus, a key part of any successful IP addressing scheme is understanding the specific routing protocol or protocols to be used.

Another important global-scale issue is the network's physical geography. An organization with a branch-office WAN usually needs a large number of small subnets for each of the branch offices. It also probably has a similar large number of point-to-point circuits (perhaps Frame Relay or ATM virtual circuits) for the actual WAN connections.

However, an organization that is concentrated on a single campus, perhaps with a small number of satellite sites, needs to break up its address ranges in a completely different way. Many organizations are a hybrid of these two extremes, having a few extremely large sites and a large number of small sites. Other organizations may start off in one extreme and, through growth, mergers, and acquisitions, find themselves at the other end. I can't really recommend a single IP addressing strategy that suits every organization, but I can talk about some principles that go into building a good strategy:

- Create large, yet easily summarized, chunks
- Set standard subnet masks for common uses
- Ensure that there is enough capacity in each chunk for everything it needs to do
- Provide enough flexibility to allow integration of new networks and new technologies

Easily summarized ranges of addresses

Take these points one at a time. First, creating large, yet easily summarized, chunks is relatively straightforward. Summarization makes it easier to build the network in distinct modules. This means that routers can deal with all of the routes for a particular section of the network with a single routing table entry. This ability is useful, no matter what sort of dynamic (or static) routing protocol is used in the network.

To be summarized, you have to be able to write the chunk of addresses with a single simple netmask. For example, if you use the 10.0.0.0 unregistered Class A range, then you might make your chunks by changing the second octet. The first chunk might be 10.1.0.0 with a mask of 255.255.0.0. This chunk will usually be written 10.1.0.0/16 to indicate 16 bits of mask. Then the second chunk would be 10.2.0.0/16, and so forth. If the mask turns out to be too small for the requirements of the network, it is easy enough to work with a shorter mask. Then you might summarize in groups of four, as in 10.4.0.0/14, 10.8.0.0/14 and so forth. Here, the mask is 255.252.0.0.

Another approach to creating easily summarized chunks of addresses uses the unregistered Class B range of addresses. In this case, you might simply start with 172.16.0.0/16 for the first chunk, 172.17.0.0/16 for the second, and so forth. Remember that only 16 of these unregistered Class B ranges are available. Instead, you might make your chunks smaller, as in 172.16.0.0/18, 172.16.64.0/18, 172.16.128.0/18, and 172.16.192.0/18.

The two key issues here are figuring out how many of these chunks are required and how big they must be to accommodate the network's requirements. If the number of chunks becomes too large, then you will need to create a hierarchy of address ranges. As I will discuss in Chapter 6, these chunks are appropriate for the size of an Open Shortened Path First (OSPF) area, but if you create too many areas, you need to be able to break your network into multiple Autonomous Systems (ASes). Then you will also require route summarization between ASes. I define these terms in Chapter 6, but for now you can just think of an OSPF area as an easily summarized group of addresses and of an AS as an easily summarized group of areas.

For a quick example of how this might be done, suppose you want to use 10.0.0.0 for the network. Then you might make your OSPF areas with a mask of 255.255.0.0, so each area has the same number of addresses as one Class B network—they will be denoted 10.0.0.0/16, 10.1.0.0/16, 10.2.0.0/16, and so forth. You might decide that for performance reasons you need to restrict the number of areas within an AS to a number like 50, for example. Unfortunately, 50 is not a nice "round" binary number, but it is not far from 64, which is.

Providing a few too many potential areas may turn out to be useful later, if you have to make one AS slightly larger than the others. It is not a bad thing to have to go to 64. In this case, the ASes are summarized on a mask of 255.192.0.0. The first one will be 10.0.0.0/10, the second will be 10.64.0.0/10, and so forth.

One final note on summarizing—the chunks do not all need to be the same size. One area can have small and large subnets, as long as the area can be summarized. Similarly, one AS can have small and large areas, as long as you can still summarize every area. You can even mix differently sized AS, as long as they also can be summarized easily.

The first AS could be 10.0.0.0/10, as noted previously. The second and third could be 10.64.0.0/11 and 10.96.0.0/11. The second 10-bit mask range is broken into two 11-bit mask ranges. Breaking up the ranges this way—by subdividing some of the larger chunks with a larger mask—is the best way to look at the problem. The same idea applies to subdividing area-sized chunks that are larger than required.

Dynamic routing protocols don't require this sort of summarization, but summarizing routes will result in a more stable and easily administered network.

Sufficient capacity in each range

How big does each chunk of addresses need to be? As mentioned before, it is easier to subdivide ranges of addresses than it is to merge them. You probably want to err on the large side, if you can. The only way to answer the question is to decide what you're going to put in this range. For the time being, suppose that the address range is for an OSPF area. The same reasoning applies to sizing OSPF AS, but on a larger scale. If you use a different dynamic routing protocol, such as RIP or EIGRP, the differences are again just a matter of the appropriate scales for these protocols. Focusing on the OSPF area version of the problem, the usual rule for area size is 50 routers in an area.

I will discuss this in more detail later when I talk about OSPF. As you will also see later, there must be a Core or backbone area that all of the other areas connect to. Thus, you have to be concerned about sizing the Core area as well as the peripheral areas.

The largest hierarchical LAN designs, discussed in Chapter 3, had two routers in each VLAN Distribution Area and a central Core with a handful of routers. Even with this design, the network would probably need at least 15 VLAN Distribution Areas before needing to be broken up into OSPF areas. Conversely, OSPF area structure becomes important very quickly in even a modest-sized WAN. The sizes of your LAN and WAN OSPF areas will probably be completely different, and one certainly wouldn't expect them to have the same sort of internal structure.

This book is about building large-scale LANs, so I will carry on with a relatively simple example involving a large campus network that connects 100 departments. Each department is its own VLAN Distribution Area in your hierarchical design model, so each department has two routers and several VLANs.

A VLAN Distribution Area is far too small to be a good OSPF area. However, all routers in each OSPF area must connect to the Core area through a small number (I will assume two) of Area Border Routers (ABRs). The main constraint in the size of each OSPF area is not the rule of 50 routers per area. Rather, you will quickly run into bandwidth limitations on those ABRs if you connect too many VLAN Distribution routers to them, so you might want to set a limit of 10 VLAN Distribution Areas per OSPF area, or perhaps only 5. A detailed bandwidth requirement study would yield the most appropriate topology.

Suppose that the network will have five VLAN Distribution Areas per OSPF area. You need to look at how many VLANs live in each Distribution Area and the netmask of each VLAN. If you know you have up to 25 VLANs, each with a mask of 255.255.255.0, then you can finish the puzzle. You need about 125 Class C-sized subnets in each OSPF area, and you need this chunk to be summarized. That number is easily accommodated in a Class B-sized range. With a mask of 255.255.0.0, you could fit in 256 subnets.

Note that this example implies that a mask one bit longer could have been used to accommodate 128 subnets. However, as I mentioned earlier, it is good to err on the high side in these sorts of estimates. The difference between 125 and 128 is only a 2% margin of error, which is far too close for such back-of-the-envelope estimates.

The whole campus has 100 departments and a total of 20 departmental OSPF areas, each containing 5 departments. In addition, the network has a Core OSPF area, with a total of 21 areas. If each area has a mask of 255.255.0.0, then the whole network has to be able to accommodate 21 masks of this size. Clearly, this network won't be able to use the 172.16.0.0/16-172.31.0.0/16 set of Class B addresses. There is more than enough room in the 10.0.0.0/8 Class A network.

This example shows the general thought process that needs to be followed when finding the appropriate sizes for the area-sized chunks of addresses. It is also easily extended to AS-sized chunks of addresses. Suppose, for example, that bandwidth and stability issues force the network engineer to break up the Core of this example campus network. To make the example interesting, suppose that the engineer has to break the network into three ASes.

There are 20 OSPF areas to divide among these three, which could mean two sets of 7 and a 6. Each of these areas has its own Core area, giving two 8s and a 7. The nearest round number in binary is 8. There is no room for growth, so once again, it is good to err on the large side and use groups of 16. This means that the ASes will have a summarization mask of 255.240.0.0. The first one would be 10.0.0.0/12, the second 10.16.0.0/12, and the third 10.32.0.0/12.

Standard subnet masks for common uses

One of the most useful things network designers can do to simplify the design of an IP network is to set up rules for how to use subnets. There are actually three types of rules:

- What subnet masks to use for what functions
- How to select a subnet from the larger group of addresses for the area
- How to allocate the addresses within the subnet

The fewer different subnet masks in use in a network, the easier it is to work with the network. Many people, particularly less experienced network personnel, find the binary arithmetic for subnetting confusing.

In many networks, it is possible to get away with only three different subnet masks. For point-to-point links that can only physically support two devices, you can safely use the longest mask, 255.255.255.252. For most regular LAN segments, you can use 255.255.255.0, which is the same size as a Class C, and relatively easy to understand. Then you can allocate one other netmask for special subnets that are guaranteed to remain small, but nonetheless contain more than two devices. A good mask for this purpose is 255.255.255.240, which supports up to 14 devices.

Since there are broadcast-efficiency issues on larger LANs, it is best to try to keep the number of devices in a VLAN below a reasonable threshold. A good natural number for this purpose is the 254 host maximum allowed by the 24-bit mask, 255.255.255.0. Nonetheless, many organizations like to expand their VLAN-addressing range by using a mask of 255.255.254.0 or even 255.255.252.0. There is certainly nothing wrong with doing this. But if a network uses a mixture of VLANs with masks of 255.255.252.0 and 255.255.255.0, it is very easy to get confused in the heat of troubleshooting a difficult problem. For this reason, I tend to avoid these larger masks. I also feel that broadcast issues make Class C–sized subnets more efficient in a VLAN, but this latter issue will not be true on every network.

Many organizations also like to try to improve their address-allocation efficiency by using other in-between-sized subnet masks. For example, for smaller user LAN segments, they might opt to use a mask of 255.255.255.224. This mask undoubtedly winds up being necessary when trying to address a large network with a single Class B address. For example, if a network designer insisted on using a registered Class B range for a network, he might find that this kind of measure is needed to avoid running out of addresses. Getting into this sort of crunch using the unregistered Class A 10.0.0.0 would take either a monstrously huge network or terrible inefficiency.

Suppose you allocate an OSPF area's address range to a set of user VLANs. Suppose you have selected a standard netmask for all such subnets, but you also need to decide how to allocate these addresses from the larger range. This allocation is largely arbitrary, but it is useful to have a common standard for how to do it. The usual way to do this is to divide the area range into different groups according to netmask. For example, suppose the area range has a mask of 255.255.0.0 and that three different types of masks are in use—255.255.255.0 (24 bits), 255.255.224.0 (27 bits), and 255.255.252.0 (30 bits).

The range consists of 255 Class C–sized units. The first mask size uses one of these units for every subnet. The second one allows you to fit up to 8 subnets into each unit. You can also fit 64 of the smallest subnets into each unit. Then work out how many of each type of subnet you expect to require.

The smallest-sized subnets actually have two uses. It is useful to assign a unique internal loopback IP address to every router. Some networks use a mask of 255.255.255.255 for this purpose, but the rules hand over one entire Class C–sized group of addresses for these addresses. There never should be more than about 50 devices in any OSPF area. Since 64 30-bit subnets are in one of these groups, and since keeping the number of different masks to a minimum is a good idea, it makes sense to use a mask of 255.255.255.252 for these loopback addresses. You then need to see how many real point-to-point subnets are needed. This step requires a better idea of the network topology. The rules should be as general as possible. In effect, I am talking about the worst cases, so I can follow the rule no matter how much the future surprises me with new technology.

I might want to say that up to 50 routers will be in an OSPF area and perhaps 3 point-to-point circuits on each one. This tells me to set aside the first 4 Class C-sized groups for 30-bit subnets. Then I need to figure out how many 27-bit subnets I will require. I can fit 8 of these subnets into one Class C–sized group, so if I think that 64 of these will be enough, then perhaps I can reserve the next 8 groups. And this will leave the remaining 242 groups for 24-bit subnets.

Note that throughout these arguments I made an effort to break up the groups along bit-mask lines. I could have said that I wanted 5 groups of 30-bit subnets, but I chose 4 groups to keep the subgroups aligned in sets that the network can easily summarize with another netmask. I did this not because I have any foreseeable need to do so, but because one day I might have to break up an area into parts. If that happens, I want to make things as easy to split up as possible. At the same time, I don't want to make life more complicated if that split is not required.

You could make up a scheme where, for example, every sixteenth group contains 30-bit subnets and the next two are used for 27-bit subnets. This scheme would work, and it might make subdividing the area somewhat easier. However, subdividing an area will be hard no matter what you do, so it's more important to make everyday life easier.

Finally, the network designer needs to have standards for how she uses the addresses within a subnet. This depends not only on the subnet mask, but also on its use. Once again, if a small number of generally applicable rules can be made up, then trouble-shooting a problem at 3 A.M. will be much easier.

A common example of this sort of rule involves the default gateway for the subnet. Most network designers like to make the first address in the subnet belong to the main router to get off this subnet. For the 24-bit subnet (255.255.255.0) 10.1.2.0/24, this address would be 10.1.2.1. In a subnet that uses HSRP or VRRP, this default gateway address would be the virtual or standby address. The real router interfaces would then have the next two addresses, 10.1.2.2 and 10.2.2.3, respectively. Many designers like to reserve a block of addresses at the start of the range just for network devices.

In a 30-bit point-to-point subnet (255.255.255.252) such as 10.1.2.4/30, only two addresses are available, 10.1.2.5 and 10.1.2.6. Devising a general rule for deciding which device gets the lower number is useful. I like to use the same rule mentioned earlier and make the lower number the address of the device leading to the Core. If this address is used to connect to a remote branch, then the remote side gets 10.1.2. 6 and the head-office side will get 10.1.2.5. Sometimes this link might be a connection between two remote sites or two Core devices. In this case, which router gets the lower number becomes arbitrary. In the case of point-to-point links between a router and a host, the router gets the lower number.

Establishing specific rules for how the addresses are allocated can be useful for any VLAN. Many organizations have rules so specific that it is possible to tell from just looking at the IP address whether the device in question is a user workstation, a server, a printer, or a network device. This knowledge can greatly simplify trouble-shooting and implementation.

Flexibility for future requirements

So far, I have tried to encourage designers to leave extra space. You need extra addresses in each subnet, extra subnets in each area, and extra room for more areas in the network. Network growth is driven purely by business factors that are largely unpredictable or, at least, unknown to the network designer.

One of the most profound challenges that a network designer can face is the acquisition of another company. This situation usually involves merging two networks that, in all likelihood, share address space and use conflicting standards. Even if this doesn't happen, healthy organizations tend to grow over time, which means that their networks must have growth capacity. A good IP addressing strategy always involves carefully overestimating the requirements, just in case.

The Default Gateway Question

The default gateway on any subnet is the IP address of the router that gets you off the segment. In fact, many routers may exist on a subnet. These routers may all lead to different destinations, but the default gateway is the one that you send a packet to when you don't know which one of the other routers can handle it.

In hierarchical network architectures, it is not common to put several routers on a segment. In this sort of design, it is generally best to use two routers and HSRP or VRRP for redundancy instead. But in a general network it is possible to have multiple routers all leading to different destinations.

The end devices need to have some sort of local routing table. In its simplest form, this routing table says two things. First, it directs all packets destined for the local subnet to just use the network interface card. Second, it contains a route for the default gateway, often expressed as a route to the IP address 0.0.0.0, with a mask of 0.0.0.0. This default gateway route is traditionally handled in one of two ways. Either it points to the local router, or it simply directs everything to use its own LAN interface without specifying a next hop. This second option requires the local router to act as an ARP proxy device for the remote networks it can route to. When the end station wants to send the packet to the unknown network, it first sends out an ARP packet for the destination device. That device is not actually on the local LAN segment, so it cannot respond to this ARP, but the router that knows how to get there responds for it. In proxy ARP, the router responds to the ARP packet with its own MAC address. The end device then communicates directly with the router at Layer 2 and the packets are routed normally.

At one time, this second option was the only way to reliably give a LAN segment router redundancy. If one router for the segment died, the second one would simply take over the traffic. Both would be configured for proxy ARP and both would handle live traffic all the time under normal operating conditions.

There are two problems with this strategy. The first is that every ARP query is a broadcast. Even in a fully switched VLAN architecture, every time a device wants to communicate outside of its subnet, it must disturb every other device in the VLAN. This disturbance is unlikely to cause large traffic overhead, but it is nonetheless inefficient. Furthermore, because it must ARP for every off-segment host separately, there is a short additional latency in every call setup.

The second problem is more serious. Most end devices use a simple ARP cache system that allows only one MAC address to be mapped to each destination IP address. If one router fails, the second will not be able to take over. Rather, the end device will continue trying the first router until the ARP cache entry times out. This timeout period is typically at least 5 minutes and often as long as 20. Clearly this time is not good enough if the network actually requires a robust fault-recovery system. But a shorter time is clearly inefficient.

This proxy ARP approach does give a convenient way to build IP-level fault tolerance for a LAN segment. However, the advent of VRRP and HSRP provides a much quicker and more efficient way of achieving the same result. In a hierarchical LAN design, the best high-availability topology involves two routers running VRRP or HSRP. Every end device on the subnet then treats the virtual address shared by these two routers as the default gateway.

DNS and DHCP

Two important IP-related applications are used in most large-scale LANs. Domain Name Service (DNS) is an application that provides mapping between host names and the corresponding IP addresses. Dynamic Host Configuration Protocol (DHCP) is a facility that provides a way to dynamically configure IP devices when they connect to the network.

The DNS client lookup procedure is built into just about every operating system. This procedure allows you to connect to your favourite web site by its name rather than having to remember the IP address. When you look up an arbitrary address on the Internet, your computer sends out a query to a preconfigured DNS server IP address. This query asks the DNS server to convert (or resolve) this name into an address. Once your local computer has the information it requires, it stores it so it won't need to ask again.

The greatest advantage to using DNS this way is not that it allows a human to remember the name rather than the address, although this feature is convenient. Rather, it is important because it allows the administrator to change IP addresses with relative ease. For example, if it is necessary to take the server offline and replace it with another, the administrator can simply set DNS to map the same name to a new address.

For efficiency, the end devices that request this name-to-address conversion generally store it in a local cache. Thus, DNS provides the ability to associate a maximum age for a particular address. For example, when the DNS server responds with the IP address, it may also tell the client device that it should only remember this address for five minutes. Once this period is over, if the client connects to this device again, it needs to do another lookup.

The naming system used by DNS is hierarchical. The various segments are separated by dots. For example, there might be a web server named *www.oreilly.com*. In this case, the top-level domain is *.com*. There are several top-level domains such as *.org*, *.net*, and *.gov*, as well as country-specific codes such as *.us*, *.uk*, and *.ca*.

The next field to the left defines the organizational domain name. There can be many hosts within that organization, one of which is called "www". In fact, DNS allows the administrators of the local domain to define more layers of hierarchy.

DHCP is a protocol that makes it possible to automatically configure end devices. The most common things to include in this configuration are the device's IP address, mask, and default gateway. It is also possible to configure several other kinds of information, such as the addresses of the DNS servers, time servers, database, or application servers. Indeed, the protocol itself is highly flexible and makes it possible (in theory) to configure just about anything the end device might need.

The interesting thing about DHCP is that, in the common example of setting up an IP address, the client device doesn't have enough information to get onto the network when it starts out. It doesn't have an IP address and it doesn't know where its default gateway is. In general, it doesn't even know the IP address of the DHCP server. All this device can really do is send out an all-hosts broadcast to 255.255.255.255 looking for a DHCP server. For its source address, it has to use the generic source address 0.0.0.0, because it doesn't know anything else to use. In the default situation, the router for this network segment refuses to pass along a broadcast of this type. You either need to have a DHCP server for every segment or the router needs to cooperate.

Usually, the router is set up to automatically forward these broadcasts to a particular IP address, which will be the DHCP server. This IP address could be somewhere very far away in the network, perhaps several hops away. The router has to not only forward the client's request packet through the network to the server, but it also has to be able to receive the configuration information from the server so it can pass it along to the client. Most routers have the ability to pass this information along. On Cisco routers, doing this requires the use of the IP Helper Address feature.

CHAPTER 6

IP Dynamic Routing

The network needs to understand how to get packets through from one side to the other. This can be accomplished in several ways. In a simple network with only one or two routers, it is probably most efficient to configure this routing information into the routers manually. However, in a large or complex network, the routers need to learn and update routing information through the network automatically. This is particularly true for networks that offer multiple redundant paths for fault-tolerance purposes.

Dynamic routing protocols give the network a way of healing around link or equipment failures. This is because they can see all of the different paths through a network and pick the best one at any given moment. When one path becomes unusable, another is selected.

The routing of IP packets is always handled by means of a routing table. This table is basically just a list of destination networks and the next hop required to get to these destinations. It may also contain other supplemental information, such as an estimate of how much it costs to use that particular route, and it may contain several different options for directing traffic to some destinations.

This concept of the cost of a route is relatively open and vague. The cost could be a function of any number of variables, such as the number of hops, the net latency of the path, the minimum bandwidth along the path, as well as other less tangible factors. For example, it may be better to avoid a particular route because of a usage charge. Or in some cases the network administrators direct traffic through networks under their direct control, instead of using a possibly shorter path through a foreign network.

It is interesting how these routing tables come into being, how they are updated when the topology changes, and how they avoid problems like loops. Several commonly used methods keep routing tables up-to-date.

The earliest and more popular routing protocols typically used a Distance Vector Algorithm. Then Link State Algorithms became popular. I discuss one popular protocol, Border Gateway Protocol (BGP), that uses a completely different algorithm relying on a Path Vector system.

All of these algorithms fulfill two main functions. First, they allow the routers on the network to keep track of changes in the state of the network that require changing routing tables. Second, they provide a mechanism for eliminating routing loops.

A routing loop is exactly what it sounds like: one router forwards a packet to its next hop to be delivered to the eventual destination. But instead of sending the packet on, the second router just forwards it back to the first one, perhaps via other intermediate routers. This is clearly a serious problem for a network, and it is relatively easy to get such loops when the routers are responsible for figuring out for themselves how to send data through the network. This is why sophisticated algorithms are required to prevent them.

Before discussing the more sophisticated dynamic methods of maintaining routing tables through a network, I start with simple static routing. This discussion helps explain the problems that dynamic routing was developed to solve. Further, it is common in large networks to use a mixture of static and dynamic routing, so it is important to understand where each method is useful.

Static Routing

Conceptually, the simplest method for maintaining routing tables is to configure them into the routers manually. This method naturally relies on the accuracy of the network administrator to avoid problems such as loops. It is also up to the administrator to update the tables whenever something changes anywhere in the network.

Maintaining a large network using static routes presents several problems, however. It is cumbersome and labor intensive. It is impossible to achieve automatic fault tolerance because changing routes in response to a network failure always takes time. It also demands that the network administrator have perfect knowledge of the state of the network.

Furthermore, when building static routing tables on a network of any size, making mistakes that isolate remote parts of the network is remarkably easy. When this happens, technicians may need to visit the remote devices and manually reconfigure them from the console. Put simply, static routing is not an effective way of handling the main routing of a network. However, it still has its place, even in a network that uses a more sophisticated dynamic routing protocol to build its tables. For example, when connecting to external networks, it is often easier to configure a few static routes than to share routing information with the external network. This is particularly true when the external network is always accessed through one point. If this Access point goes down, the network doesn't have a backup path, so there is no point in updating the route to elsewhere.

In fact, it may be worse to try more sophisticated methods. Suppose there is more than one external network, such as an Internet connection and a separate secure connection to a partner organization. If that secure connection becomes unavailable, you probably don't want the packets sent out to the Internet instead. In all likelihood, this would happen if the network exchanged routing information with the partner organization.

This is because the partner network's IP-address range is not part of the internal range. When the dynamic routing information from that network disappears, the global default static route pointing out to the public Internet is used instead. Depending on the specific type of failure and the exact network configuration, the same thing could happen if you used a static route to the partner network. For the purposes of this example, let me assume that the static route was added in a way that allows it to remain in effect even if the link goes down.

You may need to use static routes in networks involving equipment that doesn't support the preferred dynamic routing protocols. In this case, though, you would only use the static routes to get through these isolated parts of the network.

Static routes definitely have their place, but they should be used sparingly. Each time you configure a static route you have to ask whether it would be better if this routing information were learned dynamically. As you will see in the following discussion, once a static route exists on one of your routers, it is relatively easy to use the dynamic routing protocol to distribute this information throughout the rest of the network.

Floating Static Routes

Another important kind of static route is a *floating static route*. This feature is not available on all vendors' routers. A floating static route is like a normal static route, but it isn't always present. That is, if a better route is available, the router will not look at this static route. But if that better route disappears, then the router will revert to the floating static route.

The way it works is simple enough in concept. The floating static route is manually configured in the router, the same as any other static route. But it has an extremely high metric to indicate a high cost associated with this path. If there is any other path available, it will be better than this one and consequently will not be used.

This feature is commonly used in dial-backup situations, for example. When the network is working properly, a remote router receives its routing table via a dynamic routing protocol. However, when there is a failure, the router stops receiving any dynamic routing information, and it flushes all of this dynamic information out of its routing table. When that happens, the floating static route suddenly starts to look good despite its high metric. The router inserts this route into its routing table, and this triggers the dial-backup process.

The key to floating static routes is that there is a magic metric value. Normally, if a router has a static route, it will use it. On Cisco routers it is conventional to use a metric of 200 or greater for floating static routes, although values as low as 150 appear to work just as well.

Types of Dynamic Routing Protocols

It is customary to describe routing protocols by both their function and the algorithms they employ. Functionally, a routing protocol can be either an Interior Gateway Protocol (IGP) or an Exterior Gateway Protocol (EGP). There are three commonly used routing algorithms. Distance Vector Algorithms are used by RIP, IGRP, and EIGRP. OSPF, on the other hand, uses a Link State Protocol Algorithm to find the best paths through the network. BGP uses a Path Vector Algorithm.

I describe the algorithms in more detail in the context of the actual protocols, but it is necessary to clarify the difference between Interior and Exterior Gateway Protocols before I go on.

Simply put, an Interior Gateway Protocol handles routing within an Autonomous System, and an Exterior Gateway Protocol deals with updating routes between Autonomous Systems. But what is an Autonomous System?

This term replaces the more vague term network. If one organization has a network, that concept is easy to understand. If that network is connected to another organization's network, how many networks are there? Really there is just one big network, since you can send packets from a device on one side to those on the other. Is the public Internet one network, a collection of millions of small networks, or a little of both?

The word network stops having much meaning when you talk about these very large scales. It is actually the administrative boundaries between these networks that matter. Interconnecting two networks allows traffic to flow between them, but this doesn't change the fact that Company A controls the first network and Company B controls the second one.

It has been necessary to introduce the phrase *Autonomous System* (AS) to describe this separation of control. To make things more confusing, once this distinction exists, you can then break up a large corporate network into many ASes.

This brings me back to the original definition of terms. IGPs operate within an AS. You can opt to break up a network into several ASes to isolate your IGPs. It is often possible to make an extremely large or complex network operate more efficiently by splitting it up.

In most cases you can create a stable LAN with only one AS and one IGP. Most IGPs (excluding RIP) can handle all but the largest local or Campus Area Networks with one AS if they are configured properly. In extremely large networks it can become necessary to split up ASes.

There are other situations that force a network designer to interconnect distinct ASes within a smaller network. In some cases, a large enterprise network might be managed by different groups, sharing only a backbone. It's also common to connect ASes of different companies because of mergers or other cooperative business requirements. I include a discussion of BGP in this chapter to deal with these sorts of situations.

The possibility of using several ASes in a network introduces the concept of an Autonomous System Boundary Router (ASBR). These are the routers that interconnect different ASes. This term is most useful to the IGPs, as the ASBR represents a portal to the next AS.

As long as I'm talking about boundaries between hierarchical levels of dynamic routing protocols, another important type of router is an Area Border Router (ABR). This concept will be discussed in depth in the "OSPF" section. OSPF has a built-in hierarchical structure in which each AS is divided up into a number of separate areas. Using areas helps to reduce the amount of routing information that each router needs to maintain. The ABR routers act as portals between these areas.

Throughout this chapter I point out the ways that the different routing protocols contribute to the hierarchical design model favored by this book.

RIP

One of the oldest dynamic routing protocols used by IP is the Routing Information Protocol (RIP). RIP uses a Distance Vector Algorithm. It should be stressed from the outset that RIP is a poor choice for a large network. I include it in this discussion for two reasons. First, it makes a good introduction for readers who might be unfamiliar with dynamic routing protocols. Second, despite its age, it is still common to encounter specialized pieces of network equipment that support RIP as their only dynamic routing protocol. Integrating these devices into a network requires a good working knowledge of RIP.

There are two common versions of RIP called, appropriately enough, RIP-1 and RIP-2. RIP-1 is the original version introduced during the early days of ARPANET (the spiritual predecessor to the modern Internet) and is documented in RFC 1058, although the protocol was a de facto standard long before this RFC was published. RIP-2 is an updated version of RIP that improves several key operational problems with the original version. The current version of the protocol is documented in RFC 2453.

Although it is often useful in isolated pockets of a network, there are several reasons to avoid using RIP on a network-wide basis. It is slow in responding to topology changes. It is only effective in small- to medium-sized networks and breaks down completely if the distance between any two parts of the network involves more than 15 hops. It can also cause serious traffic-overhead problems in a network with a large number of routes, particularly over slow links.

The original RIP implementation was actually made for UNIX hosts because it effectively predated modern routers. Thus, every BSD UNIX operating system has always been equipped with a program called routed (for routing daemon). This is not merely an interesting quirk of history; it also represents one of the most dangerous problems with running RIP: there are end devices that expect to take part in the routing protocol.

Defenders of the routed argue that it helps these end devices find the appropriate routers for their desired destinations. However, if a network is well designed, it should be possible to simply point all end devices to a single, default gateway address that lets them reach all destinations transparently. In a well-designed network there is never any need to run a dynamic routing protocol on end devices.

End devices don't need to know how the network routes their packets. Letting them take part in the dynamic routing protocol doesn't just give these devices unnecessary routing information. It also allows these end devices to affect the routing protocol, even though they aren't in a position to understand the physical topology of the network.

As a result, it is quite easy for an end device running routed to mislead the network about the best paths. In particular, if the end device is configured with a default gateway, it will attempt to tell the rest of the network about this information. Then if something goes wrong on the network—causing real routes to disappear—the routers will look to the next best option. This often turns out to be the end device that broadcasts the false default route. Since a default route is a route to anywhere, all routing in the network suddenly becomes confused.

In most cases there is a simple way to get around this problem. You can configure the routers that connect to end-device segments so that they ignore all RIP information coming from those segments. This means that you can only use specialized router-to-router segments to carry routing protocol information. These segments cannot contain any end devices.

With RIP an end device can listen passively to routing updates without taking an active role in building the routing tables. This is significantly less dangerous. However, if a network is well designed, there should be no need for any end device to see this information. It should be able to get a packet to any valid destination just by forwarding it to its default router. This default router should respond to topology changes faster and more accurately than the end device. So allowing the end device to make important routing decisions is likely less reliable.

RIP Functionality

The main idea behind RIP is that every router maintains its own routing table, which it sends to all of its neighbors periodically. The neighbors update their own tables accordingly. Every route in the table has a cost associated with it, which is usually just the number of hops to the destination.

Figure 6-1 has a small network containing four routers and eight Ethernet segments. Router A knows about the two routes directly connected to it: 10.1.5.0/24 and 10.1.12.0/24. It also knows that it has two neighboring routers, B and C.

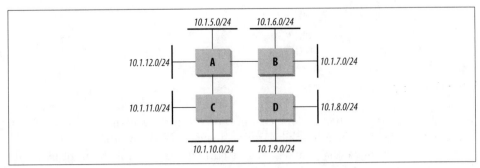

Figure 6-1. Distributing routing information with RIP

When Router B receives information about these routes from Router A, it adds these routes to its own table. For the routes that Router A indicates are directly connected, Router B has to specify some higher cost.

In RIP this cost is called a *metric*. By default, the metric just counts the number of hops. Router A uses a metric of 1 for its directly connected networks, so Router B will increment this metric and show the same entries in its routing table with a metric of 2.

At this point, Router B's routing table is shown in Table 6-1. The table lists the routes in numerical order by destination network because the routers generally display them this way. Router B now sends this same information along to Router D. At the same time, all other routers in the network similarly exchange their routing tables. Clearly, it will take a few rounds of updates before Routers C and D have one another's tables.

Table 6-1. Intermediate routing table for Router B

Destination network	Metric	Next hop
10.1.5.0/24	2	Router A
10.1.6.0/24	1	Local
10.1.7.0/24	1	Local
10.1.12.0/24	2	Router A

When the process is complete, Router A's routing table looks like Table 6-2. Note that Router A doesn't have a direct connection to Router D, which owns 10.1.8.0/24 and 10.1.9.0/24, so it has to direct traffic for these destinations to Router B.

Table 6-2. Final routing table for Router A

Destination network	Metric	Next hop
10.1.5.0/24	1	Local
10.1.6.0/24	2	Router B
10.1.7.0/24	2	Router B
10.1.8.0/24	3	Router B
10.1.9.0/24	3	Router B
10.1.10.0/24	2	Router C
10.1.11.0/24	2	Router C
10.1.12.0/24	1	Local

As long as nothing in the network changes, this routing table remains constant. If something changes, such as a link becoming unavailable, the protocol needs to make it known. To do this, every router sends its current routing table to all of its neighbors every 30 seconds. This update serves two purposes: it allows the routers to ensure that the neighbor routers are all still working, and it makes sure that everybody has the latest routing table.

Suppose the link between Routers B and D suddenly breaks. Router B finds out about this because it stops seeing updates from Router D. But Router B shouldn't react immediately. There may just be a delay or some noise in the network. Perhaps the update message was lost due to congestion caused by a random burst of traffic. There are many reasons why an individual update might not be received. So RIP waits 180 seconds before declaring the routes dead. After the route is considered dead, the protocol will wait another 120 seconds before actually removing it from the table.

This long wait time reflects, in part, the poorer network media available when the protocol was developed. It was not unusual to lose several packets in a row, so the relatively long wait time is a trade-off between wanting to respond quickly to the change in topology and wanting to prevent instability. A busy or noisy link shouldn't cause the routing tables to search continually for new paths. Doing so results in an unstable network.

When a new router is placed on the network, it needs to get a good routing table as quickly as possible. When it first comes up, the router sends out a special request message on all of its active interfaces. Any neighboring routers found on these interfaces respond immediately to this request with a full routing table, rather than waiting for the regular update cycle. The new router integrates this information into its own routing table, adding information about the new routes that are unique to this new device. Then it turns around and updates its neighbors with the resulting routing table, and the neighbors propagate the new routes throughout the network.

Instead of using the default metric just to count hops to a destination, it can be useful to specify higher values for slower links and lower values for higher bandwidth links. In this way, the network tends to prefer the fastest paths, not just the shortest.

Figure 6-2 shows an example of how this concept might work. Router R1 has connections to both R2 and R3 that can eventually lead it to the destination network, 10.1.6.0/24. The link to R2 is a standard Ethernet connection, and the link to R3 is a 56Kbps point-to-point serial link. The network should favor the faster link, so the Ethernet connection is given a metric of 3 and the serial connection a metric of 10. Similarly, suppose that the connection from router R2 to R4 is Ethernet, so this too will have a metric of 3. The connections between R2 and R3 and between R3 and R4 are Fast Ethernet, though, so these high-speed links will have a metric of 1.

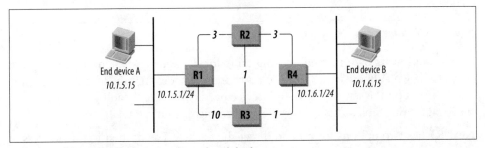

Figure 6-2. Slower links can be configured with higher metrics

There are four possible paths to get a packet from R1 to the destination network 10.1.6.0/24. It can go from R1 to R2 to R4, with a total metric of six. Or, it can go R1 to R2 to R3 to R4, for a total of five. Similarly, the packet can go R1 to R3 to R4 with a metric of 11. The final possible path is from R1 to R3 to R2 to R4, which has a metric of 14.

So the lowest metric path is the one that goes R1 to R2 to R3 to R4. Because the metric values have been adjusted, the path with the lowest metric is not necessarily the one with the lowest hop count. It is the fastest path, though, which was the point of changing the defaults.

It isn't necessary to give the same metric to all links of a particular type. In fact, you have to be very careful with RIP that you never exceed a total metric of 15 along any valid path. This requirement is too restrictive to establish set rules of different metrics for different media speeds. However this philosophical approach will be quite useful later in the section on "OSPF."

Avoiding Loops

In every dynamic routing protocol, one essential goal is to find the best way to get from A to B. This generally means that every router in the network has to figure out how to get from itself to every place else. Every router has its own routing table that says, regardless of how the packet got here, this is how to get to its ultimate destination. The problem is that, with every device making these decisions on its own, it is possible to wind up with routing loops. Figure 6-3 shows a small network that has four routers. Suppose end device A wants to send a packet to end device B.

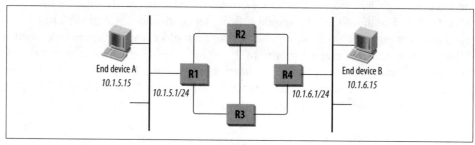

Figure 6-3. Routing loops

A first looks at its own internal routing table for B's address. The destination is not part of its own subnet, so it has to find a route to the destination subnet. Since only one router is on the segment, the end device needs only one default gateway entry in the local routing table. This entry sends everything to router R1.

Now R1 has two options for how to direct the packet. The destination IP address in the packet is 10.1.6.15, so it looks in its routing table for anything that matches this address. There are clearly two possibilities in the picture, R2 and R3. Suppose it sends the packet to R2.

Then R2 must decide how to get to the destination, and it has three possible paths from which to choose: the ones leading to R1, R3, and R4. If everything is working properly, it should see that the path through R4 is the shortest and use that. Suppose it picks one of the others, though—the one through R3, for example. This might happen if a high cost has been assigned to the link to R4, indicating that it is a slow or expensive link.

The routing tables can start to get into trouble because R3 also has three possible paths. Two of these paths, the ones to R1 and R2, send the packet back where it has already been. If R3 chooses either of these paths, it will create a loop.

Fortunately, IP includes a mechanism to break loops like this so that packets do not circulate indefinitely. Every IP packet has a Time To Live (TTL) field in its header. Originally, when network latency was very high, TTL had a real time meaning, but today it is simply a hop counter. In most IP packets the TTL field starts out with a value of 255. Each time a router receives this packet, it decrements the TTL value before forwarding it. If the value eventually reaches 0, the packet is discarded. When I talk about multicast networking in Chapter 10, I discuss another useful application of this TTL field.

You should notice a few important things about routing loops. First, they are fundamentally a Layer 3 phenomenon. It doesn't matter whether the network has multiple connections. A loop could happen if R2 forwarded the packet back to R1 so even if there are no physical loops, a network can still have routing loops.

Also realize that a routing loop happens on a per-route basis. The network might have a loop for one route, say 10.1.6.0, but have no problems with another destination, such as 10.1.5.0. This is different from a Layer 2 loop, which can take all of the traffic into the spin cycle. Every good routing protocol has several techniques for finding and eliminating loops. One of the main ways that RIP avoids loops is by *counting to infinity*.

The protocol's designers believed that RIP would not converge well in large networks. They estimated that if the distance between any two devices was more than about 15 hops, guaranteeing reliable convergence after a topology change would be difficult. So they somewhat arbitrarily defined infinity as the number 16. This may seem like a small number, but it should be as small as possible if the routers have to count to it quickly.

Look at Figure 6-4. Suppose Router R4 suddenly dies and there is no longer any router available for 10.1.6.0/24. The protocol somehow has to flush this route out of the tables of the other three routers.

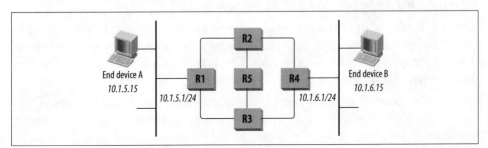

Figure 6-4. Counting to infinity

Routers R2 and R3 will both eventually time out waiting for an update and remove the route they learned from R4. However, Routers R1 and R5 both have routes to get to R4; they can send packets via either R2 or R3.

In the next updates from R1 and R5, R3 will see that they both have routes with a metric of 3 for this destination. R3 will set its own metric to 4 and try to use one of these routes. Meanwhile, R2 will see the same information and do the same thing. Both R2 and R3 will distribute this information back to R1 and R5 in the next cycle.

When R1 and R5 learn that their preferred paths for this destination have suddenly developed higher metrics, they will simply update their own tables, setting the metric to 5. The updated tables are sent back to R2 and R3, which set their metrics for this route to 6 and send it back again. It should be clear why having infinity as small as possible is a good thing. The extinct route will not be removed from the routing table until all routers agree that it is infinitely far away.

RIP has another simple but clever technique for avoiding loops. The protocol stipulates that a router can only send out information about routes that it actually uses. Even if several paths are available, the routers preselect the best one and only worry about the others if this best route becomes unavailable.

For example, look at Figure 6-4 again. Router R2 knows that it can get to the destination network 10.1.6.0/24 through R4. Even though it has heard about alternate routes from both R1 and R3, it never advertises these. Then, when the path through R4 becomes unavailable, it picks either the path through either R1 or R3 and ignores the other.

When R3 also loses its connection with R4, only one possibility remains: R1. However, R1 only advertises the path that it actually uses, which is the one through R2. Eliminating unused—and therefore unnecessary—path options allows the protocol to converge on new paths more quickly when the topology of the network changes.

The *triggered update* is another important feature of RIP helping it converge more quickly. As I described earlier, all of the routing table exchanges normally happen on a timer. However, when a router's interface physically goes down, the router knows for certain that the associated route is no longer available.

Even with static routes, when this happens the router will flush the corresponding route from its tables. When using RIP, the router follows up on this action by immediately telling its neighbors that this route has disappeared. It does this by telling the other routers that this route now has a metric of 16.

Each time a router changes its metric for a particular route, it also executes a triggered update of this information. This allows the information to propagate through the network quickly.

Meanwhile, another router might still have a connection to this network that had been considered worse because of a higher metric. This new information will propagate through the network as it is now better than the other unavailable route.

Split Horizons in RIP

The counting-to-infinity example in the previous section might have seemed slightly more complicated than necessary by including router R5 in the middle. But this was necessary because of another clever feature of RIP called *Split Horizon* that is designed to help destroy loops.

In a regular Split Horizon algorithm, routers simply refrain from passing information back to the router that originally sent it. If R1 and R2 have a link, as they do in Figure 6-4, then R1 will not bother telling R2 about the routes it heard from R2 in the first place.

In fact, RIP employs a slightly modified version of a Split Horizon algorithm called *Split Horizon with Poisoned Reverse*. To understand this, suppose again that R1 and R2 are sharing routing information. When R1 sends its routing table to R2, it includes the routes it received from R2, but it sets the metric to 16 (remember 16 = infinity in RIP). To see how this causes things to converge faster, the reader is invited to repeat the counting-to-infinity example using the network in Figure 6-3, which is the same as 6-4, but without router R5.

Variable Subnet Masks

One of the most serious drawbacks with the original RIP specification was how it handled subnets. In Version 1, RIP assumed that all of the subnets for a given network had the same mask. As I already discussed, the ability to vary subnet masks in a complex network is extremely useful. This ability is called Variable Length Subnet Mask (VLSM). It allows not only more efficient use of the address space, but also makes it much easier to summarize the routes to a particular part of the network.

Removing this restriction was a driving force behind the introduction of RIP Version 2. To accomplish this, the protocol had to be modified so that every subnet address could have its subnet mask specified with it. In the original Version 1 specification, the mask information was not included. Consequently, every subnet of any given network was assumed to have the same mask.

This issue is sufficiently serious that it eliminates RIP Version 1 as a candidate routing protocol in most modern networks. However, there are two alternative options. One is to use RIP Version 2 if the equipment supports it. The other, equally viable option, is simply to restrict the use of RIP to small portions of the network where the condition of equal subnet masks can be satisfied.

RIP Version 2 also has the advantage of using multicast rather than broadcast to send its updates. The advantages of multicast are discussed in depth in Chapter 10. In this case it makes it safer to have end devices on the same network segment as routers that communicate via RIP. Because they are broadcast, RIP Version 1 packets must be examined by every device on the network segment. If there are many routers on the network segment, this can cause CPU loading problems on the end devices, even those devices that don't know or care anything about RIP.

In fact, the only reason that RIP Version 1 is ever used in a modern network is for compatibility reasons with legacy equipment. In most of these cases, the RIP routing information is isolated to local communication between the legacy equipment and a modern router. This modern router then redistributes the RIP routes into a more appropriate routing protocol. To allow full two-way communication, this router must also summarize the rest of the network into RIP for the legacy equipment to use.

Redistributing with Other Routing Protocols

Another key difference between RIP Versions 1 and 2 is the inclusion of *Route Tags*. A Route Tag is a two-octet field used to indicate routes that come from outside of the RIP AS. These could come from another IGP or an EGP, or they could even specify routes that are statically configured on a router.

RIP does not use the Route Tag information directly while routing packets, but it is included because it is often useful to know from where different routes came. In other routing protocols Route Tags often ensure that traffic remains inside the AS wherever possible. So, any tagged route will have a higher cost than the worst interior route to the same destination.

This is not practical in RIP, however, because of the small range of allowed metrics. Since any route with a metric of 16 is considered unreachable, it is not possible to use this for exterior routes. The low value of infinity in RIP makes it extremely difficult to balance metrics so as to prefer certain paths to others.

So the Route Tag field is included primarily for information and to allow RIP to pass this information to other routing protocols (in particular, BGP) that can use it.

IGRP and EIGRP

In response to the scaling problems of RIP, Cisco developed a proprietary IGP of its own called Interior Gateway Routing Protocol (IGRP). This protocol was later updated and improved, with the result called Enhanced IGRP (EIGRP). Because these protocols are proprietary, they are only implemented on Cisco equipment. As always in this book, I recommend that readers avoid proprietary protocols for compatibility reasons. However, I include this discussion on IGRP and EIGRP because they are remarkably efficient and easy to implement. Furthermore, Cisco has produced not only IP, but also IPX and AppleTalk versions of EIGRP, making multiprotocol networks easier to administer.

IGRP and EIGRP are distance-vector algorithms just like RIP. But they are able to operate on much larger networks while consuming much less bandwidth. There are a number of differences between the original IGRP and the more recent EIGRP. One of the most important is that, like RIP Version 1, IGRP cannot handle Variable-Length Subnet Masks (VLSM). The other main difference is the use of a new algorithm called Diffusing Update Algorithm (DUAL)in EIGRP, which provides better convergence properties.

The enhancements in EIGRP make it a much more useful protocol. I recommend avoiding IGRP in favor of EIGRP wherever possible. In fact, the only place where IGRP is likely to be used is in older networks originally built before the advent of EIGRP. In most cases it is relatively easy to complete an upgrade from IGRP to EIGRP simply by configuring the protocols to redistribute routing information into one another. Then it should be possible simply to move the IGRP/EIGRP dividing line through the network one router at a time. Note that this might require the temporary use of additional static routes because IGRP does not cope well with splitting up networks in ways that cannot be easily summarized. The remainder of this section focuses on EIGRP.

Basic Functionality

An important difference between EIGRP and RIP is how they handle routing updates. While RIP sends out the entire routing table periodically, EIGRP only sends incremental updates. So, if a router has no updates to send, it sends only a tiny HELLO packet to each of its neighbors. This allows EIGRP to consume much less bandwidth than RIP.

The first thing an EIGRP router does when it comes up on the network is send out HELLO packets to establish the neighbor relationships with all of the routers on directly connected networks. As soon as it discovers a new neighbor, the router sends it a query requesting that it send its routing table.

EIGRP is uses a Distance Vector routing algorithm, like RIP. However, unlike RIP, the distances are calculated based on the speed and latency of each path. The latency is found by adding up the round-trip delays of every link in the path. The speed comes from the bandwidth of slowest link. The actual formula used by EIGRP[*] is:

$$metric = 256(\Sigma(delays)/10 + 10^7/(minimum\ bandwidth))$$

The delays in this equation are measured in microseconds; the bandwidth in kilobits per second.

Figure 6-5 shows a simple example of how these metrics work. Router R1 connects to Router R2 via a 10Mbps Ethernet connection. The delay on this link (including the latencies of the routers themselves) is 2000 microseconds (2 milliseconds). Router R2 connects to Router R3 over a 4Mbps Token Ring with a delay of 3500 microseconds (3.5 ms).

---

[*] In fact, this is the simplified version of the formula that results from using the default k values. There are five variables, k1 to k5, that control the relative weightings of the delay and bandwidth. They also introduce using the reliability and load of the link to control the metric further. However, I advise using the default k parameters to avoid confusion and instability that can result from accidentally choosing poor combinations of values. As always in networking, simplicity is a virtue.

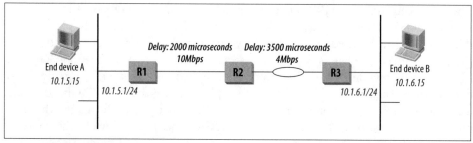

Figure 6-5. Metrics in EIGRP

In calculating the metric to the network 10.1.6.0/24, Router R1 must first figure out what the lowest bandwidth is. It gets this information from its neighbor, R2. R2 has already found out that the minimum bandwidth is associated with the 4Mbps Token Ring that it uses to connect to R3. So R1 compares this to its own link and uses the lower one. In this way, each router along a multihop path needs only to include one minimum bandwidth for each route. At each successive hop, the next router compares the reported minimum bandwidth with that of its own link and takes the slower one.

For each successive hop, the routers must also keep track of the total delay so far. Each router adds the delay for its own leg to the running total. This greatly simplifies the calculations that each router needs to perform. In this example:

$$metric = 256((2000 + 3500)/10 + 10^7/4000) = 780800$$

This metric is a large number. In RIP the maximum metric is 15. In EIGRP the maximum is $2^{32} = 4,294,967,296$. Clearly, this means that EIGRP can't use the same counting-to-infinity algorithm to get out of loops the way RIP does.

Instead, EIGRP relies on its Split Horizon implementation and on its neighbor relationships to avoid loops. Recall from the RIP discussion that Split Horizon means that the router doesn't advertise itself as a route to any device that it considers closer to the destination. In particular, if a router is using a particular next hop router to get to some destination network, then it never tells the next hop router that it knows how to get to that destination.

RIP used a modified version of Split Horizon in which it does advertise the path to the destination network, but it does so with a metric of infinity so that it is never used. This is called Split Horizon with Poisoned Reverse. EIGRP uses a similar rule for exactly the same reasons.

EIGRP only works with incremental updates rather than distributing the entire routing table. So when a router detects a topology change, it alerts its neighbors to flush this route from their tables. They can then determine a new optimal path. There is no need to count to infinity incrementally before removing the route. The DUAL algorithm eliminates routing loops.

Unlike OSPF, EIGRP does not support the use of areas. The entire AS acts as a single unit. However, EIGRP can use its autosummarization feature to achieve many of the same benefits as OSPF does using areas. In fact, the existence of areas in OSPF forces all route summarization to be done at the Area Border Routers. In EIGRP, however, route summarization can be done at multiple levels.

EIGRP is said to be a Classless routing protocol because it can summarize at any bit in the network address, without being concerned about the class of the address range. Thus, a carefully designed hierarchical network can have a very efficient routing table. Figure 6-6 shows an example of how this might work. This is a hierarchical network design with a large number of Distribution Areas. When allocating the IP addresses downstream from the Distribution Routers, one has to be careful to ensure that the routes can be summarized.

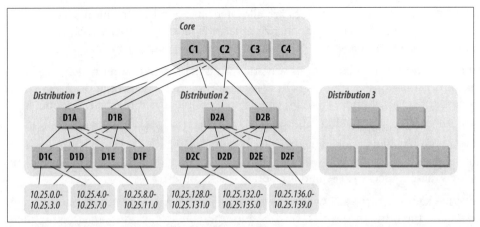

Figure 6-6. Route summarization in an EIGRP network

The most important restriction on this sort of summarization is that you cannot break up any summarized address range across multiple Distribution Areas. In Figure 6-6 a range of subnets from 10.25.0.0 to 10.25.3.0 to is given the first group of LAN segments in Distribution Area 1. These could be subnetted in whatever way is appropriate. But Routers D1C and D1D can summarize the connections to this group as 10.25.0.0/22. Then you need to be careful only that you don't assign subnets from these ranges anywhere else in the network.

Following the summarization process up the diagram toward the Core, Routers D1A and D1B can have a single summary route for both 10.25.0.0/22 and 10.25.4.0/22, namely 10.25.0.0/21. These routes then point to Routers D1C and D1D.

Suppose the designer needs to reserve a large number of subnets for growth in this Distribution Area. He might allow the summary route for the entire area to be 10.25.0.0/17. Then Distribution Area 2 could be summarized as 10.25.128.0/17. In this way, each router can have an extremely compact routing table that is easy to update throughout the network. The routers in the Core don't have to care about whether a particular subnet, such as 10.25.3.5/32, is behind router D1C or D1F. All they have to know is that D1A and D1B take care of a large range of addresses that happens to include this subnet.

The same sort of summarization also happens in the other direction. If Distribution Area 2 is summarized as 10.25.128.0/9, then every router in Distribution Area 1 will see a route for this summary network pointing into the Core. There is no need for these routers to see any more detail.

By default, EIGRP automatically summarizes whenever two different IP networks meet if the networks represent two different Classes. For example, where a section of network containing 172.16.0.0/16 meets another one using 172.17.0.0/16, they will both be summarized.

However, if the subnet addresses are allocated in a good hierarchical scheme, you can configure the routers to summarize other smaller ranges. It is a good idea to do so because every router should have a simple, concise, routing table.

If the network is not planned this way, then summarization doesn't make sense. For example, some of the subnets of 10.25.3.0 are located in Distribution Area 1 and others are in Distribution Area 2, then it is not possible to summarize either one.

EIGRP can also handle multiple routes to a particular destination. The network in Figure 6-6 has two connections from each router to the next level above it. Each of the higher-level routers will see two routes to everything downstream from it. EIGRP allows these routers to keep and use both of these routes.

In the example, there are two paths from Router D1A to 10.25.3.0: one through D1C and the other through D1D. If both of these links have the same metric, then EIGRP uses equal-cost multipath routing. In most cases, the router simply alternates the traffic flows between the different paths. The packets belonging to a particular TCP session are called a flow. So equal cost multipath routing keeps all of these packets on the same path. However, as each new session is established, the router attempts to balance the paths since they have the same cost.

If the packets from several different flows are coming sufficiently quickly, the router sends the second packet out the second path before the first packet has finished departing along the first path. This allows a simple form of load sharing between the paths. However, this form of load sharing is not terribly bandwidth efficient, so you will get considerably less than twice the bandwidth of one path in practice.

Active and Stuck-in-Active Routes

EIGRP uses an interesting technique for keeping its routing tables up-to-date. Even though it only uses the best route, the EIGRP topology table keeps a list of every path to every subnet. This way, if the best path goes away it can select a *feasible successor*. But if there are no feasible successors when a route disappears, the router puts this route into an "ACTIVE" state and queries its neighbors to find a new path to the destination. If one or more of the neighbors knows a path to this destination network (or a summary route that contains this one), they respond. But if they do not have a route, they in turn query their neighbors.

Sometimes the destination is simply nowhere to be found. This can happen because a failure somewhere in the network has isolated some subnets. Sometimes the process of trying to find a new path can fail to converge. In the ever-expanding chain of queries from one router to the next, each device is waiting for a response. If the network is too large or if it contains too many high-latency sections, it may become difficult for this process to converge.

If the queries for an "ACTIVE" route are not satisfied within the timeout period of a few minutes, the router gives the dreaded "Stuck In Active" message. It then clears the neighbor relationship with the router that failed to respond. This can happen either because the route has disappeared or because a communication problem has broken the chain of queries somewhere in the network. Either way, "Stuck In Active" represents a serious problem, particularly if it happens repeatedly.

When the routers in an EIGRP network issue large numbers of "Stuck In Active" messages, it is important to determine where thing are getting "Stuck." This is by far more serious than the "ACTIVE" problem, which just means that a route is missing. When these messages appear, the network engineer should find out which neighbor relationships are being reset. This could be happening anywhere in the network, not necessarily on or adjacent to the router that reports the "Stuck In Active."

The easiest way to find these problems is to ensure that EIGRP is configured to log neighbor status changes. Then, when the "Stuck In Active" messages appear, attempt to track where the neighbor relationships are flapping. In some cases the neighbors that are changing are randomly dispersed throughout the network. This may indicate that the EIGRP AS has simply become too large to be stable. This can happen particularly when the automatic route summarization features of EIGRP are not used effectively.

Interconnecting Autonomous Systems

EIGRP networks are grouped into Autonomous Systems (ASes). Each router that has EIGRP configured must specify the AS number. All neighbors must be in the same AS to exchange routes.

It is possible to break up an EIGRP network into multiple ASes, but these ASes cannot be directly connected to one another. The problem is that the router sitting on the border between the two ASes is a full member of both. It maintains a distinct topology database for each AS. But consider what happens when a route in one of the ASes disappears. As I discussed in the previous section, that route becomes

"ACTIVE" as EIGRP attempts to find an alternate path. When the router that is a member of both ASes marks this route as "ACTIVE," it queries all of its neighbors for a possible alternate. That includes the neighbors that belong to the other AS. So any ACTIVE route queries from one AS are forwarded over to the other AS. This means that if there are stability problems in one AS, they will be inherited by the other.

The main reason to break up a network into multiple ASes is to help convergence and stability of each of the smaller units. In doing so you must be careful to separate these ASes more effectively by using another protocol between them. Since EIGRP is an IGP, it is natural to use an EGP, such as BGP, to perform this function. However, it can also be effective simply to use another IGP such as RIP or OSPF.

Like RIP, EIGRP lets you tag routes that originate from outside of the AS. But, while RIP made it difficult to use this information to make routing decisions, it is relatively straightforward in EIGRP. This information is commonly used to keep traffic inside the AS if any internal path exists. For example, consider a network with two ASes. It might turn out that the shortest path between two segments in the same AS actually passes through the second AS. But usually this is not desirable. After all, what is the point of breaking up the network into ASes if there is no real division between them? In EIGRP, these route tags ensure that if there are two routes for a particular network, one internal and one external, then the internal one is preferred automatically.

Sometimes you might want to use that external route for administrative or cost reasons. More commonly, there might be two or more different external routes for a particular network. For example, there might be more than one Autonomous System Boundary Router (ASBR) connecting to one or more external ASes. In this case the external route with the best metric may not actually be the administratively preferred path.

For these types of situations, Cisco lets you use policy-based routing to act on these route tags. In the simplest implementation, the routers at the edges of the ASes might just add a large delay to one external route.

Although they are intended to act as IGP, IGRP, and EIGRP are sometimes used themselves as EGPs to interconnect OSPF ASes. EIGRP has excellent route-summarization properties, making it also useful for summarizing routes between ASes.

A real EGP such as BGP has better native filtering properties than EIGRP does. Furthermore, because EIGRP is a proprietary standard, it is probably not appropriate for interconnecting the networks of different organizations.

However, two or three OSPF ASes can be easily interconnected within the same organization. This is particularly true if the network designer intends to share all routes between these ASes. EIGRP is extremely simple to configure, and it works well when redistributing routing information with OSPF. So for purely internal uses like this, it may be easier to use EIGRP than BGP to function as the EGP.

Redistributing with Other Routing Protocols

Cisco has made it very easy to distribute routes between EIGRP and other routing protocols. All you need to do is configure a border router that talks to both protocols. Then, in configuring the two protocols, one just instructs each to redistribute routes from the other. But usually AS boundaries serve multiple purposes. It is usually necessary to restrict what information flows between the two protocols.

At a minimum, you must be careful about how the metrics of the external routes look to each protocol. They will be tagged as external routes, so you can always use policy-based routing if you need to. But, as I discussed in Chapter 3, policy-based routing should be used as sparingly as possible. In fact, it is best if used only at the boundary between the two protocols—that is, only on the ASBR routers.

Routers can also set default metrics for all injected external routes in both ASes. This is useful when the two protocols handle metrics in fundamentally different ways, as with RIP and EIGRP. In this case the network designer might want RIP to show all of the external EIGRP routes with a minimum metric of 5. On the EIGRP side, she might want to specify a large minimum administrative delay for all injected RIP routes. Setting default metrics in this way is often the simplest way to control the routes injected from foreign routing protocols.

The situation becomes more complicated when some routes should not be redistributed. For example, there might be a third AS, perhaps running still another routing protocol. Suppose the network has an EIGRP AS connecting to each of two different OSPF ASes. Then the designer decide must if she wants the EIGRP AS to carry traffic between these other two systems. If not, then the boundary router between OSPF AS number 1 and the EIGRP AS can simply refuse to pass along the routing information for AS number 2.

Cisco makes this easy with the use of distribute lists in the EIGRP configuration.

OSPF

Open Shortest Path First (OSPF) uses a Link State Algorithm for finding the best paths through a network. This is a completely different way of looking at dynamic routing than with the Distance Vector protocols discussed earlier. Version 2 of OSPF is the most recent. It is defined in RFC 2328.

Routers running OSPF don't exchange routing tables with one another. Instead, they exchange information about which networks they connect to and the states of these links. This *state* primarily means whether it is up or down, but it also includes information about its type of interface. Every router in the OSPF area (a term that I define shortly) carries an identical copy of this Link State database. The database of links in the network is then used to create a *shortest-path tree*, from which the routing table is calculated.

A simple example should help to explain these concepts. Figure 6-7 shows a simple network that runs OSPF. For now I avoid any questions of media type and IP addressing. These are all point-to-point links. Arbitrary cost is indicated beside each link in the diagram. Some of the links are faster than others. I use a cost of 1 for all-fast links and 10 for the slow ones.

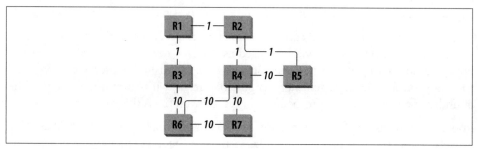

Figure 6-7. A simple OSPF network

Table 6-3 shows the Link State information for this network.

Table 6-3. Link State database

	R1	R2	R3	R4	R5	R6	R7
R1		1	1				
R2	1			1	1		
R3	1					10	
R4		1			10	10	10
R5		1		10			
R6			10	10			10
R7				10		10	

Now OSPF uses this Link State information to construct a shortest-path tree. Even though the Link State information is identical on every router, each one has its own unique shortest-path tree. Figure 6-8 shows the shortest-path tree for Router R6. At first glance it looks like just a redrawing of the same network diagram from Figure 6-8, but it is actually somewhat different.

In particular, although there is a connection from R4 to R7, R6 would never use this link because it has its own links to each of these destinations. Also, the shortest path from R6 to R5 in terms of number of hops goes R6—R4—R5. But the link from R4—R5 is slower than the apparently longer path from R4—R2—R5. Since the shortest-path tree only cares about the links the network will actually use, it shows this more circuitous (but nonetheless shorter in terms of cost) path.

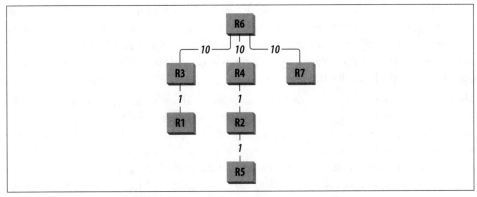

Figure 6-8. Shortest-path tree for Router R6

Every router in the network builds its own shortest-path tree and uses this information to construct its routing tables. Each entry in the routing table indicates the next hop, exactly as it did for the other routing protocols mentioned earlier.

The preceding example was deliberately constructed so that there one would be only one best path to each destination. In any real network this is rarely the case. OSPF provides a mechanism called *equal-cost multipath*. This means that the tree-building algorithm actually discovers and uses these alternate paths. This makes the picture harder to draw, but it works the same way conceptually.

Different vendors have different ways of dealing with equal-cost multipath routing. In most cases there is a configurable maximum number of paths that will be considered. If there are four equal-cost paths to a destination, the router might only use the first two that it discover. Usually this does not cause any problems, but it could result in routing tables that do not look as expected. Consult your router vendor's documentation for details on how it handles equal-cost multipath routing.

OSPF requires that every router in a grouping have the same Link State database. Scaling efficiency dictates that these groupings shouldn't contain more than about 50 routers. This number is far too small to support most large networks. So clearly there must be a mechanism for subdividing OSPF ASes.

This AS has the same meaning as it did for the discussions of RIP, IGRP, and EIGRP. It is a large administrative grouping of routers that all share routing information using a single IGP.

An area is simply a group of routers that all share the same Link State database. The process by which all routers in an area learn the Link State database from one another is called *flooding*.

When a new router connects to the network, it first attempts to establish neighbor relationships with every other router that it can see directly. Most of these neighbors will then become *adjacent*, meaning that they directly exchange Link State information with one another. There are exceptions where routers that are neighbors do not become adjacent, but I discuss this later.

Then the new router sends its current Link State to all of its adjacent neighbors. This Link State information is contained in a Link State Advertisement (LSA). Since every router taking part in this OSPF area needs to see the same Link State database, the neighbors proceed to pass this information along to all of their adjacent neighbors. These neighbors in turn send the new information to their neighbors and so on until every router in the area has updated its database. Meanwhile, the new router also receives the current Link State database from its neighbors. Very quickly every router in the area obtains the new database. They then must recalculate their shortest-path trees and the resulting routing tables.

The fact that every router in an area must have an identical copy of the Link State database poses an important scaling problem with OSPF. The more routers there are in the area, the more different links each router has, and the more memory the Link State database will consume. This is actually the smaller problem, though. A more serious scaling problem comes from the difficulty in calculating the shortest-path tree as the area becomes more and more complicated.

The usual rule of thumb is that no area should contain more than 50 routers. In a simple network design where every router's shortest-path tree is easily calculated, this number can be pushed up. This is particularly true if the routers are all configured with faster processors and extra memory.

However, it is a good idea to keep OSPF areas small and simple. This helps ensure that the network can respond quickly and accurately to topology changes.

In general, routers that are neighbors are also adjacent. But there are places where this is not the case. The exceptions happen for broadcast media like Ethernet segments and Token Rings, as well as for Nonbroadcast Multiple Access (NBMA) media. ATM and Frame Relay networks can be implemented as NBMA, as can some types of wireless networks.

If a broadcast medium such as an Ethernet segment contains several routers, then every router is a neighbor to every other router. This effectively forms a mesh of relationships. As I mentioned earlier in this book, meshes do not scale well. So OSPF allows routers on broadcast and NBMA networks to simplify their relationships by electing a Designated Router (DR) for the segment. They also elect a Backup Designated Router (BDR) to take over if the DR fails. Then every other router on the segment becomes adjacent to only the DR and BDR. This changes the mesh into a star.

The DR handles all flooding of Link State information for the segment. This router does not take on any special role in routing, however. The DR function is only used to make exchange of Link State data more efficient.

If the DR becomes unreachable for any reason, then the BDR automatically takes over for it and becomes the new DR. It remains in this role until it also fails. So in many networks the DR is just the router that has been up the longest. But this is not always desirable. For administrative reasons, sometimes a network designer wants to restrict which routers take on these functions. In this case, it is possible to set an OSPF priority on every router connected to the broadcast or NBMA medium to control the election process.

The router with the highest priority is elected as the DR, and the second highest becomes BDR. However, this election only happens if there is no DR, either because it's a new network or because the DR has failed.

Frequently there are routers that the network engineer does not want as DR for the segment. In this case the priority is simply set to zero.

Area Types

OSPF allows the designer to break up the AS into a number of smaller areas. Between these areas are Area Border Routers (ABR). An ABR controls the flow of routing information between the different areas, while maintaining distinct Link State databases for each.

There are two main types of areas and a number of subcategories. The main distinction is whether an area is capable of acting as a Transit area.

A Transit area carries traffic that originates in a different area (or a different AS) and is destined for still another area. These external destinations may be other areas, or they may even be other ASes, perhaps running different routing protocols. Conversely, a non-Transit area is one that can only carry traffic that either originates or terminates in that area.

The main reason for this distinction has to do with how external routes are summarized. If an area uses summary and default routes for everything external, then other areas can't use it to get to external or other areas. It simply doesn't have sufficient information to allow this kind of flow-through. So a Transit-capable area is one that does little or no summarization.

There are three common options for how this summarization can be done. They are called Stub, Not-So-Stubby, and Totally Stub.

A Stub area is one that uses a summary route for everything outside of the AS. If the whole network is contained in one AS, perhaps with a single default route to the Internet, then a Stub area provides very little benefit. However, Stub areas can be quite efficient in networks that have a large number of external routes.

If any of the routers in the area connect to a different AS, then the area cannot be Stub. However, it is possible to use a Not-So-Stubby Area (NSSA) for this purpose.

NSSA are defined in RFC 1587. This option allows for the summarization of some external routes but not others. If there is a router internal to the NSSA that connects to the external AS, then those external routes are not summarized. Any external routes that originate in a different area are summarized.

Finally, a Totally Stub area summarizes everything from outside of the area. So even routes that are internal to the AS but originates in a different area appear only as summary routes. This can be useful for portions of a network where routers have limited resources. It is also useful when a large number of the links in the area are slow or have high latencies. In these cases the area cannot transmit large amounts of routing information. So it makes sense to summarize everything from outside of the area.

Not all vendors implement Totally Stub areas. This feature originated with Cisco and is not included in any of the RFC documents that define the OSPF standard. Some other vendors have also implemented Totally Stub areas, however. As with all non-standard options, it should be used with caution. All of the routers in any given area must agree on the type of area. So if some routers are not capable of operating in a particular mode, they may be unable to participate in the area.

NSSA and Stub areas, on the other hand, are implemented by nearly every router vendor.

Route summarization in this discussion is similar to how it was used with EIGRP. In a normal non-Stub area, OSPF distributes routing information on every individual subnet, including those in external regions of the network. A summary reduces this information to a small number of routes that describe large ranges of addresses.

For this to work, it must be possible to reach every valid address in this range through a single Access point. In the case of summary routes for networks outside of the AS, the destination must point to the Autonomous System Boundary Router (ASBR). For summary routes of networks in other areas (or where the ASBR is in another area), every router in the area will simply direct traffic to the Area Border Router (ABR).

Because it is a Classless routing protocol, OSPF uses a system of the longest possible match when looking at summary routes. Suppose a packet has a destination of 10.2.3.5. The router forwarding this packet will look in its routing table to see how to deal with it. It might have a default route of 0.0.0.0, which it will use as a catch-all in case it can't find a better match. It might also have a summary route for 10.0.0.0/8. Again, if it can't find a better match, it will use this one. If there are several possible matches, the router will always use the one with the longest mask, which will be the most specific route. In this example, if there is a route for 10.2.3.4/30, this will be better than any either 10.0.0.0/8 or 0.0.0.0/0.

Note also that the ABR routers summarize in both directions. The routes from outside of the area are summarized when they are distributed into the area. Similarly, the internal area routes are summarized when the ABR presents them to the rest of the network. So if an area has a summary route of 10.1.4.0/22, then it is up to the ABR to distribute this summary information to the neighboring area. If it is summarizing this way, then it does not distribute any of the specific routes for this area.

Just as ASes are defined by numbers, areas also have numeric identifiers. Every AS must have at least one Transit-capable area called area 0.

Areas are sometimes called by a single number, and sometimes by numbers written out in the same format as IP addresses. So Area 0 is sometimes written as 0.0.0.0. It is usually a good idea to have the default route for an AS connected to Area 0.0.0.0. But this has nothing to do with this naming convention. In fact, the numerical identifiers for areas (except for Area 0) are completely arbitrary. Since every area must connect directly to Area 0, and only to Area 0, there need not be any relationship between the names of different areas.

However, it can make administration and troubleshooting simpler if areas have meaningful names. Some organizations make their area names identical to the summary of networks inside the area. So, if an area can be summarized with the route 10.1.16.0/22, then the area might be called 10.1.16.0.

Other organizations choose their area designations to represent administrative information. For example, they might have a group of areas belonging to each of several different divisions of the organization. One of these divisions—Engineering, for example—might be called 5.1.10.0. Then the Engineering OSPF areas would be called 5.1.10.1, 5.1.10.2, and so forth. Meanwhile, the Marketing division might have 10.2.5.1, 10.2.5.2, and so forth.

The numbers are completely arbitrary, so it is up to the network designer to come up with a scheme that is meaningful to the organization.

Area Structures

Every AS must have an Area 0. Every other area in the AS must connect directly to Area 0 and no other area. In other words, every OSPF AS is a star configuration. So OSPF lends itself well to hierarchical network design.

The routers that connect one area to another Area Border Routers (ABR). Every ABR straddles the line between Area 0 and at least one other area. Figure 6-9 shows an example of how this works.

There are three areas in this picture. Area 0.0.0.0 is called the backbone or Core area. There are six routers in this area. Four of these routers are ABRs, and the other two are purely internal. Routers that are purely internal to Area 0 are called backbone routers, so I have named them BBR 1a and BBR 1b.

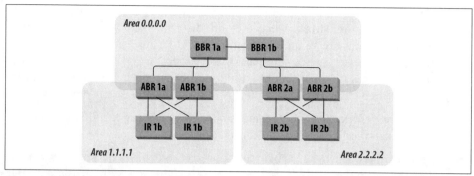

Figure 6-9. Layout of areas in an OSPF AS

There are two other areas indicated in this picture, Area 1.1.1.1 and Area 2.2.2.2. Each of these areas connects to the backbone area through a redundant pair of ABR routers. Each area also contains two other routers. Routers in nonbackbone areas that are not ABRs are called Internal Routers (IR). Most of the routers in the network will wind up being IRs.

This figure shows multiple ABRs connecting to each area. This is important because it affects how summarization is done. Suppose Area 1.1.1.1 is a Stub area. Then all of the IR routers inside this area will see two types of routes. Any route that originates inside the AS will be a full route with no summarization. But every route from other ASes will be summarized into a default route such as 172.16.0.0/14 or 0.0.0.0/0.

This summary route will then be distributed by Link State flooding to every router in the area. In the example, both of the internal routers in this area are directly attached to both of the ABRs. So they will see equal-cost multipath routes for these summary routes.

Suppose Area 2.2.2.2 is not a Stub area. Then every router in this area will see all of the full routes originating with every router in the network. They will only see the Link State database for routers in their own area, but they will see routes for everything else.

Figure 6-9 showed two ABR routers for each area. This was done to remove the single point of failure that a single ABR would represent. But it presents a special problem for OSPF to deal with. The two ABR routers must present the same information to the Core. To ensure that they are in synch, it is important to always mesh the ABRs in any one area. The same issues will be even more applicable when talking about ASBRs later in this chapter. This is because ASBRs ensure that summary routes are correct for an entire AS. ABRs only have to summarize an area, but they still need to keep the routing information up-to-date.

In many networks there is an additional reason for meshing the ABRs for any given area. It is common for every IR in an area to have connections to a pair of ABRs. Then if one of these links fails, the second ABR will take over all of the traffic. However, if the ABRs summarize the area routes when passing them to the Core, then the Core does not need to know about this failure inside the area. So, if traffic from the Core to the IR used the ABR with the failed link, the ABR-to-ABR link provides a new path to the IR. Otherwise, every little change in a remote area will cause changes in the routing tables of the backbone. The backbone area should see only routing changes that result from serious problems.

This diagram shows a pair of ABR routers that connect Area 0 to each of the non-Core areas. In fact, if the ABR routers have relatively powerful processors and lots of memory, they act as ABR for a number of non-Core areas.

One could, for example, have a single ABR router with three high-speed interfaces. The first interface connects to Area 0, the second interface connects to Area 1.1.1.1, and the third to Area 2.2.2.2. This router then acts as ABR to both areas. There need be no particular relationship between Area 1.1.1.1 and Area 2.2.2.2 in this case. The point is just to economize on the number of ABR routers required.

There are no theoretical limits on how many areas an ABR can support. But there are relatively strict practical limits imposed by CPU performance and memory capacity. Most modern routers can readily handle two areas plus Area 0. Some powerful devices can be ABR for 4 or 5 areas with relative ease. Ask your hardware vendor for guidance before attempting to support multiple areas through a single ABR router. It may require a memory or CPU upgrade.

So far, the benefits to summarization have concerned efficient use of resources. But summarization has another key benefit. If you don't summarize, then you must propagate every route through the network. In particular, if the ABRs don't summarize into Area 0, then they must propagate every individual route into Area 0. This is usually not a problem, but every time a link changes state, the route *flaps*—that is, a Link State advertisement is flooded through the area. When this information crosses into another area, such as Area 0, it also has to update the routing tables in this area.

Normally, this is not a problem. But suppose the circuit that connects a number of routers to an ABR is faulty. Every time this circuit goes up and down, the ABR must send out Link State advertisements for all of the routes that have changed state. If it happens too frequently, it can cause stability problems in the network Core. So summarization is not just a resource issue; it is also a stability issue.

I have one final comment on OSPF Area structures. In vendor documentation and even in the OSPF RFC, you frequently read about Virtual Links. These are effectively routing tunnels that allow physically remote routers to become adjacent neighbors. This is sometimes used when a router needs to be in one area, but is physically located in another.

For example, a network might consist of a chain of four areas in a row. The first area is Area 1, the second is Area 0, and the last two are Areas 2 and 3. Area 0 connects Areas 1 and 2 properly, but there is a problem in getting to Area 3. One solution is to configure a virtual link from Area 0 to the router that connects Areas 2 and 3 together. Then this router becomes an ABR for both of these areas.

It should now be clear that needing to use virtual links is a symptom of a bad design. It is far too easy for a virtual link to break and partition an area. When the area that breaks is Area 0, this is disastrous. I strongly caution against using virtual links. They may make otherwise impossible configurations possible, but they will never make a network stable.

Interconnecting Autonomous Systems

Just as with RIP and EIGRP, it is possible to join OSPF Autonomous Systems. This could happen because two otherwise separate networks need to talk to one another. Or it could be that one AS has to be divided into two or more pieces. Routers that connect one AS to another are called Autonomous System Boundary Routers (ASBR).

Technically, an ASBR can be placed in any non-Stub Area or in any NSSA. However, in a hierarchical design it is usually preferable to place the ASBR routers in Area 0. In principle, routers from anywhere in the AS will want to connect to the ASBR and the network beyond it.

However, if the ASBR is in one of the non-Core areas, then traffic from a different area must travel a potentially large distance to get to the ASBR. This tends to be rather inefficient. Also, if there are multiple ASBR routers connecting to several different ASes, all via different areas, then it can be very difficult to know which default 0.0.0.0/0 route is the best one. However, if the ASBR routers are all located in Area 0, it becomes much easier to keep tight control over external routing.

Finally, if the designer is building a hierarchical network design, then it should be hierarchical at all levels, not just within the OSPF AS. So this concept leads to the idea of a central EGP Core that interconnects a number of IGP ASes. In this view the most natural place to connect the OSPF and EGP clouds is in the Core of the OSPF AS, Area 0.

The one important exception to this is using static routes or a foreign routing protocol such as RIP to accommodate network gear that doesn't support OSPF. It is not uncommon to encounter legacy equipment in outlying portions of the network. In this case it is essentially unavoidable: you need to have an ASBR in an area other than Area 0.

It is important to make sure that this area is a Transit Area. It can be either a non-Stub Area or NSSA. The choice between these two options depends mainly on how much other routing information comes from outside of the AS. If the AS has very few external routes, then a non-Stub Area is simpler and therefore preferable. But if there are many external routes, then an NSSA should use router resources more efficiently.

Strictly speaking, since OSPF is an IGP, you should interconnect ASes using an EGP such as BGP. It is possible to use another IGP for this purpose, however. IGRP and RIP actually work relatively well for this purpose. However, it is usually not a good idea to interconnect two ASes running the same IGP without some other protocol in the middle. This is essentially to control the flow of IGP information.

I mentioned previously that it is a bad idea to connect two EIGRP ASes directly. OSPF behaves somewhat better in this regard. But it is still good practice to use a foreign protocol in the middle to help control how routes are distributed between the ASes.

There are two reasons for splitting up an OSPF AS. First, it might have grown so large that it no longer converges quickly after a link failure. This is relatively rare, however. More frequently a designer might want to split up an AS to help isolate regions of instability. Whenever a link fails, the route associated with this link must be updated throughout the AS. If the ABR routers for the area containing the failed link give Area 0 summary rather than detailed routing information, then there is nothing to update. But if every route is listed in detail, then this detailed information must be rigorously updated whenever it changes.

Now consider an AS that contains a mixture of LAN and WAN areas. Suppose that a WAN area contains a Frame Relay cloud with a single circuit supporting hundreds of remote sites. If this circuit fails, the ABR for this area must update Area 0 with all of these individual routing updates. When the circuit comes back up, all of the routes must be updated again.

If this happens frequently, it can make the routers in Area 0 extremely busy recalculating their routing tables. That can result in Area 0 itself becoming unstable. So some network designers like to separate their WAN components into one or more distinct ASes that are separate from the more stable LAN components.

Redistributing with Other Routing Protocols

The simplest example of redistributing other routing information into OSPF is the use of static routes. This is effectively the same as redistributing from one AS into another. Every route that does not come from within the AS and is not generated by the standard Link State advertisements is considered an external route and is tagged as such.

When an external route is injected by an ASBR, a cost is associated with it. This need not be a real indication of the number of hops or the speed of links on the outside of the ASBR. In fact, you only need to be careful with the costs of external routes when there are two or more different ASBRs offering connections to the same network. In this case, OSPF adds its own internal costs to each hop through the network.

To reliably control which external path is used in this scenario, all ASBR routers that connect to the external network should be located together in Area 0. Then if one ASBR is preferred, it injects the route with the best cost. If this is not done—for example, if two ASBR routers with the same external routing information are located in different Areas—then predicting which one will be used is difficult. Some routers may use one, and others may use the other ASBR. This may be desired. But it is simpler and easier to maintain if all ASBR routers are located in Area 0.

In fact, OSPF uses two different types of external routes. An arbitrary router inside an AS looking at a Type 1 external route sees a metric equal to the cost for that route at the ASBR, plus the cost required to get to the ASBR. For Type 2 external routes, on the other hand, the internal portion of the cost is ignored.

If there are two ASBR routers injecting the same Type 1 route with the same metric, then each internal router chooses the closer ASBR. But if it is a Type 2 route, then it always picks the same ASBR, regardless of which one is closer. The ASBR it picks will be the one with the best external cost. If the metrics for two Type 2 routes are equal, then the internal distance is used to break the tie.

Where both Type 1 and Type 2 routes exist for a particular network, the internal routers will always select the Type 1 route.

A special case is the injection of an external route that overlaps with address range of the AS. This is generally dangerous. But there are times when a static route must be used because OSPF is not naturally aware of the route. This might happen, for example, if there is foreign equipment in the network that does not run OSPF.

OSPF will always use the most specific route first. So, ven if there is a lower cost route that includes the subnet mentioned in the static route, the specific route will be used. For example, suppose a route to 192.168.5.0/24 is distributed through the normal Link State process. This could be distributed either as a summary route or as a normal route. Suppose there is one particular host, 192.168.5.16/32, that is connected differently, perhaps through a PPP or SLIP connection directly to a router port. Then this router could inject this host route (a host route has a mask of 255.255.255.255) with the appropriate metric for this medium. OSPF would then use this host route properly for this specific device and the network route for everything else in the segment. This should work even if the host route has a higher cost than the network route.

IP Addressing Schemes for OSPF

OSPF relies on route summarization to work efficiently. Unlike EIGRP, which allows route summarization at any point, OSPF only summarizes at ABR and ASBR routers. So where EIGRP can benefit from highly sophisticated addressing schemes that summarize on many levels, OSPF can use somewhat simpler IP addressing schemes.

Each AS must be completely summarized by a simple network/mask combination. As mentioned previously, it is always possible to inject external routes that overlap with the internal range. But this should be avoided because it is confusing. If multiple ASes are used, they should all have their own clearly summarized ranges. Then, each area within each AS should be composed strictly of a summarized subgroup from the AS address range.

For example, suppose you have a network with two ASes. The first uses the range 10.1.0.0/16, and the second uses 10.2.0.0/16. This will make it easy for the ASBR routers to summarize the links that connect them. Then the areas within the first AS may have address ranges that look like 10.1.0.0/22, 10.1.4.0/22, 10.1.8.0/21, 10.1.16.0/21, and so forth. Note that these ranges are not all the same size. There is no reason to restrict areas to summarize the same way as one another.

If you fail to create clearly summarized address ranges at the ASBR and ABR boundaries, OSPF has to work much harder than it would otherwise. This is extremely inefficient. It is also very difficult for human engineers to diagnose problems when there is no simple and clear pattern to the IP addresses.

OSPF Costs

Earlier in this chapter I indicated that the OSPF cost values are arbitrary. They are used to select the best paths through a network. So, in general, faster links will be configured to have lower costs. In fact, if you assume the same latency for every type of link (which is not true in reality), then you can define the cost to be inversely proportional to the bandwidth.

This leads to one of the most popular methods for setting OSPF costs. You can take a reference bandwidth as the fastest link in the network and make its cost 1. Then every slower link has a cost that is just the reference bandwidth divided by the slower link's bandwidth. If your reference bandwidth is a Gigabit Ethernet link in the network's Core, then every Fast Ethernet (100Mbps) link will have a cost of 10, 10Mbps Ethernet links will have 100, and a T1 (1.544Mbps) will cost 6476.

This is a relatively good system, but it has one critical flaw that makes it unworkable in many networks. The maximum value for an OSPF cost is 65,535. In fact, it is important to avoid coming anywhere close to this value because a path that includes such a link plus any number of faster links could easily have a total cost greater than the maximum. When this happens the entire path becomes unusable. This is effectively the same problem as when a RIP metric exceeds 15.

The problem is that many networks include too large a range of bandwidths. Suppose, for example, that the fastest link in the network is a Gigabit Ethernet link, and the slowest is a 9.6kbps dialup line. If the Gigabit link has a cost of 1, this implies that the 9.6kbps line must have a cost of 104,166, which is considerably larger than

65,535. This problem becomes worse in a network with a 10Gbps link in its Core, because then even relatively common 56kbps circuits have excessively high costs.

Let's revisit the reasoning behind this standard linear rule to adapt it to these real networks. The range of bandwidths available forces many network designers to use a non-linear rule. Certainly, the faster links must have lower costs than slower ones. But do links that are one-tenth as fast really need to bear a cost that is 10 times as high? This would make the net cost of a path passing through nine Fast Ethernet links better than the cost of a single 10Mbps Ethernet link. Is this realistic?

The main problem is what nonlinear method to use to include the bandwidth factor. What it really comes down to is deciding how many hops through high-speed links equals one slow hop.

Clearly, an important factor is the latency of each of these links. The latency for a short 10Mbps Ethernet is roughly governed by the length of time required to wait for carrier and inject the packet. Time of flight to the farthest part of the segment is less than the time to transmit the entire packet (or else the segment will suffer from late-collision problems). The same is true for 100Mbps Ethernet, but because the carrier frequency for 100Mbps Ethernet is 10 times as fast, the latency should be roughly one-tenth as long.

Adding more hops to the path also increases the latency because each router in the path takes some time to process the packets. In the case of Ethernet and Fast Ethernet, the amount of work is almost exactly the same. So assume that each router adds roughly the same additional latency as a Fast Ethernet segment does. Then passing through N Fast Ethernet hops will add N link delays plus N–1 router delays, for a total of 2N–1. This implies that the break-even point based on latency alone will be when 2N–1 = 10, or N = 5.

Now consider how the bandwidth should scale neglecting latency effects. Nominally, if a link is 10 times as fast, then an application can send 10 times as much data through it. But this assumes that this application is the only one using this link. In fact, the faster links usually aggregate traffic from a number of slower links. The amount of competition for the bandwidth on some remote link depends on the network design and traffic patterns. Generally speaking, these links have some constant utilization for which many devices compete, plus excess capacity that they can use fairly freely.

Putting these factors together suggests a simple formula with the cost inversely proportional to the square root of the nominal bandwidth. Note that a great deal of hand waving went into finding an appropriate formula. It is balanced so that a Fast Ethernet link is roughly three times as good as a 10Mbps Ethernet link. Similarly, Gigabit Ethernet links are roughly three times as good as Fast Ethernet. This simple rule scales the same way throughout the entire range. Best of all, it results in usable cost numbers for the slowest links in a network, as shown in Table 6-4.

Table 6-4. Suggested OSPF cost values for different media types.

Medium	Nominal bandwidth	Cost in 1/bandwidth model	Cost in 1/square root model
9.6kbps line	9.6kbps	1,041,666[a]	1020
56kbps line	56kbps	178,571[a]	422
64kbps line	64kbps	156,250[a]	395
T1 Circuit	1.544Mbps	6,476	80
E1 Circuit	2.048Mbps	4,882	69
T3 Circuit	45Mbps	222	14
Ethernet	10Mbps	1,000	31
Fast Ethernet	100Mbps	100	10
Gigabit Ethernet	1Gbps	10	3
10 Gigabit Ethernet	10Gbps	1	1
4Mbps Token Ring	4Mbps	2,500	50
16Mbps Token Ring	16Mbps	625	25

[a] These costs are all higher than the maximum cost value of 65,535, and they would be adjusted in practice.

Table 6-4 also includes the costs that result from using the more common model in which cost is inversely proportional to bandwidth. In both cases I adjusted the costs so that the fastest link, the 10Gigabit Ethernet, has a cost of 1.

Both of these models are just basic suggestions for starting points. The network designer should carefully consider the OSPF costs of every link in the network to ensure that they are appropriate. Poor choices of values can lead to serious traffic routing problems. But, as with all network design problems, simple consistent rules will usually result in a more stable network.

It is particularly important to include room for growth. If there is even a remote chance that your network will one day include Core links that are faster than the 10 Gigabit Ethernet speed suggested in this table, make sure to scale all of the cost values up accordingly. Then the new fastest link will have a cost of 1, and all of the other links will be correspondingly more expensive. Making this change after a network is built can be time consuming and highly disruptive.

There is an interesting exception to the preceding comments. OSPF areas are configured so that only Area 0 carries traffic from one area to another. If a packet starts in any area besides Area 0 and then leaves that area, then it cannot return to the area in which it started. If it then passes into another area, then it must have its ultimate destination in that area. So the problem of selecting the best path breaks up into components. First, OSPF needs to find the best path through the originating area. If the destination is in the same area, then it needs the best path to the destination. But if the destination is in some other area, then all it cares about is finding the best path to Area 0.

Once the packet is in Area, 0 OSPF needs to find the best path within this area. It may terminate in Area 0, or it may lead to an ABR for another area. Finally, in the destination area it needs to find the best path to the final device. But the point is that the protocol does not need to know the entire path from end to end unless the path is contained entirely in one area. It just needs the best path to the next ABR.

Consequently, it doesn't matter if you use different costing rules in different areas. For example, Area 0, being the Core of the network, might contain several 10 Gigabit Ethernet links. But it is unlikely that this area will contain anything slower than a T1 circuit. So you can use one set of costs appropriate to this range of bandwidths. Similarly, a destination area might contain a number of remote WAN sites connected via 56kbps circuits. But as long as the fastest links in this area are 100Mbps Fast Ethernet, you can use a consistent set of costs based on 100Mbps bandwidth. However, as with all aspects of network design, it is preferable to have a single common rule that applies everywhere. So this exception is best used only as an interim measure while readjusting metrics throughout an AS.

BGP

Border Gateway Protocol (BGP) is currently in its fourth version, which is defined in RFC1771. Although the Core protocol has not changed since 1995, there have been some additions to it.

BGP is an EGP. All of the other routing protocols that I have discussed so far in this chapter are IGP. In the usual configuration, IGP protocols function purely within an AS, while EGP protocols are used to interconnect ASes. The main exception to this rule is that sometimes an IGP can be used in a limited function to link together two ASes running a different protocol. For example, you can link two OSPF ASes using EIGRP or RIP. However, using a real EGP offers many important advantages.

BGP is by far the most popular EGP. There is an earlier EGP protocol called, confusingly enough, EGP. But BGP is much more robust and offers many more useful features for policing traffic flows. Most importantly, BGP Version 4 allows fully classless routing.

Classless routing is important because there are many cases where organizations want either to subnet or to supernet their address ranges. I have already discussed subnetting. Supernetting is a similar idea, except that it allows an organization to group together a number of contiguous smaller class networks.

For example, suppose an organization uses four unregistered Class C networks, 192.168.4.0/24, 192.168.5.0/24, 192.168.6.0/24, and 192.168.7.0/24. They could distribute routing information to these four addresses by means of the supernet route 192.168.4.0/22. Similarly, two different organizations might opt to share the Class B range 172.19.0.0/16. So one could use 172.19.0.0/17, and the other 172.19.128.0/17. They could then exchange all of their routing information with a single simple summary.

This feature, called Classless Interdomain Routing (CIDR), is becoming relatively common throughout the Internet. This is because the growth of Internet participation has led to a drastic shortage of IP addresses. So the IETF has been forced to get creative with its address allocation. Since BGP is the primary routing protocol for interconnecting organizations on the Internet, it has become completely classless.

The Internet presents some interesting challenges to a routing protocol. There are some regions of the Internet that share a common backbone. However, internationally the Internet is best viewed as a completely arbitrary collection of interconnected networks.

A large number of individuals and organizations connect to the Internet through one or more Service Provider networks. These Service Provider networks in turn connect with one another and with high-speed Internet backbone networks that are themselves essentially just fast Service Provider networks. In addition, there are a number of educational and governmental organizations that behave almost like Service Provider networks by acting as interconnection points for a number of other networks.

Internally, each Service Provider network may use any routing protocol to distribute routing information. Also internally, these networks form one or more ASes. When connecting to other networks—either client networks or other Service Providers—these networks use BGP to share routing information.

So BGP must share routing information between ASes. It must also summarize information about what routes lie behind each AS. Devices on my network need to get to some distant part of the world by first passing through my Service Provider. My Service Provider needs to know that it can reach this network through some other Service Provider, and so forth, until my packet finally reach its destination.

In short, BGP functions not router to router, but AS to AS. It resolves loops and finds the shortest path in AS-sized chunks.

BGP also has another more complex role to play in AS-to-AS routing. Some organizations might want to take part in the Internet (or, for that matter, any shared IP network). But they might not be willing to act as a conduit for traffic between other organizations. So BGP has a filtering function that allows considerable control over what routes are distributed to which AS neighbors.

BGP uses a different routing algorithm than either RIP or OSPF. Like RIP, it only keeps track of information about the nearest hops and the routes that can be reached through them. But unlike RIP, it doesn't use a simple metric to decide which path is the best. Instead, it maintains information about the entire path to the destination. The method for doing this is called a Path Vector Algorithm.

This means that every route that BGP knows about is accompanied not by a simple number representing cost or distance, but by the actual path. It is easy to avoid loops when you can look at the whole path and see that the same intermediate step appears more than once. The path is not a sequence of routers, but a sequence of ASes, which is why it is called AS_PATH.

If Autonomous Systems exchange routing information using BGP, then each one must have one or more routers that speak both BGP and the IGP. These routers are called Autonomous System Boundary Routers (ASBR). Figure 6-10 shows how three ASes might be connected.

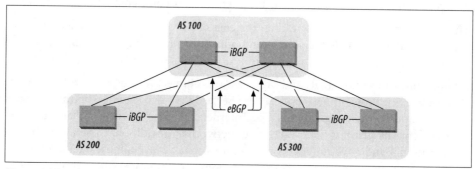

Figure 6-10. Interconnecting three ASes using BGP

Figure 6-10 shows two BGP ASBR routers in each AS for redundancy. These ASes could be running any combination of IGP protocols, such as OSPF, RIP and EIGRP. The two ASBR routers inside each AS communicate with one another using iBGP, the interior protocol. ASBR routers in different ASes use eBGP, the exterior protocol. This is an important distinction because two routers that provide access to each AS must present a unified picture of what is inside. This means they share a common view of the interior of the AS, and they also share the most up-to-date information about all of their AS neighbors.

You have to configure a full mesh of iBGP connections between all of the ASBR routers in each AS. Every ASBR connection, whether iBGP or eBGP, uses a TCP session to exchange routing information. This TCP session is not discovered, but must be manually configured on each router, and it then remains permanently active.

However, as mentioned earlier in this book, fully meshed networks do not scale very well. So there have been some additions to the BGP protocol that aim to relax this requirement. The most important of these protocol additions are Route Reflection (discussed in RFC 2796) and BGP AS Confederations (RFC 3065). These documents are both relatively recent, so not all router vendors have implemented their recommendations. Even those that have incorporated these options have only done so recently, so older equipment may not support them.

There are many different ways of connecting ASes. An AS may have only one ASBR and connect only to one other AS. In this case the routing information that it conveys to the rest of the world only concerns its own IP addresses. This is similar to an AS that has multiple Access points but does not allow traffic to pass through it. These are both called nontransit ASes.

A third option is an AS that has multiple Access points and allows traffic to pass through it. This is called a transit AS. In Figure 6-10, there is no connection between AS 200 and AS 300. To allow devices in these two networks to communicate with one another, AS 100 must pass along routing information received from each to the other. However, AS 200 and AS 300 only need to pass along their own summary routing information into AS 100.

A useful feature of BGP is the ability to restrict what routing information is conveyed. This in turn has the effect of restricting whether a particular AS is used for transit between other ASes. So, for example, an AS might be configured to provide transit services for some external networks, but not others. This can be done either per-network or per-AS. It might only pass transit information to some of its downstream neighbors.

Autonomous System Numbers

Since BGP uses AS Numbers to identify routing elements, there must be rules for how these AS Numbers are allocated. If BGP is to work on the public Internet, then clearly two organizations can't both use—for example, AS Number 100. A conflict in AS Numbers is as serious as a conflict in IP addressing. AS Numbers detect routing loops, so they must be globally unique.

The standard rules for allocating AS Numbers are defined in RFC 1930. These rules apply to all IP networks and to all routing protocols. The range from 64,512 to 65,534 (and possibly also 65,535) is reserved for private networks. These AS Numbers cannot be advertised on the public Internet. This is similar to the private use of unregistered IP address ranges such as 10.0.0.0/8. So it makes a great deal of sense to use AS Numbers from this range particularly for any AS that uses unregistered IP addresses. This way neither the addresses nor the AS Numbers will ever be in danger of reaching the public Internet.

The AS Numbers from 1 through 22,527 have been divided up among three main international Internet standards organizations[*] to allocate to networks that connect to the public Internet. Of the remaining numbers, 0 and the range from 22,528 through 64,511 are currently held in reserve by the IANA for future purposes. There is some inconsistency between IANA documents and RFC 1930 in the availability of AS Number 65,535. The IANA indicates that this number is reserved, while RFC 1930 lists it as part of the unregistered range. So it is probably best to avoid using 65,535 to avoid possible future compatibility problems.

---

[*] In the Americas, Caribbean, and sub-Saharan Africa, ARIN (American Registry for Internet Numbers, *http://www.arin.net*) is responsible for allocating all AS numbers. In Asia and the Pacific region, this is done by AP-NIC (Asia Pacific Network Information Centre, *http://www.apnic.net*). RIPE NCC (Réseaux IP Européens Network Coordination Centre, *http://www.ripe.net*) allocates these numbers for Europe.

However, in most cases it is easiest to just contact your Internet Service Provider (ISP) for assistance with registering AS numbers. They should be able to help in deciding whether officially registered AS numbers are required, or whether it is possible to get away with using only unregistered numbers.

Where to Use BGP

BGP is useful anywhere two or more ASes need to exchange routing information dynamically. If the information never changes, then it is considerably simpler to just use a static route.

Many factors lead to networks requiring continuously updated routing information. For example, there might be more than one way to get to a distant AS. Figure 6-11 shows four ASes. To get from AS 100 to AS 400, a packet can go through either AS 200 or AS 300. It might have an administrative reason for preferring one of these paths, but if the preferred path becomes unavailable, it will need to switch to the other.

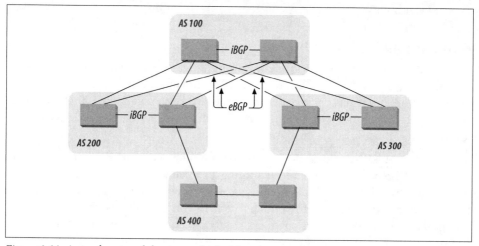

Figure 6-11. A simple network having multiple AS paths

However, there is a simpler reason for needing to use a dynamic EGP protocol in Figures 6-10 and 6-11. Both of these cases have multiple ASBR routers. For example, there are two ASBR routers in AS 100 and AS 200. There are then four paths between these two ASes. A static route would not allow the network to use these paths for redundancy.

BGP is unnecessary in the simple example of one AS connecting to the Internet via a single Service Provider. In this case the ISP can easily handle all inbound traffic with a single static route that summarizes the block of registered addresses for this client network. All outbound traffic is handled similarly by directing the route 0.0.0.0/0 to the Service Provider's network. This is the configuration that most organizations use to connect to the public Internet. So most of these organizations do not need to use BGP for their Internet connections. Consequently, they do not need to register an AS Number.

BGP becomes useful to the client, however, when the network uses two or more different ISPs. Then they can configure BGP to give redundancy in the Internet connection. In this case the network needs a registered AS Number, even if the client network is not configured to allow transit from one ISP to another. In this case the designer will want to configure BGP to distribute the routes for the internal AS only. This will prevent the client network from becoming transit capable.

CHAPTER 7

IPX

Internetwork Packet Exchange (IPX) is a Layer 3 protocol that forms the basis for Novell's network operating system (NOS) called NetWare. IPX was developed from the earlier Xerox Network System (XNS). Today, it is used almost exclusively to support networks of Novell NetWare servers. It is primarily used for file and printer sharing, but the capabilities are broader. IPX is able to carry a large variety of applications.

Unfortunately, some of the terminology adopted by Novell is different from that used in IP networks. For example, Novell calls every device that provides IPX services a *router*. This term can cause some confusion. Thus, in this book, I continue with the already adopted language. I call a device that provides application services a *server*. In this book, a router is a device that primarily performs Layer 3 network functions. As always, I strongly caution the reader against using general-purpose application servers to perform network functions such as bridging and routing.

Just running applications creates a lot of work for application servers. At peak utilization times, they frequently are unable to perform their network functions as well. Therefore, when the network is needed the most, it is unavailable for all applications, not just the ones served by this device. I mention this fact specifically in the context of IPX because Novell servers are frequently configured to either bridge or route—a situation I do not recommend.

Every device in an IPX network has a globally unique address. This address is divided into two parts. A 32-bit address called the *network number* defines on which segment the device lives and the 48-bit *node number* defines the specification on the segment. Usually, the node number is identical to the device's MAC address.

The network number is similar to IP, which also uses 32-bit addresses, but IPX does not use the same notation for its addresses. While IP shows the four octets of the address as separate decimal numbers separated by dots, IPX network and node numbers are usually written in hexadecimal format. Furthermore, in most cases, leading "0" digits from the IPX network number are dropped when the address is written.

For example, a network might include the network number A1A. This number means that its address is really 00000A1A. The first and second octets of the address are both 00. The third octet has a value of 0A (10 in decimal) and the last has the value 1A (26 in decimal).

Another difference from IP is the absence of a subnet mask. The whole network number refers to a particular network. This reference causes confusion in networks that have more than one server on a LAN segment. To get around this problem, every Novell server also has an *internal network number*. This internal number need not have a relationship to the network number of the segment.

As I discuss later in this section, if the network uses Novell Link State Protocol (NLSP) areas, it is more efficient to allocate all addresses in blocks. This allocation includes both the LAN network numbers and these internal network numbers.

The services associated with any particular server are generally associated with the internal network number. The server acts like a router that connects the external LAN segment address to this internal network number that, in turn, represents the unique server.

One of the most important issues to remember when building an IPX network is that these IPX network numbers are not administered rigorously. Novell does offer a service called the Novell Network Registry that allocates and tracks IPX network numbers. This allocation and tracking permits different organizations to interconnect their IPX networks without worrying about address conflicts. However, participation in the Novell Network Registry is optional. Thus, merging two IPX networks together can be extremely challenging.

When merging occurs, it is quite common to find that both IPX network numbers and server names appear in both networks. The only solution to this problem is to adopt a single common standard for naming and addressing servers and IPX networks. However, this standard can take a long time to implement, and corporate priorities may make it necessary to merge the networks quickly.

There is a convenient way around this problem. Usually, in such situations just a few servers actually need to be simultaneously accessible to both networks. These few servers can then be readdressed and renamed according to the new common standard. You can then build a simple IPX routing firewall between the two networks by using a pair of routers with a LAN segment between them. One router connects this common segment to the first network and the other connects to the second network.

You can then implement Access lists on the exchange of IPX routing and service information (I discuss these protocols shortly). The two routers prevent those network numbers and server names that are in conflict from entering this common segment. Then, as IPX names and addresses are migrated to the new standard, the new addresses pass through the routing firewall setup. In this way, one can gradually migrate the entire networks to a common addressing scheme. When it is complete, the firewall connection can be replaced by a common LAN infrastructure.

There are three reasons for deploying two routers with a common segment (rather than a single router) between them. First, much greater control is possible over the routing Access lists because the first can see all of the first network's routes and services and only pick and choose those that will be permitted to pass to the second network. Second, this sort of filtering can be rather CPU- and memory-intensive in a large network. Splitting the task between two routers helps ensure stability. Third, it might become necessary to implement one or more servers on this intermediate segment. For example, if both networks use IPX for their email services, then the network designer can implement an email relay server on this intermediate segment. Since this LAN segment is visible to both sides, it is also a natural place to put central file servers or servers that download common information to remote user servers.

IPX itself is a connectionless protocol and similar in concept to IP. Programmers can build connectionless applications to run over IP using UDP. For applications that require connections, with the network protocol ensuring that all of the packets arrive intact and in order, an IP programmer would instead use TCP.

IPX also has a connection-based transport layer called Sequenced Packet Exchange (SPX). Like UDP and TCP, SPX includes the concept of well-known port numbers to ensure that a server knows to which application to connect the session.

Dynamic Routing

IPX has dynamic routing protocols that are in many ways similar to those that I already discussed for IP. They fall into the same general categories of Distance Vector and Link State protocols, and they apply many of the same loop-avoidance mechanisms. The basic goals are the same—to find the best multihop path to a particular destination automatically, to converge quickly after topology changes, and to eliminate loops.

Novell RIP and SAP

The services or applications that any particular server has to offer are described by Service Advertisement Protocol (SAP) packets that are sent around the network. End-user workstations receive these SAP broadcast packets and use them to build a list of all available services on the network.

Running parallel to these Service Advertisements is a routing protocol called Routing Information Protocol (RIP). IPX RIP shares several similarities to IP RIP. Both are Distance Vector algorithms. However, while IPX RIP keeps track of the number of hops to a destination, it doesn't use the information in exactly the same way as IP RIP. Both protocols use the hop count metric to avoid loops. In the case of IPX RIP, the actual routing decisions are made according to which route has a shorter time delay to reach the destination.

Time delay is measured in *ticks*. The length of a tick is selected so that there are 65,535 ticks in an hour (65,535 is the largest number that can be expressed in 16 bits). Thus, there are roughly 18.2 ticks in a second, each one being about 55 milliseconds long. RIP makes its routing decisions based on this time delay and uses the hop count only as a "tie breaker" when two paths have the same net time delay.

RIP routing updates are made on a schedule. Each RIP packet can contain up to 50 routing table entries, and each device attempts to pass its entire routing table along to all of its neighbors. The exception to this situation is the fact that IPX RIP employs a Split Horizon algorithm that does not pass routing information back to the device from which it was originally learned. At each successive hop, the devices increment the hop counts indicated in the received routing table. They also add to the time delay a new delay that is measured by the network-interface card.

The SAP protocol carries information about what devices support what application services. This information does not change as frequently as routing information. Generally, if a server is available, then all of the services it offers are also available. Thus, SAP generally works as a query and response.

When a new workstation appears on a network, it sends out a general query looking for information about what servers are available on the network and what services they support. When a new server appears on the network, its neighbors ask it what services are available on the network. When a server stops responding to queries, its services are eventually flushed from the SAP tables of other devices on the network.

Since NetWare is intended to operate across large network environments, a user on a remote LAN segment must be able to get information about the services supported by central servers in the computer room. To make this possible, SAP information is relayed around the entire network from router to router. In this way, every device is able to see a list of available services anywhere in the network.

This SAP information includes some routing information. It is not sufficient to say only that a server named ACCOUNTING supports a database application. The network has to know where that ACCOUNTING server is. However, although these SAP packets include routing information, this information is not used to route the packets. The information used to route packets comes from RIP. Therefore, one of the most confusing problems in an IPX network comes when the RIP and SAP information is inconsistent.

This is particularly true when filtering either RIP or SAP. This filtering is often done to control the size of the routing and service tables on routers and servers. Also, because RIP periodically updates all of its neighbors with its entire routing table, network engineers often want to filter RIP to control bandwidth. Later in this chapter, I explain why too much SAP on a large network is a potentially greater problem. Thus, SAP filtering is usually more restrictive than RIP filtering.

Unless properly controlled, RIP and SAP traffic can cause serious congestion problems, particularly on low-speed WAN links. RIP and SAP, however, are distinct protocols, so they must be filtered separately.

It is not uncommon to wind up with inconsistent filters. Then the network can get into a situation in which an end-user workstation sees that a server called ACCOUNTING offers a database service, but cannot reach that server. Conversely, if the RIP but not the SAP is present, then the user will not even see this service, but might connect to other services on the same LAN segment, or even the same server. This is one of the most common network problems on a large IPX network.

An up-to-date list of registered Novell SAP numbers can be found online at *http://www.isi.edu/in-notes/iana/assignments/novell-sap-numbers/*.

EIGRP

Cisco's EIGRP protocol is capable of supporting IPX, as well as IP (it also can distribute AppleTalk routing information). EIGRP distributes both route and service information. That is, it replaces both RIP and SAP. If a network uses EIGRP, it is important to disable IPX RIP and SAP on all router-to-router links.

However, on the router-to-server links, RIP and SAP must be enabled. Because RIP and EIGRP calculate metrics differently, routing tables can become terribly confused if both protocols are present between two adjacent routers. Always take care to disable or filter out the one that is not in use.

EIGRP can provide several important efficiencies over standard RIP and SAP. First, it supports a much larger network radius. A RIP network can have at most 15 hops between any two networks. This is for exactly the same reason that the IP RIP maximum size is 15 hops. The maximum size of an EIGRP network depends on the architecture. Usually one encounters problems due to too many devices before exhausting the theoretical maximum number of hops.

IPX EIGRP works essentially the same way as IP EIGRP. The main conceptual difference is that IPX EIGRP must carry SAP information, as well as routing information. Again, these updates are performed separately and can be filtered separately. Thus, the network actually still has the same potential problems with route and SAP information being inconsistent. This situation is almost impossible to avoid.

The chief advantage of using EIGRP over RIP and SAP is its bandwidth economy. EIGRP only distributes changes to its tables, rather than sending the entire table periodically. If there are no updates, then neighboring routers only exchange HELLO packets. Conversely, RIP and SAP must periodically distribute their entire tables to ensure consistency.

Another potential advantage of using EIGRP is the availability of equal-cost multipath routing. This routing represents a significant advantage in IP networks. However, I usually try to vary routing costs so that one path is absolutely preferred in IPX. This is because some IPX applications do a poor job of recovering when packets are delivered out of order.

In general, when one has equal-cost multipath routing, the routers distribute the packets among all possible paths. This means that two successive packets will take different paths through the network. It is possible that they will arrive in inverted order. For a well-behaved application this rarely presents a problem. But some IPX applications do not cope well with packet-sequence errors.

It should be noted that some IP applications also suffer from this malady, but the IP world has had equal-cost multipath routing for a long time. Consequently, natural selection has eliminated most of these unfit applications. However, in the IPX universe, equal-cost multipath routing has been introduced relatively recently. Therefore, many legacy IPX applications behave poorly in this environment.

NLSP

Novell also has created a more efficient routing protocol to overcome some deficiencies of RIP and SAP. This protocol, called Novell Link State Protocol (NLSP), is derived from the OSI Intermediate System to Intermediate System protocol (IS-IS). IS-IS is not discussed in this book, but NLSP shares many similarities with OSPF, so I discuss it by analogy with OSPF.

As a replacement for RIP, NLSP carries all of the routing information for an IPX network. As a replacement for SAP, it also carries service advertisements. However, NLSP does not completely replace RIP and SAP. End stations still require these protocols to find their servers.

The usual mode of operation for NLSP is to run RIP and SAP on the local segments. Then the servers on these local segments speak NLSP back to the router (or routers) that provide network connectivity to this segment. Router-to-router communication then uses NLSP for the main infrastructure of the network.

NLSP works best when all servers and routers in the IPX network use NLSP and only the end station–to–server communication uses RIP and SAP.

Like OSPF, NLSP is organized hierarchically into an Autonomous System (AS) that holds several areas. Each AS has an associated NLSP System ID number that is common throughout the network. Areas in NLSP serve the same functions as they do in OSPF. They allow network address summarization, which in turn results in efficient routing. They allow the Link State database to be broken up.

All routers and servers in any particular NLSP area share a common Link State database that is updated by flooding incremental changes, exactly as in OSPF. However, like OSPF, routers and servers in one area do not see the Link State information for routers and servers in a different area.

NLSP areas are defined according to the IPX summary addresses for the enclosed networks. To use NLSP effectively, it is important to use areas for exactly the same reasons as in OSPF. As in OSPF, effective summarization is important for areas to work properly. However, unlike OSPF, areas do not function at all if the enclosed networks cannot be summarized.

An NLSP area is specified by an IPX network and mask that together summarize all IPX network addresses in the area. For example, one could specify an area with the address 00258A00 and mask FFFFFF00. Then this area would include the networks 00258A00, 00258A01, and so forth up to 00258AFF.

As with IP address masks, you can use masks that break the range at any bit. So another valid area could be 030AC000 with a mask of FFFFE000. In this case, the range included in this area is 030AC000 to 030AC1FF. Writing these pairs out in binary, as in Table 7-1, helps to show how they work.

Table 7-1. IPX address mask pair examples

	Address / Mask			
Hx	00258A00 / FFFFFF00			
Binary network	00000000 (00)	00100101 (25)	10001010 (8A)	00000000 (00)
Binary mask	11111111 (FF)	11111111 (FF)	11111111 (FF)	00000000 (00)
Allowed range	00000000 (00) only	0010101 (25) only	10001010 (8A) only	00000000 to 11111111 (00) to (FF)
Hex	030AC000 / FFFFE000			
Binary network	00000011 (03)	00001010 (0A)	11000000 (C0)	00000000 (00)
Binary mask	11111111 (FF)	11111111 (FF)	11111110 (FE)	00000000 (00)
Allowed range	00000011 (03) only	00001010 (0A) only	11000000 and 11000001 (C0) and (C1)	00000000 to 11111111 (00) to (FF)

This summarization property of areas has important design implications. It means that designers must be extremely careful about how they allocate their IPX network numbers. Most IPX networks that were initially implemented with RIP never had any requirement for this sort of summarization. Consequently, for many organizations, the conversion from RIP and SAP to NLSP requires that all servers be readdressed.

The language of NLSP diverges somewhat from OSPF. NLSP defines three different levels of routing. Level 1 routing occurs within an area, Level 2 routing occurs between areas, and Level 3 routing occurs between ASes.

OSPF requires that an Area 0 must sit at the center of the AS. Then all other areas are connected to this area directly by means of Area Border Routers. NLSP does not have this restriction. It is possible to construct NLSP areas in somewhat arbitrary configurations, with Level 2 routing taking place between them. However, the OSPF architectural model is good and should be followed in NLSP as well.

It might seem tempting to designate the central area with a network number and mask pair of 00000000 and 00000000 by analogy with OSPF's Area 0. In this way, the central area would effectively include all possible IPX network numbers. But including these numbers is not a good idea because it implies that the central area actually encloses all other areas, which is not possible. The central area is just another area, similar to all of the others. It contains a group of routers and servers that communicate using Level 1 routing. It also communicates to the other areas using Level 2 routing. Thus, the central area must have a summary address of its own that is distinct from every other area.

Figure 7-1 shows how one might use NLSP to build a hierarchical network. Note that in this picture only one connection exists between each "leaf" area and the central area. This arrangement is only to make the picture easier to read. As with OSPF, these key links should always be made redundant. In fact, NLSP supports an equal-cost multipath mode just as OSPF does. The same basic design principles for redundancy apply to both.

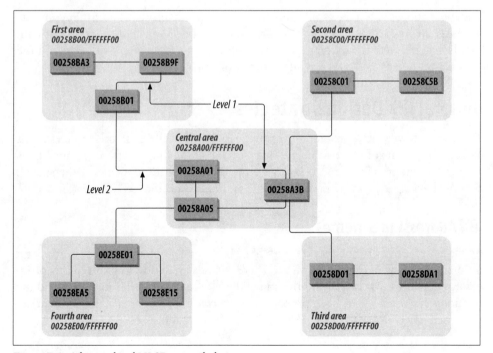

Figure 7-1. A hierarchical NLSP network design

In an IPX network of any size, it is important to limit the number of entries in the Service Advertisement table. This limitation is not merely for bandwidth reasons. Using NLSP or EIGRP makes it possible to drastically reduce the bandwidth taken to distribute this information.

The problem with a large IPX network is simply the size of the table. It is not uncommon for a large IPX network with hundreds of servers to have thousands or tens of thousands of advertised services. This is because every network-attached printer must send a SAP. Similarly, every Windows NT workstation running IPX sends out at least one SAP by default unless SAP is disabled, and every server generally runs several services besides simple file sharing, remote console, and directory services.

The table size for large networks adds up to a huge amount of information that must be distributed to every IPX router and server in the network. Each one of these devices is responsible for redistributing this information to every device downstream from it. In many cases, it represents more information than the routers can reliably handle. They start to run out of memory, and, worse, they start to run out of the CPU power required to process the data.

The vast majority of these advertised services originate with end devices such as workstations and printers. They are not required anywhere but in their originating segment. Thus, it is critically important for network stability that the routers must filter out all nonessential SAP information and prevent it from crossing the network.

The most appropriate place to do this filtering is usually on the router that connects the LAN Access segment to the network Distribution Level. Since a good network avoids using servers of any type as routers—preferring real routers—filtering on the servers isn't necessary. Rather, it all must be done on the routers.

General IPX Design Strategies

There are a few basic design strategies that can make an IPX network more efficient and reliable. Some of these strategies, like special addressing schemes, are analogous to good design principles that I have already discussed for IP networks. Others, such as those having to do with minimizing SAP traffic, are specific to IPX.

IPX Addressing Schemes

As discussed earlier in the section on NLSP, IPX route summarization can present a problem for many networks. However, there is a relatively tidy solution to this problem for networks that run IP and IPX in parallel. If the IP network runs OSPF and the IP addressing scheme has been properly constructed to allow area route summarization, then it is possible to derive IPX addresses from IP addresses.

You can derive these addresses easily. IP and IPX addresses contain the same number of bytes, and they both summarize from the left. Thus, you can do a decimal-to-hexadecimal conversion of the IP address to get the IPX network number.

For example, if the IP address of a file server is 10.1.21.15, then you can convert the four bytes to hexadecimal notation as 0A01150F. This is the address of the file server itself, so you can use this address for the IPX Internal Network Number. The External Network Number is effectively the address of the LAN segment.

In this case, the subnet's address is 10.1.21.0, so the IPX External Network Number would be 0A011500. If there was a second file server on this segment with an IP address of 10.1.21.16, then its IPX Internal Network Number would simply be 0A011510, and it would have the same External Network Number as the first server.

Now, if you have built your OSPF areas properly, you should be able to summarize all addresses inside of an area. If the area containing this example server's LAN is summarized as 10.1.0.0/16, then the NLSP area will become 0A010000 with a mask of FFFF0000. Everything maps perfectly between the two protocols if you choose to number your servers in this way.

If the IPX network does not use NLSP, then there are essentially no restrictions on how the IPX network numbers are allocated. In many networks, IPX network numbers are also randomly distributed throughout the network.

This random distribution is a poor strategy, however. It makes sense to use IPX network numbers that correspond to IP addresses for several reasons. First, most modern networks using IPX also use IP, so there is a natural convergence between the two. Second, if one day the network is converted to NLSP, there is no need to readdress every device. Third, if a simple rule gives the correlation between the IP and IPX addresses, then troubleshooting is much simpler.

This last point deserves extra comment. It is relatively common to build IPX networks that also run IP, so it is natural to bind the IP protocol to an interface on the server. When troubleshooting network problems, it is often useful to send test packets to see whether point A can reach server B.

However, IPX does not have a universally standard equivalent to the IP PING utility. IPX PING does exist, but there are several different standards, and they do not work together. Furthermore, for a server to respond to an IPX PING request, it must have the appropriate NetWare Loadable Module (NLM) loaded. Therefore, there are many reasons why an IPX PING test might not work, even though nothing is wrong with the network.

However, all IP devices should support ICMP ping (firewalls are a notable exception to this rule). If a network administrator is concerned about network connectivity between two segments, using an IP ping test can be useful, even though this is a different protocol. If an IP ping works, but there is no IPX connectivity, then the administrator can focus on IPX issues immediately. If neither work, then it is more likely that the problem is with physical connectivity.

Networks should always be designed as easy to manage, and troubleshooting is an important part of management. Anything you can do to make troubleshooting easier will give you a more reliable network in the long run.

RIP and SAP Accumulation Zones

In a large IPX network the routers are likely to have to employ significant amounts of route and SAP filtering. This filtering works in two directions. From the edges of the network into the Core, the network should prevent unnecessary SAP information from causing bandwidth or memory problems. From the Core out to the edges, it should distribute only the required routes and SAPs.

In most cases, it is not necessary for users in one department to see the local server for another department. They both may require access to a central server that handles global authentication, however.

To handle this situation, a designer can create a RIP and SAP Accumulation Zone somewhere in the Core of the network. An example of this configuration is shown in Figure 7-2. This figure shows four different user area groups. These groups may be NLSP areas, or there may be some other functional organization. Routers in each user area have redundant connections to a pair of Core routers. These connections provide extra fault tolerance.

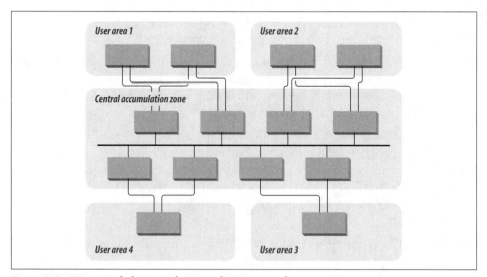

Figure 7-2. IPX network design with RIP and SAP accumulation zone

The user-area routers distribute RIP and SAP information inward to this redundant pair of routers. In the center of the picture is an Ethernet segment that I call the Accumulation Zone. Each router that is connected to this Accumulation Zone shares all of the RIP and SAP information that it receives with this segment. Note that this information need not be collected using either the RIP or SAP protocols. This model works equally well for any dynamic routing protocol.

Then RIP and SAP information is distributed back out to the user areas by the Accumulation Zone routers. Note that none of these routers actually needs to have the entire route or SAP tables. Rather, they can all just dump their tables onto this central segment for others to use as required. They can also take in only those routes and SAPs that they themselves require.

The advantage to this approach is that a central point in the network has all the RIP and SAP information that anybody could ever need. At the same time, though, keeping track of this information doesn't overwhelm any device.

Suppose there is a sudden requirement for a user in one user area to have access to a particular server in another area. Then you can simply allow its Accumulation Zone routers to receive and distribute this information to that user's own server. This provides maximum flexibility to managing the IPX network. At the same time, it avoids the most serious problems with having to support a large route or SAP table.

Efficiency in IPX Networks

I conclude this section with a brief discussion of other basic things you can do to improve efficiency in an IPX network.

I already mentioned the need to keep the number of SAPs to a bare minimum. This information can be gathered in an Accumulation Zone, as mentioned earlier. However, in a large IPX network, it can easily overwhelm the memory and bandwidth resources of the network devices to maintain all of it. Thus, the first thing to do is to create a thorough list of filters to restrict what routes and services are advertised.

Another aspect of the same issue is limiting the amount of server-to-server traffic. Usually this sort of traffic is not necessary. You often need to allow communication between user-area servers and central servers. However, you should try to keep this traffic flow in a star format as much as possible.

Finally, in any large IPX network, it is critical to avoid using RIP and SAP protocols. These protocols work well in small- to medium-sized networks. But remember that routers and servers must all take part in the routing protocols. Suppose, for example, that two servers communicate via RIP, but are separated by three routers. Then the internal network numbers of these servers are, in fact, five hops apart, so an IPX network is usually somewhat larger than it appears on the surface.

In even a moderate-sized network, it is not difficult to find distances that are greater than 15 hops, which is too large for RIP to handle. As I already mentioned, RIP and SAP scale rather poorly for bandwidth usage. It is a good idea to try to move away from these protocols in any large-scale IPX network.

It is possible to make an IPX network appear smaller than it is, however, by tunneling the IPX traffic inside of IP. For example, suppose that getting from a user-area router to the central Accumulation Zone requires several router-to-router hops. You can make it require a single hop by configuring an IPX tunnel between the Accumulation Zone router and the last user-area router before the server.

Even in this case, however, you should avoid using RIP and SAP. Although this design avoids the hop-count problem, you still have to be concerned about the bandwidth-usage problem with these protocols.

CHAPTER 8

Elements of Efficiency

Efficiency is a nebulous term. In general, it measures how thoroughly one manages to achieve some desired result as a function of the required resources. The biggest problems in implementing efficiency in a computer network are essentially matters of definition. What is the desired result for a network, and what resources are actually required?

With a relatively narrow view of the desired results in network design, it essentially comes down to the factors that I mentioned earlier when talking about network reliability. The network must deliver data to the destination. It must do so within the required application constraints. In most networks, the desired result is effectively quantified with just four parameters: latency, jitter, throughput, and dropped packets. I will define these terms when I come to talk about Quality of Service later in this chapter.

The hard part of describing efficiency is actually in defining the resources. Which resources should the definition include? Some resources are obvious. Everybody would agree that it's necessary to worry about CPU and memory utilization in their routers. The same is true for the bandwidth utilization on the various links that connect network devices. But some resources are harder to quantify or harder to see. How do you compare the relative importance of these resources? Do you want to save bandwidth, for example, at the expense of CPU load?

The ultimate resource for any organization comes down to money, and efficiency has to be defined for the entire organization. Suppose, for example, that you can save money by running a particular application on a particular type of server. The money you save has to be balanced against the extra money it costs to upgrade parts of the network. Perhaps the new implementation will turn out to be more expensive overall than the old way. But perhaps it will also allow the organization to win new business that will more than pay for the difference in cost. Doing such an upgrade is worthwhile for the organization. You just have to understand where you are drawing the line around what resources to include. Conversely, the network engineer may look at a Core router and see abnormally high CPU and memory utilization. If fixing this problem means spending hundreds of thousands of dollars, the organization may not feel that the expense is justified.

Ultimately, efficiency is a matter of the global economics of the organization. This subject, however, is far beyond the scope of this book. The resources that I can reasonably talk about here are the ones that are specific to the network. I can discuss how to make the best use of the resources already in the network, so I look at the four parameters—latency, jitter, throughput, and dropped packets—that describe how well the network works. I also look at network resources such as bandwidth, CPU, and memory utilization. It is never possible to obtain perfect efficiency, though. Therefore, a network designer's most difficult job is to decide what tradeoffs will give the best design possible under the circumstances and will fit in best with larger corporate goals.

Using Equipment Features Effectively

There are usually several ways to configure any given piece of network equipment to achieve the same basic result. These different configurations usually do not use resources in the same way, and they often do not have exactly the same performance characteristics. For example, an inefficient configuration of a router might mean that it has to do too much processing on each packet. This extra processing increases the amount of time that each packet spends inside the router and probably also increases the memory utilization of the router, as it has to buffer large numbers of packets.

A typical example of this increase happens when an engineer fails to use special features of the equipment. For example, in many routers the ability to make most common routing decisions is delegated to logic circuits supporting the interface card. This approach works well because it means that the CPU is free to coordinate the activities of the different cards. The result is vastly improved net throughput; however, the advantage can be completely lost if this engineer implements a CPU-bound process that examines the contents of every packet.

For example, the engineer might turn on a feature that prioritizes or routes packets based on their contents. This sort of feature usually requires the CPU to examine the packet. So the packet cannot be processed solely by the interface. The same CPU loading happens if the router is configured to rewrite the contents of the packets, as in an address-translation feature systematically.

This has several implications for network design. Locally, it is important to ensure that each device does only what it needs to do and that it does so by the most efficient method. Globally, it means that network designers have to be careful about what network functions are performed where.

The local issue is really a matter for the network engineer who should sit down with the manuals for the network hardware and find the most efficient way to implement the functions of this device. If special optimizations are available, such as Cisco's

Fast Switching, then they should be used. Discussing the implementation details with the hardware vendor may also help, since the vendor should be aware of the features of the equipment.

The global issue, however, is for the network designer to resolve. A good example of this resolution comes up in prioritization and Quality of Service (QoS) implementation. The best place to decide on the priority of a packet is at the point where that packet enters the network. The entry-point router should examine the packet and mark its header with the appropriate priority value. Then, each subsequent device that handles the packet reads this priority value and treats the packet appropriately. The worst thing a designer can do is make every router look at the packet in detail and decide again what its priority should be.

Looking at a single byte in the header is easy for a router and can frequently be handled in highly optimized code in the hardware. However, looking at several bytes and making a decision about each packet takes a huge amount of extra resources. In most cases, it also increases the forwarding latency and reduces the number of packets that the router can handle.

Hop Counts

Efficiency means using the smallest amount of resources to accomplish the desired result. All other things being equal, heavily used network paths should have as few hops as possible.

Efficiency is actually a natural outcome of using a hierarchical network design. Building a network in a tree-like structure so that every leaf is no more than three hops away from the central Core of the network means that the greatest distance between any two leaves is six hops. Conversely, if the network has a relatively ad hoc structure, then the only effective upper limit to the number of hops between any two end points is the number of devices in the network.

Keeping hops counts low has several advantages. First, all routing protocols that were discussed in Chapters 6 and 7 (for IP and IPX, respectively) converge faster for lower hop counts. This convergence generally results in a more stable network. More specifically, it means that the network recovers more quickly after a failure. If a path is available to route traffic around the failure point, it can be found quickly and put into use.

Other advantages all have to do with the delivery of packets through the network. Every extra hop represents at least one additional queue and at least one additional link. Each additional queue introduces a random amount of latency. If the queue is relatively full, then the packet may spend extra time waiting to be processed. If the queue is realtively short, on the other hand, it may be processed immediately. If the network is extremely busy, the packet may be dropped rather than being kept until its data is no longer relevant.

This queuing delay means that every additional hop increases the net latency of the path. Latency is something that should be kept as low as possible in any network. Because this extra latency is random, the more hops that exist, the more variation there is in the latency.

This variation in latency is called *jitter*. Jitter is not a problem for bulk data transfers. But in any real-time applications such as audio or video, it is disastrous. These applications require that the time to deliver a packet from one point to another be as predictable as possible, or the resulting application will suffer from noticeable gaps. These gaps will appear as audible pops or skips and frozen or jumping video images.

Finally, there is the problem of what happens to a packet that passes through a highly congested device in the network. The device can do two things with a new packet entering its buffers. It can either put it into a queue to be forwarded at some future time, or it can decide that the queues are already too full and simply drop the packet. Clearly, the more hops in the path, the greater the probability of hitting one that is highly congested. Thus, a higher hop count means a greater chance of dropped packets.

This rule is true even if the network is rarely congested. A relatively short, random burst of data can temporarily exhaust the queues on a device at any time. Furthermore, the more hops there are in the path, the greater the probability of hitting a link that generates CRC errors. In most LAN media, the probability of CRC errors is relatively low, but this low probability is multiplied by the number of links in the path. Thus, the more hops there are the higher the probability that the packet will become corrupted and have to be dropped.

MTU Throughout the Network

The size of the largest data packet that can pass along any particular section of network is called the Maximum Transmission Unit (MTU). Suppose, for example, that a network contains both Ethernet and Token Ring segments. The default MTU for Ethernet is 1,500 bytes. For a 16Mbps Token Ring, the maximum MTU is 18,200 bytes. If a packet travels from one of these media to the other, the network will have to find a compromise.

There are two main ways to resolve MTU mismatch problems. The network can either fragment the large packets, or it can force everything to use the smaller value. In most cases, the network will fragment packets if it can and negotiate the greatest common MTU value only if it is not allowed to fragment. The efficiency issue is that both fragmentation and MTU negotiation consume network resources. However, fragmentation has to be done with every oversized packet, and MTU negotiation is done primarily during session establishment. MTU negotiation also happens if the path changes and the new path contains a leg with a lower MTU value.

In TCP sessions, the Path MTU Discovery process starts when a packet that has the Don't Fragment (DF) bit in the IP header set is sent. This bit literally instructs the network not to fragment the packet. Fragmentation is the default. Suppose a TCP packet passes through a network and it gets to a router that needs to break that packet to send it to the next hop on its path. If the DF bit in the IP header is not set, then the router simply breaks the packet into as many pieces as necessary and sends it along. When the fragments reach the ultimate destination, they are reassembled.

If the DF bit is set, then the router drops the packet and sends back a special ICMP packet explaining the situation. This packet tells the sender that the packet has been dropped because it could not be fragmented. It also tells the sender the largest packet it could have sent. Doing so allows the sender to shorten all future packets to this Path MTU value.

Note that it is more efficient in general to reassemble at the ultimate destination rather than at the other end of the link with a lower MTU. This is because it is possible that the packet will encounter another low MTU segment later in the path. Since there is significant overhead in both fragmentation and reassembly, if the network has to do it, it should do it only once.

Many protocols do not have a Path MTU Discovery mechanism. In particular, it is not possible to negotiate an end-to-end MTU for a UDP application. Thus, whenever a large UDP packet is sent through a network segment with a lower MTU value, it must be fragmented. Then the receiver has to carefully buffer and reassemble the pieces. However, most UDP applications deliberately keep their packets small to avoid fragmentation.

If the network is noisy or congested, it is possible to lose some fragments. This loss results in two efficiency problems. First, the device that reassembles the packet from the fragments must buffer the fragments and hold them in its memory until it decides it can no longer wait for the missing pieces. This is not only a resource issue on the device, but it also results in serious latency and jitter problems. The second problem can actually be more serious. If any fragment is lost, then the entire packet must be resent, including the fragments that were received properly. Data lost due to congestion problems will make the problem considerably worse.

Obviously, it is better if the network doesn't have to fragment packets. Thus, in a multiprotocol network it is often better to configure a common MTU manually throughout all end-device segments.

This configuration is not always practical for Token Ring segments that run IBM protocols. Suppose a tunneling protocol such as Data Link Switching (DLSw) connects two Token Ring segments through an Ethernet infrastructure. Generally, it is most efficient to use the greatest MTU possible. In this case, however, there is an important advantage. The DLSw protocol is TCP based and operates as a tunnel between two routers. These routers can discover a smaller Path MTU between them.

They can then simply hide the fragmentation and reassemble from the end devices. They will appear to pass full-sized Token Ring frames.

Even here, the routers suffer from additional memory utilization, and there will be latency and jitter issues on the end-to-end session. If at all possible, it is better to reduce the Token Ring MTU to match the lower Ethernet value.

Bottlenecks and Congestion

Avoiding bottlenecks in any large network is impossible, and it isn't always necessary or desirable to do so. One of the main efficiencies of scale in a large network is the ability to oversubscribe the Core links. Oversubscribing means that most designers deliberately aggregate more network segments than the network can support simultaneously. Then they hope that these segments don't all burst to their full capacity at once. This issue was discussed in Chapter 3 in the section, "Trunk capacity."

Just oversubscribing is not a problem. The network has a problem only when it cannot support the actual traffic flow. This is called congestion, and it results in increased latency and jitter if the application is lucky enough that the network can queue the packets. If it is not so lucky, the network has to drop packets.

A little bit of congestion is not a bad thing, provided it is handled gracefully. However, systematic congestion in which one or more network links cannot support typical traffic volumes is a serious issue. The network can handle intermittent congestion using the various QoS mechanisms discussed later in this chapter. For systematic congestion, however, the designer usually has to modify the network design to reduce the bottleneck.

By intermittent congestion, I mean congestion that never lasts very long. It is not uncommon for a link to fill up with traffic for short periods of time. This is particularly true when bursty applications use the network.

QoS mechanisms can readily handle short bursts of traffic. They can even handle longer periods of congestion when it is caused by low-priority applications such as file transfers. However, when a high volume of interactive traffic causes the congestion, it is usually considered a systematic problem. In general, QoS mechanisms are less expensive to implement than a redesign of the network, so it is usually best to try it first.

Another common method for handling intermittent congestion is using a Random Early Detection (RED) system on the router with the bottleneck. The RED algorithm deliberately drops some packets before the link is 100% congested. When the load rises above a certain predetermined threshold, the router begins to drop a few packets randomly in an attempt to coax the applications into backing off slightly. In this way, RED tries to avoid congestion before it becomes critical.

However, it is important to be careful about RED because not all applications and protocols respond well to it. It works very well in TCP applications, but in UDP applications, as well as Appletalk and IPX, RED does not achieve the desired results. These protocols cannot back off their sending rates in response to dropped packets.

There are essentially two different ways to handle a systematic and persistent congestion problem at a network bottleneck. You can either increase the bandwidth at the bottleneck point, or you can reroute the traffic so it doesn't all go through the same point.

Sometimes you can get a bottleneck because some redundant paths in a network are unused, forcing all of the traffic through a few congested links. Examining the link costs in the dynamic routing protocol can often provide a way to alleviate this problem.

In many protocols, such as OSPF, it is possible to specify the same cost for several different paths. This specification invokes equal-cost multipath routing. In some cases you may find that, despite equal costs, some of these paths are not used. This may be because the routers are configured to use only a small number (usually two) of these equal-cost paths simultaneously. Many routers offer the ability to increase this number. However, it is important to watch the router CPU and memory load if the number is increased because maintaining the additional paths may cause an additional strain on the device.

Ultimately, if a subtle rerouting cannot alleviate the bottleneck, it will be necessary to increase the bandwidth on the congested links. Doing so is not always easy. If the link is already the fastest available technology in this type, then you have to do something else.

Other options are usually available to you in these situations. You might migrate to a different high-speed link technology, such as ATM or 10 Gigabit Ethernet. Or, you may have the ability to *multiplex* several fast links together to make one super high-speed link. If even this is not possible, then it is probably best to start configuring new redundant paths through the network to share the load.

Filtering

One of the most important things a designer can do to improve how efficiently a network uses resources is to filter out ill-behaved or unwanted traffic. This is particularly true for chatty protocols that tend to transmit data that is not necessary. A good example of filtering for efficiency comes from IPX networking. In an IPX network, every device that has any sort of service to offer sends out Service Advertisement Packets (SAP). This information then circulates not just over the local segment, but throughout the entire network. Although unnecessary SAP information may not have a significant effect on the bandwidth used in the network, it can have a large impact on the amount of memory that Core routers need to keep track of this information. Specifically, every printer sends at least one SAP; so does every Windows NT workstation.

In a large network, it is difficult enough to ensure that the SAP information regarding important servers is distributed correctly. If there are unneeded SAPs for every printer and workstation, then the amount of required memory can easily exceed the available resources. So this is a good example of the need for filtering. The first router that sees the unwanted SAP information simply discards it without passing it along. The information stays local to the LAN segment where it is used and does not use up key network resources.

Filtering can also restrict malicious, unwanted traffic. For example, some popular Internet-based attacks use certain types of ICMP or packets used in setting up TCP calls. If these packets are not eliminated, they may cause serious network problems. Thus, these specific types of packets can be filtered at the network boundaries.

I want to stress once again that connecting to an untrusted external network without a firewall is foolish. However, in some organizations, these same sorts of problems can arise either because of malicious employees or because of innocently executed malicious programs. In these cases, it may become necessary to filter the unwanted traffic at the user LAN segment level, just as I suggested eliminating unwanted IPX SAP information.

In many networks chatty little unnecessary applications (and network games!) can be easily filtered and prevented from crossing the network. The key is to remove the unwanted traffic as soon as possible. This usually means that the filtering should be applied at the edges of the network. If the network adjoins another network, then the border routers should perform this filtering before the unwanted traffic enters the network. Similarly, if the filtering is to restrict traffic from user LAN segments, then the best place to run the filter is on the default gateway routers for these segments.

Quality of Service and Traffic Shaping

As I mentioned before, four measurable parameters define how well a network performs: latency, jitter, bandwidth, and dropped packets.

Bandwidth is a term borrowed from transmission theory. If a signal has only one frequency that is broadcast perpetually, then it doesn't contain any information. If that carrier signal is modulated, then you can use it to carry a data signal. As soon as you do this, you introduce some fluctuation into the frequency of the carrier signal. Sometimes the carrier wave pulse comes a little bit earlier because of the modulation, and sometimes it comes a little late. If you draw a graph of the frequency, sometimes it's a little lower than the carrier, and sometimes it's a little higher. However, the average is equal to the carrier wave's frequency.

The width of this frequency curve is called the bandwidth, and it is a measure of how much information the signal carries. The width in frequencies is going to be a frequency itself, and frequencies are measured in Hz (cycles/s). If you can put one bit in a cycle of the wave, then it is exactly the same as bits per second. That's how the term originates. However, modern communications protocols use sophisticated compression and include extra overhead for error checking and so forth. Thus, using the term "bandwidth" to describe the throughput on a link is no longer accurate. The meanings of words migrate over time, and today people generally use the word bandwidth to mean the amount of data that a medium can transmit per unit time.

In any given network, several applications compete for the same bandwidth resources. Each application has a bandwidth requirement—a certain minimum amount of data that it has to send and receive. The network designer must balance these various requirements and find a way for the applications to all work well together. There are two ways to do this. You can either carve off a certain dedicated amount of bandwidth for each application, or you can make them share the total fairly. There are pros and cons to both approaches, as I describe next.

Latency is the amount of time it takes to get from one point in the network to another. Obviously, latency varies depending on the two points, how far apart they are, how many hops are between them, and the nature of the media. Three main factors affect latency: bandwidth, physical distance, and queuing time.

Bandwidth affects latency in a simple way. If the link can support a certain number of bits per second, then that is how many bits a device can inject per second into the link medium. It takes 10 times as long to inject a packet onto a 10Mbps Ethernet as it does onto a 100Mbps Fast Ethernet segment. There are exceptions to this rule for media that support carrying several bits at once in parallel. But parallel media are fairly uncommon.

Physical distance also affects latency in a simple way. The further the packet has to fly, the longer it takes. This time of flight component to latency is most relevant over WAN links, since it is governed by the speed of light in the transmission medium. The speed of light in fiber optic cable is governed by the refractive index of the medium. For glass, this index is about 1.5, so the speed of light in optical fiber is about 2/3 of its value in vacuum. In wire, the speed is somewhat slower than this, although the actual speed varies depending on the kind of cable. This effect may sound small, and usually it is for LAN- and campus-sized networks, but for WAN links it can be a large part of the total latency. The distance from New York to Los Angeles is about 4000 km. So the one-way time of flight for a signal through optical fiber is about 20 milliseconds. Signals sent around the world suffer significantly larger time-of-flight delays. Finally, queuing time introduces an additional random component to network latency, as I discussed earlier in the section "Hop Counts."

Jitter is the packet-by-packet variation in latency. Of the three components to latency that I just mentioned, only the queuing time is subject to change. So this is the main factor in causing jitter. If the latency is changing very gradually, then it will not generally cause serious application problems. The most noticeable jitter issues happen when the latency of one packet is significantly different from the latency of the next packet following it in the same data stream. This is what causes skips, pops, and frozen frames in audio and video applications. So jitter is defined as the difference in latency between any two successive packets, as opposed to a general difference or standard deviation from the mean latency.

As I mentioned, the main cause of jitter is queuing. So devices need to be careful with how they handle queuing of data streams for jitter-sensitive applications. Basically, they should queue the packets as little as possible in these sensitive data streams.

Normally routers set up their queues so that whenever one of these jitter-sensitive packets arrives, it simply sends it to the front. Equivalently, they can give this application its own queue to ensure that other applications do not interfere. As long as the application doesn't send a sudden burst of packets to cause congestion within its own flow, the jitter should be minimal.

The final performance parameter is the number of *dropped packets*. Obviously the goal is to drop as few packets as possible. But there are times when the amount of data transmitted through the network is simply greater than what it can carry. Devices can only buffer for so long before they have to start throwing some data away.

Systematically dropping excess packets is also called *policing*. It is important that it be done fairly. Low-priority data should be dropped before high priority. But some high-priority data is extremely sensitive to jitter. In these cases, it may be better to drop the packet than to hold it in a buffer until it can be transmitted. Controlling how and when devices decide to drop packets is critical to maintaining any QoS criteria on a network.

QoS Basics

QoS implementations come in three functional flavors. Any real network implementing a QoS system generally uses more than one of these.

The first option is that the network can do nothing to discriminate between different applications. This is called Best Efforts Delivery. The second functional flavor is called Preferential Delivery. In this case, network devices define certain applications as more important than others and give them precedence whenever they encounter congestion. The final option, called Guaranteed Delivery, allows the network to reserve a guaranteed minimum bandwidth through the network for each important application.

In Best Efforts Service, packets are transmitted through the network if there is sufficient capacity. If congestion occurs along the path, then the packet may be dropped.

Note that Best Efforts is not necessarily the same thing as First In First Out (FIFO). FIFO is a queuing strategy in which the router deals with packets in the order in which they are received. There are several other possible queuing (sometimes called *scheduling*) algorithms. For example, many routers use Fair Queuing or Weighted Fair Queuing algorithms instead of FIFO.

Preferential Delivery requires the network engineer to make certain decisions about which applications are more important than others. For example, an FTP file transfer might be considered low priority, since it is effectively a batch-mode bulk transfer. An interactive business-critical application, on the other hand, would have a high priority.

Generically, Preferential Delivery means that if a device is dropping packets, it will drop low priority first. If it delivers packets, it delivers the high priority first. As I describe later in this chapter, the delivery priority could be different from the drop precedence.

Preferential Delivery does not mean that devices have to use any particular queuing strategy. Standard FIFO queuing is probably not going to provide a terribly effective way of implementing Preferential Delivery, but Weighted Fair Queuing is certainly a reasonable option. However, one can also implement a Preferential Delivery mechanism simply by sorting the various priority data streams into their own FIFO queues.

The Guaranteed Delivery service model means that each application is allocated a certain minimum amount of bandwidth through the network. There are different ways of implementing this bandwidth guarantee.

In some cases, the different applications have different reserved bandwidths through certain links. Whether an application uses its reserved minimum or not, that bandwidth is set aside for it. In other implementations, the specific applications have reserved bandwidths, but if they do not use it, other applications can borrow from the unused pool.

Some implementations allow each application a certain minimum bandwidth plus an option to burst above it if there is excess capacity. In this case, it is common to specify that packets sent using this burst capacity can be dropped if they encounter congestion.

One particularly interesting implementation of Guaranteed Delivery is the so-called Virtual Leased Line (VLL). In this case, the application is guaranteed a minimum and a maximum bandwidth with no congestion, no dropping, and minimal jitter. VLL is often implemented in conjunction with a tunnel, making the VLL look like a realistic dedicated link to the routers.

In general, Guaranteed Delivery allows the designer to specify not only bandwidth but also latency and jitter limitations. This specification is necessary for real-time interactive applications such as voice and video. In these applications, the data stream is usually almost constant, and jitter is intolerable.

The queuing mechanisms required to accomplish this are naturally more complex than the algorithms that I have discussed so far. They all involve setting up different queues for the different data streams and then servicing these queues appropriately. To minimize jitter, each queue has to be serviced on a timer instead of whenever the router gets around to it.

Layer 2 and Layer 3 QoS

So far, everything I discussed has left the actual implementation fairly generic. In principle, you can implement the QoS functionality at either Layer 2 or Layer 3.

The advantage to Layer 3 is, of course, that you can set a priority parameter in the Layer 3 packet header and have it visible at every hop through the network. This results in a good end-to-end QoS implementation and allows you to ensure consistent application behavior throughout the network.

Setting a parameter at Layer 3 tells the network very little about how it should actually handle this packet as it is routed from one media type to another.

There are also Layer 2 QoS features. Token Ring has the ability to send high-priority frames preferentially to lower priority frames. ATM has extremely sophisticated QoS functionality that allows you to specify sustained and burst rates directly, for example. Ethernet, on the other hand, has no native QoS functionality. However, Ethernet VLAN tags can specify a Class of Service value to affect how the frames in trunks are handled at each subsequent switch.

Over network regions that involve hopping from one segment to another via Layer 2 switches, you need a Layer 2 QoS implementation. This implementation allows you to specify how the switches handle the frames.

Meanwhile, a network needs Layer 3 QoS to allow consistent handling of packets as they pass through routers. Ideally, the Layer 3 information should be used to generate Layer 2 QoS behavior.

When a router receives a packet that has a high Layer 3–priority indication, it should use this information at Layer 2 in two ways. First, it should copy this information appropriately into the Layer 2 header so other Layer 2 devices can handle the packet properly. Second, it should select the appropriate Layer 2 QoS functionality when delivering the packet.

Buffering and Queuing

When a router receives a packet to pass along from one network to another, it often cannot transmit immediately. The medium may be in a busy state. For example, it could be an Ethernet segment on which another device is already talking. Or, the outbound port may already be busy sending another packet.

When a packet cannot be forwarded because of a temporary situation like this, it is usually best if the router holds onto it for a short time until it can send it along. This is called buffering. The packet is copied into the router's memory and placed in a queue to be transmitted as soon as possible.

There are several different kinds of queues. The simplest, which I have already mentioned earlier in this chapter, is a FIFO queue. A router using FIFO queuing simply puts all of the packets for a particular outbound physical interface in one place and sends them in the order they were received. FIFO queues are conceptually simple and may seem to treat all applications fairly, but in fact there are serious problems with FIFO queues when the network becomes busy.

Many bulk file-transfer applications, such as FTP or HTTP, have the property of sending data as fast as the network can accept it. When this data hits a bottleneck or congestion point in the network, it fills up the router's input queue until the router has to start dropping packets. Then the application backs off until it matches the available capacity of the network. Unfortunately, if other less-aggressive applications try to use the same network, their packets are also dropped when the queue fills up. Thus, FIFO queuing tends to favor the aggressive applications.

The worst part is that these aggressive applications are relatively time insensitive. The low-rate data flows that are choked off are often used for interactive real-time applications. Thus, FIFO queuing has the worst possible behavior in this situation. To get around this problem, other more sophisticated queuing algorithms have been developed. One of the most popular algorithms is called Fair Queuing.

In Fair Queuing, the router breaks up the incoming stream of packets into separate conversations and queues these conversations separately. Then the router takes packets from each queue in a simple rotation. It can take either a single packet at a time from each queue or, alternatively, a group of packets up to a certain predefined number of bytes.

Weighted Fair Queuing is a slight modification to this algorithm. Instead of picking equally (by number of packets or bytes) from each queue, the router assigns a *weight* to each queue. This weight can be based on any of a large number of different parameters such as the rate at which packets are received into the queue or the sizes of the packets. It can also be associated with formal priority markings such as IP Precedence or DSCP. In this way, Weighted Fair Queuing actually spans the gap between Best Efforts and Preferential Delivery service modes.

By breaking up the incoming stream of packets into individual conversations, Fair Queuing algorithms ensure that no one application can take all of the available bandwidth.

Returning to the FTP file transfer example with Fair Queuing, the packets in this file transfer go into their own queue. If that queue fills up, then the router drops only FTP packets, but the other traffic streams are unaffected. When the FTP application notices that packets have been dropped, it slows down the rate that it sends data. In this way, Fair Queuing and Weighted Fair Queuing prevent any one data stream (usually called a flow) from taking over the network.

Another Queuing option commonly used with Preferential Delivery is called Priority Queuing. This term means that each incoming packet is categorized by some rule and put into a queue. There will usually be a small number, perhaps as many as five of these queues, ranging in priority from high to low. The router services these different queues, taking packets preferentially from the high-priority queues.

This servicing is typically done by specifying a maximum number of bytes or packets to take in each pass from each queue, with the highest priority receiving the best service. In the most extreme version, the first priority queue is emptied before the second priority queue is considered. However, this process is usually just a recipe for ensuring that low priority traffic is not delivered at all.

You should be aware of three main problems with any Priority Queuing model. First, because every packet must be examined to determine its priority, high CPU loads on routers can occur. Care must be taken in limiting which routers need to do this examination and in making the test as simple as possible. Preferably, it should be based on just the IP TOS or DSCP field, which is described later in this chapter.

The second problem is that a straight-priority queue model allows different traffic flows within each priority grouping to interfere with one another. Effectively, each individual queue is a FIFO queue. Thus, it is important to understand how the application traffic flows work before selecting an implementation. If there is potential for one conversation within an application group to choke off the others in that group, then Priority Queuing is not appropriate.

The third problem happens when devices have too many different priorities. Each packet must be examined and compared to some criteria to find the appropriate priority. If there are many different priorities, then there are many different tests to perform on each packet, which results in high router CPU load during peak traffic periods.

Also, using too many different priorities may divide the available bandwidth into too many pieces. This division then leaves each queue with a tiny amount of useful bandwidth, so it is always congested.

Suppose, for example, that a network has to support one extremely important application and eight less-important applications, all of which compete for a small amount of bandwidth. Each time the router services the high-priority queue, it grabs two packets. It then delivers one packet from each of the eight low-priority queues. In this example, the router winds up delivering four lower-priority packets for every high-priority packet. This situation clearly becomes worse the more queues each device has.

Furthermore, the more different queues the router has to service, the longer it takes to get back to the high-priority queue. This delay results in serious jitter problems, since there is a large random element in how long it will take to deliver any given packet. Thus, it is crucial to keep the number of different priorities as small as possible.

Integrated and Differentiated Services

The Internet Engineering Task Force (IETF) has specified two different standards for IP QoS. These standards are called Integrated Services (intserv) and Differentiated Services (diffserv).

The basic idea of intserv (also called IS in some documents) is to allow applications to request resources such as bandwidth or latency characteristics from the network. The network then keeps track of this individual conversation and ensures that it always has the reserved resources.

Although it is not required, the most common way to implement this resource request uses ReSerVation Protocol (RSVP). The end stations taking part in the user application use RSVP to request a specific performance characteristic from the network. RSVP is discussed later in this chapter.

The network then maintains state information about the individual conversations (called flows). This maintenance has an enormous overhead in a large network with thousands of simultaneous conversations. Therefore, it is not usually practical in the Core of a large network.

Integrated Services attempts to get around this scaling problem by allowing the network to aggregate the flows. In a complex network, allowing any-to-any communication, this aggregation poses further problems if it is done dynamically. In a hierarchical network, it should be possible to aggregate flows successfully at least on the in-bound direction to the Core of the network.

Differentiated Services takes a simpler approach to the same problem. By taking over the seldom-used TOS byte in the header of the IP packet, it defines an end-to-end priority. This priority value, called the Differentiated Services Control Point (DSCP), specifies how each router along the path will treat the packet.

Each router along the path reads this DSCP value. This step is easy for the routers because the information is stored in a single byte in the IP header. The DSCP value tells each router how to forward the packet, specifying a Per-Hop Behavior (PHB). There are standard PHB profiles that the router can follow. But the network engineer can configure the routers manually to interpret specific DSCP values differently.

Two standard flavors of PHB have been defined for Differentiated Services. These flavors are called Expedited Forwarding and Assured Forwarding, although the names are somewhat misleading. Assured Forwarding (AF) does not imply guaranteed delivery as the name might suggest, but expedient delivery according to priority levels. Conversely, Expedited Forwarding (EF) is not merely expedient, as it does provide service assurances.

There are three main differences between the Integrated and Differentiated Services models for QoS:

- Integrated Services must maintain state information about individual traffic flows. Conversely, Differentiated Services combines all traffic of a particular type, which results in much better scaling properties for Differentiated Services in large networks.

- To set up a nondefault forwarding behavior, Integrated Services uses an external protocol such as RSVP reserve network resources. This is done on a per-conversation basis. It also works well with multicast data streams. Differentiated Services allows the end stations to define the way each individual packet is handled. This definition is done by setting the DSCP byte in the IP header of each packet. The network can optionally change this value if it is not appropriate.

- Because Differentiated Services defines the handling properties of each packet by referring to the DSCP byte in the header, it can handle path failure and path redundancy situations transparently. Integrated Services, on the other hand, needs the robust path-tracking features of RSVP to cope well with multiple paths or with changes in path routing through the network. Even with these capabilities, however, there is a significant probability of losing reserved resources when the path changes.

Assured Forwarding in Differentiated Services

The Assured Forwarding standard for Per-Hop Behavior Differentiated Services is defined in RFC 2597. In AF, two basic properties define how each packet will be forwarded. The standard defines four Classes and three different values for Drop Precedence.

The Class value is essentially a forwarding priority. Packets with the same Class value are all queued together. The standard requires that the packets of individual conversations be forwarded in the same order that they are received, as long as they are all of the same Class.

The most common way to implement AF is to give a separate queue to each Class. This allows the network to ensure that flows from different Classes do not interfere with one another. It also permits higher-priority Classes to receive more bandwidth from the network by increasing the amount of data taken from the more important queues each time the router takes packets from them.

In addition to the four Classes, AF defines three different types of Drop Precedence. This number simply tells the router which packets to drop first in case of congestion. When the Class queue fills up and the router needs to start dropping packets, the ones with lower Drop Precedence values are protected. The router should scan through the queue and drop the packets with the highest Drop Precedence values first. If dropping the packets does not alleviate the congestion problem, then the router should drop all of the next-highest Drop Precedence packets before dropping the ones with the lowest Drop Precedence values.

In this way, AF can give important data streams better treatment as they pass through the network. Note, however, that AF does not necessarily guarantee a particular fraction of the total bandwidth for any one Class. It also doesn't give guaranteed end-to-end performance characteristics for specific data flows. Furthermore, it does not have the ability to give direct control over parameters such as jitter or bandwidth. It is merely a method for providing Preferential Delivery.

Expedited Forwarding in Differentiated Services

The Expedited Forwarding standard for PHB Differentiated Services is defined in RFC 2598. The basic goal of EF is to provide guaranteed service characteristics such as bandwidth, latency, and jitter.

One type of proposed EF implementation is the Virtual Leased Line (VLL). This implementation is essentially a reserved chunk of bandwidth through a network coupled with a queuing mechanism that restricts jitter. As with a real leased line, however, a VLL cannot handle any traffic in excess of its bandwidth limits. If an application tries to send packets too quickly, they will be dropped. Thus, EF is usually used in conjunction with some sort of Traffic Shaping.

IP TOS and Diffserv DSCP

The IP standards foresaw the need for specifying Quality of Service as long ago as 1981 in RFC 791. This document defines the current standard IP (IPv4) packet format and includes a byte called Type of Service (TOS). As QoS requirements and technology grew more sophisticated, this field has been replaced by the Distributed Services Control Point (DSCP), which includes significant backward compatibility with the older standard.

The TOS or DSCP value is typically set by the end devices. If an application knows that it needs special priority through the network, then it is able to set the appropriate value in each packet separately to affect how the network handles it. The network, however, is generally free to alter these values if they are not appropriate. If network devices change TOS or DSCP values, however, you should be careful about where it is done.

As I discussed elsewhere in this chapter, there is a lot of CPU overhead in categorizing and marking packets. Thus, the network should do it as little as possible. That usually means that it will mark the packets with the appropriate TOS or DSCP values as the packets enter the network. The first router they encounter should be the only one making this change. Then the packets can traverse the network, enjoying the appropriate service level at each hop. If they leave this network and enter another, then they might be marked again with a different value.

The original standard for the format of the TOS field is defined in RFC 791. It breaks the 8-bit field into 2 3-bit sections. The first three bits specify the Precedence, and the second three specify a particular vision of PHB. The final two bits were designated as unused and set aside for future requirements. The approximate service types defined in Table 8-1 became the standard IP Precedence values.

Table 8-1. Standard IP Precedence values

IP Precedence	Decimal value	Bit pattern
Routine	0	000
Priority	1	001
Immediate	2	010
Flash	3	011
Flash Override	4	100
Critical	5	101
Internetwork Control	6	110
Network Control	7	111

The Internetwork Control value, 110, is reserved for network purposes such as routing protocol information. The highest-precedence value, Network Control, 111, is intended to remain confined within a network (or Autonomous System). Any of the other values can be freely assigned to specific user applications.

The third through sixth bits separately designate the required delay, throughput, and reliability characteristics, respectively. If the bit had a value of 0, then it could tolerate a high delay, low throughput, or low reliability. If the bit had a value of 1, then the packet needs a low delay, high throughput, or high reliability. The standard recommends setting only two of these parameters at a time, except in extreme situations.

In RFC 2474, these definitions were updated to allow them to work with Distributed Services. The TOS byte was renamed the DS byte. It was again broken into a 6-bit component, the DSCP, and two unused bits.

The 6-bit DSCP is broken into two 3-bit sections. The first three bits define the Class, and the last three define the PHB. This definition is done to help provide backward compatibility with networks that implement IP Precedence in the older TOS format. To create the four different Classes and three Drop Precedence values for Assured Forwarding, RFC 2597 defines the bit patterns as shown in Table 8-2.

Table 8-2. Assured Forwarding DSCP values

Drop Precedence	Class 1	Class 2	Class 3	Class 4
Lowest Drop Precedence	001010	010010	011010	100010
Medium Drop Precedence	001100	010100	011100	100100
Highest Drop Precedence	001110	010110	011110	100110

It is easy to see from Table 8-2 that the first three bits define the Class and the last three bits define the Drop Precedence. With three bits, it is possible to define several more Classes than the four defined in the standard. Specifically, the values 000, 101, 110, and 111 are all unused in Assured Forwarding. The Class values 110 and 111 are reserved for network purposes such as routing protocol information. Thus, these values are not available for general users. By default, any packet with a Class value of 000 is to be given a Best Efforts level of service. However, there is room for introduction of a new Class 5, if it is required. I use this value later when I talk about Expedited Forwarding.

This set of definitions for the AF DSCP is clearly compatible with the older TOS format. The only difference is that the older definitions of delay, throughput, and reliability are replaced with a new two-bit pattern indicating drop precedence. The last bit is always equal to zero.

There is only one defined DSCP value for EF. RFC 2598 recommends using the value 101110 for this purpose. Note that this is the obvious extension to the values in Table 8-2. Since EF offers service guarantees that are not available in AF, it is in some sense a higher priority. One additional Class value is available before reaching the reserved values—the value 101, which would be Class 5. At the same time, since packets designated for EF should not be dropped, they have the highest drop precedence value, 110. This value inherently means that only one type of EF is available.

A network can't have, for example, two flavors of EF—one with low and the other with high reserved bandwidth. If this separation is required, the best strategy is to define additional Control Point values and configure the routers to recognize them. In this case, it is better to fix the first three bits at 110 and use the second three bits to specify the different forwarding characteristics. However, it is important to remember that devices on other networks (such as the public Internet) will not recognize these parameters and may not handle the packet as delicately as you would like.

Traffic Shaping

Traffic Shaping is a system for controlling the rate of data flow into a network. Networks often use it in conjunction with other QoS mechanisms.

There are two main ways to control the rate of flow of traffic. A device can either throw away packets whenever the specified rate limit is reached, or it can buffer packets and release them at the specified rate. The process of discarding packets that exceed a bandwidth parameter is usually called *policing*. Saving packets for future transmission is called *buffering*.

In any real-world application, of course, it is necessary to do both policing and buffering. If an application persistently sends data at twice the rate that the network can forward it, then it doesn't matter how many packets are put into the buffer because the network simply can't send them all along. If the traffic flow is characterized by a number of short bursts, then network devices can easily buffer the bursts to smooth them out—provided, of course, that the time average of the traffic rate is less than the available output bandwidth.

Traffic Shaping can be done either on an entire pipe of incoming data or on individual data flows. Usually, network designers implement Traffic Shaping only at network bottlenecks and at input points into the network.

EF is a good example of a place where Traffic Shaping needs to be used in conjunction with a QoS mechanism. The EF model specifies a certain sustained bandwidth level that the data flow is allowed to use. If an application exceeds this flow rate, then the excess packets are dropped. The best way to implement such a service is to ensure that the data stream entering the network is restricted to less than the reserved bandwidth. This data flow may enter the network from a user segment within the network, in which case the first router the traffic encounters does the traffic shaping.

Dropping packets, while undesirable, is not a completely bad thing in a network. Many protocols such as TCP have the ability to notice when they start losing packets because every packet has a sequence number. If packets do not follow in sequence then the end devices usually wait a short time to see if the missing packet will eventually arrive. When this time has elapsed, the receiving device sends a notification to the sending device to tell it about the missing packet.

When this happens, the sender assumes that the network has a reliability problem, and it reduces the number of packets it will send before it gets an acknowledgement (the TCP Window). Reducing the packets also reduces the amount of bandwidth that the application consumes.

By dropping TCP packets, the network can effectively control the rate that the application sends data. It tends to back off until it no longer sees dropped packets. This data-flow rate is exactly equal to the preset Traffic Shaping limit.

However, not all applications behave as well as TCP when they suffer from dropped packets. For example, UDP packets generally do not need to be acknowledged. Thus, UDP applications may not respond properly to traffic shaping. IPX has similar issues. The connection-oriented SPX protocol can respond to dropped packets by reducing its windowing, similar to TCP. But other IPX protocols are not so well behaved.

In general, it is a good idea to monitor applications that use heavily policed links to ensure that they behave well. If they do not, then you must increase the bandwidth to reduce the congestion.

Defining Traffic Types

Usually, traffic types are defined by some relatively simple parameters. Generally, looking at well-known fields within the IP packet header is fairly easy. Thus, these fields are the main factors used in identifying different traffic types.

In IP packets, five fields are typically used for classifying traffic. These fields are the source and destination IP addresses, the protocol type (primarily TCP, UDP, and ICMP), and the source and destination port numbers (for TCP and UDP).

Obviously, this amount of information is limited, but many applications can be easily identified with some combination of these parameters. Indeed, Fair Queuing applications use the set of all five fields to identify specific flows uniquely within a larger data stream.

For example, if a router needs to identify FTP file transfers, it needs only to look for a TCP protocol packet with either a source or destination port number of 20 or 21 (FTP uses 21 for control and 20 for actual data transfer). Similarly, if there is a large database server whose traffic needs to be protected, the router can simply look for its IP address in either the source or destination address field.

Note that in both of these examples the router looked in both the source and destination fields. This is because, in general, it is necessary to classify both sides of the conversation. If the router looks only at the destination address, then it will see the traffic going to the device with that address, but it will miss all of the traffic coming from it.

Similarly, a TCP session usually begins with a request on a well-known destination port from client to server. The client includes a dynamically assigned source port when it places this call. The server then uses this dynamic port number to identify the destination application when it talks back to the client.

In general, the router doesn't know which end is client and which end is server. When looking for a particular TCP port, the usual practice is to look in both the source and destination fields of a packet.

Some applications are not easily identified. For example, some applications use a dynamically generated port number. Using this port number can have important security and programming advantages, but it is extremely difficult for the network to give this session preferential treatment.

Conversely, some systems group many applications together. In some cases, such as with the Citrix system, the server passes only screen updates of applications running on a central server to the user workstation. Passing only screen updates makes it impossible to tell which packets correspond to which applications.

Citrix also includes the ability to run file transfers. In this case, however, the system's designers were thoughtful enough to include a batch-mode designation for these data streams and to put the flag specifying this mode in an easily accessible part of the packet. In this way, the network can at least distinguish between interactive and batch traffic. However, this is not always sufficient granularity.

The same problem occurs in many other network services. For example, it is sometimes necessary to give different Remote Procedure Call (RPC) applications different priorities. However, the fact that they all use the same basic Layer 4 architecture makes this difficult. In fact, this problem exists for any application built at a higher layer on the protocol stack. For programmers, building a new application on stock networking Application Program Interface (API) calls such as RPC can be extremely useful. If all of these applications wind up using the same TCP port numbers, it becomes hard to distinguish between them.

This distinction might be necessary for security reasons, as well as QoS reasons. For example, blocking Java code from being downloaded from certain web pages might be useful. However, blocking the code requires that the router distinguish between different types of URL information within a single web page. To the router, it all just looks like an HTTP connection.

One partial solution to this problem (there can never be a completely general solution because of the nature of the problem) is Cisco's proprietary Network-Based Application Recognition (NBAR) software. NBAR works with a set of specific Packet Description Language Module (PDLM) modules that tell the router how to find higher-layer information in the IP packet. When using NBAR to distinguish two applications that both use the same Layer 4 information, the router must have the appropriate PDLM module loaded. The PDLM modules then allow the router to distinguish between applications that use the same network layer information.

This information can then be applied to Access lists in the same way that Layer 3 information can be isolated. Once the information is accessible to an Access list, it is relatively easy to use it to set the DSCP or TOS bits in the IP header. The packet can then pass through the network with the appropriate QoS behavior.

The other parameter that is often used to define QoS classes is the size of the packet. Real-time applications such as packetized voice or video systems will often use a very small packet size. Small packets can usually be delivered with lower latency. If the data segment of a packet represents a constant amount of information, then it follows that a longer packet contains more data. Thus, a longer packet also represents a longer time period when capturing sound or video samples. If the application has to wait a longer time to fill up a packet before it is sent, then this clearly results in a higher latency.

Real-time applications often use shorter packets than low-priority batch-mode applications. For this reason, some networks give preferred treatment to smaller packets.

RSVP

ReSerVation Protocol (RSVP) is an IP protocol that allows end devices to request particular resource characteristics from the network. It is a control protocol similar in concept to ICMP, so it does not carry the data stream. Instead, it just reserves the resources.

The general concept is that an end device requiring certain network resources will send an RSVP packet through the network. This is an IP packet whose destination is the other end device taking part in the application conversation. The packet passes through the network, hop by hop. Each intermediate router reads the packet and allocates the appropriate resources, if possible.

If a router is unable to comply with the request, it responds back down the path with a packet indicating that the request has been refused. All intermediate routers again read the packet and release the resources. If the router is willing and able to reserve the resources for this application, it passes the packet along to the next device along the path.

If the RSVP request goes through the entire network, the end device responds with a message indicating that the request has been granted.

One clear problem with this model is that most good network designs don't have a single unique path between any two points. One of the main design principles is to use multiple-path redundancy.

RSVP includes elaborate methods for rerouting the reserved path in case of a network failure. When the routing table in a router in the middle of the network changes, it attempts to establish a new reserved path using the new routing information. Also, RSVP uses a periodic system to verify that the reserved resources are still available.

If a network failure forces a change in path, then the new path may refuse to grant the reservation request. In fact, this refusal is quite likely because the new path may suddenly find itself carrying a heavy additional load. Under these circumstances, it probably will not allow new reservation requests.

Thus, the application may suddenly lose its reserved resources without losing actual network connectivity. In a large network, this loss tends to result in considerably less-stable performance than the simpler Differentiated Service model.

Another problem arises because of multiple redundant paths through a network. There are two ways to handle redundant paths. If a router handling an RSVP request notices that it has more than one possible way to get to the destination, it could reserve bandwidth on both paths and forward the RSVP request to downstream next-hop devices. Or, it could select one of the paths and use it for the application.

The first case is clearly inefficient because the application reserves resources that it will not use. If the router shares the load among all possible paths, then reserving the full bandwidth requirement on each path individually is inefficient.

On the other hand, if the router deliberately selects only one of the possible paths for this traffic stream, then it loses one of the key advantages to a highly redundant design philosophy. Worse still, the highest level of fault-tolerant redundancy is used only for the lowest-priority traffic.

The only alternative is to have the RSVP protocol actively track all possible paths through the network. In doing so, it must have an accurate model for how effectively the network can share loads among these paths. This level of tracking is not practical in a large network.

Network-Design Considerations

The best QoS implementations readily break up into two functional parts. The first router a packet encounters upon entering the network should set its TOS or DSCP field. Then the rest of the devices in the network only need to look at this one field to know how to treat this packet.

There is a very simple reason for this division of labor. The process of reading and classifying packets can be extremely CPU intensive, so the network should do it only once.

Furthermore, when getting closer to the Core of a hierarchical network, one expects to see more traffic. The easiest place to do the classification is at the edge. In many cases, the edge router is in a unique position to do this classification. For example, if the edge router runs any sort of tunneling protocol, such as DLSw, then it can see application information in the packet before it is encapsulated into the tunnel protocol. This fact is even truer when the edge device encrypts the packet contents, as in a VPN architecture.

In this case, there is essentially no way to differentiate between applications after the packet is encrypted. The only practical place to do the classification is the edge router. Then, once the packet enters the network, it needs a design that permits treating the different traffic classes appropriately. In an Integrated Services implementation, the design must be built to respond to RSVP requests.

RSVP suffers from efficiency problems when many paths run through the network. Because it requires every router to keep track of all reserved data flows, it does not scale well to large networks. However, there is a relatively straightforward way of getting around this problem.

It is possible to use Integrated Services only at the edges of the network and build the Core with Differentiated Services. The key to making this possible is in the flow-aggregation properties of Integrated Services. These properties specify that the network is allowed to group a set of flows together if they all have similar properties and then treat them all at once. That principle is good in theory, but Differentiated Services is usually limited to either Assured or Expedited Forwarding. Thus, you have to be careful about how you map specific RSVP requests to DSCP values and how you implement the Per-Hop Behavior.

An obvious way to make a gateway between an Integrated Services edge and a Differentiated Services Core is through EF. EF allows explicit reservation of bandwidth up to and including VLL implementations.

Note that this reservation implies that the network must aggregate an arbitrary number of reserved bandwidth flows. Thus, it is possible to oversubscribe the bandwidth that has been reserved in the Core. However, if oversubscription occurs, the router that acts as the gateway between the Integrated and Differentiated Services regions simply refuses any further RSVP requests.

For packets passing through Differentiated Services networks, there are many ways to implement the required traffic-flow characteristics. The simplest method is to use Weighted Fair Queuing on every router in the Core.

This method does not strictly meet the requirements of either EF or AF PHB models because it does not have the prescribed drop precedence characteristics. However, Weighted Fair Queuing does allow the different flows to be weighted according to the DSCP Class (or TOS IP Precedence, since they are compatible).

If a strict implementation of either EF or AF is not required, this implementation is much easier. If a strict AF model is required, then you must to consult the router vendor to find out how to turn on this style of queuing.

For EF implementations, on the other hand, you should define the different performance criteria carefully. How much bandwidth is reserved? What are the latency and jitter requirements? These parameters in turn define how the software that services the queues is configured. Most importantly for EF implementations, how are the different logical paths defined?

If many physical path possibilities exist between two end points (which is a design philosophy that I strongly advocate), then the designer has to be absolutely clear on how structures such as VLL will be implemented. Is the VLL only defined along one path, or is it configured through multiple paths?

In general, I prefer to keep network design as simple as possible. In almost all cases where QoS is required, I recommend the AF model of Distributed Services. Classification is to be done at the edges of the network. Then every other device in the network needs to implement only the appropriate PHB.

If congestion within the network is kept under control, it is rarely necessary to implement any real bandwidth reservation. For light congestion, there is little or no observable difference. However, if congestion becomes severe or sustained, then it is usually easier to increase the bandwidth than it is to implement a more strict QoS system. If there is a serious congestion problem in the network, then implementing strict bandwidth reservation for one application only makes the congestion problem worse for every other application using the network.

In any QoS implementation, remember that bandwidth is a finite and limited resource. All you can with QoS is to allocate it a little more fairly. If there is simply not enough to go around, then QoS cannot solve the problem.

CHAPTER 9

Network Management

Network management is an afterthought in many networks. This is a pity because the network designer can do many things to facilitate network management. In most large organizations, the job of network manager is considered "operations," while network design is done by a different implementation group. Frequently, these two groups report to different departments of the company.

If a network can be managed easily, then it is inherently more reliable. Thus, manageability is a fundamental design goal for a good network. Before I launch into a discussion of design implications for manageability, I need to spend some time talking about what I mean by network management.

Network-Management Components

The OSI has published an official definition of network management that includes five different components: configuration management, fault management, performance management, security management, and accounting management. I usually think of performance management as being composed of two separate subcomponents. The first is a tactical performance management, and the second is the more strategic long-term capacity planning component.

Configuration Management

Configuration management actually includes two different but related activities. The first keeps track of physical hardware, serial numbers, locations, patching information, and so forth. The second part of configuration management is the process of modifying, backing up, and restoring the software configuration of network equipment. This aspect of configuration management often becomes the focus of the whole activity. Many hardware vendors for routers and switches have excellent software for building and modifying software configurations. This software usually includes the ability to do scheduled backups of running configurations. This ability is an extremely important feature. If you have a recent configuration backup, then replacing a failed router with a new one is a fast and easy operation. Without a backup, this replacement is time consuming and usually requires an experienced engineer to reconstruct the software configuration.

However, remember the physical tracking side of configuration management, especially if you deal with the configurations of Layer 2 devices such as hubs and switches. If network managers have accurate information about physical locations, MAC addresses, and cabling for end devices such as user workstations, then they can easily handle hardware moves, adds, and changes. In most organizations, business requirements force network administration to respond quickly and efficiently to requests for end-user moves and service changes. However, the cabling and hardware records are usually out-of-date, so every small move requires a technician to visit the site and carefully document the equipment and cabling. This process is expensive and slow.

Unfortunately, no software can solve this problem; it is primarily a procedural issue. Technicians making changes have to keep the records up-to-date, and the cabling and patch panels have to be periodically audited to ensure accuracy of the records. However, the network designer can do much to facilitate this process. If the patch panels are well designed and there is a clear correlation between physical floor location and cable numbers, then the technicians can at least get a running start at the job.

Fault Management

Fault management is what most people picture regarding network management. This management is the active monitoring of the various key network components to find problems and alert the appropriate people. But there is another side to fault management that is also important, particularly to the network designer—the troubleshooting process.

Troubleshooting occurs after the appropriate person knows of a problem. Usually, all that the fault-management software says is that a failure occurred somewhere near a particular device. It is usually not able to say what caused the problem, precisely which device needs attention, or even what the failure actually was. Upon receiving an alert, the network engineer must troubleshoot the problem, try to isolate the source, and look for a solution. For many problems there is a short-term solution to get the network back up immediately, as well as a long-term solution to make sure it doesn't happen again.

Performance Management

Performance management requires monitoring the network carefully and looking for bottlenecks and congestion issues. There is some overlap between performance management and fault management when performance problems become so severe that they interfere with the basic functioning of the network.

Capacity planning is the natural outcome of performance management. When network managers discover a systematic performance problem, such as a bandwidth shortage through performance management, they turn to capacity planning to resolve this problem. Capacity planning is fundamentally a network-design issue.

Security Management

Security management is the set of activities that ensure that the network's security measures work properly. Every firewall must be carefully monitored to see if it is in danger of compromise or if it is being abused in some way. Similarly, security management includes the maintenance of any filtering or encryption options.

Accounting Management

Security management leads directly into the concept of accounting management. Accounting partly deals with security. One of the main reasons for giving individual users different accounts is to ensure that they can only have access to the resources they require. This access is essentially a security issue. However, accounting management also includes the general problem of keeping track of who uses what on the network. In some cases, this information is used to bill for these services.

It should now be clear that all of the different activities of network management have network-design implications.

Designing a Manageable Network

A well-designed network has network management included in its basic requirements. At each stage of the design process, one of the key questions should be "how will this be managed"? The network designer should know from the outset where the network-management servers will be, both physically and logically, on the network. If special protocols are used for network management, then the design must ensure that this information can be delivered. If protocol analyzers or RMON probes are used to monitor network performance and assist in troubleshooting, then these devices should be placed in the design.

A probe is used to watch all of the traffic passively as it passes by. The issue of where to put probes is particularly difficult. In a switched or VLAN-based environment, probes are nearly useless if they are not deployed carefully.

Before switches, when Ethernet networks were made up of large bus configurations, it was possible to deploy a few probes and see everything. The probes would be placed near the Core of the network. From there, they could easily be switched to whatever LAN segment needed monitoring. However, in a switched Ethernet design, every end device is on its own LAN segment. This situation fundamentally changes how network monitoring has to be done.

One way to use a probe is to look at all traffic going to and coming from a particular end device by configuring the probe's switch port to mirror the port connecting to this device. This mirroring requires, of course, that a probe be available for use with this switch. In the ideal case where everything can be monitored centrally without having to leave the network operations center, this implies that there must be a separate probe on every switch. This prospect can be rather expensive. Thus, many organizations use either full or partial RMON probes built into their switches instead. The use of these probes allows good monitoring capabilities for every device in the network.

Another way to use a probe is on trunk links. In a hierarchical VLAN architecture, keeping a close watch on trunk utilization is important because this is where congestion problems usually first arise.

The discussion of hierarchical designs in Chapter 3 showed that trunks are used in four ways. They connect the Access Level to the Distribution Level and the Distribution to the Core. Internal trunks also exist within the Distribution and Core Levels. The important thing is that, while most of the switches wind up being at the Access Level, all trunks have at least one end in the Distribution or Core Levels. Thus, there is no need to deploy probes for monitoring trunk links to the Access Level. Not needing to deploy the probes at every switch should provide an important cost savings.

Chapter 3 also mentioned another important design issue for large-scale LAN environments in the discussion of hierarchical VLAN designs—the presence of a dedicated network-management VLAN. Obviously, the same VLAN cannot be present in different VLAN Distribution Areas, but every Distribution Area should have such a VLAN.

There are several reasons for having a separate network management VLAN that contains no user traffic:

- If you monitor traffic on a user VLAN, you don't want to see the probe traffic mixed in with user traffic.

- If you have to transfer configuration or software to or from the network devices, you don't want this traffic to interfere with production-application traffic.

- Separating the management VLAN from user traffic can be useful for security reasons. A router can then completely block SNMP and other management-specific traffic from passing between user and management VLANs. Blocking the traffic greatly reduces the chances of a successful attack.

- Perhaps most importantly, if there is a serious problem with a user VLAN, having a separate network-management VLAN allows the network engineer to get to the switch and hopefully fix the problem.

A network-management VLAN should always be part of the network design for every Distribution Area. This VLAN should contain the management addresses for all hubs and switches in the managed Distribution Area. It should also hold the management interfaces for all probes and protocol analyzers in the area. If any devices, such as Inverse Terminal Servers, are used for out-of-band management, then these devices should also be connected through this management VLAN.

The management VLAN can suffer failures without affecting production traffic. Thus, it is not necessary to provide the same level of redundancy for this VLAN as for the rest of the network. However, if a large number of devices are to be managed through this VLAN, then it is wise to make it fairly robust. Economy of design may mean just building this VLAN according to the same specifications as the rest of the production network.

A network designer can do several different things at the physical layer to ensure that a network is designed to be managed effectively. These steps generally involve ease of access, clear labeling, and logical layout.

By ease of access, I mean that equipment that needs to be touched frequently should be in a prominent position. It should be safe from being bumped accidentally; there should also be no obstructions such as walls or poles to prevent a technician from seeing or handling the equipment. A good example would be cabling patch panels. Patch panels are almost always the network elements that need the most frequent physical access. Fiber patch panels tend to be used less frequently than the patch panels for user LAN drops. It is common for fiber patch panels to be mounted too high or too low to access easily.

Usually, the best way to handle LAN-cabling patch panels is to mount them in logical groups in equipment cabinets with locking doors. When the technician needs to make changes, the door can be easily unlocked and opened. The changes can then be documented and the door locked again to prevent tampering.

A clear, consistent, and simple labeling scheme is critical, particularly for patch panels and patch cords. Every patch-panel port should have a unique code number, and the formats of these codes should be consistent. These codes should clarify to what this port attaches. Suppose, for example, that you want to number the patch panels in a wiring closet that supports a large number of end users. In general, there should be a consistent floor plan in which every user work area is numbered.

Then, if each work area has three or four drops, you usually label the patch-panel ports with the work-area number followed by an alphabetic character to indicate to which cable drop the port connects. Each patch-panel port has a unique number that is easily associated with a particular cable drop in a particular work area. Thus, for example, desk number 99 may have 3 jacks beside it. If two of these jacks are for data and one is for voice, then you might number them 99-A, 99-B, and 99-V, respectively. This way, which ports are for what purposes is completely clear both at the desk and in the wiring closet.

Documenting Patch-Panel Changes

There are two good methods for documenting patch-panel changes. One method is to have every change accompanied by a work order. The technician notes the changes on the work order. Then, when the work order is closed, the changes can be input into a database or spreadsheet of cabling information. The other method, which is probably more effective in most organizations, is to simply have a printed spreadsheet of the patching information taped to the inside of the cabinet door. When a technician makes a change, he immediately notes it on this sheet of paper. Then somebody needs to gather up the paper sheets periodically, input the changes, and print out new paper sheets to tape back inside the cabinets. The principle advantage to this method is that not all changes are accompanied by work orders. In particular, emergency changes usually have to be done quickly by whoever is on call. This person may not have time to access the work-order system and update databases with the small changes that they had to make to fix the problem.

If you later found that you had to run an additional data cable to this desk, you could number it 99-C. An additional voice line, perhaps for a fax machine, could be numbered 99-W.

These designations are merely intended as examples. Every network is different, so the network designer has to come up with a locally appropriate scheme.

Giving consistent labels to the patch cords that connect to these patch panels is also important. There are many different ways of doing this. Some organizations like to label the patch cord with a tag that indicates what is on the other end. For example, suppose that a cord connects panel 1, port 2 to panel 2, port 3. Then the first end plugs into panel 1, port 2, and it has a label saying "panel 2, port 3." This method is quite common, and it is generally not very good. The problem is that, at some point, somebody will need to move that patch cord. If they fail to change the label in the heat of the moment, then they will have a situation that is worse than having no labels at all because the labels cannot be trusted.

The simplest and most effective method for labeling patch cords that I have seen is simply to give every patch cord a unique number. These cables can be prenumbered and left in convenient locations in each wiring closet. Whenever a patch cable is connected between two ports, the technician writes the information on the sheet inside the cabinet. Patch panel 1, port 2 connects to patch cord number 445, which connects to panel 2, port 3. This system greatly facilitates the process of auditing patch panels. All that you need to do is go through the patch panels port by port and write down what patch-cord number connects to that port. Then you can put all of this information into a spreadsheet and sort it by patch-cord number to see all of the cross-connections immediately.

If the spreadsheets get badly outdated, and there is an emergency problem involving a particular port, then the technician will have to trace the cable manually regardless. An effective labeling scheme will be of no help if the spreadsheets are outdated.

Having universal rules for what constitutes a logical patch-panel layout is difficult. This is because what is logical depends on how the cabling is used. For example, suppose every user workstation has two LAN drops, labeled A and B. The first drop is for data and is connected to a computer. The second drop is for an IP telephone. In this case, it makes sense to separate the patch panels to put all drop As together in one group of panels and all drop Bs together in another group. Alternatively, if all drops are intended for user workstations and many users simply have two workstations, then grouping the A and B drops together may be simpler. In this case, the pattern might even alternate A and B on the same patch panel.

What is universal is that the patch-panel layout should make finding devices easy. Usually, workstations are numbered logically through the user work area. Consecutive numbers should indicate roughly adjacent workstations. Then the ports on the patch panel should be arranged in numerical order. In this way, it becomes easy for the technician who usually deals with cabling in this wiring closet to look at the patch panel and know at least approximately where the corresponding workstations are.

However, even with the best of initial intentions, the pattern can be badly broken over time. This is because you frequently have to deal with changes to the work area. Sometimes a cubicle pattern may change on the floor, and sometimes you need to run extra cabling to support extra devices. The network designer and manager have to tread a very careful line between forcing these changes into the logical flow of the entire area and wanting to minimize changes to unaffected areas. This situation usually means that any new drops are taken as exceptions and put at the end of the existing group of patch panels.

One of the most important considerations in designing a network to be manageable is deciding how and where to connect the network-management equipment. Is there a separate network-management center to accommodate? Do nonoperational staff members like the network designer sit in a different area? Do they require access to the network-management center's equipment through the network?

In general, the design should include a separate VLAN just for network-management equipment. This VLAN is not necessarily the same one mentioned earlier. That management VLAN was used to access management functions on remote network equipment. This network management–equipment VLAN houses servers and workstations used to manage the network.

This VLAN is usually as close to the Core of the network as possible. However, it is not always close to the Core. Many organizations are opting to outsource their network-management functions. This outsourcing permits highly trained staff to be available at all hours. It also means that network management must be done from offsite, usually from behind a firewall.

SNMP

No discussion of network management in IP networks would be complete without including the Simple Network Management Protocol (SNMP). I want to stress that SNMP is primarily used for fault management and, to a lesser extent, for configuration and performance management. It is definitely not the only tool required for a complete network-management system, but it is an important one.

SNMP is a UDP-based network protocol. It has been adapted to run over IPX, as well as IP. However, IP is by far the most common network protocol for SNMP.

SNMP has three general functions. It can request information from a remote device using a get command. It can be used to configure the remote device with a set command. Or, the remote device can send information to the network-management server without having been prompted, which is called a trap. A trap is usually sent when there has been a failure of some kind. In general, a trap can be sent for any reason deemed useful or appropriate for this particular device. However, the main application alerts the network-management server of a failure of some kind.

In general, two types of devices speak SNMP. The remote device that is managed has a relatively small engine called an SNMP *agent*. The agent is a piece of software that responds to get and set packets. It also monitors the functioning of the device it runs on and sends out trap packets whenever certain conditions are met.

The other general type of device is the SNMP *server*. This server is typically a relatively powerful computer whose only function is to monitor the network. The server polls remote devices using get and set commands. The IP address of the server is configured in the remote agents so that they will know where to send trap messages.

Many network engineers prefer not to use SNMP for configuration. This is because they believe there are too many serious security problems with the model, making it relatively easy to attack and reconfigure key pieces of network equipment. These problems can make configuration much more difficult. However, if there is a security concern, then turning off SNMP write access on your network devices is worthwhile.

There are several commercial SNMP server systems. They usually come with a number of complex features such as the ability to discover and map the network and display it graphically. Almost all modern network equipment includes an SNMP agent, at least as an optional feature.

The amount of information that can be exchanged with SNMP is enormous. Every device that has an SNMP agent keeps track of a few basic variables that the server can query with get commands. Thousands of other optional variables are appropriate for different types of devices. For example, a router with a Token Ring interface allows the server to poll for special parameters that are relevant to Token Ring. If this router doesn't have any Ethernet ports, then it doesn't make sense for it to keep track of collisions, since there will never be any. However, it does need to keep track of beacon events, for example.

This same router also has a number of special-purpose variables that are unique to this type of equipment and this particular vendor. All of these different variables are accessed by a large tree structure called the Management Information Base (MIB). People talk about "the MIB" and different vendor-specific "MIBs." However, it is all one large database. The only difference is that some parts of it are used on some types of devices, some parts of it are defined by particular hardware vendors, and others are globally relevant. Thus, I prefer to talk about vendor- or technology-specific "MIB extensions."

Every network-hardware vendor has its own set of MIB extensions. These extensions allow different vendors to implement special customizations that express how they handle different interface types, for example. They also allow the different vendors to give information on things such as CPU load and memory utilization in a way that is meaningful to their particular hardware configuration.

Three different revisions of SNMP are currently in popular use—SNMP-1, 2, and 3. The differences between these revisions are relatively subtle. They primarily concern factors such as security. The important thing is to ensure that your SNMP server understands to which version of SNMP the agent on each device expects to speak. Most networks wind up being a hybrid of these different SNMP flavors.

How to Monitor

In general, a network is monitored with a combination of polling and trapping. Devices are polled on a schedule—every few minutes, for example. But you need a way to determine if something bad has happened in between polls. This requires the device to send trap packets whenever important events occur. On the other hand, traps alone are not sufficient because some failures prevent the remote device from sending a trap. If the failure you are concerned about loses the only network path from the remote device to the network-management server, then there is no way to deliver the trap. Thus, failures of this type can only be seen by polling, so any successful network-management system always uses a combination of polling and trapping.

Setting an appropriate polling interval is one of the most important network-management decisions. You want to poll as often as possible so that you will know as soon as something has failed. Polling a device too frequently can have two bad side effects.

First, polling too often, particularly on slow WAN links, has the potential to cause serious bandwidth problems. For example, suppose each poll and each response is a 1500 byte packet. Then, each time you poll, you send a total of 3000 bytes through the network. If you poll each of 100 different remote devices all through the same WAN serial interface (a common configuration in Frame Relay networks), then each poll cycle generates 300 kilobytes of traffic. Therefore, if you poll each of these devices once every 30 seconds, then this generates an average of 10kbps on the link just because of polling traffic.

These numbers are relatively small, but in a large network they can become large very quickly. If instead of polling 100 devices, you have a network with 100,000 devices, then that 10kbps becomes 10Mbps. This increase will cause a noticeable load on even a Fast Ethernet segment.

The second problem with a short polling interval, however, is much more dangerous. Consider the example of 100 remote devices again. Suppose one of these devices is not available. The usual prescription is that the server will try three to five times, waiting a default timeout period for a response. The default timeout is usually between 1 and 5 seconds, so the server will have to wait between 3 and 25 seconds for this device before it can move on to the next one in the list. As a result, if there are several simultaneous problems, or a single problem affects several downstream devices, the management server can get stuck in its polling cycle. When this happens, it spends so much time trying to contact the devices that are not available that it loses the ability to monitor the ones that are still up effectively.

A number of different SNMP server vendors have come up with different ways of getting around this polling-interval problem. Some vendors allow the server to know about downstream dependencies—if a router fails, then the server stops trying to contact the devices behind it.

Another clever method for dealing with the same problem is to break up the queue of devices to be polled into a number of shorter queues. These shorter queues are then balanced so that they can poll every device within one polling cycle even if most devices in the list are unreachable. The most extreme example of this is when the queues contain only one poll each. This means that all polling is completely asynchronous, so no failure on one device can delay the polling for another device. This situation loses some of the efficiencies of using queues, however, and may consume significantly more memory and CPU resources on the server. Some servers can use some variation of both methods simultaneously for maximum efficiency.

Whether the server discovers a problem by means of a poll or a trap, it then has to do something with this information. Most commercial network-management systems include a graphical-display feature that allows the network manager to see at a glance when there is a problem anywhere on the network. This idea sounds great, but in practice, it is less useful than it appears. The problem is that, in a very large network, a few devices are always in trouble. So the network manager just gets used to see a certain amount of red flashing trouble indicators. To tell when a new failure has really occurred, it is necessary to watch the screen for changes constantly. Constantly watching the screen can strain one's eyes, which tend to get sore from such activities, so network managers have different methods for dealing with this problem.

Some people don't look at the map, but look at a carefully filtered text-based list of problems. This list can be filtered and sorted by problem type. It is even possible to have these text messages sent automatically to the alphanumeric pagers of the appropriate network engineers.

Another popular system is to use the network-management software to open trouble tickets automatically. These tickets must be manually verified by staff on a help desk. If they see no real problem, they close the ticket. If they do see a real problem, then they escalate appropriately.

Any combination of solutions like this should work well, but beware of network-management solutions that are purely graphical because they are only useful in very small networks.

SNMP monitoring has many uses. Until now I have focused on fault management. But it can also generate useful performance-management data. For example, one of the simplest things you can do is set up the server to simply send a get message to find out the number of bytes that were sent by a particular interface. If this poll is done periodically—say, every five minutes—the data can be graphed to show the outbound utilization on the port. In this way, you can readily obtain large historical databases of trunk utilization for every trunk in the network. Usually, the only limitation on this sort of monitoring is the amount of physical storage on the server.

Besides port utilization, of course, you can use this method to monitor anything for which there is a MIB variable. You can monitor router CPU utilization, dropped packets, and even physical temperature with some device types.

Another interesting, underused application of network-management information is to have automated processes that sift through the trap logs looking for interesting but noncritical events. For example, you might choose to ignore interface resets for switch ports that connect to end-user workstations. End users reboot their workstations frequently, so seeing such an event in the middle of the day is usually considered an extremely low priority. The network manager generally just ignores these events completely. But what if one port resets itself a thousand times a day? If you ignore all port-reset events, you will never know this information. This problem is actually fairly common.

It is a good idea to have automated scripts that pass through the event logs every day looking for interesting anomalies like this. Some organizations have a set of scripts that analyze the logs every night and send a brief report to a network engineer. This sort of data can provide an excellent early warning of serious hardware or cabling problems. In fact, these reports highlight one of the most interesting and troubling aspects to network management. The problem is almost never that the information is not there. Rather, there is usually so much information that the server has to ignore almost all of it.

In a modestly sized network of a few thousand nodes, it is relatively common to receive at least one new event every second. A human being cannot even read all of the events as they come in, much less to figure out what problems they might be describing. Instead, you have to come up with clever methods for filtering the events. Some events are important. These events are passed immediately to a human for support. Other events are interesting, but not pressing, and are written to a log for future analysis. Other events are best considered mere noise and ignored.

The most sophisticated network-management servers are able to correlate these events to try to determine what is actually going on. For example, if the server sees that a thousand devices have suddenly gone down, one of which is the gateway to all others, then it is probably the gateway that has failed.

The server can in principle do even more clever event correlation by examining the noncritical events. For example, it might see that a router drops packets on a particular interface. There are many reasons for dropping packets. Perhaps there is a serious contention problem on the link. If, at the same time, the free memory on the same router is low and the CPU utilization is high, then this router is probably not powerful enough to handle the load. Perhaps this router has been configured to do too much processing of packets in the CPU instead of in the interface hardware. If the dropped packets occur when the router receives a large number of broadcast packets, then it may be a broadcast storm and not a router problem at all.

Setting up this sort of sophisticated event correlation can be extremely difficult and time consuming. Some relatively recent software systems are able to do much of this correlation out of the box. They tend to be rather expensive, but they are certainly more reliable than homemade systems.

What to Monitor

In general, the network manager needs to monitor key devices such as switches and routers to see if they work properly. The simplest and most common sort of polling is the standard ping utility. Since every device that implements the IP protocol has to respond to ping, this is a good way to see if the device is currently up. In fact, a few devices, particularly firewalls, deliberately violate this rule for security reasons. However, if a device has disabled ping responses for security reasons, it will probably have SNMP disabled as well, so it has to be managed out-of-band anyway.

Ping is really not a great way to see what is going on with the device. If the device supports SNMP at all, it is better to ask it how long it has been up rather than simply ask whether it is there. This way, you can compare the response with the previous value. If the last poll showed that the device was up for several days and the current poll says that it was up for only a few minutes, then you know that it has restarted in the meantime. This may indicate a serious problem that you would otherwise have missed. The SNMP MIB variable for up time is called *sysUpTime*. It is conventional to call the difference between the current value and the previous value for the same parameter on the same device delta.

Table 9-1 shows several different standard tests that are done by a network-management system. Some of these tests, such as the *coldStart*, *linkUp*, and *linkDown* events, are traps. Note that it is important to look even for good events such as *linkUp* because the device may have an interface that flaps. In this case, the traps saying that the interface has failed may be undelivered because of that failure.

Table 9-1. Standard set of items to monitor

Parameter	MIB variable	Test	Comments
Reachability	ICMP (not SNMP)	Time > N, % not responded	All devices, including those that don't support SNMP
Reboot	coldStart	Trap	Indicates that the SNMP agent has restarted
Uptime	sysUptime	delta < 0	Number of seconds since the SNMP agent started running
	ifOperStatus	delta ! = 0	Shows that the status of the interface has changed
	ifInOctets	Record	The number of bytes received
	ifInDiscards	delta > N	Incoming packets that had to be dropped
	ifInErrors	delta > N	Incoming packets with Layer 2 errors
Interface Status (for every active Interface on the device)	ifOutOctets	Record	The number of bytes sent
	ifOutDiscards	delta > N	Outgoing packets that had to be dropped
	ifOutErrors	delta > N	Outgoing packets sent with errors (should always be zero)
	ifInNUcastPkts	delta > N	Incoming multicast and broadcast packets
	ifOutNUcastPkts	delta > N	Outgoing multicast and broadcast packets
	linkDown	Trap	Indicates that an interface has gone down
	linkUp	Trap	Indicates that an interface has come up

This set of variables tells the network manager just about everything she needs to know for most types of devices. Many other important MIB variables are specific to certain technologies, however. For example, parameters such as CPU and memory utilization are important, but these parameters are different for each different hardware vendor. Consult the hardware documentation for the appropriate names and values of these parameters.

For routers, one is usually interested in buffering and queuing statistics. Again, this information is in the vendor-specific MIB extensions. There are also certain technology-specific MIB extensions. For example, an 802.3 MIB extension includes a number of useful parameters for Ethernet statistics. Similarly, there are useful MIB variables for Token Ring, ATM, T1 circuits, Frame Relay, and so forth. In all of these cases, it is extremely useful to sit down and read through the MIB, looking at descriptions of each variable. In this way, one can usually find out if there is a convenient way to measure particular performance issues or to look for particular fault problems that may be unique to the network.

Ad Hoc SNMP

All of the SNMP polling I have discussed so far has been periodic and scheduled. However, the same SNMP server software can also do ad hoc queries. This means that the network manager can use the system to generate a single poll manually. This can be an extremely useful tool for fault isolation and troubleshooting. For example, this facility can quickly query a set of different devices to see which ones have high CPU loads, errors, or whatever you happen to be looking for. Using this facility is usually much faster than logging into all of these devices manually and poking around on the command line. In fact, the network-management software for many types of hardware makes it possible to do a large list of standard ad hoc queries on a device automatically.

Many hardware vendors make SNMP software called *instance managers*. This software gives a relatively detailed, graphical view of the complete state of one device all at once. Usually, these instance managers also provide the ability to make configuration changes via SNMP as well.

For Ethernet switches, it is often true that the instance-manager software is the fastest and most efficient way to do basic configuration changes such as manipulating VLAN memberships.

This topic actually brings up one of the most serious issues with SNMP. With SNMP Version 1 and, to a lesser extent, with Versions 2 and 3, it is remarkably easy to subvert the security. It is not difficult to load publicly available SNMP server software onto a PC. This software can then be used to reconfigure key pieces of network equipment.

Even nonmalicious users and applications can cause problems. For example, some ill-behaved server-management software automatically attempts to discover the network path to the remote managed-server devices. In doing so, this software generally does detailed SNMP polling of key network devices. Once the path is discovered, this software then periodically polls these network devices as if it were managing the network instead of just the servers.

This situation is not in itself a problem because the server-management software is only polling and not actually changing anything. Remember that the SNMP agent running on a router or a switch is a CPU-bound software process. It uses memory from the main memory pool. If a server program repeatedly polls this device, requesting large parts of its MIB, it can overload the device's CPU. Many such programs all requesting this data at the same time can cause network problems.

As I have stressed repeatedly throughout this book, there is no reason for any end device to ever have to know the topology of a well-built network. It may be necessary in these cases to implement access controls on the SNMP agents of key devices. These access controls have the effect of preventing the agent from speaking SNMP with any devices other than the officially sanctioned SNMP servers.

Some network engineers go further and actually block SNMP from passing through the network if it does not originate with the correct server. However, this measure is extreme. There may be well-behaved applications that happen to use SNMP to communicate with their well-behaved clients. In this case, the network should not prevent legitimate communication.

Automated Activities

SNMP allows much flexibility in how network managers deal with the network. They can set up the network-management server to automatically poll a large list of devices on a schedule looking for well-defined measures of the network's health. If the results are within the expected range of results, then the server concludes that this part of the network works properly. If the result is outside of the expected range, then the server treats it as a problem and somehow prompts an engineer to investigate further. As a rule, it is best if these noninvasive monitoring and polling activities are done automatically without requiring any user intervention. It is a routine repetitive task—exactly the kind of thing that computers are good at. The server can do many different types of things automatically. It is particularly useful to download a copy of the configuration information for every device in the network. This downloading is usually scheduled to execute once per night or once per week in networks that seldom change.

Sometimes a network device fails completely and needs to be replaced. When this happens, it is necessary to configure the new device to look like the one replaces. If the network-management server maintains an archive of recent software configurations for all network devices, then this task is relatively easy.

Another good reason to maintain automatic configuration backups is to note changes. For example, many organizations automatically download the configurations from every router and every switch each night. They then run a script that compares each new image to the previous night's backup. This information is encapsulated into a report that is sent to a network engineer. Usually, the only changes are the ones the engineer remembers making. But a report like this can be an extremely useful and efficient way to discover if somebody has tampered with the network.

All of these fully automatic processes are completely noninvasive. Some organizations also use a noninvasive suite of test scripts. These test scripts are executed automatically if the network-management software sees a potentially serious problem. The result of these automated tests can be helpful in isolating the problem quickly.

Sometimes network managers want to partially automate invasive procedures as well. For example, it is relatively common in a large network to have a script automatically change login passwords on routers. This way, every router can be changed in a single night. With any sort of invasive procedure, it is usually wise only to partially automate it. A user should start the script and monitor its progress. That person should then verify that the change is correct.

Some network managers go further and allow full automation of invasive procedures such as scheduled VLAN topology or filtering changes. In some cases, invasive scripts are run to reconfigure network devices automatically in response to certain failures. I do not recommend this type of automation; it is simply too dangerous in a complex network. Usually, the automated change assumes a well-defined starting point. However, it is possible to have an obscure problem in the network create a different initial configuration than what the automated procedure expects. This configuration could cause the scripted changes to give unexpected, perhaps disastrous, results. It is also possible to have an unexpected event while the reconfiguration is in progress. In this case, the network might be left in some strange state that requires extensive manual work to repair.

A large network is generally such a complex system that it is not wise to assume that it will behave in a completely predictable way. There are simply too many different things that can happen to predict every scenario reliably. If weird things happen, you should be in control, rather than allow a naïve program to continue reconfiguring the network and probably make the problem worse.

Management Problems

A number of design decisions can make network management more difficult. This doesn't necessarily mean that you should avoid these features, but it does mean that you need to be aware of their implications. It usually also means that you need to devise ways of working around the management problems that you create.

For example, sometimes parts of the network are hidden from a protocol, as in a tunnel, for example. If an IP tunnel passes through a number of devices, then it becomes impossible to see the intermediate devices in-band. If there is a problem in an intermediate device, and if there is no external way to observe that device, then it is impossible to tell which intermediate device has a problem, much less what the problem is.

In the example of tunnel-hiding intermediate devices, the most obvious workaround is to provide out-of-band access. This may mean something as simple as IP addressing in a different range. Or, it may require something as complex as putting modems on serial ports for the inaccessible devices.

Besides architectural features, certain network applications and protocols can create management problems. Again, I don't necessarily advise avoiding them, but the designer should be aware of the problems and provide alternatives.

DHCP

Dynamic Host Configuration Protocol (DHCP) is a system that allows end devices to learn network information automatically. In its minimal form, DHCP allows end devices to acquire IP addresses dynamically, while learning the correct netmask and default gateway. However, other important pieces of network information can also be conveyed by DHCP. For example, DHCP can tell the end device about its time zone, as well as the addresses for time servers (NTP), name servers (DNS), log servers, printers, and cookie servers. It can specify various network parameters such as timer values and MTU values. Literally dozens of different kinds of information can be conveyed by DHCP. It even has some open fields that convey special vendor-specific application parameters. For all of these reasons, DHCP can greatly assist in the management of end devices. The device can be set up anywhere in the network, and it will automatically discover the correct DHCP server and learn everything it needs to know to use the network.

One problem with DHCP, however, comes from its ability to assign addresses out of a pool. The first device to be turned on in the morning gets the first address, the second device gets the second address, and so on. This is by no means the only way to configure a DHCP server. It can also be set up to look for the end device's MAC address and give out a unique predetermined set of parameters that will always be associated with this device. But a simple dynamic assignment from a pool of addresses is frequently used because it is easy to implement. The problem with doing this is that there is often no easy way to determine which device has a particular IP address. This situation can be corrected by linking the DHCP server to the DNS server. When the DHCP server gives out a particular IP address, it informs the DNS server to which device it assigned this address. Then there is a simple association between the device's name and address.

However, even with a linking between DNS and DHCP, it can be difficult to do some types of fault isolation when IP addresses are assigned from a dynamic pool. In particular, when looking at historical records correlating IP addresses with actual devices can be difficult. This correlation becomes a problem when, for example, a server records in its logs that it has had network problems associated with a particular IP address. It can be extremely difficult to reconstruct which actual device this was. The only solution is to ensure that the DHCP server keeps a reliable record of historical data. It must be possible to determine which end device had a particular IP address at a particular point in time. This data has to be reliable at least as far back in history as any other logging information.

When DHCP is configured to give addresses from a pool as they are required, it often creates confusion on network-management servers, even if there is a good link between DNS and DHCP systems. These servers tend to maintain large databases of every device in the network. This information is usually discovered automatically by periodically polling ranges of IP addresses. If a particular IP address is associated with a particular DNS name when the device is discovered, the network-management software records that association permanently in its database. Then, at some later time, it may record an error associated with that IP address. However, it will often report this error as being associated with the previous DNS name, which is no longer accurate.

Some network-management software provides methods to work around this problem. It is possible simply to provide a mechanism to look up the names dynamically each time they are required, for example. However, remember that this is not usually the default configuration and that there is potential for confusion.

This first problem can be mitigated somewhat by setting the DHCP lease time to be extremely long. This setting allows each device to receive the same IP address each time it reboots. If the lease time is sufficiently long, the addresses become effectively static.

Another problem with using DHCP is its actual operation in a large network. In many networks, it is common practice to tie a particular end device's configuration information to its MAC address. This method is useful, but it means that this information must be maintained carefully. If the Network Interface Card (NIC) in the end device is changed because of a hardware problem, then the DHCP database must be updated. Similarly, if this end device is moved to another location, the DHCP database has to reflect this new information as well.

These situations are not really problems, but rather facts of life in this sort of implementation. However, they do represent a significant amount of work that is required each time maintenance work is done on an end device.

Architectural Problems

Some types of architecture can result in network-management challenges. By architectural problems I do not necessarily mean that these architectural features are bad. In fact, some of these features, such as firewalls and VLAN trunks, are extremely useful. We would not want to do without them. When we use them, though, we have to ensure that there are ways around the management difficulties. This section discusses some of these problems and suggests some solutions.

VLAN structures

Most modern LANs use VLANs and trunks. There are too many advantages to these features to avoid them. However, you should be careful about how you monitor trunks. A trunk link that contains many different VLANs treats all of these VLANs as a single stream of traffic. Consequently, if there is a physical failure, it takes out everything. However, there are two basic ways to implement the Spanning Tree protocol in a VLAN trunk. In the most common configuration, the whole trunk is replaced by a redundant trunk in case of a failure. But some vendors have features that allow Spanning Tree to operate on each VLAN separately. The principal advantage to this approach is that the backup link is configured to take some of the load during normal operation. However, determining which VLANs are using which trunks can be very difficult. Thus, if a problem involves a few VLANs is discovered, it might take a long time to determine that all affected VLANs happen to traverse the same trunk at one point in the network.

Conversely, the design could employ a system in which each trunk has a backup that is unused except when the primary fails. In this case there is the danger of suffering a secondary trunk failure and not noticing the failure because it has not affected any production traffic.

The best way around both of these problems is simply to provide the network-management system with a detailed view of the VLAN and trunk status for every switch. Furthermore, since most problems that occur will be physical problems of some sort, it is important to maintain physical monitoring of all trunk ports on the switch. This monitoring is particularly critical for trunk backup ports because they do not pass traffic. Thus, you have to rely on the switch to tell you when there is a problem.

For all higher-layer problems, it is useful to have protocol analyzers available to monitor the flow of traffic through the trunks. These devices are usually too expensive to deploy on every trunk. It is often possible to set up a system to allow probes to be patched manually into the required location quickly.

In general, there are several issues to consider when managing VLAN structures. Some hardware vendors provide useful software that allow the manipulation and configuration of VLANs. Individual ports can be readily moved from one VLAN to another. This movement is useful, but configuration management is only part of what the network managers need to do. They also need to do fault and performance management on all switches and trunks.

This management requires a system that allows you to readily determine where a given end device MAC address is connected. If you look in the MAC address tables of the switches, every switch that supports the right VLAN knows about the device. But if you have to locate it by following trunks from one switch to the next, it can be extremely time consuming. Some software can make this easy, but it shouldn't be asssumed.

There also needs to be a method for monitoring trunk traffic. This means both the gross trunk utilization and the per-VLAN portions of that overall utilization. The total trunk utilization is important because it indicates when it is time to upgrade the trunks. It also shows where trunk congestion occurs in the network. The network manager also needs to know exactly how much of each trunk's capacity is consumed by each VLAN. Knowing this shows which groups of users are actually causing the congestion problems. Then you can decide if, for example, they should be moved onto a new trunk of their own to prevent their traffic from interfering with other user groups.

This per-VLAN utilization is somewhat harder to determine. A good protocol analyzer can do it, and some switches include sufficiently powerful probes to do this sort of analysis.

LAN extension

LAN extension is a general term for providing a Layer 2 LAN protocol over a larger distance. This provision might be handled with dark fiber and a few transceivers and repeaters. Or, it could be implemented using a LAN bridge through some wide-area technology such as an ATM network.

The reason why LAN extension represents a management problem is that the actual inner workings are usually hidden from view. For example, one particularly common implementation of a LAN extension is to use RFC 1483 bridging. This simple protocol allows encapsulation of all Layer 2 information in ATM. The customer of this sort of service sees only a LAN port on either end of an ATM PVC link, which makes it possible to deliver what looks like a Fast Ethernet connection between two different cities, for example. The problem is that there is no easy way to determine if a problem exists in this link. All internal workings of the ATM network are hidden from view. All the customer's network-management software can see is an Ethernet port on either end of the link.

Ethernet link always remains up because the Ethernet signaling is provided by a port on an ATM/Ethernet switch that is physically located on the customer premises. Thus, there is no way to receive a physical indication of a failure.

The only way to work around this management problem is to configure the network management software to poll through the LAN extension links periodically. Doing this configuration requires a detailed understanding of the PVC structure within the ATM network.

Figure 9-1 shows an example ATM LAN-extension configuration. In this example, one central site talks to each of three different branch sites. To the device shown in the main site, all three remote devices appear to be simply on the same Ethernet segment.

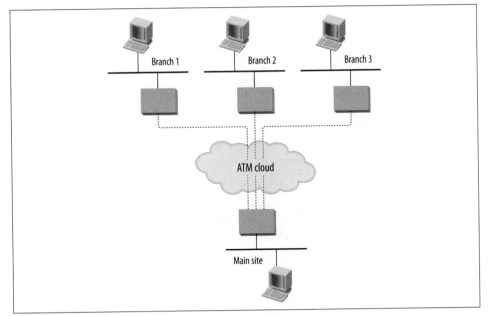

Figure 9-1. Managing a LAN-extension network

Now suppose that you suffer a failure in the ATM cloud that knocks out the PVC to Branch 1. The other two devices look fine, but you have lost contact with the first device. Most critically for network management, however, the server has not received a trap of any kind for this failure. In fact, it is almost impossible to issue a trap on this sort of failure. The only way to verify that the link is still available is to continuously poll through that link to the other side. This polling can be either SNMP or ping. Of course, even with this sort of active polling through the links, the only indication of trouble is a complete loss of the remote site. Many things could cause such a failure; power or cabling problems within the remote site can cause the same symptoms.

The best you can do is to detect that there has been some sort of problem. More troubleshooting is needed before you can conclude that there was a PVC failure in the ATM cloud.

Filtering

Another common feature in networks—one that I have advocated earlier in this book—is filtering. You can filter traffic, or you can filter routing information. In IPX, you can also filter SAP information.

Filtering represents serious potential problems for network management. In particular, if there are traffic filters, you should be sure that the network-management traffic is still allowed to pass.

There are cases in which stringent filters have been implemented for security reasons. For example, an application vendor might need to place a semitrusted server on the inside of a customer network to deliver the service. The customer might react to this situation by placing the server behind a router with strict filtering to allow only the desired application to pass through. The problem is that, at some point, there will be a problem and somebody will need to troubleshoot. If the router filters out all traffic except application traffic and the application is not working, then the network engineer is left with no way of testing. Is the server hung? Is the application broken? Or, is there perhaps a problem with its network connection? There has to be a way to verify network connectivity to the server, and this usually means ping.

For this reason, wherever traffic filters are employed, simple ICMP (ping) packets should be permitted along with the application. This way, the network-management system can at least determine if there is basic connectivity. What you lose in security, you more than make up for in the reliability that comes from swift problem analysis.

In IPX networks, SAP information is frequently filtered separately from route information. This filtering can cause a relatively common problem. It is possible for the route and SAP filters to be different in a subtle way. Either the SAP or the route is visible, but not both. When both are not visible, the network-management staff must be able to track the flow of routing and SAP information through the network. Remember to follow the whole round trip. SAP information flows from the server out to the end devices. If the end device can see the server in its server list, then the SAP must have arrived safely. There is generally no need in general for workstations to send SAP information back to the server.

Then you have to follow the routing information. Routes must exist on the workstation end that points to the server; routes must exist on the server end that point to the workstation.

Firewalls

The most extreme form of filtering is a firewall. A firewall is always called for in any location where devices on one network must communicate with devices on another untrusted network. In general, no routing information flows through firewalls. They are usually configured only with static routes. If any dynamic routing capabilities are available within a firewall, they should be restricted to BGP-4.

It can be extremely difficult to manage devices on the other side of a firewall. The typical configuration involves putting a network-management server inside of the firewall and the device to be managed on the outside of the firewall.

Firewalls are generally set up to allow just about anything to pass from the inside to the outside, but they strictly block inbound traffic. If you ping the device on the inside from the outside, you generally get no response. If you instead ping something on the outside from the inside, it usually works because the firewall knows to expect the returning ping response.

Let's look at this process in a little more detail. The network-management server sends out some kind of poll packet. For the time being, suppose that it is a ping request packet. This packet is received by the firewall. Most firewalls translate the IP source address of outbound packets. Instead of having the real network-management server's IP address, the packet has the firewall's external address when it is sent along. The external device receives this poll packet and responds. It creates a ping response packet and sends it to the firewall's IP address. The firewall has been waiting for this particular device to respond. It remembers that it passed through a ping request for this device that originated with the network-management server. Thus, it changes the destination address in the packet to the network management server's IP address and delivers the packet. If the external device had sent this packet without being prompted, the firewall would not know how to forward it internally, so it would simply drop it.

Now suppose the network manager needs something more sophisticated than ping. The firewall can be configured to pass SNMP packets, so the same pattern follows. The network-management server sends a packet. The source address is translated and the packet is delivered to the external device. The external device responds and sends the packet back to the firewall, which forwards it back to the server. Everything works well. But what about traps? SNMP traps are a critical part of the whole network-management system, but these traps are never prompted by a request. So how does the firewall know where to forward the inbound packets?

Many firewalls have the ability to define special inbound addresses. In effect, the outside of the firewall appears to have several different IP addresses. One of these addresses is configured to correspond to the network-management server. As long as the external device forwards its trap packets to this special address on the outside of the firewall, it is possible to deliver the addresses.

Alternatively, it is possible on many firewalls to deliver unexpected inbound packets based on their port number. SNMP has a well-known UDP port number of 161 for polls and poll responses, and 162 for traps. It is easy to ensure that all inbound SNMP traffic is forwarded to the network-management server.

Another interesting problem occurs when managing networks through firewalls. Sometimes the address translation works in the other direction. That is, the network-management server sees translated addresses for everything inside the managed cloud. Some network address–translation devices are capable of doing this kind of wholesale address translation, giving every device a new unique address.

This configuration especially appears in cases in which an external network-management service provider is used. The internal network may contain sensitive information and therefore require protection from the service provider by means of a firewall. The firewall may be configured to pass only SNMP and ICMP packets (and perhaps telnet, FTP, and TFTP for configuration-management purposes) and to translate all IP addresses in the internal network.

This address translation may be used for a good reason. If the network-management service provider manages two large networks, there is a good chance that both of them use the common unregistered 10.0.0.0 address range. If the service provider wants to see both networks properly, they have to do some address translation.

This configuration leads to serious complications, however. Many types of SNMP packets include IP addresses in their data segments. An IP address is just one of many pieces of management information that could be sent. However, this means that the address in the payload of the packet is different from the address in the header of the packet because of address translation. This difference causes serious confusion in many cases. There is no clean workaround. The best way to handle this situation is simply to avoid it. The network-management service provider is advised to maintain a separate, disconnected management server for each client.

In some cases, such as when managing sections of the public Internet, there may be security concerns about allowing SNMP through the firewall. In fact, there are security concerns about using SNMP at all in such hostile environments. Most frequently, the devices that are connected directly to the public Internet have SNMP disabled.

Disabling SNMP presents a serious management problem, however. How can the network manager monitor a device that doesn't use SNMP? As it turns out, a lot of devices, particularly in legacy networks, do not use SNMP. In all of these cases, it is necessary to use out-of-band management techniques. Some of these techniques are discussed later in this chapter.

Redundancy features

Redundancy is one of the most important features of a robust network design. It is also one of the most dangerous because it makes it possible to get away with extremely poor network-management procedures. Suppose, for example, that you have a large network in which every trunk is redundant. If you have a trunk failure anywhere in the network, you suffer no noticeable application failure. This is a good thing, but that broken trunk now needs to be fixed. If you have another failure in the same area, you could have a severe outage. However, if you do not manage the network carefully, you might have missed the failure. After all, the phones didn't ring.

There have been many cases of networks running for years on a backup link because nobody noticed that the primary had failed.

Just as serious, and even less likely to be noticed, is a failure of a redundant backup when the primary was still working properly. Some network managers rely on interface up and down traps that indicate that the backup link or device was activated. This is certainly a good way of telling that the primary has failed, but there is no change of state if the redundant backup systems fail first.

Both of these scenarios reinforce the same point. All systems and links, even redundant backups, should be monitored constantly.

Constant monitoring can be particularly difficult in the case of links that are protected by Spanning Tree. Spanning Tree disables links that are in the backup state. It isn't possible to just ping through these links to see if they are operational. The Spanning Tree protocol does keep track of the status of its disabled links, however. There is an SNMP MIB extension specifically for monitoring Spanning Tree.

The MIB extension is called the *dot1dStp* (for 802.1d Spanning Tree Protocol) defined if RFC 1286. It contains specific entries describing the state of every port, *dot1dStpPortState*. The values that each port can have correspond to the various allowed states: disabled(1), blocking(2), listening(3), learning(4), forwarding(5), and broken(6). Using this SNMP MIB extension should provide all of the necessary information about the health of all redundant Spanning Tree links.

The ideal management technique for these links is to configure automated periodic polling for the states of all Spanning Tree ports using this special `dot1dStpPortState` variable. This information, combined with the traps generated by Link State changes, give a good picture of all primary and backup links.

Tunnels

There are several tunneling protocols. Some, like DLSw, are used to tunnel foreign protocols through IP networks. There are also several ways of tunneling IP in IP.

There are many reasons for tunneling IP in IP. Usually, they have to do with needing to pass transparently through sections of the network that are either externally controlled or lacking in some important feature. A common example of the missing feature problem is a legacy IP network that does not support the required dynamic routing protocol. Similarly, a device might need to take part in multicast applications. If it is located behind network devices that do not support multicasting, then it might be necessary to pass a tunnel through these devices to reach the multicast-enabled portion of the network.

It is also relatively common to use tunnels to hide the network structure of a foreign network that traffic must pass through. For example, it may be necessary to interconnect two buildings by means of a network operated by a telephone company. If the telephone company's network is essentially an IP network, this company might deliver the service as a tunnel to hide their internal network structure.

Another common type of tunnel is the ubiquitous VPN. In this case, an organization extends its private internal network to include a group of devices, or perhaps a single device, on the public Internet. VPN tunnels usually have the additional feature of being encrypted as they pass through the foreign network.

To the network manager, however, tunnels represent a difficult problem. If a failure or congestion occurs anywhere in the hidden region, the only symptoms are either interrupted or degraded service.

It is not possible to narrow down the problem any further than this unless there is another way to see the actual network devices that the tunnel passes through. If the tunnel passes through a foreign network that is managed by another organization, then you can simply pass the problem over to them. For tunnels that pass through internal pieces of network, it is necessary to have an out-of-band management system of some kind.

Out-of-Band Management Techniques

Out-of-band management means simply that user data and management data take different paths. There are many ways to accomplish this. Usually, when people use this term, they mean that the device is managed through a serial port. But it is useful to consider a much broader definition.

Devices are managed out-of-band for three main reasons:

- Many Layer 1 and 2 devices are incapable of seeing Layer 3 addressing.
- Some data streams contain untrusted data, so the devices should not be managed in-band for security reasons.
- Some networks contain tunnels that hide the intermediate devices. These devices must be managed from outside of the tunnel.

First, let's look at the simplest type of out-of-band management. Transceivers, modems, and CSU/DSU type devices are almost impossible to manage in band. This is because these devices function at the physical layer. They do not even see the Layer 3 signaling that would allow them to send and receive SNMP packets. They could be given this capability, but it would require that they look at all frames that pass through them. That generally means that a faster CPU is needed. It can also introduce serious latency problems.

However, many of these types of devices can be managed through a serial port. In fact, in many cases, there is full SNMP (and even RMON, in some cases) support by means of a SLIP or PPP connection through an RS-232 serial port.

Not all lower-layer devices must be managed out-of-band. Many Ethernet and Token Ring hubs are managed in-band, for example. These Layer 2 devices are typically managed by a special purpose management card. This card is connected to the network as if it were an external device, but it lives inside the hub's chassis. In this way, the card can monitor the functioning of the hub without interfering with it.

Security presents another common reason for out-of-band management. The classic example is a router that is connected directly to the Internet. It is dangerous to allow such devices to respond to SNMP gets and sets. The security within SNMP is too simplistic to prevent a dedicated saboteur from modifying the configuration.

Many small organizations with only one router on the public Internet can get away with SNMP management of the device. They can apply access-list restrictions that drop all SNMP packets coming from or going to the Internet. Many organizations also prevent ICMP packets, but these restrictions would not be applied to the internal network. These devices can then be safely managed in-band through the port that faces the private network.

However, this strategy does not work for any organization with several devices connected directly to the untrusted network. If there are several such devices, then it is possible that the topology has become complex, with multiple different paths to the Internet. This complexity makes a simple path-based restriction impractical. Also, if several different devices are all connected directly to the untrusted network, it is possible to compromise one device and then use it as a base. From this base, the other devices can be compromised more easily. Thus, for all but the simplest connections, security restrictions mean that devices directly connected to the Internet should be managed out-of-band.

It can be useful to think of a special variety of management that is only partly out-of-band. This is the case for any tunnel that contains IP traffic. The tunneled traffic does not see any of the intermediate devices. However, these hidden devices can be managed using IP and SNMP through the same physical ports that contain the tunneled data.

For management purposes, there are effectively two types of tunnels. The tunnel can pass through a section of network that has directly accessible IP addressing. Or, the tunnel might pass through devices that cannot be reached in-band from the network-management server.

In the first case, a tunnel might pass through a group of legacy devices. This could be necessary because the legacy devices do not support the preferred dynamic routing protocol, such as OSPF. Or, it may be necessary because they do not support some key part of the IP protocol that is required for the data stream. This might be the case if there are MTU restrictions on the application, or if there are special QoS or multi-cast requirements. Or, maybe the tunnel is there to trick the routing protocol into thinking that a device is in a different part of the network, such as a different OSPF area. However, in these cases, the tunnel passes through devices that are managed in-band. They are part of the same IP-address range and the same Autonomous System (AS). In effect, these devices are managed out-of-band from the tunnels, but through the same physical interfaces that tunnels use. In this case, the management is essentially in-band.

There are also times when a tunnel passes through a different AS. The devices in the other AS could even be part of a distinct group of IP addresses that the network cannot route to directly. This is where the line between in-band and out-of-band becomes rather blurred.

This construction is relatively common when a network vendor uses an IP-based network to carry the traffic of several different customers. They can get excellent fault tolerance through their networks by using dynamic IP-routing techniques, but they must prevent the different customer data streams from seeing one another. This prevention is easily done by simply passing tunnels through the vendor's network Core. The vendor places a router on each of the customer's premises and terminates the tunnels on these routers. Thus, no customer is able to see any of the Core devices directly, nor even the IP-address range used in it. In fact, the IP-address range in the vendor's Core can overlap with one or more different customer-address ranges without conflict. Everybody can use 10.0.0.0 internally, for example, without causing routing problems.

In this case, however, the customer would not do out-of-band management on the vendor's network. It should be managed by the vendor. I mention this configuration, though, because sometimes an organization must be this sort of vendor to itself. This happens in particular during mergers of large corporations.

In effect, all of these different options come down to management through either a LAN port or through a serial port. Management through a LAN port effectively becomes the same as regular in-band management. The only difference is that it might be necessary to engineer some sort of back-door path to the managed LAN port. However, management through a serial port always requires some sort of special engineering. Serial-port management is usually done in one of two ways. In some cases, a higher-layer protocol can run through the serial port using SLIP or PPP. In most cases, there is only a console application available through this port.

If SLIP or PPP options are available, they can make management of these devices much easier. I recommend using it wherever possible.

Figure 9-2 shows one common configuration for out-of-band management using a SLIP link.* The managed device is not specified, although it could be a CSU, a microwave transmitter, or any other lower-layer device that does not see Layer 3 packets directly.

In this case, a low-speed serial port on the router is configured for SLIP. A serial cable is then connected to the management port on the device. As anybody who has set up such a link will attest, there are many ways to misconfigure such a setup.

---

* The example indicates the use of SLIP on the serial link, but any other serial protocol, such as PPP or HDLC, would work in exactly the same way. I specifically mention SLIP because it is common for this type of application.

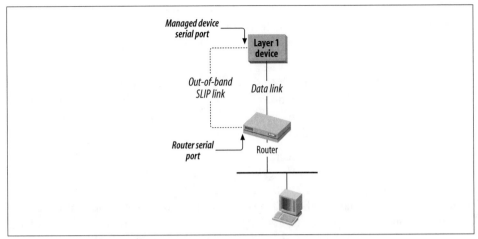

Figure 9-2. Out-of-band management using a SLIP link

Usually, SLIP links assume asynchronous serial connections. Conversely, most router serial ports are synchronous by default. Thus, the router's port must be configured to operate asynchronously.

SLIP creates a point-to-point IP link over the serial line. Therefore, both ends must have IP addresses and the managed device must have its default gateway configured to point to the router's address on this link. Usually, the managed device will not run nor need to run any dynamic routing protocols, so ensure that these are turned off on the router for this port. However, the router needs to distribute the route to this device into the dynamic routing protocol so that the management server knows how to reach it.

In many cases, the managed device uses the same physical serial port for SLIP that it uses for regular console connections. It is important to ensure that the port is configured for SLIP rather than console mode before connecting. This configuration usually just involves connecting a terminal to the console and switching the mode, then disconnecting the terminal and connecting the router in its place.

With any serial connection, make sure that the DTE and DCE relationships are made correctly. This relationship is not just the physical pins on one end the cable being male and female on the other. It also specifies which pins are used for sending and receiving. The relationship becomes more involved for synchronous connections, in which you also have to worry about which device provides the clock signal. In most cases, the manufacturer assumes that the device is talking to a modem. Modems are always DCE, so the serial interface on the device is almost always DTE. Thus, the router must be configured to be DCE.

Once this has all been done properly, it should be possible to do SNMP management of the device. It will have an IP address, and it should respond to ping and SNMP polling. Some of these devices also support telnet to allow a remote-console connection.

For SNMP management, remember to set up the network-management station as the SNMP on the device. This usually does not restrict polling, but rather specifies where the device will send traps when it sees important error conditions. In general, it is a bad idea to specify a large number of trap recipients. One or two should be sufficient.

If too many trap recipients are specified, then each time the device encounters a serious problem, it has to send trap packets to all the devices. Over a slow serial line, sending these packets can take a relatively long time, perhaps as long as a second or more. In a disaster situation, this is a very long time, and it may mean that the device is unable to send the trap to every recipient. It may also mean that the device's CPU is temporarily overloaded by creating and sending traps, which could worsen disaster situation.

For devices that do not support SLIP or PPP, remote out-of-band management can become messy. Somehow, there has to be a console connection between the device's console serial port and the network-management server. If there are more than a few of these devices or if they are physically remote, it is not practical to use direct serial cables. Thus, you have to come up with other methods for making these connections. Once you have these physical connections, you need to have a way to use them automatically. As I said earlier in this chapter, all network monitoring should be automated, and it should have a way to report problems to humans for investigation.

Some network-management software provides the ability to build arbitrary scripts for managing nonstandard devices. If there is a way to connect physically to a device, the software has a way to ask that device about its health. In most cases, the network manager would then automate this script to run every few minutes. If there are no problems, the result is simply recorded in a log. If the device reports an error condition of some kind, it can trigger an alarm to allow a human to investigate.

This fact alone indicates why having hardware standards is so important. If you have a thousand identical devices that you have to manage this way, you can do it all with the same script. You can also afford to take the time to make this script robust and useful. However, if you have a thousand different devices from different hardware vendors, coming up with a thousand such scripts is impractical.

Physically, there are two main ways to create these out-of-band physical connections. For remote locations, the best method is simply to attach a modem to the console port. This attachment allows the device to be contacted for maintenance even if the primary network is down. It is also problematic because the server cannot do a frequent poll of the device's health.

Doing regular polling of serially managed devices requires a way to get this serial data into the network's data stream. A convenient device for doing this is called an inverse terminal server. An inverse terminal server is in many ways very similar to a normal terminal server. In fact, many commercial terminal servers are able to function as inverse terminal servers as well. Some low-speed multiport routers can also be used for this purpose.

A terminal server has a LAN port and one or more serial ports. They were once extremely common, as they provided a way to connect dumb terminals to the network. Each terminal would connect to a serial port on the terminal server. Then, from the terminal server, the user could use a text-communication protocol, such as telnet, to connect to the application server.

An inverse terminal server is similar, except that it makes connections from the network to the serially connected devices, rather than the other way around. Usually, this server works by making a telnet connection to the IP address of the terminal server, but on a special high-numbered TCP port that specifies a particular serial port uniquely.

As Figure 9-3 shows, you can use an inverse terminal server to manage a number of different devices through out-of-band serial connections.

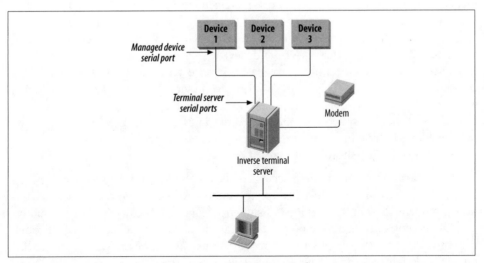

Figure 9-3. Out-of-band management using an inverse terminal server

The network-management server is configured to telnet to the appropriate set of IP address and TCP ports that represent a particular device. It then runs a script that queries the device about its health.

As noted previously, when connecting a serial console port to a router, you have to be careful to configure the DCE and DTE relationships properly. However, unlike the SLIP example, in the case of text-based console ports, there is no common standard for the gender of the console connection.

In some cases, the console port is DCE; in other cases, it is DTE. There are even pathological examples in which the gender of the cable does not match the Layer 1 signaling on the port. For example, it may be a female (DCE) connector physically, but with DTE pin arrangement. In this case, it is necessary to use a null-modem adapter with the cable to convert DCE to DTE instead of just swapping female to male connectors.

In other cases, you need to convert the gender, as well as the DCE/DTE relationship. There are no set rules to make this conversion. Therefore, it is usually a good idea to have a supply of gender-changer plugs and null-modem adapters on hand. To make matters worse, some devices require special cables because they use extra or nonstandard RS-232 signaling. Others do not use RS-232 standards. Consult the documentation of the device being connected.

With many inverse terminal server devices, it is possible to also run SLIP or PPP on the various serial ports. In this way, you can combine several console ports on one inverse terminal server. Since a network-management failure never affects service, it is not necessary to build redundancy. This permits the inverse terminal server to act as a router for several very slow links. The network-management server can then do direct SNMP polling to the out-of-band devices. Of course, if you can do SLIP or text-based console connections through an inverse terminal server, you can do a combination of the two. This configuration can provide a useful way of managing a group of these devices. For example, several CSU devices, firewalls, and other hard-to-manage devices may exist in the same computer equipment room. By running serial cables to a common inverse terminal server, it is possible to provide convenient secure management to all of them at once.

The advantages of remote modem access can be combined with the ability to do periodic polling out-of-band. Most inverse terminal servers provide the ability to connect a modem to one of the ports, as shown in Figure 9-3. This connection allows periodic polling of the console ports of the various serially attached devices through the network. If a serious network failure leaves this part of the network unreachable, the network manager can still get to it by dialing to the modem.

With SLIP-type connectison on an inverse terminal server, you will definitely have a DCE/DTE issue with the ports. As I said earlier, usually the SLIP port on the managed device expects to talk to a modem, so it is usually DTE for the modem's DCE. Those ports on the inverse terminal server connecting to SLIP managed devices will likely be configured as DCE. However, the port that connects to the modem have to be DTE. As always, have a handful of gender changers and null-modem adapters on hand whenever setting up this sort of configuration.

One final issue should be mentioned when connecting modems or terminal servers to a console port. This connection can represent a serious security problem on many devices. Most pieces of network equipment provide the ability to override the software configuration from the console during the boot sequence. This override is frequently called *password recovery*.

Password recovery means that an intruder can take advantage of a power failure to take control of a network device. From there, it might be possible to gain control of other network devices, perhaps even the Core of the network. Gaining control of these devices is a lot of work, requiring a skilled attacker, but it is possible. For this reason, some network-equipment vendors (particularly Cisco) actually include two serial ports, one called Console and the other Auxiliary. The Console port, but not the Auxiliary port, can be used for password recovery. In this case, it is safest to connect any out-of-band management equipment to the Auxiliary port.

CHAPTER 10
Special Topics

This chapter deals with a few other topics that are too important to leave out, but didn't readily fit into other parts of this book: IP multicast, IPv6, and security. Not every site needs to employ these topics initially. To varying extents, they can all be retrofitted into existing networks.

IP Multicast Networks

Most TCP/IP applications operate like a telephone conversation. That is, one device makes a connection with another, they exchange information, and then they disconnect. This activity is appropriate and efficient for some types of applications. Allowing any device to call up any other device avoids the overhead of maintaining a mesh network in which every device is permanently attached to every other.

There are some types of applications that do not work well in this telephone-call model, though. For example, it would be extremely inefficient to run a radio station this way. Radio stations work by broadcasting a single signal. This common signal is received by many end devices simultaneously. Thus, everybody who listens to this station hears the same news or music at the same time. It would be extremely inefficient if this simultaneous broadcast required sending the same signal separately to every device.

Sending the same signal thousands of times is not only inefficient on the server; it also uses the network bandwidth poorly. Radio and television broadcasting are effective partly because the signals are sent only once. Sending the signals once allows a much higher-quality signal to be transmitted than what would be possible if the available bandwidth had to be broken into a separate channel for every listener or viewer. All receivers share the same signal and the same bandwidth.

IP networks have exactly the same problem of limited bandwidth resources, so the IETF has developed a set of standards that allow for multicast IP applications.

There are three parts to a successful implementation of a multicast application. First, the server and the application must have a sensible way of sending multicast information. This means in part that the application must have enough duplication of information that it makes sense to send it as a multicast.

Second, the network must be able to handle multicast traffic. There are many subtle aspects to this ability. The multicast information should reach only those devices that want to see it to avoid wasting the resources of devices that don't care about this application. The network needs a way to duplicate the flow whenever it hits a fork in the road. The network also needs some way of figuring out which end devices listen to each multicast stream so that it can deliver them appropriately.

Third, the end devices that receive the multicast data need a way to identify this traffic and process it into something meaningful. By definition, it is not addressed to them directly. Yet somehow it must be addressed so that only those devices that listen in on this data stream will pick it up.

Multicast Addressing

Chapter 5 pointed out that the range of IP addresses from 224.0.0.0 to 239.255.255.255 is reserved for multicast addressing. Chapter 4 noted that in Ethernet, the lowest bit in the first octet of any multicast Ethernet MAC address is always 1.

The IETF reserved a block of Ethernet MAC addresses for IP multicast purposes. The addresses fall into the range spanning 01:00:5E:00:00:00 to 01:00:5E:7F:FF:FF. Looking at this in binary, 23 bits can be used to express each multicast address uniquely. That is, there are 2 full 8-bit bytes plus 7 bits of a third byte.

However, in the multicast range of IP addresses, there are three full bytes plus four bits in the first byte of the address. So this gives a total of 28 bits to specify unique multicast IP addresses. No matter how these IP addresses are encoded into MAC addresses, there will be some overlap.

The rule for converting between multicast IP addresses and Ethernet MAC address is to copy the 23 lowest-order bits of the IP address into the 23 lowest-order bits of the MAC address. For example, the multicast IP address 224.0.0.5 is used by OSPF for routers to update one another efficiently. The corresponding MAC Ethernet address is 01:00:5E:00:00:05. However, there could easily be a multicast application using a multicast IP address of 225.0.0.5, or even 224.128.0.5. The corresponding Ethernet MAC addresses for both of these addresses are exactly the same as the OSPF address, 01:00:5E:00:00:05.

This situation is not a problem because the IP protocol stack on the device that is listening for OSPF updates always checks the IP address to make sure that it has the right data stream. The same end device can even take part in both applications because the multicast protocol simply delivers the two data streams to the appropriate applications by using their destination IP addresses.

For Token Ring networks, the addresses come from a similar rule, but with a different byte ordering. The byte-ordering rule for converting Ethernet to Token Ring addresses is discussed in Chapter 4.

As discussed earlier in this book, there are IP-address ranges that anybody can use anywhere for any purpose, provided that they don't appear on the public Internet. These address ranges, like 10.0.0.0, allow network designers to develop flexible, internal addressing standards.

The same is also true for multicast IP addresses. The range of IP multicast addresses from 239.0.0.0 to 239.255.255.255 is reserved for "administratively scoped multicast" purposes. This means that these multicast addresses are purely local to a network. No multicast applications using an address in this range can pass into the public Internet.

In addition to this address block for administratively scoped multicasting, there are a two other important blocks of multicast IP addresses. For multicast traffic that is local to a segment and used for low-level network-topology discovery and maintenance, such as OSPF and VRRP, there is a block of addresses from 224.0.0.0 to 224.0.0.255.

However, all other well-known multicast applications are assigned addresses in the range from 224.0.1.0 to 238.255.255.255. These addresses must be registered to be used—in contrast to the administratively scoped multicast addresses, which can be used freely. A current list of registered multicast addresses can be found online at *http://www.iana.org/assignments/multicast-addresses/*.

Multicast Services

The way a multicast application works is relatively simple in concept. It is quite similar to the earlier example of a radio transmission. The server has a designated multicast IP address for the application. When it wants to send a piece of information to all of the listening devices, it simply creates a normal IP packet and addresses it to this designated multicast IP address. The network then distributes this packet to all devices that take part in this multicast group. The server generally knows nothing about who those group members are or how many there are. It just sends out packets to these multicast addresses and relies on the network to deliver them.

The most common type of multicast application operates in a simple one-to-many mode. That is, a central server sends the same information to a large number of client devices. This server might send out stock quotes or news stories, for example. Each time it has a new piece of information to disseminate, it just sends it out in a single multicast packet to the common multicast IP address.

The listening devices have some special work to do, however. Usually, an IP device just listens for its own IP address and its own Layer 2 MAC address. When an appropriately addressed packet comes along, it picks it up and reads it. If this device takes part in one or more IP multicast applications, it must also listen for these multicast IP addresses and the corresponding multicast MAC addresses. Conceptually, this is not difficult to understand, but it means that these devices need to have special multicast extensions to their IP protocol stack. Thus, not all end devices are capable of running multicast client software.

The listening devices can receive the multicast packets in two ways. They might be on the same Layer 2 medium (the same Ethernet segment, for example), in which case they receive the multicast packets directly. Or, they might be somewhere else in the network, in which case the network has to figure out a way to get the packet to the clients.

The network knows where the clients are by using the IGMP protocol, which is discussed in the next section. That protocol only works once the clients and the server know about the multicast IP address for this application. This address can be assigned statically, as in the previous OSPF example.

Multicast applications are deployed dynamically in some cases. This deployment requires another protocol that is responsible for dispensing and managing multicast IP addresses, similar to how DHCP dispenses and manages normal IP addresses. The protocol for doing this is called MADCAP. It is defined in RFC 2730.

Some organizations might find it useful to use dynamically assigned, multicast IP addresses. However, there is significant overhead in using MADCAP, just as there is in DHCP. It requires the existence of one or more specialized MADCAP servers to manage and dispense these addresses. Of course, these servers must be maintained, just as DHCP servers are. Before deploying a MADCAP server, it is important to figure out how frequently the organization needs to allocate dynamic multicast IP addresses. In many cases, it is easier to simply work with static addressing.

There is one important multicast example that makes extensive use of dynamic multicast addresses. This is the general class of conference-type applications. In this case, a large number of end devices wish to share data with one another, similar to a telephone conference call or a mailing list. In this case, all (or many) of the devices either send or receive data to the multicast group address. There is no central server in this configuration, as it is the multicast equivalent of peer-to-peer communication. To let these conference groups spontaneously form and then spontaneously disband again, it is necessary to use dynamic multicast addressing. This, in turn, requires one or more MADCAP servers to manage this dynamic addressing process.

Note that multicasting in IP is always essentially one-way communication. Each multicast server is the base of a tree. The leaves of this tree are the devices that listen to the multicast. There is no backward communication from the client to the server. If the application requires that the multicast client devices talk back to the server, then this must be done through some other method. A common example would be to use standard unicast UDP packets to communicate from the client to the server. In that case, each device that can send multicast packets to the group is itself a root to a multicast tree.

The point is that the network must work out each of these paths separately. The existence of more than one server talking to the same group means extra work for the network in determinining how the downstream relationships work.

Also note that the multicast server is not necessarily a member of the multicast group. If it is a member, then it will receive the packets that are sent to all group members, including the ones that it sends.

In an application with one multicast server, it would be quite reasonable for this server to not be a member of the group. However, if there are several servers, then it might be useful to the application if these different servers kept track of what information the others were sending.

IGMP

The protocol that handles multicast group membership is called Internet Group Management Protocol (IGMP). It is currently in its second version, which is defined in RFC 2236. A third version is currently under development, but is not yet published.

IGMP operates locally between end devices and their first-hop routers. Some version of IGMP is required on every device that supports IP multicast functionality.

The basic operation is relatively simple. When an end device wishes to join a multicast group, it sends a multicast packet to the local LAN segment reporting that it is now a member. If this device is the first member of the group on that segment, then the router has to start forwarding multicast packets for this group onto this segment. IGMP doesn't tell the router how it should find this multicast group if it isn't already receiving it. That router-to-router functionality is the responsibility of other protocols such as MOSPF and DVMRP.

Periodically, the router polls the segment to find out if all members of a group have stopped listening. If there are no responses for a group, then it stops forwarding multicast data for that group.

The idea is simply to avoid congestion that would be caused by sending all multicast packets everywhere in the network. IGMP makes it possible to restrict multicast traffic to only those LAN segments where devices listen to that specific multicast data stream. The router doesn't keep track of which specific devices are members of which groups. It only registers that there is at least one member of a group. As long as there is one member, it forwards the group's multicast data stream.

The main differences between Versions 1 and 2 have to do with groups that change membership quickly and bandwidth-intensive multicast applications. If the membership in a group changes quickly, it can be difficult to know when the last member of the group left. Thus, IGMP Version 2 includes a number of features to help with this termination process. This process is particularly important for multicast groups that consume large amounts of bandwidth. For these applications, the network needs to keep track of membership very closely. Keeping track of it allows the network to conserve bandwidth resources that would otherwise have been consumed by this heavy data stream.

Versions 1 and 2 interoperate well. It is possible to have a mixture of both Version 1 and 2 routers and end devices on the same LAN segment without causing problems. The segment is not able to gain the full benefits of Version 2 in this case, however.

A third version is currently under development. Although it has not yet been published, at least one router vendor has already started to release equipment that uses this new version. Version 3 includes new features to restrict which devices are allowed to send multicast data streams. The receiving devices can specify multicast servers by their source IP address. Specifying these servers has security benefits, as it makes it more difficult for unwanted devices to act as multicast servers. A malicious multicast server can insert unwanted data into another multicast data stream. In most security-sensitive multicast applications, the data stream is encrypted. This encryption makes it difficult for the malicious server to insert bad data. However, it is still possible to use this technique to launch a denial-of-service attack.

The new features of Version 3 also make it possible to optimize bandwidth better by restricting which multicast servers are received on which LAN segments.

Although it is not the best way to solve the problem, source-address restrictions of this kind can be used to help enforce scope. This issue is discussed later in this chapter.

One of the most useful recent developments in multicast networking is the ability to run IGMP on LAN switches, as well as routers. If devices are connected directly to switch ports, then, ideally, the switch should forward only multicast traffic for the groups to which each device belongs. Suppose, for example, that a switch connects to four devices that receive multicast data, as shown in Figure 10-1. The device on Port 1 receives group 239.0.1.15. The device on Port 2 receives 239.0.1.16. The device on Port 3 receives both of these groups, and Port 4 has no multicast membership.

If the switch understands the IGMP packets as these devices join their respective multicast groups, then it can forward the multicast data selectively. If the switch doesn't understand IGMP, then all four devices will see all of the multicast traffic. This is not a problem for Port 3, which sees both groups anyway, but Port 4 doesn't require any of this traffic. Ports 1 and 2 only want to see the groups to which they belong. This is particularly useful in a VLAN environment, where there can be large numbers of devices sharing the same broadcast domain.

Not all switches support IGMP, but it is an increasingly popular feature. It is most frequently seen on switches that have other Layer 3 functionality, such as Layer 3 switching.

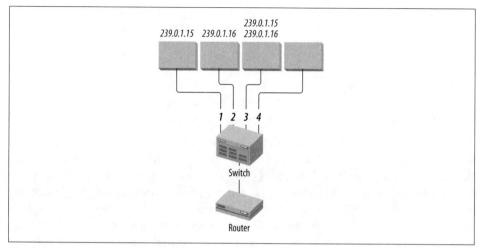

Figure 10-1. A simple multicast network

Group Membership

Although IGMP does a good job of managing groups at the network layer, it does not include application-level functionality. That is, it allows individual devices to join existing groups only if they know the multicast IP address corresponding to that group. It does not provide a way for users to find out what multicast services are offered. It cannot determine the dynamically generated, multicast IP address for a particular application. Suppose, for example, that a user wants to join a multicast group that disseminates a news service. This service might be set up so that it always uses the same multicast IP address. In this case, the application can simply have this static address hardcoded into its configuration. If this application uses dynamically generated addresses or if the client application simply doesn't know the multicast address, then none of the protocols discussed so far provide a way for it to learn this information.

This deficiency is well known, and a group within the IETF called the Multiparty Multimedia Session Control Working Group (MMUSIC) is currently working on solving it. The focus of this group is to develop protocols that are appropriate for large-scale multimedia applications. Small-scale applications do not have the same scaling problems as large-scale applications. If there are only three clients to a server, then it is much easier to build the application so that the server simply talks to the clients directly.

The reason for the focus on multimedia applications is simply that the applications are the most likely areas where multicast transmission will be useful.

MMUSIC currently has several higher-layer protocols in development used to manage groups and their members. The problems have been broken down into a number of key phases such as group creation and destruction, announcing new groups, and inviting members to join. To accomplish this task, they have worked on protocols such as Session Initiation Protocol (SIP), Session Description Protocol (SDP), and Session Directory Announcement Protocol (SDAP). As of the time of writing this book, these protocols were still not fully adopted as standards, and there were no available commercial products based on them.

For the time being, multicast applications must rely on other methods for handling group membership. Thus, most applications currently work with static addressing, or the clients query a known server to find information about the multicast groups it currently uses.

Multicast Routing

Routing of multicast traffic is different from standard IP routing. Because multicast traffic is essentially one way, the network only cares about how to route traffic from the multicast server to the various listening devices. All devices share the same multicast IP address. They are scattered throughout the network randomly. To make the problem harder, these end devices can join and leave multicast groups as often as they like.

The edge routers communicate with the end devices directly using IGMP. These routers always know which multicast groups they need to forward. In a large network, there is a significant possibility that the edge routers are not already receiving this multicast group. In this case, these routers have to have a way to look for the required groups from other routers in the network.

A few multicast routing protocols have been developed to allow routers to find and forward multicast groups as required. The most popular protocols are Multicast OSPF (MOSPF), Distance Vector Multicast Routing Protocol (DVMRP), and Protocol Independent Multicast (PIM). It is not possible to implement a multicast network involving more than one router that doesn't involve such a protocol.

Not all of the following were considered official standards at the time of writing this book, however. Therefore, it may prove difficult to find commercial equipment that supports one or more of them. For all of its promise, IP multicast networking is still in its infancy.

MOSPF

MOSPF is a set of extensions to OSPF that efficiently handles routing of multicast traffic. As in OSPF, MOSPF is a Link State algorithm. All multicast routers in an MOSPF area have identical copies of the Link State database. The Link State database for conventional OSPF keeps track of the status of the various IP connections on all routers in the area. In MOSPF, on the other hand, the Link State database keeps track of where all of the multicast group members are. For each multicast group, there are one or more servers and one or more group members. Every router running MOSPF builds a shortest-path tree not from itself, as in OSPF, but from the source to all of the destinations. In this way, MOSPF builds a reliable and loop-free multicast routing table for every group. This table updates dynamically as the group membership changes.

At many points in this shortest-path tree, there will be branch points where the same packet has to go to two downstream neighbors. MOSPF attempts to minimize the number of branch points, using common links wherever possible. At a certain point, however, it is necessary to split these data streams.

MOSPF takes care of not only the routing, but also tells the router where and how to forward and duplicate packets. This information will be different for every different multicast group. The branch points will change as group membership changes. The packets for each group are only forwarded down links that lead to group members. Bandwidth efficiency means that this information should not be sent anywhere it isn't needed. All of this information must be dynamically updated.

One of the biggest advantages to MOSPF is that it scales well over large networks, just like OSPF. It also interoperates well with OSPF. Thus, MOSPF is a natural choice for the multicast dynamic routing protocol in any network that already uses OSPF.

DVMRP

DVMRP is, as the name suggests, a distance vector protocol. It was the first dynamic, multicast routing protocol. As such, it is missing many useful features and optimizations that are available in later protocols. However, it is simple and easy to configure in most networks, especially for networks that use another distance vector protocol such as RIP or IGRP, for regular IP routing. It may be the most natural choice in these cases.

DVMRP uses IGMP as one of its basic tools. When an end device joins a multicast group, it informs its local router using IGMP. This router then uses IGMP to tell all of its neighbors that it, too, is a member of this group. Then, to eliminate loops, DVMRP takes advantage of the fact that the path back to the source is unique. It assumes that this same path can be used in the forward direction as well. Using it in the forward direction allows each router to calculate the best path back to the source. It can then simply request multicast packets for this group from whatever router is one hop closer to the multicast source.

Unfortunately, DVMRP suffers from many of the same scaling problems as other distance vector protocols. It is probably not the best choice in a large network.

PIM

PIM can operate either in *dense* or *sparse* mode. Dense mode means that routers send all group information to all neighbors. They then prune back the links that do not require particular groups.

Dense mode is efficient when there are relatively few groups and when membership is widespread throughout the network. However, if the network supports a large number of dynamic multicast applications, dense mode is extremely inefficient. (Technically, DVMRP is also considered a dense-mode protocol.)

In sparse mode, on the other hand, individual routers send their neighbors explicit messages asking that they be included or excluded from forwarding particular groups, as downstream devices join or leave these groups. Protocol Independent Multicast—Sparse Mode (PIM-SM) is defined in RFC 2362. This protocol is much more complex than either MOSPF or DVMRP. It includes the ability, for example, to switch from a semistatic forwarding structure based on "rendezvous points" to a dynamic shortest-path tree depending on traffic volume. This switch can be made on a group-by-group basis, according to a locally configured volume trigger.

PIM-SM scales very well to large networks, although setting it up is complicated. This protocol is a good choice for a large network whose unicast IP routing protocol is not OSPF. EIGRP networks, for example, are good candidates for PIM-SM multicast routing.

BGMP

Since most of the unicast routing information through the public Internet is maintained with BGP, the IETF has added multicast extensions to this protocol as well. The extended protocol is called Border Gateway Multicast Protocol (BGMP). However, the public Internet does not fully support multicast routing yet. Isolated pockets of the Internet do support it, including an experimental multicast backbone called MBONE. The main use of BGMP is to enable inter–Autonomous System multicast routing within an organization. In this case, it is often easier to simply use DVMRP or PIM instead.

Network-Design Considerations for Multicast Networks

If a network is going to support multicast traffic, it is a good idea to carefully evaluate which protocols will be used. This decision depends on what protocols are used in the handling of regular unicast traffic, as well as the nature of the applications. In particular, if a network uses OSPF for its unicast routing protocol, it is natural to use MOSPF for the multicast routing. These two protocols interoperate well. It is not even necessary to convert all routers in the network. Conversion can be done in stages.

However, there is one important case when OSPF and MOSPF can cause problems for one another. On any LAN segment that holds several OSPF routers, one of these routers will become designated router (DR) for the segment. A second router will become backup designated router (BDR), and the others will have no special status. The DR router will then handle all Link State flooding for the segment, and it will also summarize all routing information for this segment to the rest of the network. The DR for OSPF will also be the DR for MOSPF.

So if a segment has a mix of OSPF and MOSPF routers, it is critical that an MOSPF router must be the DR. Otherwise, no multicast routing will be correctly handled on this segment. This routing is easily handled by setting the OSPF priorities to zero for all non-MOSPF routers on the segment.

Other than this, MOSPF can be easily deployed to any network that already runs OSPF. The area structures, including the Area Border Routers (ABRs), and Autonomous System Border Routers (ASBRs) all map readily from one to the other. Naturally, this implies that if multicast traffic is to flow between areas, the ABRs must run MOSPF.

Similarly, to allow multicast traffic to flow between Autonomous Systems (ASes), the ASBR devices must also have MOSPF. Of course, having MOSPF also implies that some sort of exterior gateway protocol that supports multicast routing exist between the ASes.

Another important design consideration for multicast networks is whether the LAN switches can take part in IGMP. By default, only the routers run IGMP. Consequently, every time one device on a VLAN joins a multicast group, the entire VLAN sees all of the group traffic. The traffic load can become rather heavy if there are many multicast groups, each with a small number of members.

Many newer LAN switches see the IGMP requests. As each device joins a particular multicast group, the switch starts allowing traffic to pass to the corresponding LAN port. Ports connecting to devices that are not members of this multicast group do not receive this traffic.

If the switches can go further than this and support IGMP over trunk links, then the protocol is much more efficient. If none of the downstream switches contain members of a particular multicast group, then there is no need to forward multicast traffic out of the trunk port. Not forwarding the traffic may save a great deal of valuable trunk bandwidth.

Multicast administrative zones

So far, I have avoided talking about one of the most important potential problems with multicast networks—scope. Returning to the earlier radio analogy, radio stations have severe restrictions about how much power they can use to transmit signals. These restrictions have the effect of limiting how far these signals travel. A local radio station in one country might broadcast using the same frequency as another radio station in another country. There may even be other radio stations in a distant part of the same country using the same frequency.

If every radio station in the world had to have a distinct frequency, radio receivers would become much more cumbersome. A lot of transmissions, such as weather or traffic reports from a distant part of the world, are probably not of universal interest.

Multicast applications have exactly the same characteristics. Worse still, many commercial multicast application vendors always use the same static multicast address. If Company X and Company Y both implement multicast applications on their networks using the same type of server, then they probably use the same multicast IP address. Thus, it is often necessary to restrict how far multicast traffic goes. Even within a particular organization this restriction is often important, as one department may not care about the multicast applications in another department.

The original method for controlling this sort of scope was to use the IP Time to Live (TTL) field. This is a standard field in the IP packet header that is used only for loop elimination in conventional traffic.

Most unicast applications don't restrict how far apart the client and server can be. These applications simply set the value to its maximum value, 255. As I mentioned in Chapter 6, the main use for this field is to help to eliminate loops. However, for multicast applications in particular, TTL can also be a good way to restrict scope.

TTL is a standard field in the IP header that is always 8-bits long. Thus, it can have a value between 0 and 255. If it has a value of zero, the packet is dropped. However, if the value is anything other than zero, the router receiving this packet decreases it by one. For example, whenever a multicast packet is intended only for the local segment, it always has a TTL value of 1. This is the case with all IGMP traffic, for example.

If there is an application that must be restricted to a small area in the network, the server might set the TTL field to a small number like 4. Then the packet will travel three hops before being dropped. It is possible to go even further when restricting traffic. Many routers can be configured to drop any incoming packets that have a TTL value lower than some defined threshold.

A multicast region can be confined by having the server generate the multicast packets with a value that is high enough to reach the farthest corner of the required region. Then all routers that border on the required region would set a TTL threshold value that is high enough to prevent the packets from passing any farther. For example, you might decide that a TTL value of 8 is high enough to get to the entire required area. Then, at all boundaries of the area, you would set a TTL threshold that is high enough to stop the traffic from going farther. Certainly, a value of 8 would be high enough no matter where the server is located in the region.

The trouble with this TTL-based scheme for limiting the scope of multicast zones is its inflexibility. Some applications may need to be confined to the zone, while others need to cover a larger area. Furthermore, it is relatively easy to misconfigure one or more routers and allow multicast groups to leak out of the zone. This leaking could cause serious problems if the same multicast IP address is in use in a neighboring zone for another application.

To address this problem, RFC 2365 defines the concept of administratively scoped IP multicasts. One of the key points in this document is the reservation of the address ranges from 239.0.0.0 to 239.255.255.255 for purely local purposes. Any organization can use these multicast addresses for any purpose. The only restriction is that, like the reserved IP addresses such as 10.0.0.0, they cannot be allowed to leak out onto the public Internet. Furthermore, RFC 2776 defines a protocol called Multicast-Scope Zone Announcement Protocol (MZAP) that handles the boundaries of these multicast zones automatically, preventing leakage between zones.

For most networks, the multicast requirements are far too simple to require MZAP. Indeed, most organizations should be able to get by with a simple TTL-based scope implementation.

Multicast and QoS

Several of the most interesting uses for multicast technology revolve around multimedia applications. However, as discussed in Chapter 8, multimedia applications generally have serious latency and jitter limitations.

For multimedia multicast applications, latency is usually less of a factor than jitter. In live television broadcasting, it is not important if a delay of a few seconds occurs between the actual event and the time remote viewers see it. In fact, television stations use this fact to allow them to edit and censor the outgoing signals.

Latency is not a problem, but jitter is critical. If a stream of video or audio data is sent out to a number of remote receivers, the packets have to arrive in the same order and with the same timing as they were sent. Otherwise, the end application needs to do extensive buffering. In many cases, this buffering is not practical, however. In these cases, the multicast application requires some sort of QoS.

The RSVP protocol is capable of reserving network resources along a multicast path. Many designers developing multicast networks like to use RSVP. But, as I indicated in Chapter 8, a simpler technique based on the IP TOS or DSCP field is usually easier to deploy and frequently more effective in a large network. This is as true for multicast applications as it is for unicast. Before going too far in deploying any QoS system based on RSVP or Integrated Services, it is worthwhile to consider whether Differentiated Services could do the same job with less overhead.

IPv6

In the early 1990s the IETF recognized that it was starting to run short of IP addresses. The common practice at that time was for large organizations to connect their networks directly to the public Internet. Every device had to have a registered IP address.

To make matters worse, there was extensive wasting of IP addresses caused by how the address ranges were subnetted. Address ranges were only allocated as Class A, B, or C ranges. It was clear at that time that IP was heading for a terrible crunch as the number of available addresses dwindled away. Thus, the IETF undertook a number of important initiatives to get around this problem. One of these initiatives developed a new version of the IP protocol that had a much larger address space. The result, IPv6, was first published in late 1995.

IPv6 was an ambitious project because, not only did it increase the address range, it also included many of the new optional features that were added to the previous IP protocol (frequently called IPv4) over the years. The engineers who developed this new protocol wanted to build something that would last.

At the same time, two other important initiatives helped alleviate the pressure of the addressing shortage. These initiatives included Classless Inter-Domain Routing (CIDR) and the combination of Network Address Translation (NAT) and unregistered addressing. These topics were discussed earlier in this book.

The problem for IPv6 is that these other developments worked too well at reducing the pressure. After an initial urgent push, adoption of IPv6 has been slow. But these developments only fixed one of the most pressing problems with IPv4—the shortage of address space.

In truth, IPv6 includes many significant improvements over IPv4, not just an increase in address space. There are several good reasons to migrate to IPv6 even though the urgency is gone. However, it will be a long, difficult, and expensive process for most organizations to make this transition, despite the advantages that it may bring. This process has created a barrier to acceptance of the new protocol that will probably persist until external factors force the change. This could happen because of the eventual shortage of IPv4 address, or because of important new services that, for either technical or ideological reasons, are available only over IPv6.

Although several commercial IPv6 networking products are currently available, the protocol has not enjoyed wide acceptance. Very few large organizations have built IPv6 networks. Consequently, a lot of the discussion that follows is somewhat theoretical, as the practical hands-on experience doesn't yet exist.

This is particularly true when it comes to security. The existing IPv4 public Internet is an extremely active testing ground for security concepts, much as a war zone is an active testing ground for military tactics. Whenever a new security measure is developed, somebody tries to violate it. IPv6 has not yet had the opportunity to demonstrate its real-world reliability in this way. Thus, it seems quite likely that there will be some serious growing pains as it reaches wider acceptance.

The presence of this discussion in this book does not mean that I recommend rushing out and implementing IPv6 networks. Rather, it's here because knowing what sorts of technology are coming along in the future is important. If a network designer knows that the network will eventually have to support IPv6, then it can be designed with that eventual migration in mind.

I may be accused of being a Luddite, but I never like to be the first kid on my block with the latest technology. It's usually better to let somebody else find the problems and then get the improved version. This is particularly true when the technology replaces something that has been tested and refined over the course of almost 20 years, as is the case for IPv4. Inevitably, there will be unforeseen problems with the first releases of IPv6 software. It is also inevitable that they will be found quickly and fixed as more networks adopt the new technology. Where you fit into this time line is largely a matter of choice.

Header Structure

The IETF has taken advantage of the opportunity represented by a new protocol version to simplify the Layer 3 header structure. IPv4 headers have a fixed format involving a large number of optional fields that are frequently unused (or unnecessary). IPv6, on the other hand, uses a much simpler modular approach. The IPv6 header involves several components that can be combined in various ways. The first header is always the standard IPv6 header that contains the source and destination addresses. Figure 10-2 shows this first header format. The layout used in this diagram is becoming a relatively common way to show large binary structures. The marks along the top show the 8-bit boundaries. The marks down the left side show every 32-bit division. In this layout, it is easy to see how the various fields line up with the byte boundaries.

The first field in the IPv6 header is a version code whose value is, simply enough, 6. This field is 4 bits long.

Next comes the 8-bit traffic class field. This field is identical to the DSCP field discussed in the previous chapter. It is used for defining Quality of Service levels.

The third field is the first that is new with IPv6. This field is the flow label. The discussion of IPv4 queuing mechanisms in the previous chapter frequently mentioned traffic flows. In IPv4, these flows are defined by looking at a common set of source and destination addresses along with protocol information. It is important for mechanisms such as fair queuing to identify particular traffic flows uniquely. However, in IPv4, it is extremely difficult to identify them, which causes significant router overhead in identifying and classifying flows. IPv6 gets around this problem by creating a new field that identifies each flow uniquely. The end devices are responsible for assigning a value to

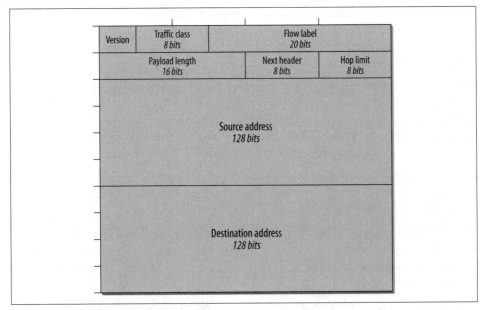

Figure 10-2. IPv6 header options

this particular traffic stream. This assignment is expected to reduce the CPU and memory loading on routers. At the same time, it should reduce both latency and jitter caused by busy routers having to buffer packets before classifying them.

The payload length field comes next. It is always 16 bits long, making the maximum packet size 65,535 bytes long, although an IPv6 specification exists for longer packets. The value does not include the length of this initial header.

The next header field replaces the Protocol field in the IPv4 header. For the most part, it uses the same protocol identification numbers as IPv4. In IPv6, though, it is also possible to use this field to specify that this header is followed by an IPv6 extension header to give additional functionality. I discuss why this header is important later in this section.

Next comes the hop limit field. This field renames the IPv4 TTL parameter, which is appropriate since the value has nothing to do with time.[*] This is an 8-bit field, which allows for a maximum of 255 hops between any two devices. The IETF believes that this number should theoretically be high enough to accommodate the highest complexity that will ever be seen in the Internet.

Finally, the bulk of this header consists of the 128-bit source and destination addresses.

---

[*] The "time" in the name is actually a vestige of the earliest IP implementations. In the early days, the TTL field counted seconds. The meaning gradually shifted from counting time to counting hops as typical per-hop latencies dropped.

Remember that this header is always exactly the same length and that the important features, such as the destination address, are always at exactly the same offset. This arrangement was done deliberately to help routers to find these fields easily; it should also help to improve router performance.

After this basic IPv6 header, the packet can have a standard IP data payload. For example, if it is a TCP packet, then everything that follows would look identical to a TCP packet in IPv4. The next header field indicates what comes next. This field is the same as the IPv4 Protocol field. In the case of TCP, a value of 6 is used in the next header field to indicate that what follows will be TCP information.

There are several new options with IPv6. The new header types are called Hop-by-Hop Options, Destination Options, Routing, Fragmentation, Authentication, and Encapsulating Security Payload.

The Hop-by-Hop Options header communicates with each router along the path. As the packet passes through the network, it may be necessary to have each router do something special. For example, the router might include special QoS information or it might be used to help trace a path.

The Destination Options header allows similar special control, but only the ultimate destination of the packet is allowed to react to these options.

A type of source routing is possible with the Routing header. It allows a packet to loosely specify which routers it would like to pass through on its path. A similar feature is present in IPv4, but it is not widely used.

Fragmentation is never done by the network in IPv6. This is another way IPv6 differs from IPv4. In the new protocol, end devices are expected to do a path-MTU discovery procedure and fragment their own packets. The standard specifies a minimum MTU of 1280 bytes. Any device that wants to avoid fragmentation problems and doesn't want to do a path-MTU discovery can always default to this MTU value to avoid problems. Media that cannot support this MTU, such as ATM, are supposed to emulate it with lower-level fragmentation.

The last two types of extension headers, Authentication and Encapsulating, are used for security purposes. These headers will be discussed later in the section "Security."

Addressing

While IPv4 uses a 32-bit address, the IPv6 address has 128 bits. This capacity allows over 3×10^{38} different addresses, which is a vast improvement over the IPv4 capacity of roughly 4×10^{9}. Increasing the available range of addresses was one of the driving forces behind the creation of IPv6. One disadvantage to having these large-number addresses is that they are cumbersome—even to write down. Therefore, the protocol designers have come up with a set of textual conventions for expressing IPv6 addresses.

The 128-bit address is broken down into 8 16-bit segments that can be expressed as hexadecimal numbers separated by colons. Each 16-bit segment is represented by 4 hexadecimal digits. For example, a valid address would be:

1A30:5BFE:0000:48C9:8A10:03BF:7801:0A3F

The sixth and eighth fields in this address have leading zeros. It is not necessary to write down leading zeros. This situation also applies to the third field, which is composed of all zeros. This same address can also be written as:

1A30:5BFE:0:48C9:8A10:3BF:7801:A3F

The IPv6 specification allows any field, including the first and last, to have a binary pattern of either all zeros or all ones (FFFF). In fact, fields with all zeros are expected to be so common that there are special rules for them.

Consider an address with several fields of all zeros:

1A30:0:0:0:8A10:0:0:A3F

The rule is that any string of adjacent zeros can be replaced by the compact form ::. Because this replacement could be extremely confusing, it can only appear once in an address. Thus, this address can also be written as follows:

1A30::8A10:0:0:A3F

To take this notation to extremes, the new loopback address to replace the IPv4 127.0.0.1 is 0:0:0:0:0:0:0:1, which can be written simply as ::1.

Another notation for these addresses is used for expressing IPv4 addresses for IPv6. This notation is used to allow tunneling IPv4 packets through IPv6 networks without requiring explicit tunnels—a technique that is discussed later in the section "Migrating from IPv4 to IPv6."

There are two ways that IPv4 addresses can be encoded within IPv6 addresses. IPv6 devices, such as routers able to communicate in both IPv4 and IPv6, have addresses that are simply 6 16-bit groups of 0s (96 bits) followed by the 32 bits of the IPv4 address. Pure IPv4 devices whose traffic is tunneled dynamically through an IPv6 network have a slightly different address format. In this case, the address consists of 5 16-bit groups of 0s (80 bits), then 1 16-bit group of 1s, followed by the 32 bits of the IPv4 address.

To see some examples of this, imagine an IPv6 part of the network, and suppose that it must communicate with an IPv4 device. Suppose there is an IPv6 device whose IP address appears to the IPv4 world as 10.1.15.223. This device communicates with an IPv4 device whose address is 10.0.192.17.

In the IPv6 part of the network, these addresses are written with the last 2 16-bit groups written out in IPv4 format. The first 1 will be 0:0:0:0:0:0:10.1.15.223, and the second will be 0:0:0:0:0:FFFF:10.0.192.17. Of course, these addresses can also be written as ::10.1.15.223 and ::FFFF:10.0.192.17, respectively.

To denote address prefixes, the notation is derived from the IPv4 CIDR notation. A subnet that has an address range from 1A30:5BFE:0:0:0:0:0:0 to 1A30:5BFE:FFFF:FFFF:FFFF:FFFF:FFFF:FFFF would be written as 1A30:5BFE::/16.

As with CIDR, this address could represent a number of smaller subnets, such as 1A30:5BFE::/48 and 1A30:5BFE:1::F300/120.

The IPv6 addressing architecture defines several reserved ranges for special purposes. This definition is based on the leading bits in the address. I already mentioned a few special cases such as loopback addresses and the embedding of IPv4 addresses. These adresses both fall into the first reserved range, which begins with eight bits of zeros. Table 10-1 shows the initial address allocations.

Table 10-1. IPv6 address allocations

Binary	Hex of first field	Allocation
0000 0000	0000 to 00FF	Reserved
0000 0001	0100 to 01FF	Unassigned
0000 001	0200 to 03FF	NSAP
0000 010	0400 to 05FF	IPX
0000 011	0600 to 07FF	Unassigned
0000 1	0800 to 0FFF	Unassigned
0001	1000 to 1FFF	Unassigned
001	2000 to 3FFF	Aggregatable Global Unicast Addresses
010	4000 to 5FFF	Unassigned
011	6000 to 7FFF	Unassigned
100	8000 to 9FFF	Unassigned
101	A000 to BFFF	Unassigned
110	C000 to DFFF	Unassigned
1110	E000 to EFFF	Unassigned
1111 0	F000 to F7FF	Unassigned
1111 10	F800 to FBFF	Unassigned
1111 110	FC00 to FDFF	Unassigned
1111 1110 0	FE00 to FE7F	Unassigned
1111 1110 10	FE80 to FEBF	Link-Local Unicast Addresses
1111 1110 11	FEC0 to FEFF	Site-Local Unicast Addresses
1111 1111	FF00 to FFFF	Multicast Addresses

Note that in this allocation, most of this range is initially unassigned—but there are some interesting allocations. In particular, the address architecture sets aside space for mapping IPX and OSI NSAP addressing. This space is intended to allow these other protocols to exist effectively as subnets of IPv6 space and to allow communication between the protocols. This space is most likely to be useful as an interim measure when migrating a network from one of these protocols to IPv6.

The Aggregatable Global Unicast Addresses indicated in Table 10-1 are used as the main method of connecting to the public IPv6 Internet. The basic idea is to break down the address range into a hierarchy of ranges and then to assign these ranges to Internet service providers.

Top Level providers connect directly to the Internet backbone. These providers are specified by a 13-bit identifier, so there can be up to 8192 of these Top Level providers.

Below the Top Level providers are so-called Next Level and Site Level address ranges. A Top Level provider allocates a range of addresses to each of their Next Level providers. The Next Level providers allocate 80-bit Site Level address ranges.

If the site then uses the autoconfiguration mechanism described next, 16 bits are left to specify every local network. This is the same size as the Class B range in IPv4.

The point of this hierarchy is to allow several levels of aggregation. Allowing these levels should have the same effect of reducing routing tables that is achieved by using route summarization, as discussed earlier in this book. Achieving this benefit globally across the entire Internet should improve its scalability.

Because IPv6 has so much more address space than IPv4, it should be possible to avoid Network Address Translation (NAT). By eliminating NAT, it should also be possible to eliminate the problems that it causes. For example, the previous chapter discussed how NAT can complicate network management, and earlier sections of this book talked about how address translation can break or complicate many applications.

There are two main reasons for using NAT in IPv4 networks. The first is to allow the use of unregistered addresses. A network of thousands of nodes can be represented by a small number of registered addresses. NAT just replaces the internal unregistered addresses with these few registered ones as the packets cross out of the network. IPv6 also has ranges of unregistered address space. However, the amount of registered adress range is expanded so much that an organization should be able to address every internal device.

The second reason for using NAT in IPv4 networks is security. NAT makes it possible to obscure the internal network architecture. This information can be useful to an attacker. However, IPv6 includes several special security features that should improve the overall security of the network, even without address translation.

Quality of Service

Quality of Service (QoS) in IPv6 is essentially similar to that of IPv4. Differentiated Services works in exactly the same way, using the traffic-class field in the main IPv6 packet header. Similarly, Integrated Services accompanied by a reservation protocol, such as RSVP, are supported by the new protocol.

The main thing that is new is the flow-label field in the IPv6 header. This field facilitates much of the work of differentiating and classifying traffic for routers. They are no longer forced to look at several fields to establish when two packets are part of the same conversation. As discussed in Chapter 8, looking at several fields is necessary for many popular queuing algorithms, such as Fair Queuing. IPv6 makes the process much easier.

In some cases, the fields that are used in IPv4 to identify flows are not readily available. For example, when the data stream is encrypted, it is sometimes difficult for the routers to see all of the required fields. By putting a flow-identification field right in the Layer 3 header, IPv6 allows much better control over queuing. As a simple example, suppose a device is connected to the network via a VPN tunnel. This tunnel will carry all of the device's traffic in encrypted form. As this encrypted tunnel passes through a router, all traffic inside of it will appear as a single flow in IPv4. However, this situation may not be desirable. If this device is a user's workstation, it means a file transfer has the ability to choke off an interactive session.

Because IPv6 identifies these different flows separately, it can treat the traffic within the tunnel appropriately. This is extremely difficult to accomplish in IPv4; it requires that different flows be given different DSCP or TOS values before they enter the encrypted tunnel.

Security

IPv6 includes both authentication and encryption options in the protocol at Layer 3. These options make it possible to include in the packet's header an authentication fingerprint that verifies that this packet came from the right source. It is also possible to encrypt packets either as a whole tunnel, as in a VPN, or on an individual basis.

The packet-authentication option is the most important new feature here because it is possible to use VPN-style encryption with IPv4. Authentication of individual packets is much harder in IPv4.

Some common types of Internet security attacks involve *spoofing* and *hijacking*. A spoof is when the source address in the packet is not the actual source, but is some other device. Spoofing can be used in many ways. For example, it is possible to send an ICMP ping packet that requests a response from a device. The device that receives this packet sends its response to the source address in the packet. If this source address has been spoofed, then the response is sent somewhere else. If thousands of devices around the Internet all suddenly send unsolicited ping responses to a single device, serious problems can occur. Furthermore, this attack is essentially untraceable.

A hijack attack is similar, except that it involves sending a source-spoofed TCP packet. In this case, the destination has an open TCP session already in progress with the real source device. Thus, it happily accepts the source-spoofed TCP packet that actually originates somewhere else.

In IPv6, these problems should be reduced by the presence of the authentication header. This header is a digital signature that validates the source of the packet. Cryptographers say that the scheme should be extremely difficult to break.

Technically, IPv4 also has the same packet-authentication mechanism available through IPsec. However, IPsec is optional in IPv4, and very few end devices take advantage of it.

Encryption in IPv6 uses the encryption header extension. This extension allows any packet to be encrypted. Of course, it is necessary to have a reasonable way to decrypt the packet when it reaches its destination. Thus, it is probably not practical to encrypt individual packets in a flow. Rather, encrypting an entire conversation is far more effective. Of course, IPv4 has several mechanisms to accomplish the same thing. The industry standard is called IPsec, which forms the basis for the IPv6 implementation as well.

Autoconfiguration

One of the features that IPv6 supporters mention frequently is autoconfiguration of IP-addressing information on end devices. The concept is fairly simple, and it takes advantage of the greatly expanded address space.

Autoconfiguration can occur in either a stateless or stateful way. The stateful method involves the use of an explicit configuration protocol and server, as in DHCP. This method is essentially the same as in IPv4. It is called stateful because the server maintains information about the states of every end device. The stateless autoconfiguration mechanism, on the other hand, allows end devices to deduce enough information by listening to the network, that they can configure themselves.

Combining these two mechanisms is also possible. For example, a device might get its initial basic configuration with the stateless method and then obtain the rest of the information from a server.

The stateless autoconfiguration method is defined in RFC 2462. It is a multiple step process.

In the first step, the device constructs a temporary unicast address using a link-local prefix and its own MAC address. This link-local prefix is a well-defined address prefix that is present on the router, but is not routed off the local segment. Before the device assigns this address to its interface, it sends out a Neighbor Solicitation packet. In IPv4 terminology, this packet is essentially a ping. If there is a response, then there is a conflict, and the address cannot be used.

If the temporary address is not in conflict, the device can carry on with the autoconfiguration process. The next step is to send a multicast Router Solicitation packet to the All-Routers multicast address. This packet finds any routers that have interfaces on the same LAN segment.

One or more of the routers on the segment respond to this query with a Router Advertisement. The response packet can tell the end device that it needs to talk to a DHCP server for either its address, for other required information, or both. Talking to the server is necessary for sites that do not wish to use stateless autoconfiguration or that have important server information that needs to be configured. In the default case, the Router Advertisement packet contains information about the address prefix, which is essentially the same as the IPv4 concept of a subnet and netmask. At the same time, the packet inherently tells the end device about a router that can be used for off-segment traffic.

The device then generates its final address using this address prefix and its own MAC address. Once again, it needs to poll the segment to see if any other devices already use this address. If there is a conflict at either this stage or the earlier link-local address stage, then it is necessary to configure the device manually.

The stateless autoconfiguration method uses the MAC address for the last 64 bits of IP address. On any given VLAN, there is sufficient address space to address over 18×10^{18} devices. This space is extremely wasteful of addresses, but the remaining 64 bits of address range that can be used for the prefix is still far greater than the 32 bits available in the entire IPv4 address.

However, the important issue is not how many bits are in the entire address, but how many bits the organization has available. IPv6 is intended to provide a hierarchical addressing scheme that allows many levels of subnetting. It is possible that an organization will have to use an Internet provider that is many steps removed from the backbone. In this case, it may turn out that they have too few bits to use this stateless autoconfiguration method. For example, suppose that the address prefix for the entire organization is only 72 bits. Then using 64 of these bits for local addressing leaves only 8 bits for defining all of the network segments. This means that the organization can have at most 256 LAN segments, which is definitely not sufficient for many large organizations.

Fortunately, in these cases it is still possible to use an IPv6 version of DHCP to configure the addressing. Using this option immediately opens up the organization's internal address range far beyond the size of the entire IPv4 Internet.

This autoconfiguration method has an extremely important architectural consequence. If end devices listen to the network to determine an appropriate address prefix, then there can only be one address prefix on each LAN segment. Note that this situation is different from IPv4, where a single LAN segment can hold several subnets. In fact, the entire method bears a close resemblance to the system of autoconfiguration used in IPX networks. See Chapter 7 for a discussion of IPX.

Multicast and Anycast

The multicast functionality of IPv6 is similar to that of IPv4. The most important difference is that IPv6 no longer has any broadcast functionality. Everything is done with multicasts of various scopes.

This fact is important because the various broadcast types of IPv4 have caused great confusion. For example, IPv4 tried to make distinctions between all-hosts broadcasts and all-networks broadcasts. However, the all-networks broadcast turned out to be incompatible with the hierarchical addressing structure of CIDR, so it had to be dropped.

IPv6 brings back the same functionality by using multicast. Because it allows good control over multicast scope, the problems IPv4 had with controlling the scope of all-networks broadcasts are no longer relevant.

There are several basic levels for the scope of multicast addresses in IPv6. The difference is defined in the last 4-bit section in the first field of the address.

As I mentioned in the "Addressing" section after "IPv6," any address whose first field is in the range from FF00 to FFFF is a multicast. The third hexadecimal number actually has only two defined values: 0 or 1. If the value is 0, then it indicates a permanently assigned, static multicast address. A value of 1, on the other hand, specifies that this multicast address is *transient*. Transient addresses can be generated dynamically for short-lived applications. The rest of the range from 2 to F is left open for future assignment.

The final hexadecimal number in the first field of the multicast address specifies the scope. Only a few of the possible values were assigned. These values are listed in Table 10-2.

Table 10-2. IPv6 multicast scope

Assignment	Value
Reserved	0
Node-local	1
Link-local	2
Site-local	5
Organization-local	8
Global scope	E
Reserved	F

For example, the multicast address FF01::1 is a static address that is local to the end device. Similarly, any address beginning with FF02 is confined to the local Layer 2 medium, just as IPv4 broadcasts are. Thus, the link-local all-nodes multicast address FF02::1 effectively fills the same role as the IPv4 broadcast address.

For multicasts that leave the segment, there are three defined levels of scope. The multicast can be site-local, organization-local, or global. Global scope means that the multicast reaches the entire Internet. These definitions leave several gaps for future scope definitions.

Anycast is a new feature with IPv6. It was previously proposed in RFC 1546 as a feature for IPv4, but was never implemented. I think anycast is one of the most interesting and potentially useful new features in the protocol. Basically, it is halfway between a unicast and a multicast. It allows the multicast server to send a packet to any group members—usually just the closest group member.

In practice, the network may opt to deliver the packet to more than one group member, and it is also possible that subsequent packets will be delivered to different group members. Therefore, anycast communication is not appropriate for any conversation that needs a concept of what was already said. Instead, it can be used only for stateless applications.

Anycast addresses are taken from the regular unicast address ranges, so there is no intrinsic way of distinguishing them. In effect, each anycast address is simply a unicast address that is assigned to many different hosts. These addresses are then distributed through the network as host routes. This distribution has some potential scaling problems. If the anycast addresses are drawn from a different address range that cannot be summarized easily, then these addresses must exist as host routes in the routing table of every router on the network. If anycast addressing is not allocated carefully, it has the potential to cause serious problems in the future.

Anycast can be useful in many ways. The server can use it, for example, to determine whether it still has any subscribers. By sending an anycast packet that requests a response, the server can discover that it is not currently required and go to sleep. Then it can wake up periodically and do an anycast poll to see if new group members have signed on.

The most exciting possibilities for this feature actually work in the other direction—allowing any of a group of servers to respond to a client request.

IPv4 has several well-known problems with using redundant network devices. For example, it is common to use some sort of traffic-director device to distribute packets to a group of identical servers. This arrangement is most commonly used for web servers. With a traffic-director device, it is necessary to have all servers located both logically and physically together on the network behind this device.

Another method IPv4 uses to accomplish similar levels of redundancy or load sharing is a protocol such as VRRP or HSRP. Typically, these protocols are just used to allow two routers to share the same IP address. Two devices sharing the same address must be able to communicate directly with the same LAN segment.

With anycast, it should be possible to eliminate extra elements such as traffic director boxes and special protocols by just using a single anycast address that represents all servers. The same technique could be used for DNS servers, NTP servers, or any other situation when multiple servers are used for redundancy and load sharing.

In fact, this feature is exciting because an organization could have servers in a dozen countries around the world and users could automatically access whichever one was closest by using the anycast address. Furthermore, if one of these servers was unreachable for any reason, the network would simply find another one transparently.

In general, one would probably not use anycast to provide router redundancy in IPv6. Instead, the specification allows two or more devices to share an IP address on the same LAN segment. There are a number of ways that this sharing could be implemented. This feature will probably emulate VRRP.

Migrating from IPv4 to IPv6

The IPv6 protocol has several features designed specifically to help with migration from IPv4. These features include the ability to tunnel IPv6 traffic in existing IPv4 networks, as well as IPv4 in IPv6 networks.

The tunneling of IPv6 in IPv4 requires the manual creation of point-to-point tunnels between IPv4 routers. When IPv4 is tunneled in IPv6, it is possible to have these tunnel generated dynamically. But this tunneling requires the use of a special reserved range of IPv6 addresses.

Many organizations have had to do protocol migrations in the past. For example, some migrations from IPX or Appletalk to IPv4 have allowed users to access the Internet. In the previous generation of networks, migrations involved Banyan, DEC-NET, and LAT. Thus, the methodology for doing a successful protocol migration has been worked through a few times in different contexts.

Usually, the best way to proceed is to build parallel infrastructure. Building the infrastructure doesn't necessarily mean that all of the equipment needs to be replaced, though. It should be possible to build most of this parallel network over the same gear, using the same physical links, but there must be software changes on the routers and end devices. The equipment all needs to support IPv6, which usually means that a new protocol stack needs to be installed.

In any organization, there will necessarily be legacy equipment that cannot be upgraded and will never run the new protocol. This situation is not a showstopper, however. It can be handled readily using gateway devices to do the protocol conversion. These gateways have a relatively simple job because they only need to replace Layer 3 information in a packet. Everything from Layer 4 up is unchanged in IPv6.

The first step should be to obtain registered IPv6 addresses and decide on a final IPv6 addressing structure. This step, in many cases, simply copies the existing IPv4 structure. Whenever one is given a chance to eliminate flaws in an existing system, however, it's a good idea to at least think about it.

For example, the age of the network may have caused an imbalance in the OSPF areas. Cisco has already announced an IPv6 version of EIGRP. Similarly, an IPv6 RIP and an IPv6 OSPF now exist, so it should not be necessary to change routing protocols. However, the change may provide an opportunity either to change or restructure the routing protocols if the network has outgrown the existing IPv4 structure.

Once the target architecture is clear, the designer needs to figure out how to get there incrementally without taking down the whole network. Only in the smallest offices is it practical to take everything down at once and spend the weekend rebuilding the network.

The other thing to remember is that you don't want just to get to IPv6; you should get to your target architecture. Thus, the migration plan needs to take the network to the ultimate goal as directly and painlessly as possible.

This means, for example, that you probably don't want to make widespread use of temporary IPv6 addressing. IPv6 makes autoconfiguration possible for end devices, and it even includes the concept of a deprecated address to allow a device to change addresses gracefully without losing packets sent to the old address. However, the more changes that you make, the more trouble you will have, so try to go directly to your final addressing structure whenever possible.

Special features, such as dynamic tunnel generation of IPv4 through an IPv6 backbone, will require introducing an extra readdressing phase late in the migration project. Instead, I advocate a migration strategy that involves running both networks in parallel for a period of time and migrating devices from one to the other gradually. The way to implement this migration strategy is to provide dual protocol stacks on both the routers and end devices. The migration can start at the Core by simply upgrading the backbone routers to support IPv6 and defining IPv6 addresses on their interfaces. For the initial phase, there will be no user traffic over this IPv6 backbone structure. Having no user traffic allows the network engineers a chance to test everything.

From the Core, the upgrade can proceed outward to include at least one user community and the servers that they use. It should be possible to keep everything running over the IPv4 infrastructure while observing one or two end devices using IPv6.

At the same time, implementing IPv6 versions of certain network services, such as DHCP and DNS, is necessary. These services can be used to help control the migration, as the end devices consult these servers for their configurations and for information about their servers. When you want a particular user to start using a particular network server through IPv6 instead of IPv4, the DHCP server simply directs the end device to consult the IPv6 DNS server. This DNS server then instructs the end device to use the IPv6 application server. Converting these users to IPv6 should be simply a matter of setting their workstations to prefer the IPv6 view of their applications. If there are problems, converting back to the IPv4 network is simply a user-by-user software change. It should be possible to make most of these changes centrally without extensive use of field technicians.

The converted user workstations need to retain their IPv4 protocol stacks for a while because they still have to access systems that were not converted. However, as more of the network is converted, you will reach a point where the number of legacy IPv4 services is relatively small. At this point, it should be possible to implement IPv4 to IPv6 gateway devices that will do the protocol conversion.

These gateways could even be ordinary routers that are configured to do the conversion. They will probably continue to exist even after the main migration is complete. They will be required to support any legacy IPv4 equipment that is still required but for whatever reason cannot be converted. Once these gateways are in place, it should be possible to eliminate native IPv4 from the end devices gradually, and finally from the routers as well.

Other migration strategies have been suggested in some protocol RFCs. For example, RFC 2529 suggests using a particular range of IPv6 addresses that maps onto the IPv4 address range. Using this range of addresses allows a very direct conversion process because the routers inherently act as gateways between the two protocols. Thus, it should be possible to migrate an entire network quickly by first setting up dual protocols on the routers, as shown previously, and then changing end devices. The new addresses will be IPv6 representations of the old IPv4 addresses.

This method should be quite effective, but remember that it is necessary to then renumber the entire network to the target IPv6 addressing structure. As this renumbering is in progress, the dynamic routing protocol has to keep track of two different ranges of addresses. More importantly, it will have problems summarizing these addresses.

Also note that the IPv6 autoconfiguration mechanism implies that each LAN segment can have only one IPv6 prefix (analogous to the IPv4 subnet address) at a time. Each segment must be converted all at once. This is the second en masse conversion that has to be done. Because of this additional step, I prefer the previously mentioned procedure.

Security

I have talked about security in several places throughout this book already, but there are a few points that warrant special consideration. In general, security is far too broad of a topic for even a single book. I usually take the view that the network cannot be the police. By this, I mean that there are too many ways to get around security restrictions. Placing too much reliance on the network is like locking the doors but leaving the windows open.

In particular, many organizations have policies about such things as outgoing email. In some cases, they have active email filtering to try to block users from sending out corporate secrets. This is a good idea in many cases, as email makes an extremely convenient medium for espionage. However, many organizations appear to forget that it's just as easy to put a floppy disk with those same secrets in your pocket and walk out the door.

The same is true for incoming data. Many organizations try to prevent viruses from coming in by scanning email as it arrives. Scanning is definitely a good idea, but it has to be accompanied by a general virus-scanning process that catches them when they come in through the window instead of the door.

To complicate matters further, no matter how good the network scanning is, it misses a lot. The outgoing file of corporate secrets could be in code. Even firewalls can be circumvented rather easily if one has access to the inside of the network.

See, for example, the April Fool's joke RFC 3093, which describes a way to make a tunnel through HTTP. Since most firewalls readily pass all HTTP packets, it is possible to hide an interactive session inside of an HTTP session. To the firewall, though, it just looks like legitimate web traffic.

Network security should never be considered actual security; it is just one element of a corporate security policy. It is, in effect, just one small tool that should be used to protect the organization.

Every organization should have a standard corporate security policy. This is a short document that describes what activities are allowed and what are not. To be effective, it needs to be backed up by well-defined penalties when somebody deliberately violates the policy. Usually, these penalties involve anything from a reprimand to dismissal, and perhaps even criminal action in some cases. To be effective, everybody in the organization needs to be aware of the policy.

This security policy document is sometimes combined with an appropriate use policy. Appropriate use policies generally define certain activities, such as distribution of pornography or engaging in abusive or criminal behavior using corporate resources, as unacceptable.

The problem with these sorts of documents is that they are frequently too vague to be enforceable. Not everybody would agree on what constitutes pornography or abusive behavior. Thus, it is possible to have a situation in which somebody believes that she is respecting the policy, while her supervisor believes that she is not.

For this reason, I personally prefer to keep security policy separate from appropriate use policy. It should be easier to create a well-defined security policy that does not need to be rewritten to solve problems of vagueness like this. If the appropriate use policy is a separate document, it can be rewritten without throwing the security policy into doubt at the same time.

A security policy needs to address two main issues: espionage and sabotage. *Espionage* is theft of information. *Sabotage* is deliberate disabling or damage of systems or information.

Sabotage using a sledgehammer is usually more effective than using the network. Espionage using a torch to cut your way into a safe of secret documents is also very effective. But neither of these methods has anything to do with the network, so they aren't covered by the network security policy. If you aren't extremely careful about restricting your definitions, building and enforcing this sort of policy can become an impossible task.

There are arguably more ways to do effective sabotage than espionage because the goal is simpler. These methods usually take the form of denial-of-service attacks. However, sabotage can also involve the network equivalent of simple graffiti, as in web site vandalism.

The security policy should be quite general. Once it is complete, you should think of ways to implement it. Think about what sorts of attacks are actually expected and where they are likely to originate. For example, do you believe that employees can be basically trusted, so that enforcement efforts can focus on external threats? Sometimes an organization has different internal groups who would benefit from one another's secrets.

The classic example is an investment bank. These organizations typically include a group of stock traders and a group of corporate financiers. The finance people arrange for large loans and help companies issue stocks and bonds to raise capital. If the stock traders were aware of these activities, they could benefit greatly; unfortunately, being aware of them constitutes illegal insider trading, and it carries severe penalties when the authorities find out about it. Thus, investment banks have to be careful about internal espionage.

In many organizations, the payroll department has computers that issue paychecks to employees. There has to be an appropriate level of security to prevent employees from giving themselves unauthorized bonuses.

Usually, the most serious threat is external. If the organization can't trust its employees, then it has far more serious problems.

The issue of auditing is extremely important but frequently forgotten. There is no point in just locking the doors and assuming that they will remain locked. You have to check them periodically.

In networking, every network Access point has to be monitored carefully. There are several standard things to look for. For example, are the remote-access accounts used properly? Do the accounts belonging to users who are on holiday appear to have heavy use? Futhermore, when a user is in the office, their remote access ID shouldn't be in use.

To look for firewall-evading tunnels like the one discussed earlier in this chapter, you can examine firewall logs. In most cases, these connections should be fairly short-lived, and most of the information should flow inward. If long-lived connections have a lot of outbound information, then this activity should be considered suspicious.

What is considered suspicious varies from one organization to the next, so somebody has to spend a lot of time with the log files to try and identify what sorts of things to look for. Once this is done, it is usually best if the logs are examined by an automated process. Firewall logs tend to be enormous files that are far too big for a human to read through and make sense of.

Most importantly, every suspicious event should be investigated. Suspicious events that keep happening are even more suspicious.

Hub and Switch Port-Level Security

Many organizations use a Layer 2 security mechanism on their hubs and switches. Most high-end access devices have the ability to detect and compare the MAC addresses connected on each port to an expected address. If the device doesn't have the right address, then the port is disabled and a security trap is sent to the network management station. This situation radically increases the amount of work involved in maintaining these access devices. It also has a number of benefits as well.

First, using a system like this means that all network records have to be kept at least somewhat up-to-date. If a PC moves from one place to another or if somebody rearranges a patch panel, things stop working.

The security rationale behind this precaution, though, is to prevent unauthorized access to the network. Most networks are vulnerable to somebody walking in and leaving a small computer plugged in behind a filing cabinet. This device can then make a connection through the firewall to a server somewhere out on the Internet. By running a tunnel through this connection, it's easy for somebody to then have relatively free access to the entire network.

Alternatively, this device could run an autonomous program to gather information or to disrupt the internal network.

This sort of attack can be prevented in two important ways. First, any LAN ports that are not in use should be disabled. Disabling the ports prevents a device from being plugged into a random port on the wall that is no longer in use. Second, port-level MAC-address security needs to be enabled on the access device, whether it is a hub or a switch. Enabling the device is necessary to prevent somebody from taking a legitimate workstation connection and splitting it with a hub. Then the workstation that is supposed to be on the port and the unauthorized device can share the Access point.

On many hubs, there is another reason for using this kind of security. While a switch port only receives traffic destined for that MAC address and multicasts, a hub port receives traffic that is intended for every other port as well. This reception allows a "packet-sniffer" type device to sit passively on the port and listen to everything that goes past on the network. Any PC can be easily converted to execute this type of attack by simply installing publicly available software. Then whomever runs the attack can analyze the data that was gathered and use it to reconstruct secret information.

Note that this process is possible on any hub-access device. Even the device that has a legitimate claim to be on a specific port can have this software loaded onto it. Some hubs have gone even further and have implemented *jamming*.

Ethernet rules require that each time a packet is sent through a hub, it has to be sent out every port. However, it is possible to jam the information in the packet by replacing it with a string of nonsense. Usually, this string is just a bit pattern such as 1010101.... The real packet is transmitted only to the port that should receive it, and every other port receives the jammed version.

This situation is less common now than it once was because access switches are now cost competitive with hubs—particularly hubs with this level of sophistication. On a switch, this is not necessary, as the only port that receives the packet is the one to which it was addressed. There are still methods for attacking a switch with a "packet-sniffer" type device, but they are much more invasive and difficult to execute.

Filtering Traffic

In several places throughout this book, I mentioned the idea of using routers to filter traffic for security reasons. Using routers to filter traffic basically means using the router as a simple firewall. It is configured to look for particular types of packets and to restrict where they are sent.

One common example involves putting a semitrusted server or router connection on the internal network. Doing so is sometimes necessary to deliver a service from an external service provider. No external service provider should ever be trusted fully, since they are intrinsically not subject to your organization's security policy.

This issue becomes a bit fuzzy when it comes to WAN links. The WAN provider has much control over the link medium and can, in theory, see the data that you send through them. Thus, some organizations choose to encrypt data over such links. I discuss the methods for doing this in the "IPsec" section.

This issue also becomes fuzzy when the external service provider's function includes back-office processes such as manipulating important corporate data such as financial information. In these cases, the organization may just decide to treat the external organization as if it were trusted.

For organizations that do not feel comfortable about this situation, however, several techniques improve the security. If the external service provider is considered potentially hostile, then a firewall may be required. However, in most cases, a simpler solution with a filtering router is probably sufficient.

Remember that the threat may not be from the service provider's organization, but from your own organization's competitors who may be using the same service. Suppose, for example, that Company A and Company B both use Service Provider C. If C's network doesn't prevent A from accessing B's network, then corporate espionage through this path is possible.

Many organizations choose to put these Access points behind routers. The routers are configured to allow only certain applications through. Usually, this configuration is specified by means of TCP port numbers, but it can also be easily restricted to certain IP addresses. Restricting on IP addresses can be useful when the service provider's server always uses the same address. The same can be effective internally when the access is always to the same internal device.

Filtering on IP addresses alone is rarely completely reliable; it doesn't do anything about spoof attacks in which the source address of the packet is altered. It also doesn't help in cases when the service provider's server has been compromised by the attacker.

The most reliable mechanism is to filter on everything that you can. If the application is always on the same TCP port number, then make sure that only this port can pass the filter. If this port is combined with IP-address filtering, then the security is that much better.

Note, though, that it is still possible in this case to launch an attack from inside the service provider's network using a spoofed source address and the known application TCP port number. This sort of attack can be extremely difficult to defend against. If it is considered likely, then a robust firewall is necessary.

IPsec

IPsec is a set of security mechanisms for use with IP. RFC 2401 defines the current version. A detailed discussion of this sophisticated cryptographic system is beyond the scope of this book. But discussing its network design implications is useful.

IPsec is a public-key network security system that is used for both authentication and encryption of IP data. It is optional with IPv4. However, many of its functions have been integrated into the main IPv6 specification.

Public-key security means that both communicating devices share an encryption key or password. Each device has a public and a private key. The public key is generated from the private key using a nonreversible process and is then shared.

Device B knows device A's public key, and vice versa, but neither knows the other's private key. Device B can send secret information to device A by encrypting it using an algorithm that can be reversed using A's private key. The data can only be encrypted using information that only the sender has. Then it can only be decrypted using information that only the recipient has.

IPsec actually doesn't restrict the specific algorithm used. There are several good encryption algorithms such as DES, Triple DES, and RSA. They all have strengths, but legal restrictions exist on the use of Triple DES outside of the United States.

IPsec specifies how these algorithmic techniques can encrypt and authenticate IP packets. It is possible to use either or both encryption and authentication.

Encryption or authentication can be deployed using IPsec in two ways. It can be done for all of the traffic between two nodes, as a tunnel. Alternatively, individual traffic flows or conversations can be encrypted or authenticated separately. This process is called *IPsec transport*.

The tunnel mode is generally preferred because it can be used to hide information about the ultimate traffic destinations. For example, suppose a user has a PC connected to the internal network from the Internet via an IPsec tunnel (which is one way to implement a VPN system). In this case, somebody else might intercept and view the packets as they cross through the Internet. However, they will be encrypted, so they can tell very little from this process.

Suppose this session is encrypted per-flow rather than across the whole tunnel. Then it is possible for the person intercepting packets to do what is called traffic analysis. Traffic analysis means that they might tell from the IP addresses and TCP ports that large numbers of files are passing between two specific individuals. In many cases this much information could be sufficient to guess the contents of the packets. By analogy, if you see several pizza delivery cars all arriving at the same house, you can be pretty certain that there's a party going on. You don't need to know what's on the pizzas. Thus, whenever possible, it is usually better to use a fully encrypted tunnel.

There are cases when using this tunnel is not particularly feasible, however. For example, if the user communicates simultaneously with many different hosts that are not all behind the same gateway, it may be easier to use the per-flow system.

Understanding when authentication and encryption are needed is also important. Encryption is used to provide privacy. Authentication is used to verify the source. Clearly these functions are distinct but complementary. Authentication is particularly important if there is some question about the authenticity of the source. For example, if there is a danger that somebody will attempt to spoof or hijack a conversation, then authentication is critical. Encryption, on the other hand, is just used to make sure that nobody else can read the information. It doesn't necessarily mean that it comes from the expected source.

The best security is achieved by using both authentication and encryption together. However, as with the per-tunnel versus per-flow implementations, this usage varies with the particular network application.

Appendix:
Combining Probabilities

Start with one flip of a coin. If you flip the coin once, you know the answer. Call the probability of getting heads P, so the probability of getting tails is $(1-P)$. The symbol $_kP_n$ represents the probability of getting k heads in n flips.

$$_0P_1 = (1 - P)$$

$$_1P_1 = P$$

Flip the coin a second time. Now there are several possibilities. You could have two tails, two heads, a head and a tail, or a tail and a head. I wrote down the probabilities for one flip. The probabilities for the second flip are the same, but I have to multiply the first flip by the second. The probability of getting two heads in a row is the probability of getting heads on the first toss times the probability of getting heads on the second toss:

$$_0P_2 = {_0P_1} \cdot {_0P_1}$$

$$_1P_2 = {_1P_1} \cdot {_0P_1} + {_0P_1} \cdot {_1P_1}$$

$$_2P_2 = {_1P_1} \cdot {_1P_1}$$

The most interesting example is the $_1P_2$. It says that the probability of getting one head in two tosses is the probability of getting a head then a tail, plus a tail then a head. Substituting in the values for $_0P_1$ and $_1P_1$ from the previous example gives:

$$_0P_2 = (1 - P)^2$$

$$_1P_2 = 2P(1 - P)$$

$$_2P_2 = P^2$$

I want to flip the coin one more time before moving on to the general case:

$$_0P_3 = {}_0P_1 \cdot {}_0P_1 \cdot {}_0P_1$$

$$= (1-P)^3$$

$$_1P_3 = {}_1P_1 \cdot {}_0P_1 \cdot {}_0P_1 + {}_0P_1 \cdot {}_1P_1 \cdot {}_0P_1 + {}_0P_1 \cdot {}_0P_1 \cdot {}_1P_1$$

$$= 3P(1-P)^2$$

$$_2P_3 = {}_1P_1 \cdot {}_1P_1 \cdot {}_0P_1 + {}_1P_1 \cdot {}_0P_1 \cdot {}_1P_1 + {}_0P_1 \cdot {}_1P_1 \cdot {}_1P_1$$

$$= 3P^2(1-P)$$

$$_3P_3 = {}_1P_1 \cdot {}_1P_1 \cdot {}_1P_1$$

$$= P^3$$

With the three-flip case, what is happening becomes more obvious. It finds all the ways that I can select k heads from n flips, and it multiplies by P^k to give the probability for this number of heads. Then I multiply again by $(1-P)^{n-k}$ to give the probability for this number of tails. Any statistics text will tell you that the number of ways of picking k from n is:

$$\frac{n!}{k! \cdot (n-k)!}$$

So:

$$_kP_n = \frac{n! \cdot P^k (1-P)^{n-k}}{k! \cdot (n-k)!}$$

Checking this equation against the values already calculated for $n = 3$ in the previous example shows that it is correct:

$$_0P_3 = \frac{3! \cdot P^0 (1-P)^3}{0! \cdot 3!}$$

$$= (1-P)^3$$

Note that 0! and 1! are both equal to 1:

$$_1P_3 = \frac{3! \cdot P^1 (1-P)^2}{1! \cdot 2!}$$

$$= 3P(1-P)^2$$

$$_2P_3 = \frac{3! \cdot P^2(1-P)^1}{2! \cdot 1!}$$

$$= 3P^2(1-P)$$

$$_3P_3 = \frac{3! \cdot P^3(1-P)^0}{3! \cdot 0!}$$

$$= P^3$$

Glossary

Numerics

10Base2

A specification for 802.3 Ethernet that uses 50Ω (ohm) coaxial cable. 10Base2 transmits data at 10Mbps using baseband signaling and is sometimes also called *thin-net*. It has a distance limit of 185 meters.

10Base5

A specification for 802.3 Ethernet that uses thick coaxial cable. 10Base5 transmits data at 10Mbps using baseband signaling and is sometimes also called *thick-net*. It has a distance limit of 500 meters.

10BaseF

Any of a group of baseband fiber optic implementations for 10Mbps 802.3 Ethernet. See also *10BaseFB*, *10BaseFL*, and *10BaseFP*.

10BaseFB

A baseband specification for 802.3 Ethernet that uses a fiber optic medium and runs at 10Mbps. It has a distance limitation of 2000 meters. 10BaseFB has special signaling properties that make it useful on trunk links.

10BaseFL

A baseband specification for 802.3 Ethernet that uses a fiber optic medium and runs at 10Mbps. It is an updated version of the earlier FOIRL standard and interoperates with that standard. It has a distance limitation of 2000 meters.

10BaseFP

A baseband specification for 802.3 Ethernet that uses a fiber optic medium and runs at 10Mbps. The FP stands for fiber-passive. It is intended for connecting end devices. It has a distance limitation of 500 meters.

10BaseT

A specification for 802.3 Ethernet that uses a twisted pair cable, Category 3 or higher. 10BaseT has a distance limit of 100 meters and runs at 10Mbps.

100BaseFx

A specification for 802.3 Fast Ethernet that uses a fiber optic cable of up to 400 meters in length. It runs at 100Mbps using baseband signaling.

100BaseT

A specification for 802.3 Fast Ethernet that uses a Category 5 or higher twisted-pair cable. 100BaseT has a distance limit of 100 meters and runs at 100Mbps.

100BaseT4

A specification for 802.3 Fast Ethernet that uses a Category 3 or higher twisted-pair cable. 100BaseT4 has a distance limit of 100 meters and runs at 100Mbps.

100BaseTX

A twisted-pair implementation of 802.3 Fast Ethernet that is similar to 100BaseT. 100BaseTX is also able to run over shielded twisted-pair cable.

100VG-AnyLAN

A 100Mbps networking standard developed by Hewlett Packard and standardized as 802.12. It is able to use a Category 3 or higher cable. 100VG-AnyLAN does not use the same congestion control mechanisms as Ethernet, but it was developed to run over the same cabling.

1000BaseT

An implementation of 802.3 Gigabit Ethernet that runs over an enhanced Category 5 cable. 1000BaseT uses baseband signaling and runs at 1000Mbps.

802.1

A core part of the IEEE set of specifications that deals with issues related to bridging. The 802.1 specifications are applicable to all IEEE standard LAN protocols such as Ethernet and Token Ring.

802.1d

The specific part of the 802.1 standard that deals with the Spanning Tree protocol. See *Spanning Tree*.

802.1q

The specific part of the 802.1 standard that deals with VLAN tagging. See *VLAN*.

802.2

A core part of the IEEE set of specifications that deals with Logical Link Control. The 802.2 specifications are applicable to all IEEE standard LAN protocols such as Ethernet and Token Ring.

802.3

The part of the IEEE set of specifications that deals with Ethernet. It defines the Physical Layer specifications, as well as Data Link Layer specifications for all Ethernet protocols.

802.5

The part of the IEEE set of specifications that deals with Token Ring. It defines the Physical Layer specifications, as well as Data Link Layer specifications for all Token Ring protocols.

802.11

The part of the IEEE set of specifications that deals with Wireless LANs. It defines the Physical Layer specifications, as well as Data link Layer specifications for all IEEE Wireless protocols.

802.11a

A specific physical implementation of the 802.11 Wireless LAN specification that uses the 5 GHz frequency band and operates at speeds of 72Mbps.

802.11b

A specific physical implementation of the 802.11 Wireless LAN specification that uses the 2.4 GHz frequency band and operates at speeds of 11Mbps.

A

AAL1

ATM Adaptation Layer 1. AAL1 is a specification for ATM networks that transmit data at a constant bit rate (CBR). AAL1 is useful for circuit-emulation applications.

AAL2

ATM Adaptation Layer 2. AAL2 is a specification for ATM networks that transmit data at a variable bit rate (VBR) such as packetized audio and video signals.

AAL3/4

ATM Adaptation Layer 3 and 4. AAL3/4 is similar to AAL2 except that it does not keep timing information intact through the network.

AAL5

ATM Adaptation Layer 5. AAL5 is a specification for ATM networks that transmit data at a variable bit rate (VBR) that is specifically suited to LAN protocols.

ABR

Area Border Router. In OSPF, an ABR is a router that acts as the gateway between two areas.

ABR

Available Bit Rate. In ATM networks, a Quality of Service specification in which cells are delivered on a best-effort basis.

Access Point

In wireless networking, the transmitter and receiver that acts as a hub for the BSS.

Address Resolution Protocol

See *ARP*.

Anycast

A Layer 3 concept in which the destination address specifies any of a set of possible specific destination devices. The network delivers the packet to one or more of these devices, but not necessarily to all of them.

AppleTalk

A set of routable protocols developed by the Apple Computer Corporation.

Area Border Router

See *ABR*.

ARP

Address Resolution Protocol. In TCP/IP networks, the ARP protocol provides the mechanism for devices to find Layer 2 MAC addresses associated with Layer 3 IP addresses.

ARP Cache

In TCP/IP networks, a table maintained by each device correlating Layer 2 MAC addresses with their associated Layer 3 IP addresses. This table of information is stored locally on each device and is called the ARP Cache. See also *ARP*.

ARPA

Advanced Research Projects Agency. ARPA is the research-and-development division of the US Department of Defense, which developed much of the core TCP/IP standards and set up the ARPANET.

ARPANET

An early predecessor to the modern public Internet. The ARPANET was the first large TCP/IP network. Devices in this network were addressed using the Class A address range 10.0.0.0. This address range, now unregistered, is sometimes called the ARPANET range. See also *ARPA*.

AS

Autonomous System. In dynamic routing protocols, an Autonomous System is a region of a network that uses a single Interior Gateway Protocol.

ASBR

Autonomous System Boundary Router. In dynamic routing protocols, an ASBR is a router that forms the gateway between two or more different Autonomous Systems.

ASCII

American Standard Code for Information Interchange. A standard system for encoding character-based data using 8-bit bytes.

ATM

Asynchronous Transfer Mode. A network protocol in which very short "cells" of fixed size are relayed between switches over virtual circuits. ATM is capable of very high transfer rates and low latency. It is commonly used to emulate an Ethernet LAN by means of the LANE standard. See also *LAN*, *LANE*, and *ELAN*.

ATMARP

In ATM LAN emulation, the protocol that provides the ability to map Layer 2 MAC address information to Layer 3 IP addresses. See also *ATM* and *ARP*.

Attachment Unit Interface

See *AUI*.

AUI

Attachment Unit Interface. In 10Mbps Ethernet, AUI provides a generic physical-layer specification that allows the connection of a transceiver to give the desired physical connection. See also *MII* and *GMII*.

Autonomous System

See *AS*.

Autonomous System Border Router

See *ASBR*.

Available Bit Rate

See *ABR*.

B

Bandwidth

A networking term that specifies the nominal peak throughput of a link.

Baseband

In contrast to broadband, a baseband network medium uses only one carrier frequency. See also *Broadband*.

Basic Service Set

See *BSS*.

Beacon

In Token Ring networks, a frame that is sent to indicate that a serious physical problem has occurred.

BGP

Border Gateway Protocol. A particular exterior gateway protocol that is used extensively on the Internet. As with all exterior gateway protocols, it allows the dynamic exchange of routing information between Autonomous Systems. The current version of BGP is BGP Version 4, which is sometimes written BGP-4.

BIA

Burned-In Address. In Ethernet and Token Ring systems, the BIA is a globally unique MAC address that is specified in the hardware of the network interface card (NIC). See also *LAA*, *MAC*, and *NIC*.

Bluetooth

A wireless networking standard that is intended primarily as a cable replacement system. Bluetooth network links typically have a bandwidth of 1–2Mbps.

Border Gateway Protocol

See *BGP*.

bps

Bits Per Second. The transmission rates of various network media are usually represented in bps.

Bridge

A Layer 2 device that connects two or more distinct physical domains. In Ethernet networks, a bridge is used to break up collision domains, while in Token Ring, networks bridges break up token-passing regions. In both cases, the network segments on either side of a bridge belong to the same broadcast domain, however.

Broadband

A network medium that uses several carrier frequencies simultaneously. This medium allows a single cable to carry many different independent signals. See also *Baseband*.

Broadcast

A piece of packet data that is destined for all other devices taking part in the same Layer 2 network.

Broadcast Domain

The region of a network that a broadcast packet will cover. Broadcast domains cross through bridges, but they terminate at routers.

Broadcast and Unknown Server

See *BUS*.

BSS

Basic Service Set. In 802.11 wireless networks, a BSS is the equivalent of a LAN segment. It includes all devices that use a particular Access point for their LAN communications.

Buffer

Used as a noun, a piece of memory used to contain a packet that must be stored temporarily until it can be delivered. Used as a verb, buffering a packet means temporarily putting it in memory.

Burned-In Address

See *BIA*.

Bus

As a basic network topology, a bus is a linear network in which signals sent by each device are carried throughout the length of the network.

BUS

Broadcast and Unknown Server. In ATM LAN Emulation networks, the BUS is a device that is used to forward packets destined for broadcast or unknown addresses. It forwards these packets by means of the ATM multicast facilities.

C

Cable Plant

The set of all LAN wiring and connection panels in a building. This set includes both fiber and copper wiring.

Campus Area Network

A computer network that encompasses all Local Area Networking technology in a set of closely situated buildings.

CAN
See *Campus Area Network*.

Carrier Sense Multiple Access/Collision Avoidance
See *CSMA/CA*.

Carrier Sense Multiple Access/Collision Detection
See *CSMA/CD*.

Category 3 Cable
Also called Cat-3, a specification for unshielded twisted-pair copper cabling. It was commonly used for 10Mbps Ethernet and 4 and 16Mbps Token Ring networks. It can also be used for Fast Ethernet with the less common 100BaseT4 standard.

Category 5 Cable
Also called Cat-5, a specification for unshielded twisted-pair copper cabling. It can be used anywhere Category 3 cable is used, as well as for higher speed networks such as Fast Ethernet and, with limits, Gigabit Ethernet.

Category 5e Cable
Enhanced Category 5 Cable, also called Cat-5e. This specification is an updated version of the Category 5 Cable specification that includes features designed to make it appropriate for Gigabit Ethernet.

Category 6 Cable
Also called Cat-6, a further refinement on previous standards for unshielded twisted-pair copper cabling that is designed for higher-speed networks.

CAU
Controlled Access Unit. For Token Ring network, a CAU is a manageable version of a MAU. See also *MAU*.

CBR
Constant Bit Rate. In ATM Quality of Service, CBR is used for applications that require reliable delivery of cells with end-to-end clocking to ensure minimal jitter.

Cell
In ATM networking, the basic unit of data transmission. Each ATM cell consists of a 5-byte header followed by 48 bytes of data.

Channel Service Unit
See *CSU*.

CIDR
Classless Inter-Domain Routing. Defined in IETF RFCs 1518 and 1519, CIDR is a standard for addressing and routing in IP networks. It abandoned the earlier Class-based system in favor of being able to divide up ranges of 32-bit IP addresses at any bit.

Class of Service
See *COS*.

Classless Inter-Domain Routing
See *CIDR*.

Collision
In Ethernet networks, what happens when two devices attempt to send frames onto the same segment simultaneously.

Collision Domain
In 802.3 Ethernet networks, a network segment. The name comes from the fact that if any two devices in the same collision attempt to transmit simultaneously, they will cause a collision.

Concentrator
A Layer 2 device, such as a hub or a switch, that is used to connect several other devices or groups of devices into a larger network.

Constant Bit Rate
See *CBR*.

Controlled Access Unit
See *CAU*.

COS
Class of Service. In 802.1q VLAN tags, the COS field contains a code that specifies how the frame should be handled by the Quality of Service mechanisms in times of congestion.

CRC
Cyclic Redundancy Checksum.

CSMA/CA
Carrier Sense Multiple Access/Collision Avoidance. This is the name for the method that 802.11 wireless LAN protocols use to handle congestion. It is similar to the Ethernet CSMA/CD system except that it is not possible to reliably generate collision information in a wireless network.

CSMA/CD

Carrier Sense Multiple Access/Collision Detection. This is the name for the method that 802.3 Ethernet uses to handle congestion. The name means that before any device attempts to transmit, it first listens for a carrier signal that would indicate that another device is already using the network. Then, if another device starts transmitting before the first device has finished transmitting, both devices detect the collision and send a jamming signal to prevent either packet from being partially received. They then both wait a random back-off period before trying again.

CSU

Channel Service Unit. When connecting network equipment to WAN circuits, the CSU enables the connection of the user device, such as a router. See also *DSU*.

CSU/DSU

See *CSU* and *DSU*.

Cyclic Redundancy Checksum

See *CRC*.

D

Datagram

A logical chunk of data that is sent through a network as a unit.

DCE

Data Communications Equipment. When connecting a device to a network, particularly in serial-type connections, the DCE device represents a network end, which generally sends the clocking signals. See also *DTE*.

DECNET

Digital Equipment Corporation Network. This is a group of communications protocols developed by the Digital Equipment Corporation.

DHCP

Dynamic Host Configuration Protocol. This protocol allows end devices to learn their network configuration at boot time from a central server.

Differentiated Services

Also called *diffserv*, this specification is a Quality of Service mechanism for TCP/IP. It defines a method of prioritizing IP packets relative to one another that uses the DSCP field in the IP header.

Diffserv

See *Differentiated Services*.

Distance Vector Algorithm

A Distance Vector Algorithm is one type of dynamic routing protocol. Every router in the Autonomous System using this protocol possesses a routing table that shows, for each route, a distance to the destination and a next-hop. This table is then shared with adjacent routers to keep the information current.

Distributed Services Control Point

See *DSCP*.

DLSw

Data Link Switching. This is a standard defined in RFC 1434 that makes it possible to tunnel unrouteable protocols such as SNA through TCP connections.

Domain Name Service

See *DNS*.

DNS

Domain Name Service. This network service provides a lookup database for converting between device names and IP addresses.

DSCP

Distributed Services Control Point. In IP Quality of Service schemes for both IPv4 and IPv6, the DSCP is a field in the packet header that allows an application to mark high- or low-priority packets. The DSCP differs from the earlier IP TOS field in that it also includes the concept of drop precedence.

DSL

Digital Subscriber Line. This method of delivering high-speed access uses telephone-grade copper wiring. There are several different variants such as ADSL, VDSL, and HDSL.

DSU

Data Service Unit. Often used in conjunction with a CSU, a DSU makes the connection to the transmission facility, such as a T1 circuit. See also *CSU*.

DTE

Data Terminal Equipment. When connecting a device to a network, particularly in serial-type connections, the network end generally sends the clocking signals. The DTE end represents the end device, which listens for these clocking signals. See also *DCE*.

DVMRP

Distance Vector Multicast Routing Protocol. This protocol distributes IP Multicast routing information. It uses a Distance Vector algorithm.

E

Early Token Release

See *ETR*.

EBCDIC

Extended Binary Coded Decimal Interchange Code. This 8-bit encoding scheme for character data was developed by IBM. See also *ASCII*.

eBGP

Exterior Border Gateway Protocol. This is the part of the BGP protocol that ASBR devices use to communicate with other ASBR devices from different Autonomous Systems.

EGP

Exterior Gateway Protocol. Generically, an exterior gateway protocol is a dynamic routing protocol used to connect two or more Autonomous Systems. A good example is BGP. However, an older protocol called EGP performs a similar function.

EIGRP

Enhanced Interior Gateway Protocol. Based on the earlier IGRP protocol, EIGRP is a dynamic routing protocol developed by Cisco systems. It uses a Distance Vector algorithm and is capable of providing dynamic routing for TCP/IP, IPX, and Appletalk.

ELAN

Emulated LAN. In ATM LAN Emulation, an ELAN is the equivalent of a VLAN.

End Device

Device that does not take part in any network functions such as bridging or routing.

ESS

Extended Service Set. In 802.11 wireless LAN technology, an ESS is a collection of BSS units. It may or may not support roaming, depending on the architecture.

Ethernet

A LAN technology defined by the IEEE in the 802.3 specification. In one common set of implementations, Ethernet uses a bus topology with the CSMA/CD collision mechanism for handling congestion. Alternatively, Ethernet can be configured as a star topology using full-duplex communication to avoid collisions.

Ethernet II

Ethernet II is an older version of Ethernet that predates the more modern 802.3 specification, although it interoperates well with it. Almost all TCP/IP implementations use Ethernet II.

ETR

Early Token Release. In Token Rings, Early Token Release is the ability of some devices to distribute a new token on the ring after they have finish sending but before they received confirmation that all of their frames were received.

Extended Service Set

See *ESS*.

Exterior Gateway Protocol

See *EGP*.

F

Fast Ethernet

The 100Mbps Standard for 802.3 Ethernet. Fast Ethernet has been implemented on several different physical media including varieties of copper and fiber cabling.

FCS

Frame Check Sequence. A Layer 2 checksum applied to Ethernet and Token Ring frames.

FDDI

Fiber Distributed Data Interface. A 100Mbps fiber optic token-passing LAN system consisting of dual rings for redundancy.

Fiber Optic Inter-Repeater Link

See *FOIRL*.

FIFO

First In First Out. The simplest possible queuing algorithm puts every incoming piece of data into a linear queue and handles them in the order in which they arrived.

File Transfer Protocol

See *FTP*.

Firewall

A network security device. Essentially all commercial firewalls are used for securing TCP/IP data streams. Some operate at Layer 2, but most operate at Layer 3. Most firewalls are capable of hiding the internal structure of the network they protect.

FOIRL

An early version of a fiber optic implementation for 802.3 Ethernet. FOIRL was later updated and replaced by the newer 10BaseFL standard. The acronym has remained in casual use and loosely refers to any fiber optic Ethernet implementation.

Frame

In most Layer 2 networks (excluding ATM), the basic chunk of information. The networks generally include source and destination information (including the possibility of broadcast and multicast destinations). When transporting user-application data, a frame generally holds the packet from a higher-layer protocol. See also *Packet*.

Frame Check Sequence

See *FCS*.

Frame Relay

A Wide Area Network protocol that is capable of connecting one circuit to many other circuits. Frame Relay is a Non-Broadcast Multiple Access (NBMA) medium.

FTP

File Transfer Protocol. FTP is one of the earliest applications built using TCP/IP. It uses a TCP connection and is capable of transferring an arbitrary stream of data from one host to another.

Full Duplex

A Full Duplex link is one that is capable of sending and receiving data simultaneously.

G

Gateway

A device that acts as an intermediate connection point in a network data stream. It terminates the session on one side and starts another on the other. To a Layer 2 network, a router is an example of a Gateway because it rewrites all of the MAC information in each frame received on one side before sending it to the other side. Similarly, special-purpose Gateway devices are capable of connecting different Layer 3 or higher protocols.

Gbps

Gigabits per second. Equal to 1024 Megabits per second, or approximately one billion bits per second.

Gigabit Ethernet

The 1000Mbps Standard for 802.3 Ethernet. Gigabit Ethernet has been implemented on several different physical media, including varieties of copper and fiber cabling.

Gigabit Media Independent Interface

See *GMII*.

GMII

Gigabit Media Independent Interface. A physical sublayer for Gigabit Ethernet that provides the ability to have a number of different possible physical media for a Gigabit Ethernet connection. See also *AUI* and *MII*.

H

Half Duplex

A link that is not able to send and receive data simultaneously. Consequently, in Half Duplex connections, it is necessary to wait until one is finished receiving data before any can be sent.

Hexadecimal

Base 16. The usual notation for hexadecimal is from 0 to 9, followed by A through F, where F represents the number 15. Hexadecimal is useful for representing the contents of 16-bit fields.

HSRP

Hot Standby Routing Protocol. This is a Cisco proprietary standard that allows two routers to possess the same IP and MAC addresses, but to have only one active at a time while the other is a backup. This way, if the primary device fails, the backup can take over for it quickly. See also *VRRP*.

HTTP

Hypertext Transfer Protocol. This TCP-based protocol is used by web browsers to transfer data from web servers.

Hub

Sometimes called a MAU in Token Ring networks, a Layer 2 device that allows connection of end devices into a network. In Ethernet networks, a hub is basically a multiport repeater.

Hub and Spoke

One of the basic network topologies. In this book, the term *star* is used instead to avoid confusion with the network device called a hub.

I

IANA

Internet Assigned Numbers Authority. This international organization is responsible for maintaining records of all well-known numbers associated with the Internet Protocol. This includes, for example, all IP addresses, all registered TCP and UDP port numbers, and all Autonomous System numbers.

iBGP

Interior Border Gateway Protocol. ASBR devices use this part of the BGP protocol to communicate with other ASBR devices within the same Autonomous System.

ICMP

Internet Control Message Protocol. A core part of the IP protocol used primarily for management and reporting network error conditions. ICMP plays a crucial role in allowing TCP protocols to adapt to MTU and congestion problems.

IEEE

Institute of Electrical and Electronics Engineers. The IEEE is an international standards body that develops and publishes standards for many things. Of particular interest for this book are the LAN standards embodied in the set of documents in the 802 series.

IETF

Internet Engineering Task Force. An organization consisting of many diverse groups whose mandate is the ongoing development and publication of Internet standards.

IGMP

Internet Group Management Protocol. IGMP is the protocol used by devices taking part in IP multicast applications to allow them to join and leave multicast groups.

IGP

Interior Gateway Protocol. An Interior Gateway Protocol is a dynamic routing protocol that operates within a single Autonomous System.

IGRP

Interior Gateway Routing Protocol. IGRP is a proprietary Interior Gateway Protocol developed by Cisco. It has been updated and effectively replaced by the more flexible and modern EIGRP protocol, also a Cisco proprietary protocol.

In-Band

Management or control information that is transmitted using the same physical and logical network pathways such as those used by application data.

Integrated Services

Also called *intserv*, a Quality of Service mechanism for TCP/IP. It is intended to offer a mechanism for giving specific applications guaranteed reserved bandwidth. It is normally used in conjunction with a bandwidth-reservation protocol such as RSVP.

Inter-Frame Gap

In Token Ring and Ethernet networks, as well as other networks, the Inter-Frame Gap is the time a device must wait after sending one frame and before sending the next.

Interior Gateway Protocol

See *IGP*.

Internet

Either the Public Internet or any private network of devices that use the Internet Protocol.

Internet Control Message Protocol

See *ICMP*.

Internet Engineering Task Force

See *IETF*

Intserv

See *Integrated Services*.

Internet Protocol

See *IP*.

Inverse Terminal Server

A device that has at least one LAN port and several low-speed RS-232 serial ports. These serial ports can be connected to various devices to access serial-based applications. Then it is possible to use the TCP/IP Telnet protocol to make an IP connection to these serial-attached devices, emulating a direct terminal connection. This connection device can be useful for legacy serial applications and for many network management applications.

IOS

Internetwork Operating System. In Cisco routers, the IOS software runs the device.

IP

Internet Protocol. Sometimes called TCP/IP, this a popular Layer 3 protocol.

Its popularity is largely due to the growth of the public Internet.

IPsec

Internet Protocol Security. This set of protocols is used to provide additional security to the IP protocol suite.

IPv4

Internet Protocol Version 4. This is the current common standard for IP. The extra information is usually provided in this form to distinguish the existing standard from the newer IPv6 standard.

IPv6

Internet Protocol Version 6. This updated version of the IP protocol suite provides many enhancements over the existing version, IPv4. One of the most visible differences is the vastly expanded address space available in IPv6.

IPX

Internetwork Packet Exchange. This protocol was developed by Novell for its NetWare NOS. It is a routable Layer 3 protocol that shares several similarities with IP.

ISL

Inter-Switch Link. ISL is a Cisco proprietary standard for VLAN trunks.

ISO

International Organization for Standardization. The ISO is an international organization that develops and publishes standards relevant to many industries, including networking. The commonly used OSI model for network protocol is one of the ISO's many contributions to networking.

JKL

Jitter

The variation in packet-to-packet latency. Jitter causes distortion in real-time signals such as audio and video data streams.

Kbps

Kilobits per second. Equal to 1024 bits per second.

LAA

Locally Administered Address. In Ethernet and Token Ring networks, it is often possible to override the globally unique MAC address that comes encoded onto a NIC (the BIA). The new address created this way is called an LAA.

LAN

Local Area Network. A computer network confined to a relatively small geographical region such as a single building. The term blends gradually into the term Campus Area Network. However, as distances grow, it becomes increasingly difficult to use common LAN technology and the network tends to require the addition of long-haul technologies. At that point, it ceases to be considered a pure LAN.

LAN Emulation Client

See *LEC*.

LAN Emulation Configuration Server

See *LECS*.

LAN Emulation Server

See *LES*.

LANE

Local Area Network Emulation. LANE specifies a method for making an ATM network emulate the functioning of a large-scale LAN. To do this, it provides mechanisms for encapsulating LAN protocols, such as Ethernet, into the ATM cells. It also provides tools for creating and tearing down ATM virtual circuits (SVC) as they are required.

LAT

Local Area Transport. This very old nonroutable protocol was developed by Digital Equipment Corporation. It is primarily intended to provide terminal access to mainframe computers over bridged networks.

Latency

The time delay involved in sending a piece of information from one point on a network to another. Network latency includes only the transmission delays and does not consider any additional delays that take place within the end devices.

LEC

LAN Emulation Client. In an ATM LANE environment, the LEC is the edge device that performs the encapsulation and switching of LAN protocols into the ATM network. Usually an ATM switch contains a number of Ethernet or other LAN ports.

LECS

LAN Emulation Configuration Server. In an ATM LANE environment, this device keeps track of which devices belong to which ELAN. Usually just one LECS exists for each network, controlling all ELANs, although there could be a backup LECS.

Legacy equipment or protocols

Unfortunately, this term is often used negatively to refer to equipment or protocols that are not at the cutting edge of current technology. However, more accurately, it refers to equipment or protocols that include deprecated features that are difficult to support.

LES

LAN Emulation Server. In an ATM LANE environment, this device controls the functioning of a particular ELAN. There is only one LES for each ELAN.

Link State Advertisement

See *LSA*.

LLC

Logical Link Control. In the 802 protocol suite, a separate logical-link sublayer is defined in 802.2. This sublayer operates in conjunction with the various MAC sublayers, such as Ethernet and Token Ring, to create the Data Link Layer.

Local Area Network

See *LAN*.

Locally Administered Address

See *LAA*.

Logical Link Control

See *LLC*.

Loopback

A logical port on a device that connects to the device itself. Loopback ports exist in the software of a device and provide a way to make a network connection from the device to itself without going onto the network. For routers in particular, it is useful for network management purposes because it provides a Layer 3 address that is always up regardless of which physical ports on the device are down.

LSA

Link State Advertisement. In Dynamic Routing Protocols that are based on a Link State Protocol, such as OSPF, individual routers do not distribute their entire routing tables (as do Distance Vector Protocols). Instead, they just distribute information about the states of their own links, plus the links of other devices they have heard about. This information is distributed by Link State Advertisements.

M

MAC

Media Access Control. In IEEE protocols such as Ethernet and Token Ring, the MAC sublayer to the Data Link Layer defines how devices access the medium. This definition includes any congestion-control mechanisms, such as token passing or collisions, as well as Layer 2 addressing. This Layer 2 addressing is often called the MAC Address.

MADCAP

Multicast Address Dynamic Client Allocation Protocol. This protocol was developed to support multicast IP applications. It is defined in RFC 2730. MADCAP allows the dynamic creation and destruction of temporary multicast groups.

MAN

Metropolitan Area Network. Usually in an urban area, a MAN is a network that allows communication between buildings that are up to a few kilometers apart. With this density and distance limitation it is possible to take advantage of high-speed network technology such as ATM and SONET.

MAU

Multistation Access Unit. In Token Ring networks, a MAU is a device that automatically handles the electrical insertion and removal of individual devices and provides the network pathways for device-to-device communication.

MBGP

Multicast Border Gateway Protocol. This exterior gateway protocol was built as a set of extensions to BGP to support routing of multicast traffic between Autonomous Systems.

Mbps

Megabits per second. Equal to 1024 Kilobits per second, or approximately one million bits per second.

Mean Time Between Failures

See *MTBF*.

Media Attachment Unit

See *MAU*.

Media Independent Interface

See *MII*.

Mesh

A basic network topology in which every device has a point-to-point link to every other device. A special variant of the meshed network is a partial mesh, in which many devices have point-to-point connections to many other devices, but where there isn't a full set of connections.

Metric

In a routing table, a number that represents a cost to get to the destination. In the simplest case, the metric simply represents the number of routing hops required to reach the destination. It can also represent a more sophisticated measure of distance based on the cost of sending the packet through each path.

Metropolitan Area Network

See *MAN*.

MIB

Management Information Base. In SNMP, the MIB is an organized table of data that describes the functioning of the device in detail. The table is organized in a tree structure.

MII

Media Independent Interface. A physical sublayer for Fast Ethernet that provides the ability to have a number of different possible physical media for a Fast Ethernet connection. See also *AUI* and *GMII*.

Modem

Modulator Demodulator. A modem is a device used to convert digital signals into analog electrical impulses for transmission through analog network equipment such as telephone lines. A second modem at the other end of the line converts these analog signals back to digital form. Modern modems contain many advanced features for noise reduction and data compression, which allows significantly higher effective bandwidth through the link.

MOSPF

Multicast OSPF. MOSPF is a set of extensions to the OSPF protocol that allows it to act as a routing protocol for multicast traffic.

MPOA

Multi-Protocol Over ATM. MPOA is an updated version of LANE that makes it more effective as a general LAN emulator by allowing it to carry any LAN protocol.

MTBF

Mean Time Between Failures. In any complex system, it is necessary to treat random individual events, such as device failures, by means of statistical estimates. The MTBF represents how long, on average, a device of a particular type is expected to run continuously before it suffers a failure.

MTU

Maximum Transmission Unit. This is the greatest packet size that can be transmitted over a given network link.

Multicast

A signal that is sent to several, but not all, devices in a particular network region. To work properly, this signal implies that devices must be able to join multicast groups to receive those transmissions that are relevant to them.

Multimode Fiber

There are two general types of fiber optic cable—multimode and single mode. Multimode is capable of supporting light signals of several different wavelengths. It can also operate with an inexpensive low-powered Light Emitting Diode (LED) to inject the signal, since these devices do not have pure single-wavelength light output. The lower costs coupled with lower power requirements means that multimode fiber is perfectly suited to shorter distances such as in a LAN.

Multistation Access Unit

See *MAU*.

N

N+1 Redundancy

In any system where a collection of N identical devices is required for the system to operate effectively, one additional device is added to the system in case one of the N fails. N+1 Redundancy is commonly used for redundant power supplies, as well as redundant trunk links in large networks.

NAT

Network Address Translation. NAT means that IP addresses on one side of a device (usually a firewall, but the feature is available on many routers as well) are transparently rewritten as the packets are passed through to the other side. In many cases, the device rewrites other portions of the IP packet, such as TCP port numbers and sequence numbers, at the same time.

NBMA

Non-Broadcast Multiple Access. Some Layer 2 network media are capable of supporting many devices simultaneously, but without having the capability to support broadcasts. This means that the broadcasts sent by one of the attached devices will not reach all of the other devices in the same media group. Such media are called NBMA.

NetBEUI

NetBIOS Extended User Interface. This is a nonroutable Layer 2 protocol that is frequently used to carry NetBIOS packets. It is most commonly seen in workgroup products such as LAN Manager and Microsoft Windows products.

NetBIOS

Network Basic Input/Output System. This is a simple higher-layer protocol that has frequently been used for building peer-to-peer file, print, and application-sharing services over LAN workgroups.

Netmask

In IP, a binary string that is used to distinguish the network part of the address from the host part. Anywhere the bit pattern has a 1, the corresponding bit in the address is part of the network address. Conversely, the bits in the address that correspond to a 0 in the netmask are interpreted as belonging to the host part of the address.

Network Device

Any device that performs basic network functions such as bridging, routing, or other gateway functions.

Network Interface Card

See *NIC*.

Network Operating System

See *NOS*.

NIC

Network Interface Card. The physical component that allows any device to connect to the network.

NLSP

Novell Link State Protocol. A dynamic routing protocol for IPX that is based on a Link State Protocol.

NNI

Network to Network Interface. In ATM networks, there are two main types of connections. At the edges of the ATM network, switches connect to user devices through UNI links. The connections from switch to switch through the ATM network use NNI links.

NOS

Network Operating System. A NOS is a system that facilitates basic network functions such as file and print sharing, although it could also include other application services.

NTP

Network Time Protocol. This is an IP protocol that allows devices to synchronize their clocks with one another. Generally, at least one of the devices taking part in NTP for a given network is a master, and it is synchronized with an atomic clock or other reliable time source.

O

OC

Optical Carrier. This represents a set of physical carrier protocols using fiber optic signal transmission. There are several OC protocols such as OC-3, OC-12, and OC-48. The number in each case represents the nominal bandwidth of the link. The actual bandwidth for each is found by multiplying this number by 51.84Mbps. For example, OC-3 runs at 155Mbps, OC-12 at 622Mbps, OC-48 at 2488Mbps (2.48Gbps), and OC-192 at 9953Mbps (roughly 10Gbps).

Octet

An 8-bit byte. Network people tend to use the term octet to avoid possible confusion over the number of bits.

OSI

Open System Interconnection. A set of standards, including the OSI model for network layers, defined by the ISO.

OSPF

Open Shorted Path First. A Link State routing protocol for IP. OSPF is an open standard that is implemented by most network-hardware vendors.

OSPF Area

In OSPF, it is necessary to break up the larger Autonomous System into smaller groups called areas. This breakup allows faster and more reliable convergence of the routing protocol.

OUI

Organizationally Unique Identifier. In Ethernet MAC addresses, the first three bytes are called the OUI. This code specifies the vendor of the NIC and helps ensure that BIA MAC addresses are globally unique.

Out-of-Band

Refers to management or control information that is transmitted using a different physical or logical network pathway from that used by application data.

P

Packet

A basic Layer 3 unit of transmission.

Path Vector Algorithm

A Path Vector Algorithm is a particular type of dynamic routing protocol used by BGP. In this protocol, each destination route is accompanied not by a single metric indicating the cost of this path, but by a detailed list of all Autonomous Systems that the path includes.

PDU

Protocol Data Unit. A logical grouping of information.

PHB

Per-Hop Behavior in QoS scheme.

PIM

Protocol Independent Multicast. This dynamic routing protocol is used with multicast networking.

PIM-DM

Protocol Independent Multicast Dense Mode. A particular flavor of the PIM protocol in which all routers in an Autonomous System are assumed to care about all multicast groups.

PIM-SM

Protocol Independent Multicast Sparse Mode. A particular flavor of the PIM protocol in which only some routers in an Autonomous System are assumed to care about all multicast groups. This is generally much more difficult to handle in than Dense Mode.

Ping

An application used to send ICMP echo-request packets to specified destination IP addresses and watch for the ICMP echo response. One often loosely refers to the ICMP echo request and response as *ping packets*, although this term is rather imprecise.

PNNI

Private Network to Network Interface. In ATM networks, there are actually a few different ways to handle the communication between switches. PNNI is one method that is particularly useful in isolated private ATM network.

Policing

When network congestion is encountered, dropping the excess packets is often necessary, particularly if their flow rate has exceeded the amount subscribed to. This process of discarding excess packets is called policing.

PPP

Point-to-Point Protocol. A general Layer 2 protocol that is frequently used over point-to-point links such as serial connections.

PPPoE

Point-to-Point Protocol over Ethernet. A special adaptation of PPP that allows the emulation of a point-to-point link on an Ethernet connection. A PPP connection can then run through this virtual link. This is a popular way of implementing DSL-based Internet connections.

Protocol Analyzer

A device that is able to listen to and decode all of the traffic on a LAN segment. One of the most popular commercial protocol analyzers is called the Sniffer by Network Associates. Frequently, one hears protocol analyzers generically (and incorrectly) referred to as "sniffers."

Protocol Data Unit

See *PDU*.

Proxy ARP

When an appropriately configured router receives an ARP request for a device that it knows (from its routing table) is on a different segment, it will respond to the ARP request on behalf on this device. It can then route the packet normally. This routing generally happens when the device sending the ARP request does not have an appropriate default gateway configured.

PVC

Permanent Virtual Circuit. In many packet-switching networks, such as ATM and Frame Relay, logical connections called Virtual Circuits are set up between end point devices. If this Virtual Circuit is permanently configured through the network, it is called a PVC.

QR

QoS

Quality of Service. This term refers to any of a number of different traffic-prioritization schemes that allow the network to treat different streams of data differently.

Quality of Service

See *QoS*.

Repeater

A device that amplifies, restores, and propagates network signals. In Ethernet networks, a repeater effectively extends a segment including both broadcasts and collisions. This extention is different from a bridge, which relays broadcasts, but not collisions. See also *Bridge*.

RFC

Request For Comments. The IETF publishes its standards, proposed standards, and recommended practices in the form of RFC documents. Each document is given a sequential-order number that is used when referring to the document.

RIF

Routing Information Field. Primarily in bridged networks, but also to a lesser extent in routed networks, it is possible for a frame to specify a RIF that indicates the path that it would like to take.

Ring

As a basic network topology, an architecture in which devices are connected to each of an upstream and a downstream neighbor device. These devices are connected in this way to form a circle so that following these neighbor-to-neighbor connections eventually leads back to the original device.

RIP

Routing Information Protocol. There are actually two distinct protocols called RIP discussed in this book. Both protocols are distance vector routing protocols. One is used for distributing TCP/IP routing information, and the other for IPX routing information.

RJ45

Registered Jack Type 45. RJ45 is standard modular jack and socket used for connecting network cables. In LAN applications, these jacks are primarily used with Category 3 and higher twisted-pair cabling, although there are other applications.

RMON

Remote Monitoring. Originally described in RFC 1271, RMON is a set of SNMP MIB extensions that are useful for many remote network management functions.

Roaming

In wireless technology, describes the ability to change association from one BSS or ESS to another.

Root Bridge

In Spanning Tree, the device at the center of the network. Every bridging device in the network looks for the shortest path to the Root Bridge to eliminate loops.

Router

A Router is a device that connects segments with different Layer 3 network addressing. It is able to forward packets between these segments based on Layer 3 information.

RPC

Remote Procedure Call. An intermediate network layer that allows client-server applications to have a consistent framework. Two distinct popular implementations of this concept share the same name. One was developed by Sun Microsystems and the other by Microsoft.

RS-232

One of the main standards for low-speed serial interfaces.

RSVP

Resource Reservation Protocol. This protocol, described in RFC 2205, allows applications to request particular network resources such as bandwidth or latency characteristics.

RWHO

Remote Who. A broadcast-based protocol developed for the early BSD UNIX platform that allowed each server on a segment to keep track of which users were logged in on which server.

S

SAP

Service Advertisement Protocol. In IPX networks, SAP is the protocol that disseminates information about what servers provide which services.

SDLC

Synchronous Data Link Control. This serial protocol was developed by IBM for use with SNA.

Service Advertisement Protocol

See *SAP*.

Single Mode Fiber

There are two general types of fiber optic cable—multimode and single mode. Single mode is capable of supporting light signals from only a narrow range of wavelengths. This means that it must operate with a more expensive higher-powered laser device to inject the signal, since these devices have a nearly pure, single-wavelength light output. The higher costs coupled with higher power requirements means that single mode fiber is perfectly suited to longer distances such as those in a campus or Metropolitan Area Network.

SLIP

Serial Line Internet Protocol. SLIP is a standard for running IP over low-speed serial lines.

SNA

Systems Network Architecture. SNA is a set of protocols developed by IBM.

SNAP

Sub-Network Access Protocol. Defined in IEEE 802.2, SNAP is a Logical Link Control protocol that is used with Ethernet and Token Ring systems.

SNMP

Simple Network Management Protocol. SNMP is a standard network-management protocol that provides the ability to monitor and configure network devices, as well as send alerts.

SONET

Synchronous Optical Network. SONET is a high-speed optical-network architecture that is commonly used in Metropolitan Area Networks.

Spanning Tree

A protocol and algorithm for ensuring that redundant Layer 2 connections are free from loops. Spanning Tree also enables backup links when primary links fail.

Split Horizon

In dynamic routing protocols, refers to the constraint that devices should not send the same routing information back to the device from which they originally received that information.

SPX

Sequenced Packet Exchange. In the Novell IPX protocol, SPX is a connection-based Layer 4 protocol.

Star

As a basic network topology, represents the configuration where many devices all connect to a single central device. This configuration is also sometimes called Hub and Spoke.

STP

Shielded Twisted Pair. A type of cabling in each run of cable contains a bundle of several strands of copper wire. The individual strands are separately insulated and are twisted around one another in pairs to improve the electrical impedance characteristics. The entire bundle is wrapped in a conducting sheath to provide further protection against electromagnetic radiation. See also *UTP*.

Subnet

In IP networking, a contiguous group of addresses that represent a logical subset of a larger network. Subnet addresses are formed by combining the IP address for the larger network with a netmask to define the contiguous smaller range. See also *Supernet*.

Sub-Network Access Protocol

See *SNAP*.

Supernet

Similar to a subnet except that, instead of subdividing larger network numbers, a supernet consists of several contiguous networks joined together by means of a common netmask. See also *Subnet*.

SVC

Switched Virtual Circuit. In many packet-switching networks such as ATM and Frame Relay, logical connections called Virtual Circuits are set up between end point devices. If this Virtual Circuit is dynamically set up and torn down by the network, it is called an SVC.

Switch

A Layer 2 device that connects different Layer 1 or 2 network domains. It forwards frames between these different network domains based on Layer 2 addressing information. Many switches are capable of grouping these domains into VLANs.

T

T1 Circuit

A long-haul network technology that is able to send data synchronously at 1554Mbps. T1 circuits are often broken up in distinct channels to create a *fractional T1*.

TCP

Transmission Control Protocol. TCP is a connection-oriented Layer 4 protocol built on top of the IP Network Layer. It provides reliable delivery of packets across an IP network.

TCP/IP

Transmission Control Protocol/Internet Protocol. TCP/IP refers to the suite of IP protocols to make a distinction from IP, which can just refer to the Layer 3 part of the protocol.

Telnet

Telnet is a terminal-access program that runs over a TCP connection. It allows character-based interactive access to remote IP devices.

Terminal Server

A device that has a number of low-speed serial ports and a LAN port. Terminal servers are used primarily to connect a number of character-based user terminals to a network.

TFTP

Trivial File Transfer Protocol. TFTP is a simple file transfer protocol that is frequently used to download configuration information into devices at boot time.

Thick-net

See *10Base5*.

Thin-net

See *10Base2*.

Token

In token-passing networks, a small frame. This frame is passed around the network from device to device. Only the device that is currently in possession of the token can transmit data onto the network.

Token Ring

A standard LAN protocol that is defined in the IEEE document 802.5. It consists of a simple-ring topology where devices pass a small token frame from neighbor to neighbor to indicate permission to transmit data.

TOS

Type of Service. The TOS field is a standard component of the IP packet header. It is renamed as Distributed Services Control Point (DSCP) and used slightly differently in some implementations.

Traceroute

A program that sends out a series of probes to attempt to determine the actual path that the network provides to a particular destination. It is a useful troubleshooting tool.

Traffic Shaping

Refers to the technique of flattening out bursts of traffic by means of buffering some packets and dropping others.

Transceiver

Transmitter/Receiver. Referred to as a Media Attachment Unit (MAU) in some literature, this book uses the term Transceiver to avoid confusion with the Token Ring device mentioned in this glossary. A transceiver is generally a device that connects one network's physical medium to another. The most common implementations connect the generic physical sublayers such as AUI, MII, and GMII to specific physical implementations such as 10BaseT, 100BaseT, and 1000BaseT. But there are also transceivers that connect, for example, 100BaseT to 100BaseFx.

Transmission Control Protocol

See *TCP*.

Trap

In SNMP, an unsolicited packet sent from a device to its server, usually to indicate an error condition.

Trunk

A network link that is used to aggregate the traffic from several downstream sources into a single stream.

TTL

Time To Live. In IP networks the TTL field is a number between 0 and 255 that indicates how many more hops the packet can be forwarded through before it is dropped. The TTL field is used to limit scope in some multicast applications, and more generally, it helps break routing loops.

Tunnel

A general term that means that one protocol is carried inside of another temporarily. Tunnels are used to create connections between separate parts of a network. This is sometimes done because the tunneled protocol is not able to propagate through the intervening network for technical reasons. Tunnels are also frequently used for security reasons.

Type of Service

See *TOS*.

U

UBR

Unspecified Bit Rate. In ATM QoS, UBR means that packets are delivered on a "best-efforts" basis, with no guarantees of delivery or delay.

UDP

User Datagram Protocol. UDP is a non–connection oriented Layer 4 protocol built on top of the IP Network Layer. Because it is not connection oriented, it is not able to verify delivery of packets.

UNI

User to Network Interface. In ATM network, UNI specifies the connection point between the first ATM switch at the edge of the ATM network and the device that it connects to. This device may be an end device, or it may be an switch that provides both ATM and LAN interfaces. In many cases, the UNI device connects the ATM network to a port on a LAN router.

Unicast

A piece of data that is sent from one source to only one destination device.

User Datagram Protocol

See *UDP*.

UTP

Unshielded Twisted Pair. A type of cabling in each run of cable contains a bundle of several strands of copper wire. The individual strands are insulated separately and are twisted around one another in pairs to improve the electrical impedance characteristics. See also *STP*.

V

VBR
Variable Bit Rate. In ATM QoS, VBR specifies that the data stream is entitled to a particular average rate and well-defined burst properties.

VC
Virtual Circuit. In many packet-switching networks, such as ATM and Frame Relay, logical connections called Virtual Circuits are set up between end-point devices.

VCI
Virtual Channel Identifier. The VCI is a 16-bit number that appears in the ATM UNI cell header. The VCI defines a particular channel within a Virtual Path (see VPI) that together specify a particular VC.

Virtual Private Network
See *VPN*.

VLAN
Virtual Local Area Network. A VLAN is a logical grouping of devices. The switches that define a particular VLAN ensure that it is treated as a broadcast domain distinct from any other VLANs in the network.

VLSM
Variable Length Subnet Mask. When creating IP subnets, using VLSM means that not all of these subnets must be of equal size.

VPI
Virtual Path Identifier. The VPI is an 8-bit number that appears in the ATM UNI cell header. The VPI defines a bundle of Virtual Channels. See *VCI*.

VPN
Virtual Private Network. A VPN is a tunneled connection that is usually encrypted. It is used primarily to create a secure connection between two points that are separated by an untrusted network.

VRRP
Virtual Router Redundancy Protocol. This protocol is an open standard defined in RFC 2338. It allows two routers to possess the same IP and MAC addresses for redundancy. While only one router is active at a time, the other is capable of quickly becoming active in case it fails. See also *HSRP*.

WXYZ

WAN
Wide Area Network. As opposed to a LAN, a WAN is a network that can have extremely large geographic distances between devices. These distances are generally larger than an immediate metropolitan area and can be arbitrarily large.

WEP
Wired Equivalent Privacy. In 802.11 wireless networking, WEP defines the security standards used in making connections between an end device and an Access point.

Wide Area Network
See *WAN*.

X.25
An older packet-switching network technology. X.25 was similar in many ways to modern Frame Relay except that it operated at slower speeds and included more error-correction functions. X.25 VC's also tended to be switched (SVC) rather than permanent (PVC), as in Frame Relay.

XNS
Xerox Network System. XNS was an early suite of networking protocols that influenced the development of many later protocols, including both IP and IPX.

Bibliography

Requests for Comments

Nearly all TCP/IP-related protocols discussed in this book are described in RFC documents. These documents can be freely downloaded from many sites on the Internet, including *http://www.faqs.org*. Some RFC documents listed here are referenced in the text explicitly; others provide useful background material.

RFC 791
> *Internet Protocol*, J. Postel, September 1981, 44 pp.

RFC 922
> *Broadcasting Internet Datagrams in the Presence of Subnets*, J. Mogul, October 1984.

RFC 950
> *Internet Standard Subnetting Procedure*, J. Mogul and J. Postel, August 1985.

RFC 1058
> *Routing Information Protocol*, C. Hedrick, June 1988, 32 pp.

RFC 1112
> *Host Extensions for IP Multicasting*, S. Deering, August 1989.

RFC 1191
> *Path MTU Discovery*, J. Mogul and S. Deering, November 1990.

RFC 1286
> *Definitions of Managed Objects for Bridges*, E. Decker, P. Langille, A. Rijsinghani, and K. McCloghrie, December 1991, 40 pp.

RFC 1483
> *Multiprotocol Encapsulation over ATM Adaptation Layer 5*, Juha Heinanen, July 1993, 15 pp.

RFC 1518
> *An Architechure for IP Address Allocation with CIDR*, Y. Rekhter and T. Li, September 1993.

RFC 1519

  Classless Inter-Domain Routing (CIDR): An Address Assignment and Aggregation Strategy, V. Fuller, T. Li, J. Yu, and K. Vanadhan, September 1993.

RFC 1546

  Host Anycasting Service, C. Partridge, T. Mendez, and W. Milliken, November 1993, 13 pp.

RFC 1587

  The OSPF NSSA Option, R. Coltun and V. Fuller, March 1994, 15 pp.

RFC 1633

  Integrated Services in the Internet Architecture: An Overview, R. Braden, D. Clark, and S. Shenker, June 1994.

RFC 1700

  Assigned Numbers, J. Reynolds and J. Postel, October 1994.

RFC 1716

  Towards Requirements for IP Routers, P. Almquist and F. Kastenholz, November 1994.

RFC 1771

  A Border Gateway Protocol 4 (BGP-4), Y. Rekhter and T. Li, March 1995.

RFC 1918

  Address Allocation for Private Internets, Y. Rekhter, B. Moskowitz, D. Karrenberg, G. J. de Groot, and E. Lear, February 1996.

RFC 1930

  Guidelines for Creation, Selection, and Registration of an Autonomous System (AS), J. Hawkinson and T. Bates, March 1996.

RFC 2205

  Resource ReSerVation Protocol (RSVP)—Version 1 Functional Specification, R. Braden, L. Zhang, S. Berson, and S. Herzog, September 1997.

RFC 2225

  Classical IP and ARP over ATM, M. Laubach and J. Halpern, April 1998.

RFC 2236

  Internet Group Management Protocol, Version 2, W. Fenner, November 1997.

RFC 2328

  OSPF Version 2, J. Moy, April 1998.

RFC 2338

  Virtual Router Redundancy Protocol, S. Knight, D. Weaver, D. Whipple, R. Hinden, D. Mitzel, P. Hunt, P. Higginson, M. Shand, and A. Lindem, April 1998.

RFC 2362

  Protocol Independent Multicast-Sparse Mode (PIM-SM): Protocol Specification, D. Estrin, D. Farinacci, A. Helmy, D. Thaler, S. Deering, M. Handley, V. Jacobson, C. Liu, P. Sharma, and L. Wei, June 1998.

RFC 2365

Administratively Scoped IP Multicast, D. Meyer, July 1998.

RFC 2373

IP Version 6 Addressing Architecture, R. Hinden and S. Deering, July 1998.

RFC 2375

IPv6 Multicast Address Assignments, R. Hinden and S. Deering, July 1998.

RFC 2401

Security Architecture for the Internet Protocol, S. Kent and R. Atkinson, November 1998.

RFC 2453

RIP Version 2, G. Malkin, November 1998.

RFC 2462

IPv6 Stateless Address Autoconfiguration, S. Thomson and T. Narten, December 1998.

RFC 2474

Definition of the Differentiated Services Field (DS Field) in the IPv4 and IPv6 Headers, K. Nichols, S. Blake, F. Baker, and D. Black, December 1998.

RFC 2475

An Architecture for Differentiated Services, S. Blake, D. Black, M. Carlson, E. Davies, Z. Wang, and W. Weiss, December 1998.

RFC 2529

Transmission of IPv6 over IPv4 Domains Without Explicit Tunnels, B. Carpenter and C. Jung, March 1999.

RFC 2597

Assured Forwarding PHB Group, J. Heinanen, F. Baker, W. Weiss, and J. Wroclawski, June 1999.

RFC 2598

An Expedited Forwarding PHB, V. Jacobson, K. Nichols, and K. Poduri, June 1999.

RFC 2638

A Two-bit Differentiated Services Architecture for the Internet, K. Nichols, V. Jacobson, and L. Zhang, July 1999.

RFC 2730

Multicast Address Dynamic Client Allocation Protocol (MADCAP), S. Hanna, B. Patel, and M. Shah, December 1999.

RFC 2776

Multicast-Scope Zone Announcement Protocol (MZAP), M. Handley, D. Thaler and R. Kermode, February 2000.

RFC 2796

> *BGP Route Reflection—an Alternative to Full Mesh IBGP*, T. Bates, R. Chandra, and E. Chen, April 2000.

RFC 2815

> *Integrated Service Mappings on IEEE 802 Networks*, M. Seaman, A. Smith, E. Crawley, and J. Wroclawski, May 2000.

RFC 2900

> *Internet Official Protocol Standards*, J. Reynolds, R. Braden, and S. Ginoza, Editors, August 2001.

RFC 2932

> *IPv4 Multicast Routing MIB*, K. McCloghrie, D. Farinacci, and D. Thaler, October 2000.

RFC 2998

> *A Framework for Integrated Services Operation over Diffserv Networks*, Y. Bernet, P. Ford, R. Yavatkar, F. Baker, L. Zhang, M. Speer, R. Braden, B. Davie, J. Wroclawski, and E. Felstaine, November 2000.

RFC 3002

> *Overview of 2000 IAB Wireless Internetworking Workshop*, D. Mitzel, December 2000.

RFC 3065

> *Autonomous System Confederations for BGP*, P. Traina, D. McPherson, and J. Scudder, February 2001.

RFC 3093

> *Firewall Enhancement Protocol (FEP)*, M. Gaynor and S. Bradner, 1 April 2001.

Books and Articles

Albitz, Paul, and Cricket Liu. *DNS and BIND, Fourth Edition.* Sebastopol, CA: O'Reilly & Associates, 2001.

Borisov, N., I. Goldberg, and D. Wagner. "Intercepting Mobile Communications: The Insecurity of 802.11," *Proceedings of the Seventh Annual International Conference on Mobile Computing and Networking.* (July 16–21, 2001.)

Cunningham, David G., and William G. Lane. *Gigabit Ethernet Networking.* Indianapolis, IN: Macmillan Technical Publishing, 1999.

Geier, Jim. *Wireless LANs: Implementing Interoperable Networks.* Indianapolis, IN: Macmillan Technical Publishing, 1999.

Hunt, Craig. *TCP/IP Network Administration, Second Edition.* Sebastopol, CA: O'Reilly & Associates, 1997.

Ibe, Oliver C. *Essentials of ATM Networks and Services.* Menlo Park, CA: Addison-Wesley, 1997.

Mauro, Douglas, and Kevin Schmidt. *Essential SNMP*. Sebastopol, CA: O'Reilly & Associates, 2001.

Miller, Brent A., and Chatschik Biskidian. *Bluetooth Revealed*. Upper Saddle River, NJ: Prentice Hall PTR, 2001.

Oppenheimer, Priscilla. *Top-Down Network Design*. Indianapolis, IN: Cisco Press, 1999.

Retana, Alvaro, Don Slice, and Russ White. *CCIE Professional Development: Advanced IP Network Design*. Indianapolis, IN: Cisco Press, 1999.

Rose, Marshall T. *The Simple Book: An Introduction to Network Management*. Upper Saddle River, NJ: Prentice Hall PTR, 1996.

Scott, Charlie, Paul Wolfe, and Mike Erwin. *Virtual Private Networks*. Sebastopol, CA: O'Reilly & Associates, 1998.

Spurgeon, Charles E. *Ethernet: The Definitive Guide*. Sebastopol, CA: O'Reilly & Associates, 2000.

Stevens, W. Richard. *TCP/IP Illustrated, Volume 1*. Menlo Park, CA: Addison-Wesley, 1994.

Vegesna, Srinivas. *IP Quality of Service*. Indianapolis, IN: Cisco Press, 2001.

In addition to these references, the Institute of Electrical and Electronics Engineers (IEEE) publishes the defining standards for several lower-layer LAN protocols, including Token Ring. These documents can be found online at the IEEE web site at *http://www.ieee.org*.

Index

Numerics

10Base2, 6, 127, 130
10Base5, 130
10BaseF, 131
10BaseFB, 131
10BaseFL, 131
10BaseFP, 131
10BaseT, 6, 130
  hubs and, 140
    throughput, 60
10 Gigabit Ethernet, 146–149
  signaling standards for, 146
100BaseFx, 6
100BaseT
  Gigabit Ethernet and, 146
  hubs and, 140
100VG-AnyLAN, 132
10/100 hubs, 140
1000BaseT, 146
5-4-3 Repeater rule, 139
80d5 format, 142
80/20 rule, 68
  distribution level, 83
802.1d (Spanning Tree), 61
802.1Q (VLAN Tagging), 105, 111, 152
802.2 LLC sublayer, 134
802.3 (Ethernet), 132–136, 144, 165
  full-duplex mode, 138
802.5 (Token Ring), 141, 145, 165
802.11, 155, 157
  802.11a/802.11b, 157

A

ABR (Area Border Router), 197
ABR (Available Bit Rate), 151
access level, 85, 114
  augmenting with hubs, 128
accounting management, 275
Address Resolution Protocol (see ARP)
addresses
  broadcast, 135
  globally unique, 234
  IP, 170–175, 182–191
    classes, 173–175
    default gateways, 190
    flexibility, 189
    loopbacks, 188
    for OSPF, 224
    ranges, 184–187
    standard subnet masks, 187–189
    unregistered addresses, 182
  IPv6, 322–325
    allocations, 324
  IPX, 242–244
  MAC, 54, 132, 135
    broadcast/multicast, 135
    DECNET protocol, 135
    Ethernet, 135
    fault recovery and, 27
    IP ARP packets and, 48
    security and, 99
    updating, 63

We'd like to hear your suggestions for improving our indexes. Send email to *index@oreilly.com*.

addresses (*continued*)
   multicast, 135
      (see also addressing, multicast)
      (see also addressing, dynamic
         multicast; IP multicast networks)
addressing
   dynamic multicast, 309
   multicast, 307
      anycast and, 329–331
      IPv6 allocation, 324
AF (Assured Forwarding), 261
   classes, 262
   design considerations, 270
   Drop Precedence, 262
   DSCP and, 265
algorithms
   Distance Vector, 197, 207, 236
   DUAL, 206
   dynamic routing protocols and, 194
   Fair Queuing, 259
   Link State, 213, 236
   Priority Queuing, 260
   Split Horizon, 205
      Split Horizon with Poisoned
         Reverse, 208
   Weighted Fair Queuing, 259
anycast, 330
API (Application Program Interface), QoS
      classes and, 268
Apple Ethernet protocol reserved type, 133
AppleTalk, 169
application control, filtering for, 94
application layer (OSI model), 9
Application Programming Inteface (API),
      QoS classes and, 268
architectural problems in network
      management, 290–298
Area Border Router (ABR), 197
ARP (Address Resolution Protocol), 175
   ATMARP, 152
   cache, 98
   packets, 136
   proxy, 25
   switching vs. routing, 79
AS (Autonomous System), 196, 215
   BGP and, 229
   EIGRP and, 211
   NLSP and, 239
   RIP and, 197–206
   (see also OSPF Autonomous Systems;
      RIP)
AS numbers, BGP and, 231

ASBR (Autonomous System Boundary
      Router), 197
   BGP and, 230
   OSPF and, 218, 222
Assured Forwarding (see AF)
Asynchronous Transfer Mode (see ATM)
ATM (Asynchronous Transfer Mode), 6,
      149–154
   ATMARP, 152
   bottlenecks and, 253
   collapsed backbones, 71
   cost efficiency, 149
   LAN services, 151–154
   on large-scale LANs, 149
   routing and, 11
   telephony and, 149
   WANs and, 149
Attachment Unit Interface (AUI), 140
AUI (Attachment Unit Interface), 140
autoconfiguration, IPv6, 327–328
Autonomous System Boundary Router (see
      ASBR)
Autonomous System (see AS)
Available Bit Rate (ABR), 151

B

backbone routers, 219
backbones, 70
   collapsed, 70–74
      capacity, 72
      cost efficiency, 72
      redundancy, 73
   distributed, 74–78
      trunk capacity, 75–77
      trunk fault tolerance, 77
   Gigabit Ethernet as, 148
backoff interval, 137
Backup Designated Router (BDR), 216
backups, 19
   automatic, 24–30
      via load balancing, 28–30
      network management and, 274, 296
      Spanning Tree, 63–65
      (see also fault recovery, automated)
   distributed backbones, 78
bandwidth, 3, 16, 254
   latency and, 255
Banyan Network Operating System Ethernet
      types, 133
Banyan Vines VIP, 169
baseband signaling, 131
Basic Service Set (BSS), 156

BDR (Backup Designated Router), 216
beacon frame, 143
Best Efforts Delivery, 256
    FIFO compared to, 257
    Weighted Fair Queuing and, 259
BGMP (Border Gateway Multicast
        Protocol), 315
BGP (Border Gateway Protocol), 228–233
    Autonomous System numbers, 231
    dynamic routing capabilities in
        firewalls, 294
    where to use, 232
BIA (burned-in address), 132, 135
blocking ports, 62
Bluetooth, 155, 157
Border Gateway Multicast Protocol
        (BGMP), 315
Border Gateway Protocol (see BGP)
border routers, 213
bottlenecks
    collapsed backbones, 72
    efficiency and, 252
    (see also congestion)
bridges
    design issues, 139
    (see also bridging; switching)
bridging
    Ethernet to Token Ring, 11
    root bridges, 62
    routing vs., 10–12
    source-route, 145
    stability and, 51
    (see also switching)
broadband signaling, 131
broadcast, 54
    address, 135
    all-subnets, 180
    domains, 85, 169
    multiple subnet, 179–181
    storms, 48, 98
    switching strategies and, 96–98
Broadcast and Unknown Server (BUS), 153
BSS (Basic Service Set), 156
buffering, 258–261, 266
    monitoring statistics about, 286
buffers, 16
    congestion and, 46
bugs in routers/switches, 48
    (see also troubleshooting)
burned-in address (see BIA)
BUS (Broadcast and Unknown Server), 153
bus topology, 54

business requirements, 1–4, 16
    bandwidth (see bandwidth)
    expenses, 2
    geography, 2
    installed base, 3
    security (see security)
    vs. technical requirements, 1

C

cables
    cable plants, 57
    Categories 3 and 5, 57, 130, 163
        Enhanced Category 5, 163
    Categories 6 and 7, 163
    fiber optic, 131
        Fast Ethernet/Gigabit Ethernet, 146
        single mode/multimode, 167
    Type 3, Token Ring, 6
    (see also cabling, structured)
cabling, structured, 162–168
    horizontal, 163–166
    vertical, 166
caches, ARP, 98
capacity planning, 275
Carrier Sense Multiple Access/Collision
        Avoidance (CSMA/CA), 155
Carrier Sense Multiple Access/Collision
        Detection (CSMA/CD), 54
carrier sense phase (Ethernet), 136
CAU (Controlled Access Unit), 145
cells (ATM), 150
CIDR (Classless Inter-Domain
        Routing), 174, 229
    multiple subnet broadcast, 181
circuits, point-to-point, 6
Citrix systems, QoS classes and, 267
Class A–D networks, 173, 180
Class of Service (CoS), Ethernet and, 148
Classical IP, 152
Classless Inter-Domain Routing (see CIDR)
classless routing, 228
collapsed backbones, 70–74
    capacity, 72
    cost efficiency, 72
    redundancy, 73
collision
    detection
        Ethernet, 136–138
        full-duplex access and, 137
        late collision, 137
    rates, 59, 60
    wireless LANs, 155

complexity
  redundancy, implementing, 23
  traffic anomalies and, 47
configuration management, 273
  tracking physical changes, 274
congestion, 45
  efficiency and, 252
  hop counts and, 250
  RED and, 252
  RIP, 238
  routers and, 86
  SAP, 238
  (see also bottlenecks)
console ports, management problems
    with, 305
containment, 48
Controlled Access Unit (CAU), 145
core level, 85
core links, oversubscribing, 252
CoS (Class of Service), Ethernet and, 148
cost efficiency, 2, 247
  ATM, 149
  collapsed backbones, 72
  failures and, 15
  Gigabit Ethernet on desktops, 147
  hierarchical design, 82
  horizontal cabling, 164
  installed base, 129
  LAN technologies, 126–129
  manageability and, 12
  performance and, 16, 127
  redundancy and, 42
  switching vs. routing, 80
  Token Ring, 144
  trunks, 109
  VLANs, 66
  (see also efficiency)
cost-to-bandwidth ratios, ATM, 149
CRC errors, 250
CSMA/CA (Carrier Sense Multiple
    Access/Collision Avoidance), 155
CSMA/CD (Carrier Sense Multiple
    Access/Collision Detection), 54
CSU/DSU devices, out-of-band management
    of, 298

D

data link layer (OSI model), 6
  LLC sublayer, 134
  network congestion and, 47
Data Link Switching (see DLSw)

DECNET protocol, 135, 169
  TCP/IP operating with, 135
design
  bridges/hubs/switches, 139
  constraints
    expenses, 2
    installed base and, 3
  efficiency and, 248, 270–272
  goals, 51
  hierarchical, 81–113
    cost efficiency, 82
    hop counts and, 249
    OSPF Autonomous Systems, 222
    routing strategies, 83–95
    switching and bridging
      strategies, 95–100
    VLAN-based topologies, 100–113
  human errors in, 51–54
    limiting, 49
  IP multicast networks, 315–318
    multicast administrative
      zones, 316–318
    QoS and, 318
  management considerations, 275–280
    ease of access, 277
    equipment, location of, 279
    probes, location of, 275
  reliability, implementing, 113–115
  strategies
    for IP, 182–191
    for IPX, 242–246
  switching vs. routing
    modern style, 80
    old style, 78–80
  top-down philosophy, 12
  (see also design types)
design types, 50–125
  concepts, 50–58
  LAN topologies, large-scale, 115–125
    core-level routers, 116–118
    dedicated network-management
      VLANs, 276
    distribution-level routers, 118
    multilevel routers, 119
    remote sites, connecting, 121–124
  topologies, 54–58
    bus, 54
    mesh, 57
    ring, 55
    scalability of, 58–61
    star, 56

token bus, 54
(see also design types, LAN topologies,
large-scale)
Designated Router (DR), 216
devices
BIAs and, 135
collision detection and, 136–138
connecting, 114
efficient use of, 248
end, 51
bridging/switching and, 96
broadcasts and, 96
connections, 81
cost efficiency and, 127
DHCP and, 289
dynamic routing protocols and, 54, 65
HSRP and, 65
hubs and, 139
network functions, performing, 25, 52
reliability and, 53, 114
routing and, 25
stability and, 51
traffic and, 83
VLANs and, 110
VRRP, 65
network, 51, 53
automated fault recovery and, 26
design philosophy and, 13
Ethernet framing standards, 132
redundancy and, 18
stability, 31
number of per Ethernet segment, 59
out-of-band management of, 298
CSU/DSU devices, 298
nonstandard devices, 302
serial, inverse terminal servers, polling
with, 303
Spanning Tree and, 63–65
DF (Don't Fragment) bit, 251
DHCP (Dynamic Host Configuration
Protocol), 191
end devices, managing, 289
network-management problems with, 289
Differentiated Services, 261–263
design considerations, 270
diffserv (see Differentiated Services)
Diffusing Update Algorithm (DUAL), 206
Digital Subscriber Line (DSL), 9
Distance Vector algorithm, 197, 207, 236
Distance Vector Multicast Routing Protocol
(DVMRP), 314

distributed backbones, 74–78
trunk capacity, 75–77
trunk fault tolerance, 77
Distributed Services Control Point (see DSCP)
distribution
areas, 110–113
network-management VLANs
and, 276
sizing, 112
level, 85
80/20 rule, 83
switches, 114
DLSw (Data Link Switching), 251
tunnel protocol, 142
DNS (Domain Name Service), 191
servers, linking to DHCP servers, 289
Domain Name Service (see DNS)
Don't Fragment (DF) bit, 251
double-ring topology, 55
DR (Designated Router), 216
DSCP (Distributed Services Control
Point), 261, 263–265
AF and EF values, 265
DSL (Digital Subscriber Line), 9
DUAL (Diffusing Update Algorithm), 206
duplicating equipment, 19
DVMRP (Distance Vector Multicast Routing
Protocol), 314
Dynamic Host Configuration Protocol (see
DHCP)
dynamic routing protocols
end devices and, 53
fault recovery, automated, 65
IPX, 236–242
RIP and SAP, 236–238
types of, 196
(see also IP dynamic routing; OSPF; RIP)

E

Early Token Release (ETR), 143
EF (Expedited Forwarding), 261
design considerations, 270
DSCP and, 265
traffic shaping, 266
VLL and, 263
efficiency, 247–272
bottlenecks and congestion, 252
buffering and queuing, 258–261
equipment features and, 248
filtering and, 253

efficiency (*continued*)
　hop counts and, 249
　MTU and, 250–252
　QoS and, 256–258
　　design considerations, 270–272
　　DSCP and TOS, 263–265
　　Integrated and Differentiated
　　　Services, 261–263
　　Layers 2 and 3, 258
　　RSVP and, 269
　queuing
　　Fair Queuing, 259
　　FIFO, 259
　　Priority Queuing, 260
　　Weighted Fair Queuing, 259
　traffic
　　defining types, 267–268
　　shaping, 265
　(see also cost efficiency)
EGP (Exterior Gateway Protocol), 196, 223,
　　228
EIGRP (Enhanced Interior Gateway Routing
　　Protocol), 84, 206–213
　active and stuck-in-active routes, 210
　functionality, 207–210
　interconnecting autonomous systems, 211
　IPX on, 238
　redistributing with other routing
　　protocols, 213
ELANs (Emulated LANs), 152
Emulated LANs (ELANs), 152
encryption, 8, 275
　WEP and, 158
end devices
　bridging/switching and, 96
　broadcasts and, 96
　connections, 81
　cost efficiency and, 127
　DHCP and, 289
　dynamic routing protocols and, 54, 65
　HSRP and, 65
　hubs and, 139
　network functions, performing, 25, 52
　reliability and, 53, 114
　routing and, 25
　stability and, 51
　traffic and, 83
　VLANs and, 110
　VRRP and, 65
Enhanced Interior Gateway Routing Protocol
　　(see EIGRP)

equal-cost multipath routing, 210, 215, 253
　EIGRP and, 238
　NLSP and, 241
equipment
　dedicated management, location of, 279
　efficient use of, 248
errors
　CRC, 250
　ICMP and, 176
ESS (Extended Service Set), 156
Ethernet, 6, 130–141
　ATM compared to, 153
　backoff interval, 137
　bridges/hubs/switches, 139
　carrier sense phase, 136
　collapsed backbones, 74
　collision
　　detection, 136–138
　　rates, 59
　congestion and, 47
　cost efficiency, 126
　framing standards, 132–136
　　addresses, 135
　IEEE 802.2/802.3, 7
　jamming pattern, 137
　MTU default, 250
　physical implementations, 130
　protocol types, 133
　QoS and, 258
　routing IP to Token Ring, 11
　segment, scalability of, 59
　in star topology, 56
　Token Ring and, 141, 144
　　bridging, 11, 142
　transceivers, 140
　(see also Ethernet II; Fast Ethernet; Gigabit
　　Ethernet; 10 Gigabit Ethernet)
Ethernet II, 7, 142
Ethertype, 133
ETR (Early Token Release), 143
Expedited Forwarding (see EF)
Extended Service Set (ESS), 156
Exterior Gateway Protocol (see EGP)

F

failures, 15
　cost efficiency and, 15, 23
　dynamic routing protocols and, 193
　hard, 45
　modes, 44–49
　　congestion, 45
　　human error, 49

software problems, 48
traffic anomalies, 47
MTBF, 36
combining values, 39–44
multiple simultaneous, 23
MTBF and, 37–39
predicting, 35–44
probability of, 23, 45
single point of
collapsed backbones, 73
isolating, 31–35
star topologies, 57
trunk, Spanning Tree, 64
Fair Queuing, 259
Fast Ethernet, 6, 57, 130–141
bridges/hubs/switches, 139
bridging through, 142
collapsed backbones, 72
cost efficiency, 127
distributed backbones, 76
Gigabit Ethernet and, 146
physical implementations, 130
switching
modern style routing vs., 81
strategies, 96
fault management, 274
information, hubs and, 128
fault recovery, automated, 24–30
examples of, 27–30
intrinsic vs. external, 26
for large-scale networks, 61–66
Spanning Tree, 61–65
Layer 3, 65
OSPF, 65
fault recovery, manual, 30
fault tolerance, 14, 24–30
bus topology, 55
distributed backbones, 77
via load balancing, 28–30
ring topology, 55
star topologies, 57
(see also fault recovery, automated)
FCS (Frame Check Sequence), 134
FDDI (Fiber Distributed Data Interface), 6,
55, 154
collapsed backbones, 71
Fiber Distributed Data Interface (see FDDI)
fiber optic, 131
Fast Ethernet/Gigabit Ethernet, 146
Fiber Optic Inter-Repeater Link
(FOIRL), 131
FIFO (First In First Out), 257, 259

File Transfer Protocol (see FTP)
filtering, 275
application control, 94
efficiency and, 253
ICMP and, 254
IPX, 93
network-management problems with, 293
policy-based routing, 94
RIP, 237
routing strategies, 92–95
SAP and, 237, 253
security and, 92, 337
switching strategies, 99
firewalls, 275
IP addressing and, 178
LANs and, 160–162
network-management problems
with, 294–296
routers as, 161
wireless LANs and, 159
First In First Out (see FIFO)
floating static routes, 195
flooding, 215
flows, 91, 261
FOIRL (Fiber Optic Inter-Repeater Link), 131
forward delay timer (Spanning Tree), 64
Frame Check Sequence (FCS), 134
Frame Relay WAN links, ATM and, 151
framing standards, Ethernet, 132–136
addresses, 135
frequency, 255
FTP (File Transfer Protocol), 8
IP traffic classification fields, 267
presentation layer and, 8
queuing and, 259
full-duplex
access, collision detection and, 137
connections, end devices to Gigabit
Ethernet, 147
transmission, trunks and, 76
fully meshed topology, 57

G

gateways
default, 190
LANs and, 160–162
proxy host, 161
web proxy, 161
Gigabit Ethernet, 146–149
as backbone protocol, 148
bottlenecks and, 253

Gigabit Ethernet (*continued*)
    bridging through, 142
    on desktops, 147
    Fast Ethernet and, 146
    signaling standards for, 146
Gigabit Media Independent Interface
        (GMII), 146
globally unique address (GUA), 234
GMII (Gigabit Media Independent
        Interface), 146
GUA (globally unique address), 234
Guaranteed Delivery, 256
    VLL and, 257

H

hard failures, 45
hello timer (Spanning Tree), 64
hops
    hop counts, 249
    PHB and, 261
horizontal cabling, 163–166
Hot Standby Router Protocol (see HSRP)
HSRP (Hot Standby Router Protocol), 65
    collapsed backbones, 74
    redundancy, 88
HTTP (Hypertext Transfer Protocol)
    queuing and, 259
    security and, 334
hub and spoke topology, 56
hubs, 56
    10/100, 140
    augmenting access level with, 128
    bus topology and, 55
    design issues, 139
    fault-management information and, 128
    security and, 336
    switches vs., 95
Hypertext Transfer Protocol (see HTTP)

I

IBM protocols on Token Ring segments, 251
ICMP (Internet Control Message
        Protocol), 176
    filtering and, 254
    ping, 69, 284
    Redirect message, 176
IEEE 802.1d (see Spanning Tree)
IETF (Internet Engineering Task Force), 169
    queuing standards, 261
IGMP (Internet Group Management
        Protocol), 310–311

IGP (Interior Gateway Protocol), 196, 223
IGRP (Interior Gateway Routing
        Protocol), 206–213
    (see also EIGRP)
installed base, 3
    cost efficiency, 129
    LAN technologies, 129
instance managers (SNMP), 286
Integrated Services (see IS)
Interior Gateway Protocol (see IGP)
Intermediate System to Intermediate System
        (IS-IS), 239
Internet, 170
    routing, 174
        routing protocols and, 229
Internet Control Message Protocol (see ICMP)
Internet Engineering Task Force (IETF), 169
Internet Group Management Protocol
        (see IGMP)
Internet Protocol (see IP)
Internetwork Packet Exchange (see IPX)
intserv (see IS)
inverse terminal server, polling serial devices
        with, 303
IP ARP packets, 48
IP dynamic routing, 193–233
    BGP (see BGP)
    IGRP/EIGRP (see IGRP; EIGRP)
    OSPF (see OSPF)
    RIP (see RIP)
    types of protocols, 196
IP (Internet Protocol), 7, 169–192
    addressing, 170–175, 177, 182–191
        classes, 173–175
        default gateways, 190
        flexibility, 189
        loopbacks, 188
        for OSPF, 224
        ranges, 184–187
        standard subnet masks, 187–189
        unregistered addresses, 182
    all-subnets broadcast, 180
    ARP and, 175
    Classical IP, 152
    DHCP and, 191
    DNS and, 191
    dynamic routing (see IP dynamic routing)
    hop counts, 249
    ICMP and, 176
    IPX and, 7
        comparison, 234

multiple subnet broadcast, 179–181
NAT and, 177–179
precedence values, 264
routing, 11
traffic classification fields, 267
VLANs and, 66, 69
(see also IP multicast networks)
IP multicast networks, 306–318
    addressing, multicast, 307
    design considerations, 315–318
        multicast administrative
            zones, 316–318
        QoS and, 318
    group membership, 312
    IGMP, 310–311
    multicast routing, 313–315
        BGMP and, 315
        DVMRP, 314
        MOSPF, 313
        PIM and, 315
    services, 308–310
IPsec, 338
IPv4 (see IP)
IPv6, 319–333
    addressing, 322–325
        allocations, 324
    autoconfiguration, 327–328
    header structure, 320–322
    IPv4 to IPv6, migrating, 331–333
    multicast and anycast, 329–331
    QoS, 325
    security, 326
    (see also IP)
IPX (Internetwork Packet Exchange), 7, 169,
        234–246
    addressing, 242–244
    design strategies, 242–246
        efficiency, 245
        RIP and SAP accumulation zones, 244
    dynamic routing, 236–242
        EIGRP, 238
        NLSP, 239–242
        RIP and SAP, 236–238
    Ethernet types, 133
    filtering and, 93, 253
    hop counts, 249
    IP and, 7
        comparison, 234
    merging networks, 235
    VLANs and, 66

IS (Integrated Services), 261–263
    design considerations, 270
IS-IS (Intermediate System to Intermediate
        System), 239

J

jamming pattern (Ethernet), 137
jitter, 250, 255

L

LAA (Locally Administered Address), 132,
        135
labeling, patch panels and cords, 277
LAN Emulation Client (LEC), 153
LAN Emulation Configuration Server
        (LECS), 153
LAN Emulation (see LANE)
LAN Emulation Server (LES), 153
LANE (LAN Emulation), 149, 152
    SVCs and, 150
late collision, 137
latency, 16
    bandwidth and, 255
    hop counts and, 250
    jitter, 250, 255
    MTU and, 251
    routers vs. switches, 83
Layer 3 switches, 10, 84–87
    routing vs., 11
LEC (LAN Emulation Client), 153
LECS (LAN Emulation Configuration
        Server), 153
LES (LAN Emulation Server), 153
Link State Advertisement (LSA), 216
Link State algorithm, 213, 236
Link State information, 213
    NLSP, 239
LLC (Logical Link Control), 134
load balancing, 28–30
    distributed backbones, 78
Locally Administered Address (see LAA)
Logical Link Control (LLC), 134
logs, monitoring, 283
LSA (Link State Advertisement), 216

M

MAC addresses, 54, 132, 135
    ARP and, 175
    broadcast/multicast, 135

MAC addresses (*continued*)
  DECNET protocol, 135
  fault recovery and, 27
  IP ARP packets and, 48
  multicast IP addresses, converting
    between, 307
  security and, 99
  updating, 63
MAC (Media Access Control), 11
MADCAP protocol, 309
maintenance
  LAN technologies, 129
  redundancy and, 18
MAN (Metropolitan Area Network), 3
  Gigabit Ethernet as backbone on, 149
manageability
  cost efficiency, 12
  redundancy, implementing, 23
  VLANs, 67
  (see also network management)
Management Information Base (see MIB)
MAU (Media Attachment Unit—see hubs)
maximum age timer (Spanning Tree), 64
Maximum Transmission Unit (see MTU)
MBONE (multicast backbone), 315
Mean Time Between Failures (see MTBF)
Media Access Control (MAC), 11
Media Attachment Unit (MAU—see hubs)
mesh topology, 57
metrics (RIP), 199
Metropolitan Area Network (see MAN)
MIB (Management Information Base), 281
  extensions
      monitoring networks, 286
      for Spanning Tree, monitoring, 297
MMUSIC (Multiparty Multimedia Session
      Control Working Group), 312
modems, out-of-band management of, 298
monitoring, 281–286
MOSPF (Multicast OSPF), 313
MPOA (Multiple Protocol Over ATM), 152
MTBF (Mean Time Between Failures), 36
  combining values, 39–44
  multiple simultaneous failures and, 37–39
MTU (Maximum Transmission
      Unit), 250–252
  mismatch problems, 250
  Path MTU Discovery process, 251
multicast address, 135
multicast backbone (MBONE), 315
Multicast OSPF (MOSPF), 313

Multiparty Multimedia Session Control
      Working Group (MMUSIC), 312
Multiple Protocol Over ATM (MPOA), 152

N

NAT (Network Address Translation), 161,
      177–179
  SNMP and, 179
NBAR (Network-Based Application
      Recognition), QoS classes and, 268
NBMA (Nonbroadcast Multiple Access), 216
NetBEUI, 169
netmasks, 170, 171
  standard, for common uses, 187–189
Network Address Translation (see NAT)
network devices, 53
  automated fault recovery and, 26
  design philosophy and, 13
  Ethernet framing standards, 132
  redundancy and, 18
  stability and, 31
Network Interface Cards (see NIC)
network layer (OSI model), 7
  protocols commonly in use, 169
  VLANs and, 21
network management, 273–305
  accounting management, 275
  capacity planning, 275
  configuration management, 273
    tracking physical changes, 274
  dedicated equipment for, location of, 279
  design considerations, 275–280
    ease of access, 277
    equipment, location of, 279
  fault management, 274
  out-of-band techniques, 298–305
  performance management, 274
    SNMP and, 283
  problems with, 288–305
    backups, 296
    DHCP, 289
    filtering, 293
    firewalls, 294–296
    LAN extension, 292
    nonstandard devices, 302
    redundancy, 296
    tunnels, 297
    VLAN structures, 291–292
  security management, 275
  SNMP, 280–288
    monitoring with, 281–286

network number, 234
Network Operating System (see NOS)
Network-Based Application Recognition
    (NBAR), QoS classes and, 268
Network-Network Interface (NNI), 150
NIC (Network Interface Card), 132
    multiple, 53
    stability and, 51
NLSP (Novell Link State Protocol), 235,
    239–242
    areas, 239
    routing, 241
NNI (Network-Network Interface), 150
Nonbroadcast Multiple Access (NBMA), 216
nontransit areas, 217
NOS (Network Operating System), 7, 234
Not-So-Stubby area (NSSA), 217
Novell Link State Protocol (see NLSP)
Novell Network Registry, 235
NSSA (Not-So-Stubby Area), 217

0

objectives, 1
    reliability, 247
one-armed routers, 84–87
Open Shortest Path First (see OSPF)
Organizationally Unique Identifier
    (OUI), 135
OSI model, 5–10
    application layer, 9
    breakdown of, 9
    data link layer, 6
        network congestion and, 47
    layers of, 5–9
    network layer, 7
        VLANs and, 21
    physical layer, 6
    presentation layer, 8
    session layer, 8
    transport layer, 7
OSPF (Open Shortest Path First), 84,
    213–228
    areas, 185, 188, 215
        structures, 219–222
        types of, 217–219
    Autonomous Systems, 185, 215
        interconnecting, 222
    bottlenecks and, 253
    costs, 225–228
    end devices and, 53
    fault recovery, automated, 65
    interconnecting Autonomous Systems, 222

IP-addressing schemes for, 224
redistributing with other routing
    protocols, 223
traffic anomalies, 47
    resolving, 48
OUI (Organizationally Unique Identifier), 135
out-of-band network-management
    techniques, 298–305

P

Packet Description Language Module
    (PDLM), QoS classes and, 268
packets
    ARP, broadcast address, 136
    buffering, 266
    Drop Precedence, 262
    dropped, 256
    fragmentation, 250
    hop counts and, 249
    IP ARP, 48
    latency and (see latency)
    policing, 266
    prioritizing, 249
    SAP, filtering and, 253
    size of, QoS classes and, 268
    TTL field, 202
partially meshed topology, 57
patch panels, 277
    IBDN, 57
Path MTU Discovery process, 251
PDLM (Packet Description Language
    Module), QoS classes and, 268
PDU (Protocol Data Unit), 134
peer-to-peer networks, collapsed backbones, 70
performance, 16–17
    cost efficiency and, 16, 127
    LAN technologies, 130
    management, 274
        SNMP and, 283
    peak load, 14
    (see also efficiency)
Per-Hop Behavior (see PHB)
Permanent Virtual Circuit (PVC), 150
PHB (Per-Hop Behavior), 261
    AF and EF, 261
physical layer (OSI model), 6
PIM (Protocol Independent Multicast), 315
ping, 176
    for monitoring, 284
    VLANs and, 69
PNNI (Private Network-Network
    Interface), 150

point-to-point circuits, 6
point-to-point protocol (see PPP)
policing, 266
polling, 281
port numbers, 8
    QoS classes and, 268
    TCP/UDP, filtering for security, 93
ports
    blocking, 62
    console, management problems with, 305
    forwarding state, 63
    LAN, out-of-band management and, 300
    learning state, 63
    monitoring utilization, 283
    serial, out-of-band management and, 300
    (see also port numbers)
PPP over Ethernet (PPPoE), 9
PPP (point-to-point protocol), 155
    out-of-band management and, 300
PPPoE (PPP over Ethernet), 9
Preferential Delivery, 256
    Priority Queuing, 260
    Weighted Fair Queuing and, 259
presentation layer (OSI model), 8
Priority Queuing, 260
Private Network-Network Interface
    (PNNI), 150
probabilities, combining, 341–343
probes, location of, 275
Protocol Data Unit (PDU), 134
Protocol Independent Multicast (PIM), 315
protocol stack model (see OSI model)
protocols
    analyzers, network management and, 291
    congestion and, 46
    dynamic routing
        end devices and, 53
        fault recovery, automated, 65
        Internet and, 229
        types of, 196
        (see also IP dynamic routing; OSPF;
        RIP)
    IBM run on Token Ring segments, 251
    MADCAP, 309
    network layer, commonly used, 169
    routable/nonroutable, 169
    VLANs based on, 68
proxy
    ARP, 25
    host, 161
PVC (Permanent Virtual Circuit), 150

Q

QoS (Quality of Service), 256–258
    ATM and, 151
    classes, 267
    congestion and, 252
    design considerations, 270–272
    DSCP and TOS, 263–265
    implementing, 249
    Integrated and Differentiated
        Services, 261–263
    IP multicast networks and, 318
    IPv6 and, 325
    Layers 2 and 3, 258
    RSVP and, 269
    traffic shaping and, 266
    traffic shaping (see traffic, shaping)
Quality of Service (see QoS)
queues
    monitoring statistics about, 286
    polling and, 282
    (see also queuing)
queuing, 258–261
    Fair Queuing, 259
    FIFO, 259
    Priority Queuing, 260
    Weighted Fair Queuing, 257, 259

R

Random Early Detection (RED), 252
RED (Random Early Detection), 252
redundancy, 17–44
    ATM, 153
    BUS/LECS/LES servers, 153
    collapsed backbones, 73
    complexity and manageability, 23
    core-level routers, 116
    cost efficiency, 42
    distributed backbones, 77
    failures
        hard, 45
        modes, 44–49
        MTBF, 36, 39–44
        multiple simultaneous, 23, 37–39
        predicting, 35–44
        probability of, 45
        single point of, 31–35
    fault recovery, automated, 24–30
        examples of, 27–30
        intrinsic vs. external, 26

implementing, 18–20
  backups, 19
  duplicating equipment, 19
network-management problems with, 296
by protocol layer, 21–23
routing strategies, 88–92
  physical diversity, 90–92
  router-to-router segments, 88–90
Spanning Tree, multiple connections, 115
switching strategies, 98
reliability, 14, 26
  failures and, 15
  Gigabit Ethernet, 146
  implementing, 113–115
    multiple connections, 114
  networks as end devices, 53
  TCP/UDP and, 7
  (see also fault recovery, automated; fault
    tolerance; performance)
Remote Procedure Call (RPC) applications,
  QoS classes and, 268
Request for Comment (RFC), 169
requirements
  business, 1–4, 16
    bandwidth (see bandwidth)
    expenses, 2
    geography, 2
    installed base, 3
    security (see security)
    vs. technical, 1
  philosophical, 4
  user, 17
Reservation Protocol (see RSVP)
RFC (Request for Comment), 169
ring topology, 55
RIP (Routing Information Protocol—IP), 25,
  84, 197–206
  end devices and, 53
  functionality, 199–201
  loops, avoiding, 202–204
  metrics, 199
  redistributing with other protocols, 206
  split horizons in, 204
  variable subnet masks, 205
RIP (Routing Information Protocol—
  IPX), 236–238
  accumulation zones, 244
  avoiding, 245
  EIGRP and, 238
roaming (wireless LANs), 156
root bridges, 62
route tags

EIGRP, 212
RIP, 206
routers, 83, 234
  backbone, 219
  border, 213
  bugs in, 48
  core-level, 116–118
    redundancy, 116
  distribution-level, 118
  efficient use of, 248
  fault recovery, automated, 27
  as firewalls, 161
  flows, 91
  as gateways, 161
  ICMP Redirect message, 176
  installing, 84
  latency, 83
  monitoring, 284
    buffering and queuing statistics, 286
  multilevel, 119
  NLSP and, 239
  one-armed, 84–87
  physical diversity, 90–92
  queuing and, 255
  redundancy and, 25
  remote sites, connecting, 121–124
  router-to-router segments, 88–90
  as single points of failure, 31
  TCP/IP and, 161
  trunking through, 102–104
  (see also routing; routing strategies)
routing
  ATM and, 11
  bottlenecks and, 253
  bridging vs., 10–12
  classless, 228
  Internet, 174
  IP dynamic (see IP dynamic routing)
  multicast, 313–315
    BGMP, 315
    DVMRP, 314
    MOSPF, 313
    PIM, 315
  policy-based, 94
  stability and, 51
  static, 194–196
    floating static routes, 195
  switching vs., 78–81
    modern design, 80
    old-style design, 78–80
  (see also Layer 3 switches; routing
    strategies)

Routing Information Protocol (see RIP)
routing loops, 194
  avoiding, 202–204
routing strategies, 83–95
  filtering, 92–95
    for application control, 94
    policy-based routing, 94
    for security, 92
  Layer 3 switches, 84–87
  one-armed routers, 84–87
  redundancy, 88–92
    physical diversity, 90–92
    router-to-router segments, 88–90
routing tables, 193, 199
RPC (Remote Procedure Call) applications,
    QoS classes and, 268
RSVP (Reservation Protocol), 261
  efficiency and, 270
  QoS and, 269

S

SAP (Service Advertisement Protocol), 136,
    236–238
  accumulation zones, 244
  avoiding, 245
scalability
  congestion and, 47
  of Ethernet segment, 59
  meshed topologies and, 58
  routing vs. bridging, 11
  of topologies, 58–61
security, 4, 333–340
  filtering and, 92, 337
    switching strategies, 99
  firewalls, 161
  hub and switch port-level security, 336
  IPsec and, 338
  IPv6 and, 326
  management, 275
    out-of-band, 299
  password recovery, 305
  routers and, 52, 84
  SNMP and, 280, 286, 296
  VLANs and, 69
  VPNs and, 9
  wireless LANs and, 158–159
  (see also firewalls; gateways)
Sequenced Packet Exchange (SPX), 236
Serial Line Internet Protocol (SLIP),
    out-of-band management and, 300

servers
  BUS, 153
  DNS, linking to DHCP servers, 289
  inverse terminal, polling serial devices
    with, 303
  LECS, 153
  LES, 153
  NetWare, 234
  network-management monitoring, 284
  NLSP and, 239
  routers as, 53
  SNMP, 280
Service Advertisement Protocol (see SAP)
Service Advertisement table, IPX and, 242
session layer (OSI model), 8
signaling, baseband/broadband, 131
Simple Network Management Protocol (see
    SNMP)
single point of failure
  collapsed backbones, 73
  star topologies, 57
single-ring topology, 55
SLIP (Serial Line Internet Protocol),
    out-of-band management and, 300
SNA (Systems Network Architecture), 8, 169
SNAP (Sub-Network Access Protocol), 134
SNMP (Simple Network Management
    Protocol), 179
  agents/servers, 280
  monitoring with, 281–286
    ad hoc queries, 286
    automated activities, 287
    instance managers, 286
    items to monitor, 285
    Spanning Tree, 297
    sysUpTime, 285
  network management and, 280–288
  security and, 280, 286, 296
soft expense, 15
software problems (see bugs in
    routers/switches)
SONET, 55
source-route bridging, 145
spaghetti factor, 68
Spanning Tree, 61–65
  backup links/devices, activating, 63–65
  collapsed backbones, 74
  loops, eliminating, 62
  multiple connections, 115
  network-management problems with, 291
  SNMP monitoring of, 297

timers, 64
  values, 64
  traffic anomalies and, 47
  trunk failures, 64
  trunk redundancy, 107
Split Horizon algorithm, 205
  Split Horizon with Poisoned Reverse, 208
SPX (Sequenced Packet Exchange), 236
stability
  analyzing, 31–35
  end devices and, 51
  redundancy and, 45
  single points of failure and, 31
star topology, 56
static routing, 194–196
  floating static routes, 195
STP (Spanning Tree Protocol—see Spanning
    Tree)
structured cabling, 162–168
  horizontal, 163–166
  vertical, 166
stub areas, 217
subnets, 171
  counting from the left scheme, 172
  masks, 171
    standard, for common uses, 187–189
  variable subnet masks, 205
  (see also IP)
Sub-Network Access Protocol (SNAP), 134
SVC (Switch Virtual Circuit), 150
switches
  augmenting access level with, 128
  bugs in, 48
  bus topologies and, 55
  design issues, 139
  distribution, 64
  fault-management information and, 128
  hubs vs., 95
  latency, 83
  Layer 3, 84–87
    routing vs., 11
  monitoring, 284
  redundant core, 64
  security and, 336
  as single points of failure, 31
  (see also switching)
switching
  Layer 3, 10
  routing vs., 78–81
    modern design, 80
    old-style design, 78–80
  store-and-forward, 11

strategies, 95–100
  broadcasts and, 96–98
  filtering, 99
  redundancy, 98
  (see also bridging)
Systems Network Architecture (see SNA)

T

TCP (Transmission Control Protocol), 7
  congestion and, 46
  DF bit, 251
  IP traffic classification fields, 267
  NAT and, 179
  packets, dropping, 266
TCP/IP
  bridging through Fast or Gigabit Ethernet
      segments, 142
  DECNET operating with, 135
  Ethernet types, 133
  routers and, 161
  (see also IP)
telephony, ATM and, 149, 151
telnet, 8
thick-net, 131
thin-net (see 10Base2)
throughput, 10BaseT hub, 60
Time To Live (TTL), 202
token, 143
  bus topology, 54
  mesh topology, 57
  ring topology, 55
  star topology, 56
Token Ring, 6, 55, 141, 141–145
  ATM compared to, 153
  collapsed backbones, 74
  collision rates, 60
  congestion and, 47
  cost efficiency, 126, 144
  Ethernet and, 141, 144
    bridging, 11, 142
  ETR, 143
  IBM protocols on, 251
  MTU default, 250
  QoS, Layer 2, 258
  routing, IP from Ethernet, 11
  scalability, 59
  in star topology, 56
  VLANs, 145
topologies, 54–58
  bus, 54
  hub and spoke, 56

topologies (*continued*)
    LAN, large-scale, 115–125
        core-level routers, 116–118
        distribution-level routers, 118
        remote sites, connecting, 121–124
    large-scale, 70–81
        collapsed backbones, 70–74
        distributed backbone, 74–78
        multilevel routers, 119
        switching vs. routing, 78–81
        (see also topologies, LAN, large-scale)
    mesh, 57
    ring, 55
    scalability of, 58–61
    star, 56
    token bus, 54
TOS (Type of Service), 263–265
totally stub areas, 217
traceroute, VLANs and, 69
traffic, 4
    anomalies, 47
    congestion, 46
    Ethernet segment and, 59
    hierarchical design, 83
    human error and, 49
    IP classification fields, 267
    shaping, 265
    types, defining, 267–268
    (see also bandwidth; congestion)
transceivers, 140
    out-of-band management of, 298
Transit areas, 217
Transmission Control Protocol (see TCP)
transmission, full-duplex, trunks and, 76
transport layer (OSI model), 7
traps, 280
    logs, monitoring, 283
trouble tickets, automated, 283
troubleshooting
    fault management and, 274
    VLANs, 67
trunks, 75, 104–110
    capacity, distributed backbones, 75–77
    congestion and, 47
    cost efficiency, 109
    design, 100–102
    failures, Spanning Tree, 64
    fault tolerance, distributed backbones, 77
    probes on, 276
    trunking through router, 102–104
    VLANs and, network-management
        problems with, 291–293

TTL (Time To Live), 202
tunnels
    management of
        out-of-band, 299
        problems with, 297
    OSI model and, 9
Type 3 cabling, 6
Type of Service (see TOS)

U

UBR (Unspecified Bit Rate), 151
UDP (User Datagram Protocol), 7
    packets, dropping, 266
    Path MTU Discovery process and, 251
UNI (User-Network Interface), 150
unicasts, 54
Unshielded Twisted Pair (UTP), 146
Unspecified Bit Rate (UBR), 151
User Datagram Protocol (see UDP)
User-Network Interface (UNI), 150
users
    locations of, 2
    requirements of, 17
UTP (Unshielded Twisted Pair), 146

V

Variable Bit Rate (VBR), 151
Variable Length Subnet Masks (VLSM), 206
VBR (Variable Bit Rate), 151
VC (Virtual Circuit), 150
VCI (Virtual Channel Identifier), 150
vertical cabling, 166
Virtual Channel Identifier (VCI), 150
Virtual Circuit (VC), 150
Virtual LAN (see VLAN)
Virtual Leased Line (see VLL)
Virtual Path Identifier (VPI), 150
Virtual Private Network (see VPN)
Virtual Router Redundancy Protocol (see
       VRRP)
VLAN (Virtual LAN), 3, 21, 66–70
    cost efficiency, 66
    IP addressing and, 186
    management VLANs, dedicated, 276
    probes and, 275
    protocol-based, 68
    spaghetti, avoiding, 67–68
    subnet masks, 187
    Token Ring switches, 145
    topologies based on, 100–113
        distribution areas, 110–113

trunking through router, 102–104
trunks, 100–110, 276, 291–293
VLL (Virtual Leased Line), 257
    EF and, 263
VLSM (Variable Length Subnet Masks), 206
VPI (Virtual Path Identifier), 150
VPN (Virtual Private Network), 9
    wireless LANs and, 159
VRRP (Virtual Router Redundancy
        Protocol), 65
    collapsed backbones, 74
    redundancy, 88

W

WAN (Wide Area Network), 3
    ATM and, 149
    congestion and, 47
    Gigabit Ethernet as backbone on, 149
    LANE and, 149
    latency and, 255
    polling on, 282
    PVCs and, 150
web proxy, 161
Weighted Fair Queuing, 257, 259
WEP (Wired Equivalent Privacy), 158
Wide Area Network (see WAN)
Wired Equivalent Privacy (WEP), 158
wireless LANs, 155–159

About the Author

Kevin Dooley earned his Ph.D. in physics from the University of Toronto in 1993, having financed much of his schooling as a network and system administrator. He then immediately started a career in networking and has never looked back. He now lives in Toronto, Canada, where he works as a consultant and runs a consulting company called Manageable Networks (*http://www.manageablenetworks.com*). In this capacity he has designed and implemented large-scale Local and Wide Area Networks for some of Canada's largest companies.

In his spare time, Kevin is a jazz pianist and composer. He has a particular interest in chamber music and has served on the board of directors of a chamber music society. One day he plans to try his hand at writing film scores.

Colophon

Our look is the result of reader comments, our own experimentation, and feedback from distribution channels. Distinctive covers complement our distinctive approach to technical topics, breathing personality and life into potentially dry subjects.

The animal on the cover of *Designing Large-Scale LANs* is a reindeer. Reindeer, or caribou, can be found in the arctic tundra, the mountain tundra, and the northern forests of North America, Russia, and Scandinavia. Though the wild caribou and the domesticated reindeer are members of the same species, North America is the only place where a naming distinction is made between the two. Reindeer were first domesticated in Europe and Asia about 5,000 years ago. Most domesticated reindeer come from that same stock, as more recent attempts to tame wild caribou have been unsuccessful. Once domesticated, reindeer were used as food, for their hides, and for transportation (some were saddled and ridden, while others pulled sleds).

Reindeer (or caribou) are the only members of the deer family in which both sexes grow antlers. After mating, adult bulls shed their antlers around November or December, while cows and young often carry their antlers throughout the entire winter. During growth, the antlers have a fuzzy covering, or *velvet*, which contains blood vessels that carry nutrients.

In addition to their antlers, reindeer have lateral hooves that allow their feet to spread on snow or soft ground. The hooves also act as paddles, making them excellent swimmers. Due to breeding, the colors of reindeer vary from white and gray to brown and black. Colors often vary even within the same herd.

Jeffrey Holcomb was the production editor and proofreader for *Designing Large-Scale LANs*. Ann Schirmer was the copyeditor. Sheryl Avruch, Claire Cloutier, Tatiana Apandi Diaz, and Sue Willing provided proofreading assistance. Rachel Wheeler and Mary Brady provided quality control. Phillip Dangler, Darren Kelly, Edie Shapiro, and Sarah Sherman provided production assistance. Nancy Crumpton wrote the index.

Ellie Volckhausen designed the cover of this book, based on a series design by Edie Freedman. The cover image is an illustration from the *Illustrated Natural History: Mammalia*. Emma Colby produced the cover layout with QuarkXPress 4.1 using Adobe's ITC Garamond font.

Melanie Wang designed the interior layout, based on a series design by David Futato. Mihaela Maier converted the files from Microsoft Word to FrameMaker 5.5.6 using tools created by Mike Sierra. The text font is Linotype Birka; the heading font is Adobe Myriad Condensed; and the code font is LucasFont's TheSans Mono Condensed. The illustrations that appear in the book were produced by Robert Romano and Jessamyn Read using Macromedia FreeHand 9 and Adobe Photoshop 6. The tip and warning icons were drawn by Christopher Bing. This colophon was written by Linley Dolby.

Whenever possible, our books use a durable and flexible lay-flat binding.